Cold War Paradise

Cold War Paradise

Settlement, Culture, and Identity-Making among
U.S. Americans in Costa Rica, 1945–1980

ATALIA SHRAGAI

University of Nebraska Press | Lincoln

© 2022 by the Board of Regents of the University of Nebraska

An earlier version of chapter 6 was first published as "'As Luck Would Have It': Privilege, Agency, and Happenstance in the Life Stories of US American Immigrants to Costa Rica, 1960–1980," *Oral History Review* 44, no. 2 (2017): 278–300.

Portions of chapter 4 were first published as "In the Service of Their Homeland and Themselves: The U.S. Women's Club in Costa Rica 1945–1980," *Journal of Social History* 52, no. 2 (2018): 412–38.

This book was published with the support of the Israel Science Foundation.

All rights reserved

The University of Nebraska Press is part of a land-grant institution with campuses and programs on the past, present, and future homelands of the Pawnee, Ponca, Otoe-Missouria, Omaha, Dakota, Lakota, Kaw, Cheyenne, and Arapaho Peoples, as well as those of the relocated Ho-Chunk, Sac and Fox, and Iowa Peoples.

Library of Congress Cataloging-in-Publication Data
Names: Shragai, Atalia, author.
Title: Cold war paradise: settlement, culture, and identity-making among U.S. Americans in Costa Rica, 1945–1980 / Atalia Shragai.
Other titles: Settlement, culture, and identity-making among U.S. Americans in Costa Rica, 1945–1980
Description: Lincoln: University of Nebraska Press, [2022] | Includes bibliographical references and index.
Identifiers: LCCN 2021054494
ISBN 9781496220301 (hardback)
ISBN 9781496230799 (paperback)
ISBN 9781496232021 (epub)
ISBN 9781496232038 (pdf)
Subjects: LCSH: Americans—Costa Rica—Social life and customs—20th century. | Americans—Costa Rica—Interviews. | Identity (Psychology)—Costa Rica. | National characteristics, American. | Immigrants—Costa Rica—Social life and customs—20th century. | Counterculture—Costa Rica—History—20th century. | Costa Rica—Emigration and immigration—History—20th century. | Costa Rica—Civilization—20th century. | BISAC: HISTORY / Latin America / Central America | SOCIAL SCIENCE / Emigration & Immigration
Classification: LCC F1548 .S54 2022 | DDC 972.8605—dc23/eng/20211123
LC record available at https://lccn.loc.gov/2021054494

Designed and set in ITC New Baskerville by Laura Buis.

For my family

Costa Rica is a forgiving place. You can get by.
  —BUDDY SMITH, author interview

Contents

List of Illustrations xi

List of Tables xiii

Acknowledgments xv

Introduction 1

1. Crossroads: The Movement of Individuals within the Sociopolitical Context 33

2. Places and Networks: Settlement, Community-Building, and Identity-Making 59

3. From Cowboys to the Guardians of Eden: Identity Work in Costa Rican Nature 93

4. Becoming a U.S. Woman in Costa Rica: Gender, Immigration, and Transnationalism 125

5. Material Culture on the Move: Things and Meanings between the United States and Costa Rica 161

6. Looking Back in Amazement: Negotiating Identities as Privileged Immigrants 199

Epilogue 221

Notes 233

Bibliography 277

Index 299

Illustrations

1. Map of Costa Rica   xx
2. U.S. president John F. Kennedy being driven past crowds of cheering onlookers in Costa Rica, 1963   15
3. Ad offering a property in Costa Rica, early 1970s   49
4. Ad inviting U.S. Americans to a joint homesteading in Costa Rica, early 1970s   50
5. Ticas observing a U.S. American hippie on the streets of San José, 1974   53
6. John Stam, missionary from the United States, in Santa Cruz, Guanacaste, 1956   68
7. Tom Clairmont, known as "Captain Tom," in Playa Cacao, 1972   70
8. Poster for the San José LTG production of *Alice in Wonderland*, 1973   90
9. Walter Fiala pictured with a tiger on his farm in southern Costa Rica   112
10. *Roots*, drawing by Lucky Guindon of Monteverde, Costa Rica   115
11. WCCR's president handing a check to Costa Rica's minister of culture, 1978   141
12. An application form for the U.S.A. International Women's Club, circa 1965   143
13. Elizabeth Dyer, first editor of the *Tico Times*, with fellow staff members, late 1950s   150

14. The compound of Tom Clairmont in Playa Cacao, 1973   167
15. Cover of WCCR recipe book, *Postres / Desserts*   194
16. Cover of WCCR recipe book, *Casseroles*   195
17. Cover of WCCR recipe book, *Kitchen Pleasures*   196

Tables

1. Foreign population in Costa Rica, 1950–73   16
2. U.S. Americans according to their place of residence in Costa Rica   62

Acknowledgments

It has been many years since Itai and I went backpacking in Costa Rica, gradually noticing that there were actually a lot of Americans living there (I didn't know then that I should call them U.S. Americans), that they have a special hunger for the country's irresistible beachfronts and interesting relations with the local population, and that they never seemed to know quite what to say when you asked them about their own identities.

Many people and institutions contributed much labor, money, and love in order to transform this backpacker's experience into a book. It began as a PhD dissertation at the School of Historical Studies at Tel Aviv University, where I was fortunate to be mentored by two inspiring and dedicated scholars. Billie Mellman opened for me a horizon of knowledge, research, and thinking and gave me the constant encouragement to enable me to get there. I am grateful for her devotion and the stirring spirit and imagination with which she inspired this work. For his part, Raanan Rein showed me the way to Latin American studies. I thank him for his friendship and his boundless confidence in me, which enabled him to foresee a book in what was barely a research proposal, as well as the practical help that he has extended to me over the years.

Immense thanks is also due to Jeffrey Lesser, inspiring scholar and invaluable friend—or vice versa—who was extremely generous with his ideas, practical advice, and much-needed sense of humor. My academic hub during the writing of the dissertation was the Sverdlyn Institute for Latin American History and Culture at Tel Aviv University. I would like to thank Rosalie Sitman, Gerardo Leibner, and Ori Preuss for their teaching and support and the academic and administrative staff at the School of Historical Studies for the stimulating academic atmosphere. Fellow graduate students have become friends and colleagues. I am grateful to Claudia Kedar for her help at crucial moments and for her friendship throughout, and to Lior Ben David for his endless positive and supportive attitude. My friends and colleagues at the Faculty of Humanities and Social Sciences at the Kibbutzim College of Education have made the past few years enjoyable and meaningful, and I thank them for their support during the final leg of this journey. I would like to thank Rosiny Morales, Itamar Folman, and Esteban Fernández Morera for their skillful research assistance. I am grateful to Andrea Meli, Nirit Amir, and Susan van Hengstum for their excellent design tips, to Ronit Segev for Photoshop and good karma, and to Lilach Pery for collateral support. Special thanks to Ayelet Bechar for her clear mind and generous heart, which has saved me over and over again during the process of working on this book.

Most of all, I would also like to wholeheartedly thank the men and women who were interviewed for this book, who, despite the fact that I was a total foreigner and complete stranger on so many levels, generously shared with me their memories, experiences, and writings. Most particularly, I would like to thank a very special woman, Dery Dyer. To a considerable extent the book is based on her family's newspaper and life work, the *Tico Times*. Dery opened the *Tico Times'* office for me and recounted the story of her life and her familial enterprise. I do hope that my interpretations do justice to both. I would also like to extend my thanks to the ladies of the Costa Rica Women's Club and the members of the Little Theater Group and American Legion posts in Costa Rica, for sharing with me their stories and archives. I am grateful to Rebecca Stam and the Stam family and to Elsie Mae Fiala, David Fiala, and Jean Birkland for their generous permission to use family photos. Most of the informants' names have been changed, in order to protect their privacy.

A study on U.S. Americans in Costa Rica by an Israeli scholar requires generous financial support throughout its various stages, and my sincere thanks go to Tel Aviv University's Zvi Yavetz School of Historical Studies, the Sverdlin Institute for Latin American History and Culture, the S. Daniel Abraham Center for Regional and International Studies, the Lady Davis Fellowship Trust, the Harry S. Truman Center for the Advancement of Peace at the Hebrew University of Jerusalem, and the Department of History, Philosophy, and Judaic Studies at the Open University of Israel. I extend my gratitude to the Research Authority of the Kibbutzim College of Education for its trust in and support of this book, and me.

I could not hope for a better publisher than the University of Nebraska Press. Bridget Barry believed in the manuscript from the very beginning, and with great skill and sensibility shepherded it from two trial chapters into a published book. I deeply thank her for her encouragement and enthusiasm. Also at UNP, thanks to Emily Wendell for her engagement through the publication process, to Elizabeth Zaleski, my devoted project editor, to Irina du Quenoy for her meticulous and intelligent copyediting, to Tish Fobben for her attentiveness, and to the wonderful designers for their great work. I thank the anonymous readers of the manuscript whose comments brought to it new dimensions of research and storytelling. Many thanks to Natalie Melzer and Fray Hochstein for the linguistic editing—and much beyond—of numerous draft versions.

My mother and father, Anat and Shaul Shragai, always inspired me to read, travel, and study—and then did everything possible to enable me to do so. I could not have done this without them. My incredible siblings, Tamir Shragai and Orna Shragai-Zak, were the epitome of support and interest and made me laugh through my tears during serious crises. Many thanks to my parents-in-law, Yael and Iri Kahn, for their complete support (and endless babysitting). My beloved aunt, Roberta Steinberg, was in charge of arranging the airlift of books from the United States to Israel and for unlimited support. All my love to my daughters, Alma and Noam, who are my greatest source of inspiration and who always remind me, sometimes against my will, that there is more to life than this book. Finally, I would not have been able to write a single word if not for the unconditional backing and confidence with which I was surrounded by Itai, the love of my life and the one who makes everything possible. You are in every page of the book (though I know you would rather be on the beach in Santa Teresa).

Cold War Paradise

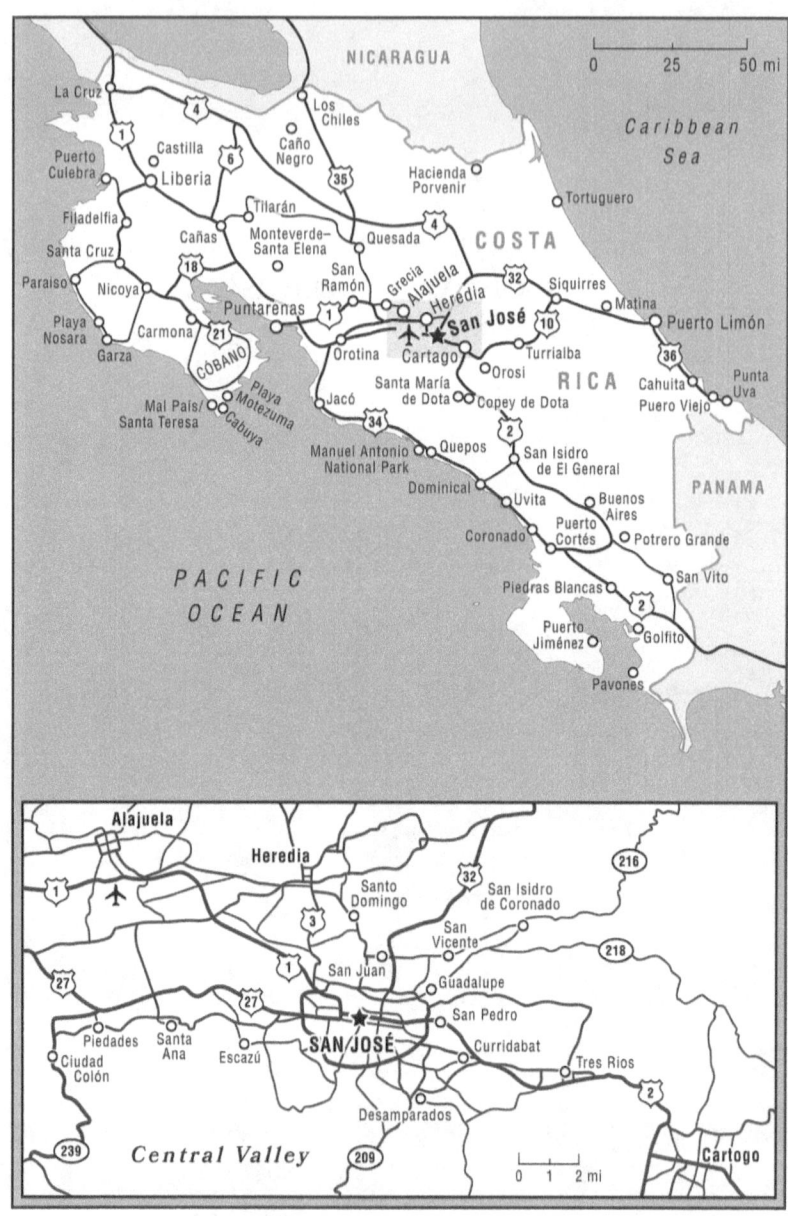

Fig. 1. Map of Costa Rica. Created by Erin Greb.

Introduction

> I like the States, admire it, and always consider myself
> an American. I just don't like to live there.
> —MARK BACH, author interview

Costa Rica's skies were dark during the rainy season of 1979. The stagnation in the country's economy, which within a year would become a full-blown economic crisis, and the political unrest in neighboring Nicaragua where the Sandinistas had just seized power, troubled both *ticos* (the colloquial term for a native of Costa Rica) and foreign residents of Costa Rica. Among the latter were several thousand U.S. Americans who had immigrated to the small Central American republic and settled there in the decades following World War II.[1] In response to rumors of a mass exodus of U.S. Americans in the face of the twin crises, an article on the front page of the *Tico Times*, the largest English-speaking paper in Costa Rica (henceforth *TT*), explained their struggle to accurately analyze the situation: "Opinions are as varied as the overworked imaginations and delicate egos of many expatriate Gringos—that strange and very un-homogeneous group of investors, retirees, businessmen, school-teachers, artists, poets, con-men, hangers-on, taggers-along and droppers-outs.... Trying to separate facts from fantasy is almost impossible—when it comes to opinions on why North Americans choose to either live or leave here, anything goes."[2]

This book is a historical ethnography of the phenomenon of a countercurrent of immigration in the Americas—from the United States to Costa Rica—from the end of World War II to the late 1970s.

Its main focus is on the process of identity work and the creation of distinct migratory identifications that took place under specific global and transnational conditions, first and foremost the U.S. dominance in Central America as part of the Cold War in general and the perceived special relations between the United States and Costa Rica in particular.

The Cold War was not only a political reality but also the generational and cultural background of most of the U.S. Americans who moved to Costa Rica.[3] Many of these immigrants were baby boomers who had been born into the Cold War and spent their childhood and early adulthood in the United States during the first years of the global standoff. They grew up in homes whose domestic culture and gendered regimes were designated as the U.S. answer to the communist threat;[4] they experienced life in a consumerist, materialist society and imbibed the moral and political values associated with capitalism, eulogized as superior to socialism and Marxism;[5] and they witnessed the rise of their homeland to the status of global superpower and its exercise of military force in Asia. Some of them served in the Vietnam War but later identified with the U.S. antiwar movement and were involved to varying degrees in the U.S. and international counterculture. As a significant cultural and mental background, the Cold War facilitated the consequences or the motivation for the move—whether for formal representatives of the United States whose work took them to Costa Rica, or, conversely, for U.S. Americans who went over there precisely to distance themselves, physically and ideologically, from Cold War–era U.S. militaristic policies and imperialistic agenda. Costa Rica, as a small Central American republic situated relatively close to the United States, both geographically and politically, yet boasting a pacifist image based on its abolition of the national army, was well positioned to sustain the identity constructions of both parties.

The book considers the individual and collective identity formation of this diverse group of U.S. Americans, who came from varied ethnic, economic, and religious backgrounds with marked educational, occupational, and political differences. Yet once in Costa Rica, by dint of their language and passport, and to some extent their material privileges, they were grouped together as U.S.

Americans, Norteamericanos, Estadosunidenses, or simply by the general and derogatory term *gringos*. While this "othering" by the Costa Rican society did serve to create a sense of community among U.S. Americans in Costa Rica, the social, ideological, and economic baggage they brought with them—which increased with the social and cultural upheavals of the 1960s—resulted in a fairly fractured and divisive sense of collectiveness.

The various practices and discourses U.S. Americans in Costa Rica employed as part of their construction of individual and communal identity are considered here as part of what David Snow and Leon Anderson have termed "identity work," that is, "the range of activities individuals engage in to create, present, and sustain personal identities that are congruent with and supportive of the self-concept as it is done individually and collectively."[6] So defined, identity work may involve a number of complementary activities, such as the arrangement of one's material environment or human associations. But it may also be performed discursively, through verbal construction and the assertion of personal identities, which Snow and Anderson refer to as "identity talk."[7] Given its consideration of identity-making and belonging, the book is also concerned with issues of gender. Throughout the constitutive narratives of the U.S. immigrants featured in this study, gender continuously intersects with other categories of identity, such as class, ethnicity, and nationality and recurs both as a factor for the act of immigration between the United States and Costa Rica (entities that in themselves are perceived in gendered terms) and as a key component in the creation of new selves, on both the individual and collective levels.[8]

I consider this identity work and identity talk along three complementary dimensions. The first is the local, which stresses the importance of places and emplacement as cultural practices, especially among immigrants of a privileged background, who are supposedly more disposed to forgo attachment to a physical place in favor of more fluid, nonterritorial identifications.[9] The second dimension is the transnational one, which encompasses practices that straddle the two countries and involves the move between them and adaptation to life in Costa Rica.[10] The third dimension is the international one, consisting of a reflection on U.S. emigration to Costa Rica as part of larger trends of international flows, such as counterculture movements and lifestyle migration; this aspect allows for a comparative consideration of this phenomenon.

Considering the international flows of migration, it is important to grasp the significance of this countercurrent of U.S. immigration in both its directionality and its cultural-ideological impetus. The flow of U.S. Americans to Costa Rica took place against the common trends of immigration in the Americas insofar as it was a north to south phenomenon rather than the more common south to north transition (which are of course not neutral geographical descriptors but carry specific cultural and political baggage and embody relations of power grounded in both the recent and the past history of the Americas). In focusing on this north to south immigration in the Americas, the book contributes to and is in dialogue with a growing body of literature that conceptualizes new forms and patterns of late twentieth- and early twenty-first-century immigration, sometimes described as "amenity migration" or "lifestyle migration." The latter is perhaps more accurately described by Michael Janoschka and Heiko Haas as lifestyle-*oriented* migration, which they define, following Michaela Benson and Karen O'Reilly, as "the temporary or permanent spatial movement of relatively affluent persons of all ages who travel and move between meaningful places with an individually imagined and collectively perceived potential to provide a better quality of life."[11] It is important to note that Costa Rica, like other destinations of immigration, was not *essentially* meaningful but rather became a geography of meaning, to use Benson and O'Reilly's term, through distinct practices of emplacement and discursive work that made the country desirable to U.S. Americans and led them to view it as providing an opportunity for a better life and, perhaps even more importantly, a better *self*.[12] Yet unlike recent work on lifestyle immigration, I trace such patterns of flow back to the decades following World War II and contextualize them within the broader power relations derived from the U.S. hegemony in Cold–War Central America and the identity work that this hegemony often generated.

In the context of the Cold War and the turbulent postwar decades in the United States, the countercurrent of immigration points also to the affiliation and identification of many of these immigrants with the U.S. and international counterculture. They perceived their immigration either as part of a direct resistance, initially to the Korean War and later to the Vietnam War, or as partaking in the more fluid "dropping out" or escape from mainstream society in favor of a self-searching journey. In this respect, the book also considers the transformation of a specific culture from the United States and its implementation in and adaptation to life in Costa Rica.

Why study these people, at this particular time and place? Costa Rica was not a prominent territory of the informal U.S. American empire in Central America, and the U.S. Americans who came there were ordinary people, not remarkable historical figures.[13] Yet I suggest that herein lies the illuminative power of the Costa Rican case for both immigration studies and Americas studies. Borrowing Laura Putnam's observation regarding a different context of migration, sometimes "the experiences and ideas of not-very-powerful people in not-very-prominent places" attest to important changes on the regional, national, and transnational levels.[14] While most of the U.S. immigrants were not powerful, or wealthy, in their homeland—indeed, their life stories suggest a strong sense of marginality—their U.S. American citizenship (even when their immigration was an act of objection to the United States) granted them a privileged status that was the result of global power relations.[15] As I demonstrate in the chapters that follow, a close examination of the U.S. American population in Costa Rica following World War II yields new insights regarding immigration under conditions of asymmetrical power relations and the role played by U.S. power in the identity work of U.S. American immigrants.

The United States and Costa Rica: Imagining Resemblance in a Hegemonic Framework

Despite the vast differences in the size and global importance of their respective countries and nations, Costa Rican and U.S. policymakers forged a discourse that stressed a kind of resemblance and affiliation between the two parties. This discourse, which was echoed also in the writings and conversations of ordinary U.S. Americans and Costa Ricans, highlighted the exceptional nature of both countries in terms of their historical development, democratic heritage, and supposedly shared political interests, which in fact were grounded in the hegemony of the United States in Central America and its acceptance, by and large, by Costa Rica.

The alleged exceptional character of Costa Rica was articulated already in the early nineteenth century. In a 1829 congressional speech, Juan Mora Fernández, the country's first president following its independence from the Spanish Crown, stated that while "the whole . . . Central American Republic appears divided, consumed and covered in blood . . . Costa Rica presents a [small] painting . . . illuminated . . . by the rainbow of peace."[16] From the nineteenth century onward, Costa Rican sources regularly dubbed the country the "Switzerland of Central America."[17] The official national narrative maintained that Costa Rica is not only Central America's most peaceful but also its most democratic, egalitarian, and "white" (i.e., not indigenous or racially mixed but exclusively European) republic, a law-abiding and democratically oriented society, and therefore more similar to the United States than to its Central American neighbors.

Like any national narrative, this account holds some truth. During the Spanish conquest most of the indigenous population in Costa Rica was exterminated, and African slavery never reached substantial levels in the country. As a small, marginal province of the Spanish empire, Costa Rica was allegedly established not as a stratified colonial society based on class and ethnicity but rather as an egalitarian community of small agricultural households of purportedly white origin. These communities were concentrated in the Central Valley, which in 1824 was home to four-fifths of Costa Rica's sixty thousand inhabitants and thus perceived as the nation's core and essence.[18] This concentration resulted in close ties and, in many cases, kinship among the Central Valley denizens, which lasted for centuries. These long-standing close family ties astonished and appealed to some U.S. Americans, who came from a very different society, one that was heterogeneous and often estranged; however, they also made it difficult for the newcomers to integrate into Costa Rican society.[19]

As the categories of nationality and race are, of course, socially and historically constructed, it is important to notice that in this process of "imagining" the Costa Rican community, race played a crucial role, with particular ramifications for the construction of national identity through immigration policies.[20] Like all societies in the Americas, Costa Rica was a settler society and therefore explicitly multiethnic. However, unlike many other Latin American nations that often asserted racial mixture as part of the core of their national identity (such as Brazil and Cuba), and similar to Uruguay and Argentina, Costa Rica staked a claim for "whiteness," which was then implemented through the manipulation of the national census and modes of public representation.[21]

This narrative of a white, egalitarian, and peaceful society has been rebutted since the 1970s by historians, geneticists, social scientists, and other scholars, from within and without Costa Rica, who point to the account's ahistorical and racist components. These studies draw attention to, for example, the existence of a robust use of Black slaves in plantations along the Atlantic coast during the seventeenth century and the fact that in the late eighteenth century less than one-tenth of the Costa Rican population was directly descended from the Spanish conquerors while over half were Black, mestizos, and mulatos.[22] The national narrative also ignored the large-scale migration, beginning in the late nineteenth century, of Afro-Caribbean workers to the Costa Rican Atlantic coast; it also obscured the significance of Chinese immigration to the country.[23]

Regardless of historical evidence, the narrative of Costa Rica's exceptionalism was not only shared by officials and presented in national modes of representations but also infiltrated the masses and was sustained as a myth about the Costa Rican character.[24] Like any nation, Costa Rica constructed its self-image both internally and vis-à-vis the ways in which it was perceived from the outside. The country's welcoming attitude toward U.S. Americans and Europeans was designed to reinforce the country's "whiteness" in its own eyes; the immigrants' arrival served as further proof of this "whiteness" by suggesting that they "feel at home" in the country. Indeed, the basic tenets of the Costa Rican national narrative of exceptionalism were largely adopted by U.S. travelers, journalists, and policymakers from the late nineteenth century on. Returning from a visit to Costa Rica in 1859, U.S. politician Thomas Francis Meagher not only echoed this view but also identified in Costa Rica an example of the Jeffersonian ideal of a society of small households: "Almost every man has his farm . . . This—more than the purity of their Spanish blood . . . is the secret of their industry. This is the secret of their manhood."[25]

Although Costa Rica boasted about its exceptional status in the Central American isthmus, and U.S. Americans largely accepted this belief, Costa Rica was actually much more similar to other Central American countries than it admitted being, in both its agricultural export-based economy and the consequent intervention of U.S. power designed to protect the interests of U.S. corporations. Costa Rica was never subjected to direct U.S. control in the form of a political or military regime, as was the case with the post-1898 U.S. empire of island colonies and neighboring Nicaragua; however, as a Latin American republic, the country was part of what Greg Grandin has called the "imperial workshop" of the United States: a site on which U.S. policymakers developed and enhanced their imperial strategies, and one, moreover, where U.S. citizens cultivated what Mary A. Renda dubbed, in the context of Haiti, an "imperial consciousness."[26]

Costa Rica played a significant role in this rise of U.S. power in Central America, serving as an early model of a "banana republic." From the 1880s onward, its Atlantic coast was the main hub of the United Fruit Company (UFC), a Boston-based corporation that, in a manner characteristic of the exercise of U.S. influence in Central America, served as the vanguard of U.S. presence in the country and contributed to the undermining of its sovereignty.[27] Soon after the arrival of the company, the influence of the United States in Costa Rica began to be directed through governmental channels, and in the second decade of the twentieth century the Wilson administration exerted severe diplomatic pressure on Costa Rica to secure U.S. access to its oil and other natural resources.[28] Despite such exercises of U.S power, in the 1930s, under the administration of President León Cortés Castro, a representative of the German coffee oligarchy in Costa Rica, the country was a strong supporter of Nazi Germany. This deviation from U.S. patronage was short-lived, and at the Pan American Congress of 1940 Costa Rican president Rafael Ángel Calderón Guardia made the strategic decision to join the Allies, assuring the U.S. ambassador in Costa Rica that he should "feel free to express to me frankly any views that you may have as to *both* foreign and domestic affairs" (my emphasis).[29]

During World War II, the United States stepped up its military and civil intervention in Costa Rica, and the latter's dependency deepened accordingly. As early as 1940, the United States sent a military contingent to Costa Rica to provide support for the defense of the Panama Canal. The same contingent also served as Calderón's security force, making the United States an active player in the Costa Rican political sphere. At the time, U.S. aid, totaling $63 million, was the only source of funding for Costa Rica's military.[30] In return, Costa Rica allowed the United States to use all its military and naval bases. In addition to military aid, Costa Rica also received loans, as well as a moratorium on debt repayments to the United States and international banks. It also received preferred quotas for its coffee in the U.S. market, which thus replaced the German market upon which this industry previously relied, propping up the Costa Rican economy during the war. In the civilian sphere, U.S. companies took over the Costa Rican electricity sector and handled the manufacturing of raw materials, mainly rubber, crucial to the war effort on terms that once again favored U.S. conglomerates and bypassed local Costa Rican manufacturers.[31] The cumulative effect of these projects and their dynamics was a deepening of Costa Rica's subordination, prompting increasingly widespread feelings that Costa Rican national interests—and national honor—were being subjugated to U.S. demands. In 1943 political and economic thinker Rodrigo Facio Brenes strongly condemned U.S. corporations and defined Costa Rica as a "semicolonial" entity, a claim that at once echoed Costa Rican sentiments that had existed since the late nineteenth-century United Fruit regime and anticipated similar assertions that were to arise in the future.[32]

Another important step that drove the United State deeper into Costa Rica and advanced, symbolically and literally, the arrival of U.S. Americans in the country, was the progress of the Costa Rican section of the Inter-American Highway, motivated by the need to secure a continental road to the Panama Canal during the war. The early 1940s construction of the road over the highest ridge in

Costa Rica—named Cerro de la Muerte (mountain of death) after the numerous casualties among those who tried to cross it—was represented in U.S. sources as a huge achievement of technology and modernity, that is, of the United States, over nature (identified with Costa Rica).[33] The highway, which aimed at creating a direct route between the United States and Costa Rica, also put Costa Rica on the map, figuratively and symbolically, rendering it more accessible to U.S. tourists and immigrants, who would indeed flow into the country in the years to come.

World War II therefore significantly increased U.S. involvement in Costa Rica, on both the political and administrative level, and spurred the arrival of U.S. Americans who set the foundations for the U.S. communities there. The founders of the English-speaking amateur theater in Costa Rica, the Little Theatre Group, for example, were members of the military contingent to Costa Rica, and it was also during the war years that the U.S. Women's Club of Costa Rica was established, its members taking upon themselves to contribute to the Allied war effort and to the image of the United States in the country. The club members' ambition exemplifies what became a recurring blurring of the line between formal and informal agents of the United States in Costa Rica during the Cold War, while also underscoring the critical role that gender came to play in the practices and image of the U.S. presence in Central America as well as the significance of U.S. power in the gendered identity work of ordinary U.S. Americans in Costa Rica.[34] Conversely, the exposure of Costa Ricans to U.S. Americans and to the United States also increased after the war, as the GI Bill enabled Costa Rican men who served in the Allied forces to study in the United States and led some of them to return home to Costa Rica with U.S. American wives.

Cold War Encounters: Shared Interests and Their Advantages

While the foreign policy of President Calderón subordinated Costa Rica to U.S. policy, his domestic policies broke with it rather dramatically, with far-reaching implications for the future relations of the United States and Costa Rica and for the country's appeal to a certain segment of the U.S. American population. An exceptional reform coalition, composed of Calderón's Partido Republicano Nacional (PRN) and the communist party (Partido Vanguardia Popular, later renamed Partido Comunista de Costa Rica [PCCR]) and supported by the Catholic Church, ruled Costa Rica from 1940 to 1948 and was responsible for radical social reforms, including pro-labor legislation that enraged U.S. corporations. After World War II, as the United States was no longer dependent on Costa Rican support, and as the rhetoric of the U.S. administration shifted from democracy vs. authoritarianism to democracy vs. communism, the U.S. administration felt free to express its resentment of the participation of the communist party in the ruling coalition. The Cold War was being transplanted into the context of the Western hemisphere, opening the door to a new era of interventionist polices in which Costa Rica, regarded always as a strategic and sensitive site due to its proximity to the Panama Canal, was a crucial arena for the pursuit of U.S. interests.[35]

The short-lived, relatively contained Costa Rican civil war, which broke out in March-April 1948, served as a test case for the U.S. intentions in the region. While brought about by the long-term social confrontation of the 1940s, the immediate trigger for the war was the political crisis following the annulment of the 1948 elections, in which the Calderonistas sought to preserve their authority while the Costa Rican communist party had increased its power by more than a quarter, a result that alarmed the U.S. administration.[36] On March 12, 1948, fighting broke out between a front of opponents, led by José (Pepe) Figueres, and pro-government troops.[37] The war continued for six weeks, until the implementation of a peace agreement, in which the United States was deeply involved. Nathaniel Davis, a former diplomat who was considered an expert in communism and who had spent a considerable part of his career stationed at the U.S. embassy in Moscow, was nominated in 1947 as the new U.S. ambassador to Costa Rica. There, he very quickly came to play a critical role in the resolution of war, to the satisfaction of the United States. The agreements included PRN-backed president Teodoro Picado's resignation and the installation in power of the Partido Liberación Nacional (PLN), headed by Figueres, first as a de facto junta, paving the road for the PLN's rise to power, which it proceeded to hold until the 1970s. Immediately after the war, the communist party was outlawed, and the ruling junta dissolved some sixty trade unions, exiled three thousand supporters of the communist party, and executed at least fourteen union and leftists activists, in what Carmen Kordick describes as a clear attempt to get close to the United States.[38] While these actions received less traction on the world stage, Costa Rica did gain international renown for its decision in December 1948 to abolish the national army. President Figueres's dissolution of the military is frequently presented as additional evidence—if not the centerpiece—of Costa Rican exceptionalism. In 1951 Figueres further strengthened Costa Rica's egalitarian image by declaring, "We are the government of the middle class."[39] And it is unsurprising to find that Davis reiterated this Costa Rican narrative of exceptionalism and democratic heritage in his memoirs, stating that "the settlers [in Costa Rica] were much like those who came to early New England: sturdy, industrious, self-reliant yeomen, the stuff of which a democratic society is made."[40] Kordick argues that this narrative, which became a Costa Rican constitutive myth celebrating the country as the isthmus's peaceful, democratic, white, and egalitarian exceptional republic, was further bolstered in the context of the Cold War. This narrative later served the United States as a means of explaining why Costa Rica avoided the violent civil wars that rocked the rest of the regions in the 1960s, '70s, and '80s and enabled U.S. officials to lay the blame for the region's politically motivated violence in the twentieth century entirely on the supposedly savage Central American nature rather than on its own interventions in the region.[41]

As the Cold War unfolded, Costa Rica, headed by Figueres, managed to maneuver between the raindrops. Figueres himself (who had been a successful abaca grower before turning to politics) spent several formative years in the United States during President Roosevelt's New Deal, was fond of quoting Thomas Jefferson, read the *New York Times* daily, and was married twice, both times to U.S. American women. As president, he carefully orchestrated Costa Rican internal policies and hemispheric Cold War politics. The nation's post–civil war constitution of 1949 enshrined the national healthcare system, progressive labor reforms, and modern social security system as constitutional rights. This ensured Costa Rica's relative political stability during the Cold War, since it reduced economic pressures on the masses—who might otherwise have been drawn to Marxist revolutionary ideas—and created a prosperous, egalitarian, and peaceful image of Costa Rica, which attracted foreigners.

In his conduct of foreign affairs, Figueres walked a thin line. During his 1952 visit to the United States he presented himself as a citizen of a banana republic and stated that Costa Rica was not interested in foreign investments; however, in his 1953 inauguration speech, Figueres identified Costa Rica with the United States and accepted its hegemony in the region, stating that "we are on the side of the Western countries which uphold our democratic and Christian civilization, and we give our backing to the leadership of United States of North America."[42] Figueres endorsed U.S. involvement in the 1954 coup against Jacobo Árbenez Guzmán in Guatemala, which gained him popularity and favors in Washington and the U.S. media. In 1954 *World Affairs* heralded Figueres as "a model that other Latin American reformers could well follow."[43]

In the early days of John F. Kennedy's term in the White House, relations between the United States and Costa Rica drew even closer. Kennedy cited Figueres in the inaugurating speech of the Alliance for Progress program in March 1961.[44] Charles Ameringer, a U.S. scholar who wrote a biography on Figueres, maintained that in the early days of President Kennedy's administration, the latest trends in Washington DC were Afro-American rights, modern art, and José (Pepe) Figueres.[45] Among Costa Ricans, the sentiment was apparently mutual. When Kennedy visited Costa Rica in March of 1963 to take part in the Central American summit designed to secure support for U.S. policy against Cuba, his presence in San José created mass hysteria. The day of his arrival was declared a national holiday and the streets of the Costa Rican capital were blocked in what was known as Operación Kennedy. Some three hundred thousand people, almost a quarter of Costa Rica's entire population at the time, packed San José's Avenida Central and the road leading to the Juan Santamaría airport, waving flags of Costa Rica, the United States, and the Alliance for Progress (fig. 2). Throughout the night, tens of thousands remained gathered under the windows of Kennedy's suite at the San José Grand Hotel, enjoining him to greet them.[46]

The following day, *La Nación*, Costa Rica's largest newspaper, stated, "It was an enormous, honest demonstration, an explosion of emotions and solidarity between two people who are equally democratic and fond of liberty."[47] In newspaper advertisements, Costa Rican businessmen saluted Kennedy, with some even comparing him to Bolívar and the Alliance for Progress to the Columbian general's plan to unite South America.[48]

Costa Rica's explicit affiliation with the United States may be viewed as the expression of a genuine sentiment of political and cultural affinity, or, more cynically, as an enforced political narrative (dissident media were shut down during Kennedy's visit, for example) and yet another political strategy to distinguish Costa Rica from the rest of Central America during the Cold War. But the fact of the affiliation is undeniable. And while scandals, such as the escapades of Robert Vesco (the infamous fugitive U.S. financier who faced charges of fraud and found refuge in Costa Rica in the early 1970s) and the massive land-purchasing by U.S. Americans in Costa Rica since the 1970s, did cast a shadow on the image of the United States and U.S. Americans, they did not create a mass anti-gringo sentiment or movement.[49] In this context, the welcoming attitude toward U.S. Americans who arrived in Costa Rica can also be seen as designed to boost Costa Rica's pro-U.S. image. Indeed, the rise in the numbers of U.S. immigrants to Costa Rica was regarded as evidence of the success of such efforts.

From United Fruit to Flower Children: The Arrival of U.S. Americans in Costa Rica

Disparate trickles of U.S. Americans began arriving in Costa Rica in the middle of the nineteenth century, encouraged by its immigration laws. These statutes accorded with the country's ethnic self-perception and desire to strengthen the allegedly white population and thus restricted if not outright banned Asian or Black immigration; they did, however, serve to attract Europeans and North Americans.[50] The majority of U.S. Americans arriving in the country by the end of the nineteenth century were merchants and agriculturists, followed by employees of U.S. corporations, such as the UFC, independent businessmen, and professionals of various

Fig. 2. U.S. president John F. Kennedy being driven past crowds of cheering onlookers after arriving in Costa Rica, March 18, 1963. Francisco Orlich, Costa Rica's president, is standing next to him in the car. Bettmann/Getty Images.

types. The U.S. Americans who arrived in Costa Rica prior to World War II played a secondary role in the Anglo-American community, which was still dominated by British people and culture.[51] In 1942 Henrietta Boggs, a young woman from Alabama, came to visit her family in San José, where her ambitious aunt was successful in introducing her to the city's high society (Boggs went on to become the first wife of José Figueres). In her memoir, she recounts the end of a formal dinner at which all the guests rose and turned to face a full-size portrait of George V: "Moved by a signal which escaped me, we raised our glasses and in one voice solemnly said, 'The King.'"[52] In retrospect, the salute Boggs described was, to a certain extent, the swansong of European hegemony in Costa Rica. According to official Costa Rican censuses, between the 1950s and the 1970s the number of Europeans in the country declined by 80 percent, from 10,616 to 2,483 people, with the sharpest decline being in the number of British citizens—from 7,000 in 1950 to 200 in 1963—a reflection of the changes in the global arena.[53]

The number of U.S. citizens, on the other hand, rose in a linear fashion. In 1948 the three U.S. consulates in Costa Rica, located in San José, Puntarenas, and Puerto Limón, documented 1,424 U.S. Americans in the country. Dominant among them were "representatives and employees of American commercial concerns" and people who were in the "employ of U.S. government."[54] The publication of U.S. consulate reports was halted in 1951, but the Costa Rican census indicates a growth of 60 percent over the next three decades, from 2,129 U.S. Americans in 1950 to 3,453 in 1979. In 1973, for example, the census shows that the size of the U.S. American population in the country had surpassed that of the overall European population. Between 1950 and 1970, U.S. Americans were the fastest-growing minority in Costa Rica, although in absolute numbers they always lagged behind immigrants from Nicaragua. In terms of gender, Costa Rican censuses indicate a close ratio of women to men (see table 1).

Table 1. Foreign population in Costa Rica, 1950–73

YEAR / NATIONALITY	1950	1963	1973
United States	2,219 (0.26)	2,051 (0.15)	3,453 (0.17)*
Europe (total)	10,616 (1.3)	3,735 (0.27)	2,483 (0.12)
Nicaragua	16,559 (2)	18,722 (1.4)	17,335 (0.8)
Total population of Costa Rica	800,875	1,336,274	1,955,776

Source: Adapted by the author from Costa Rican national censuses for the years 1950, 1963, and 1973.

* Percentage of a given foreign population compared to the total Costa Rican population

The U.S. Americans who came to Costa Rica from the 1950s to the 1970s were a diverse group that included employees of the U.S. administration and representatives of U.S. corporations and their dependents, as well as U.S. missionaries who were part of the proliferation of U.S. Protestant missions.[55] Another category of U.S. Americans who came to Costa Rica as a consequence, if indirect, of the hegemonic role the United States played in the Western hemisphere is that of U.S. women who married Costa Rican men. These relationships were formed when the latter took advantage of the 1944 GI Bill of Rights and came to study in the United States after fighting with the Allied forces during World War II.[56]

In addition, starting in the early 1950s Costa Rica became a haven for U.S. dissidents and counterculturists. Quakers, mainly from southern United States, objecting to the Korean War and the U.S. war economy and in some cases wanting to avoid being jailed due to their resistance to the draft, arrived in Costa Rica between 1951 and 1953 and established the colony of Monteverde in the province of Puntarenas. They were followed in the late 1960s and 1970s by U.S. Americans who were objectors to the Vietnam War and part of the emerging counterculture in the United States. This group, interesting and significant in itself, should also be considered as part of a larger international movement of young people from the United States and Europe who were on the move to less-developed countries, breaking family ties and resisting sociopolitical identification with their home countries.[57]

Costa Rica fitted that narrative perfectly. The country's long-held national myth of exceptionalism as a beacon of democracy and egalitarianism was augmented after 1948 by the abolition of the national army and social reforms untainted by a subversive Marxism. Despite the severe repression of trade unions and political dissidents, the decades following the short 1948 civil war and up to the economic crisis of the 1980s are known as the years of the "Costa Rican Dream."[58] Meanwhile, during those same decades, the United States was being torn and buffeted by social and ethnic conflict and becoming increasingly embroiled in Vietnam—and later troubled by the consequences of these confrontations. Seeing in Costa Rica a mirror image of sorts of their own homeland, many U.S. citizens, disillusioned with the American Dream, sought to substitute it with its Costa Rican analogy.

Another trend of immigration from the United States to Costa Rica, which occurred around the same time but was very different in its social and cultural composition, was the wave that followed the 1964 Pensionado Law. The law, which granted foreigners (regardless of their age) residency status in Costa Rica in return for a monthly deposit in Costa Rican banks, drew thousands of U.S. Americans to the country in the early 1970s, in a surge of immigration that starkly highlighted the asymmetrical economic power relations between the two countries.[59]

Immigration without Immigrants? Power Relations, Privilege, and Self-Designs

Whereas the Costa Rican censuses conducted between the 1950s and the 1970s estimated the number of U.S. Americans in the country as between two and three thousand (see table 1), a senior U.S. American in Costa Rica estimated that in the 1970s this number was closer to tens of thousands, a discrepancy that is common in data concerning immigrants of this type.[60] Indeed, the policies of both the United States and Costa Rica regarding the documentation of the flow of U.S. Americans into Costa Rica facilitated, to a large extent, such unrecorded immigration: whereas undocumented immigration is usually associated with poor, illegal migrants, here it was precisely the privileged status of U.S. Americans in Costa Rica—their national origin, their perception as white, their economic status—that enabled them to move below the radar of the United States, which did not document emigration, and Costa Rica, which was eager to receive them.[61] The acquisition of citizenship—a formal and symbolic act that attests to the immigrant's intention to become part of the receiving country, was neither required of U.S. Americans in Costa Rica nor desired by them.[62] The reluctance to give up their native citizenship was common among U.S. Americans abroad (dual citizenship was not allowed by the United States until 1990) and can be attributed to patriotic sentiments but also, and perhaps mostly, to practical considerations: U.S. citizenship enabled a circular immigration and frequent visits to the United States for work or family needs, and perhaps more importantly, served as a sort of insurance policy in case Costa Rica became dangerous or unstable. As one U.S. immigrant related the tendency to view Costa Rica as the Switzerland of Central America, "It's Switzerland—*but* in Central America."[63]

Costa Rica's loose policies regarding U.S. immigration prevailed until the mid-1970s. It was only after the Robert Vesco scandal, the rising acrimony over the privileged status granted to U.S. retirees, and the growing public attention to large-scale land purchases by U.S. Americans that Costa Rica began requiring foreigners to regularize their legal status. Mark Bach, who arrived in Costa Rica in 1968, described the nonchalant manner in which this change was communicated to the U.S. milieu: "In the beginning, when you came here you didn't need a residency. There wasn't even [any such thing]. . . . We'd been here for years, ten-fifteen years, they called us up and said, 'Would you please come down and register? We have so many of you now.' So we all went down and got our residency."[64]

While some U.S. Americans did take Costa Rican citizenship, for practical reasons mainly related to doing business in the country, for most of them residency and not citizenship was the preferred option. This choice both reflected and shaped deeper self-perceptions regarding the status of U.S. American immigrants in Costa Rica and their identity work vis-à-vis both their homeland and their adoptive country. Several thousand of them lived in Costa Rica for many years and raised families there, sometimes with Costa Rican spouses; acquired property, sometimes of substantial value; and forged complex, multilayered identifications, as is often the case with immigrants. Yet both their civic status—as undocumented immigrants or residents rather than citizens—and the fact that almost none of my informants defined themselves as immigrants—either upon arriving in Costa Rica or in many cases even after many years of living there—attest to their reluctance to perceive themselves as such. Furthermore, over the years neither the *TT* nor bulletins of U.S. social organizations used the term immigrants, preferring instead labels such as "privileged guests," "U.S. Americans in Costa Rica," or "expats." This serves to highlight both the linkage between power relations of the sending and receiving society, which are the result of long histories of colonialism and postcolonial relations, and the explicit and implicit ways through which privilege is structured and articulated in the identity work of immigrants.[65] Tracing the different identifications that U.S. Americans in Costa Rica adopted or rejected enables us to situate their process of identity work within a specific historical and geopolitical context. This in turn contributes to the refinement of scholarly definitions more broadly and thus stands to deepen our understanding of the nature of immigration.

The traditional definition of immigrants describes them as people who move from one country to another in order live there permanently.[66] However, many of the U.S. Americans in Costa Rica tended to think of themselves as people who *happened* to leave the United States for various reasons (often related to lifestyle and ideology rather than economic conditions), were then attracted to Costa Rica (or else arrived there by chance), and *happened* to stay there for many years. "I never decided to stay or leave," said Joan Stevens, who arrived in Costa Rica from Minnesota in 1967 for a three-month professional assignment and has lived there ever since.[67] Her comment reflects both the ambivalence of many U.S. Americans in Costa Rica toward their own migratory status and identity and their ongoing process of coming to terms with their post factum immigration. This ambivalence has much to do with the political, economic, and cultural baggage attached to the terms "immigrant" and "immigration" both in the United States and Costa Rica. In both cultures the terms generally connote an Other, a person of lower economic class, nonwhite, acting from a position of lack of volition, which was very different from the profile and self-perceptions of U.S. Americans in Costa Rica. In Costa Rica, the conception of who is an "immigrant" and the immigration problem are associated more specifically with Nicaraguans or Columbians, and it is partly against these populations that national identity and the individual and collective identifications of other migratory populations are defined.[68]

In recent decades, the research categories of lifestyle immigration, high-end immigrants, or privilege immigrants have emerged, attempting to bridge the gap between the act of movement and the population involved and to conceptualize the inconclusive nature of such flows.[69] These late twentieth- and twenty-first-century categories encapsulate various forms of migratory flows by relatively affluent individuals of all ages, who move either part-time or full-time to places they perceive as offering a better quality of life, usually in the sense of leisure and self-realization rather than job opportunities or other conventional kinds of economic betterment.[70] As Matthew

Hayes suggests, the term lifestyle migration itself "is tied up with the coloniality of global regimes of mobility," as it underscores the difference between work migration and lifestyle migration.[71]

This body of research, which has only recently expanded to include an examination of migration from north America to its center and south, addresses the historical consequences of the undeniable asymmetries of power between the sending and receiving societies and suggests that these factors are responsible both for the arrival of U.S. Americans in these territories and for their processes of identity work vis-à-vis both the United States and the receiving countries.[72] Even though the term is commonly applied to late twentieth- and early twenty-first century migrations, I suggest that lifestyle migration is a useful category for examining segments of the 1950s to 1970s U.S. immigrants to Costa Rica and the pattern of their settlement there, specifically with regards to the counterculture immigrants and the retirees.

Another term that recurs in the literature on U.S. Americans outside the United States is *expatriates*, a term popularized after World War I as referring to prominent American artists and writers, such as Josephine Baker, Gertrude Stein, Ernest Hemingway, and F. Scott Fitzgerald, who left the United States to live elsewhere. This association lends two meanings to the term, which were highly significant for the self-definition of U.S. Americans in Costa Rica: firstly that being an "expatriate" (or *expatriating*, as an ongoing, sometimes lifelong, process) involves an element of withdrawal or disassociation from one's native country, and secondly that it carries somewhat of a bohemian air. Sociologist Erik Cohen broadened the definition of expatriatism, suggesting that it serves to "fill the gap between the tourist, on the one hand, and the semi-permanent immigrant, on the other," a definition that applies both to the reasons that led many of the U.S. Americans in Costa Rica to settle there and to their reluctance to change their citizenship.[73] Cohen sharpens the term's definition by emphasizing transience and privilege as the factors that distinguish expatriates from immigrants, settlers, and sojourners.[74] Dorothy Backer, a U.S. expatriate in Asia, offered a definition of expatriatism that echoes Cohen's emphasis on privilege and transience while at the same time expressing the ethnic and racial overtones of this phenomenon and the power relations it generates: "Expatriatism is power, freedom from all the restraints of home. One is uncommitted, yet cannot be judged. One is an exception to every rule, *a freckled blond among the swarthy, a free man among the slaves, a person in movement among the fixed*" (my emphasis).[75]

While "expatriate" is applicable to their civic and mental status, the U.S. Americans in Costa Rica I interviewed for this book were typically ambivalent about the term. On the one hand, many of them preferred it to the designation "immigrant" because it is a more ambiguous and loose definition that captures the transitory and unrooted nature of their presence as well as their freedom from responsibility vis-à-vis both their homeland and their adoptive country, or indeed vis-à-vis any national framework ("The Vietnam War kind of took that out of me . . . I'm somewhat disillusioned, or very disillusioned, depending on what day you talk to me, with government in general and just that whole thing of flag and country and stuff like that," a veteran U.S. army paratrooper told me).[76] On the other hand, some expressed an opposite concern about the term's anti-U.S. connotation. Mark Bach, for instance, explained, "Because that is *ex*, that means in the past you were a patriot, and I just stayed a patriot, I guess. I like the States, admire it and like it, and always consider myself an American; I just don't like to live there."[77]

In sum, as O'Reilly argues, this picture suggests that acknowledging a continuum of human movement with varying degrees of agency and privilege is a more profitable framework than labeling.[78] In the chapters that follow, I use the informants' own self-definitions but also refer to them as immigrants, even if their immigration was an unintentional, post factum one. Definitions aside, I aspired to be attentive to the choice of terminology, particularly when used self-referentially, and to what it conveys about the informants' personal, cultural, and political belonging.

Identity Work and Identity Talk: A Note on Sources and Methodology

At the core of this book lie the diverse experiences and respective identity work conducted by U.S. women and men in Costa Rica, as a means to understanding processes of identity-making among immigrants in specific relations of power. Indeed, even when looking at their material culture, relations to natural surroundings, or social associations as a means of identity work, the main methodology used was the analysis of their identity talk through the oral histories that I conducted with them. The book is therefore based on a close listening to their voices, often quite literally, as they depict the passage to Costa Rica and the establishment of their lives and forging of their identifications in their adoptive country.

For this research, a total of sixty-five people were engaged in semistructured interviews.[79] All interviewees had lived in Costa Rica between 1944 and 1980 (intermittently). The interviews took place in the interviewees' domain, mostly in their homes and on several occasions in their place of work. Structurally, the interviews followed the informants' life-course chronologically, but they were not dictated by a standard questionnaire.

I did not aspire to reconstruct some sort of "representative" experience of U.S. Americans in Costa Rica through my interviews, since the "typical," as Alistair Thomson has remarked, "can be oppressive."[80] On the contrary, my intention was to expose heterogeneous experiences, marginal and exceptional as they may seem in terms of generational, geographical, gender, and class conventions.

Of the interviewees, forty (61 percent) were women, and twenty-five (39 percent) men. Such a gender imbalance is common in volunteer-based oral history research, yet it has important implications for the knowledge acquired in this research and the picture it paints of U.S. Americans in Costa Rica.[81] The majority female make-up of the body of interviewees, neither intended nor presupposed, was due, perhaps, to the "snowball sampling technique" that I employed in gathering the body of interviewees. It enabled me not only to consider the case of U.S. women in Costa Rica but also to situate it in the larger framework of U.S. female immigration and examine the ways in which gender intersects with other sociocultural and political identities in the experience of immigration. As Sheila Croucher suggested with respect to U.S. immigration to Mexico, gender is inscribed everywhere in the constitutive narratives and experiences of these immigrants. It is implicated in the immigration decisions and the settlement experiences of even relatively affluent immigrants, yet is rather absent in scholarship about lifestyle migration.[82] The life stories of U.S. women enabled me to examine the gender-specific opportunities and challenges that immigration presented for them; the ways in which they negotiated their identifications as women on the move across transnational gendered regimes, to use Sara Mahler and Patricia Pessar's term;[83] the extent to which sex and gender intersect with other identities and social hierarchies, such as national origin; and the implications of this intersection for the immigrants and the communities they established. The dominance of women among the interviewees determined, to a large extent, the type of information gathered in this research. Through frequent references to the changing status of women and womanhood spatially (between the United States and Costa Rica) and temporally (from the 1950s to the 1970s), my informants constantly negotiated the idea of being a U.S. woman abroad.[84] As a consequence, the book focuses rather heavily on feminine practices and institutions, such as the U.S. Women's Club, but lacks alternative knowledge that can only be gathered from a more gender-balanced set of interviewees.[85]

As for their seniority in the host country, fourteen interviewees (22 percent) arrived in Costa Rica in the 1940s and 1950s; another fourteen (22 percent) came in the 1960s; and the majority, thirty-six (56 percent), arrived in the 1970s. The bias toward interviewees from the 1970s can be explained by the fact that prior to this decade Costa Rica was a less-known destination on the map of U.S. emigrants and tourists; of the few who came, some were either too elderly to be interviewed or had passed away by the time I conducted the interviews. During the 1970s, however, the U.S. population in Costa Rica grew substantially, and those who arrived in this decade were still actively involved in the community.

Even before the interviews themselves took place, drawing up the list of interviewees taught me a great deal about the diversity of the communities of U.S. Americans in Costa Rica. As the U.S. population in Costa Rica lacks both strong communal institutions (such as a general U.S. club) and self-documentation in the form of community books or lists, I had to create my own indexes. Each of these began with a contact person in one of the social networks of U.S. citizens in Costa Rica that I identified in the early stages of my research, such as the U.S. Women's Club, a counterculture commune, a church, or a particular neighborhood or region. Then, using the snowball sampling technique, I asked my informants to refer me to additional potential interviewees.[86] This method proved to be very useful in exposing the fragmentation of the U.S. community in Costa Rica as well as the weakness, in some cases, of the national component in the immigrant's identifications. One rainy afternoon I talked, separately, with two women: both had come to Costa Rica from the United States in the late 1960s when they were in their early twenties, and both were white middle-class women who had been living in the very same barrio in San José for dozens of years. Yet because of their different lifestyles and social circles—one of them was a former hippie and the other the wife of a Costa Rican businessman from an elite family—they did not know each other. Since the snowball sampling technique is based on personal referral, it painted a clear picture of the patterns of attachment and detachment among U.S. Americans in Costa Rica and the ways in which these patterns are based not so much on national origin as on more nuanced criteria like class, gender, ethnicity, and lifestyle.

Yet the snowball method does not eliminate what Alessandro Portelli has called "communal censorship," which appears to be as strong as state censorship or the semiformal censorship of social organizations, if not stronger.[87] Relations of love and hate, economic interests, and various other agendas kept hidden from my eyes many informants who might have been pivotal to my research. Yet, what is not said—the silences and omissions, either conscious or subconscious—is no less important than what is said. By and large, individuals and social groups I contacted referred me to interviewees who would endorse and confirm their own narratives of their passage to Costa Rica and their lives there, not to those who would undermine them. One of my glorious failures involved trying to reach the leader of a counterculture commune that had bloomed and declined in the southern Pacific coast of Costa Rica in the early 1970s. More than thirty years after the commune fell apart and its members scattered all over Costa Rica and the United States, both his admirers and his detractors refused to divulge his name and contact information. Yet the bits of information and rumors these informants did provide about him ("he's back in the United States"; "he has vanished"; "he lives in the Central Valley with a very young partner") were telling in their own way.

Unlike this mysterious guru and a handful of other potential interviewees who declined to be interviewed, most of the U.S. Americans I contacted were accessible and responded positively, even enthusiastically, to my request. Beyond the fact that they are now retirees, with the time and inclination for self-reflection, I gradually came to identify a further motivation for their cooperation, namely a tendency toward what I term "self-spectacle-ization"—a sense on the part of interviewees that they have lived an extraordinary life, coupled with the desire to elaborate on it. Moreover, in the face of what many of these interviewees experienced as a certain alienation toward their Costa Rican surroundings and conversely a negative attitude toward U.S. Americans in Costa Rican public opinion, they felt a particular need to justify themselves and tell "their side of the story."

The interviews I conducted were therefore part of the interviewees' ongoing process of constructing and reconstructing their life stories. Dan McAdams rightfully argues that when people talk about their lives they tell stories, and these stories retrospectively create order in the chaos of experience and provide the storytellers with identity, both individual and collective.[88] Charlotte Linde further stresses that the strength and importance of a life story lies in its position at the crossroads of private experience and public norms: it reveals much about the narrator's self, but it also touches upon the common ground of social structures and groups; as such, life stories are extremely useful tools for exposing the construction of both the individual and the collective immigration experience.[89]

The narratives depicted here follow the interviewees life course from the United States to Costa Rica, with special attention to the act of immigration and the years immediately following. They are retrospective evaluations of the informants' past and sometimes also reflections on their future, with many of the interviewees considering, for example, the place in which they wish to be buried as yet another significant mark of their identity work. These stories are therefore biographical narratives, which enables me to situate the move from the United States to Costa Rica within the wider context of histories and sociopolitical processes. My analysis of these stories proceeds on two levels, informative and discursive. Despite their highly constructed nature, these narratives contain an abundance of empirical data and information, such as names, places, institutions, and so on, which, due to the shortage of written sources, could only have been gathered through oral history. As such, they enable me to reconstruct individual and collective practices of life for U.S. Americans in Costa Rica. However, given that this research focuses on processes of identity formation, the true value of the oral histories lies in the light they shed on how U.S. Americans in Costa Rica conceptualized their lives and themselves. By tracing repetitive rhetoric and verbal strategies as well as the avoidance of certain verbal patterns, I consider the life stories as a form of identity talk that is a crucial part of the informants' identity work, on the individual and collective level.

Daniel James has aptly argued that narrators make use of a wide spectrum of possible roles, self-representations, and available narratives.[90] More specifically pertinent to the immigration stories I consider here, McAdams contends that "stories rework deep and vexing issue in our cultural heritage."[91] In the stories of U.S. immigrants in Costa Rica one indeed finds echoes of biblical myths of creation and of the Garden of Eden and its loss; allusions to the conquest of the North American West and images of twentieth-century U.S. popular culture; and paraphrases of colonial narratives of the Spanish conquest in the Americas. These stories therefore allow us to examine how U.S. immigrants in Costa Rica have, over the years, interpreted and reinterpreted their experiences and endowed them with meanings and thus to trace the formation of a wide range of identifications vis-à-vis the immigrants' homeland and adoptive country. Whether portraying the narrators as refugees or exiles from the militaristic and materialistic United States, or as Anglo-Saxon agents of progress in backward Costa Rica, the stories U.S. Americans in Costa Rica tell about their lives illuminate the ways in which they have connected their individual histories to the broader context of the U.S. presence in Central America during the Cold War.

Leo Spitzer has pointed out that memory works by rendering into an experience "something that happened to me," which in itself is an act of interpretation when put into words. He further noted that "transmitting the past through memory is problematic in another way: the recollection of any event or 'experience'—as well as 'forgetting it'—is a socially constructed act undertaken from the perspective of 'a present.'" Moreover, factors like "where" the remembering takes place, the social and political background of the narrators, their gender, age, and economic situation, as well as the relations with the interviewer, all affect recollection and the shape of memory.[92] The inherent subjectivity of the impressions and interpretations depicted here has to do not only with their reconstructed nature but also with the fact that they were produced for a specific research. Oral history is a collaborative effort, and the text it yields reflects the relationship between the interviewer and the interviewee.[93] A scholar is never a complete "insider" or a complete "outsider," but rather both at the same time, and in my own research I tried to stay attentive to the complex effects of my identity and positionality on interactions with interviewees and on outcomes. National, ethnic, religious, class, and gender factors were all at play on various levels. So, for instance, in terms of my Caucasian ethnicity, I was similar to my U.S. Americans interviewees. My Israeli nationality marked me as an outsider among both U.S. Americans and Costa Ricans, though my native country is a close ally of and in many ways even subordinate to the United States. The fact that I am neither Costa Rican nor U.S. American allowed the interviewees to talk to me freely about the "mentality" of these groups, yet probably prevented me from fully grasping much of *their* mentality. Being Jewish is for me a less significant part of my identity than others, but it was apparently meaningful to my Jewish and Christian-Evangelical interviewees. Being a woman and a mother, and especially the fact that I was pregnant during my fieldwork, generated another level of identification: many U.S. women shared with me their ideas about femininity, reproduction, and medical practices in the context of their passage from the United States to Costa Rica, ideas that always carry broader cultural meaning. And I can only speculate about the various experiences my interviewees did not share with me precisely because of these very personal affiliations.

Another form of identity talk of U.S. Americans in Costa Rica—directed at themselves as well as at external readers—was their diverse writings. The impulse I mentioned earlier for self-spectacle-ization, alongside an often artistic-bohemian lifestyle as well as a life of relative leisure, drove many of them to engage in extensive writing of various types—letters, autobiographies, memoirs, and fictional or pseudo-fictional texts, which some of them were happy to share. These texts, which unlike the retrospective life stories related in the interviews were sometimes produced in real time, reveal much about the immigrants' experience, either through facts and reports of empirical experiences or through accounts lying somewhere along the continuum that stretches from the factual to the desired or the imagined.

The main arena in which the collective identity talk took place was the *TT*, the most widely read and influential English-speaking media outlet in Costa Rica. Its publication began in 1956 under the editorship of Elizabeth Dyer, with Richard Dyer, her husband, serving as publisher. It halted in 1960, when the Dyers left the country due to Richard's job relocation as a public relations agent for the UFC. The publication was resumed in 1972, this time under the editorship of the Dyer's daughter, Dery, who had graduated from Wellesley College in the United States and returned to Costa Rica. The history of the *TT* allows us to trace two significant processes: (1) a transformation of the U.S. American experience and self-perception from that of a community of expats consisting mainly of embassy people or employees of U.S. corporations to that of a diverse body of residents and (2) the influence of social and cultural changes in the United States, such as the 1960s protest movements, on the identity work of U.S. Americans in Costa Rica. The generational shift at the helm of the newspaper, from Elizabeth Dyer to her daughter Dery, and the special attention devoted in its pages to the life experiences of U.S American women in Costa Rica, enable us to consider the *TT* also as a gendered cognitive space. The *TT* is therefore examined here as a "textual club" in which the multilayered identifications of writers and readers alike and their contested models of what it means to be a U.S. American man or woman living in Costa Rica were negotiated.

A crucial component of the identity work of U.S. Americans was the selective association or disassociation with other individuals and groups, through the inclusionary and exclusionary mechanisms of the "U.S. clubland," that dense network of social, philanthropic, and business associations.[94] As part of my research I attended several meetings of U.S. organizations in Costa Rica, but as my project is a historical ethnography, I was more interested in their archival writings, which I analyze as another form of identity talk. Such talk was carried out through the vast corpus of textual and visual materials produced in the various social and cultural associations of U.S. Americans in Costa Rica that include, inter alia, monthly bulletins, cookbooks, programs of the English-speaking Little Theatre Group, and so forth. These sources, whose authorship and readership were in many cases limited to the members of a specific social organization, reflect the distinct identity work of diverse circles of U.S. Americans in Costa Rica both toward the Costa Rican surroundings and toward other U.S. Americans.

My analysis of the oral and textual sources of identity work was significantly affected by knowledge that is external to these sources, including knowledge gained through my experience of living in Costa Rica for several periods between 2008 and 2011 and my participant observation in many interactions of U.S. Americans in the country. Like my informants, who often commented in the interviews that things were very different "back then," I faced the challenge of reconstructing the past from the point of view of a very different present. As a researcher living in the Central Valley of Costa Rica in the early years of the twenty-first century, a place filled with U.S. Americans and U.S. American restaurants and medical clinics, condominiums, and businesses, I had to constantly remind myself that things were not always so and that I was searching for the roots of this current reality. And of course, in trying to reconstruct a "thick description" of the experience and self-identifications of U.S. Americans in Costa Rica between the 1950s and the late 1970s, I had also to come to terms with Clifford Geertz's famous remark, namely that "what we call our data are really our own constructions of other people's constructions."[95]

A Road Map

U.S. immigration to Costa Rica was a countercurrent relative to the common trend of immigration in the Americas, yet it was of a piece with other patterns that characterized immigration from the United States and with contemporaneous global immigration patterns of movement. In chapter 1 I situate this immigration in its sociohistorical context and consider the push-and-pull factors for leaving the United States and for choosing Costa Rica. Drawing on Douglas Massey's argument that immigration occurs at the crossroads between an individual, private decisions, and national and international circumstances, the chapter relates broader social and demographic trends (such as the baby boom) and sociopolitical events (wars and political turmoil) to the life stories of U.S. Americans in Costa Rica.[96]

In recent decades, scholarly discourse on immigration has highlighted the evolution of transnational identities and modes of identification based allegedly on social networks, ideologies, and lifestyle rather than attachment to specific places.[97] Yet even in a globalized world and among privileged immigrations, people still move between places, and these places retain a significant role in the creation of their desired selves.[98] Chapter 2 maps, first, the geographical settlement of U.S. Americans in Costa Rica and the practices of emplacement that they generated, and second, the U.S. clubland. It thus considers the dynamics and tension between these two complementary modes of identity work that places and social networks facilitated for U.S. Americans in Costa Rica.

Costa Rica was experienced and represented by U.S. Americans first and foremost as Nature—in contrast to the United States, which was identified with Culture. Chapter 3 examines the identity work that such perceptions entailed through the realization of two myths: of the pristine Amazonia and of the conquest of the North American frontier in the nineteenth century, transplanted into the geopolitical context of Cold–War Central America. The chapter further considers the intersection of gender and ethnicity as it played out in the identity work of U.S. American settlers in the Costa Rican rain forests and beachfronts and concludes with an analysis of the shift that occurred in their practices and self-perceptions with regards to the Costa Rican natural surroundings—from cowboys and capitalist entrepreneurs to paternalistic ecologists.

Examining U.S. American immigration to Costa Rica through the lens of gender, chapter 4 looks at the ways in which the crossing of geographical borders contributed to the creation of various gender-specific repertoires of U.S. American womanhood in Costa Rica, which were negotiated, advanced, and restricted through distinct practices and discourses on the individual, organizational, and communal level. This cultural process of *becoming* a U.S. American woman in Costa Rica is examined through the intersection of gender and U.S. power in the U.S. Women's Club; the discourse of public condemnation of U.S. mothers for allegedly allowing immigration to weaken their familial obligations; and the adaptation of the ideas and texts of the U.S. women's liberation movement to the lives of U.S. American women in 1970s Costa Rica.

Chapter 5 considers materiality as a crucial component of identity work among U.S. Americans in Costa Rica. Whether the move to Costa Rica was perceived as a step down from the affluence of U.S. consumer society to a place of lack, as in the case of the 1950s immigrants, or as a liberation from an overly materialistic society in the late 1960s and 1970s, practices related to material culture—homemaking, use of objects and things, and culinary repertoires—were a crucial arena in which gender, class, nationality, and ethnicity came into play in the construction of distinct identifications among U.S. Americans.

Identity talk is a crucial component of identity work. In chapter 6 I examine the rhetorical strategies and patterns used by U.S. immigrants in the telling of their life stories and the ways in which these shaped individual and collective identity-making among them. Focusing mainly on life stories of those who arrived during the late 1960s and 1970s, I argue that in refusing to understand themselves as immigrants, they articulated and perpetuated imperialist narratives. I further suggest that the core of these accounts lies in a narrative of coincidence and happenstance, which in turn enhances their sense of innocence and lack of agency and thus mitigates feelings of guilt and shame regarding their life in Costa Rica as privileged immigrants.

one

Crossroads
The Movement of Individuals within the Sociopolitical Context

> I have always had a fascination with the tropics . . .
> And also, dollars go a lot further in Costa Rica.
> —SHARON HAGE, author interview

On November 4, 1950, two vehicles, one a canvas-topped truck and the other a Land Rover jeep, drove out of Fairhope, Alabama, and headed south to San José, Costa Rica. The eight bachelors and one family they carried were all Quakers who had decided to leave the United States over their objection to the Korean War (some had already been jailed or were facing imprisonment for their conscientious objection) and, more broadly, because of their reluctance to take part in and support through their taxes what they perceived as militaristic U.S. policies. The group sought to establish an agricultural colony outside the United States and, following a preparatory trip to Central America in 1949, chose Costa Rica (over Guatemala and Mexico) due to its pleasant climate and stable government, eager to attract white, particularly U.S. American, immigrants. Costa Rica's decision in 1948 to abolish its national army, motivated of course by internal politics, provided the ideological rationale for the immigration of this pacifist group.[1]

The 1950 vanguard, which initially resided in San José while looking for a permanent property suitable for an agricultural colony, was soon followed by twenty-five more families and several additional bachelors, most of them from Alabama. In 1953 they established their colony in Santa Elena, in the province of Puntarenas, and named it Monteverde (green mountain). A statement written on the occasion of the colony's sixth anniversary asserted that their move was a permanent one and that it would be followed by a cultural integration: "We hope as speedily as possible to fit ourselves into the life of Costa Rica so that we will no longer be 'foreigners.'"[2] Monteverde endured, and survived, many hardships, and descendants of the original immigrants still live there. It became the only longstanding U.S. American collective settlement in Costa Rica and a focal point for many U.S. American and other immigrants to the country.

Contrary to the Quakers' well-organized immigration and their professed intention to become Costa Ricans, Mark Bach's arrival in the country in 1968 was perceived by him—or at least constructed that way forty years later—as thoroughly coincidental. A Vietnam War veteran and student of geology, Bach and several college friends left school to look for gold in Ecuador. Things, however, did not go exactly as planned. As Bach casually recounted, "We went to Costa Rica on a couple of motorcycles because we didn't have enough money to buy a plane ticket [to Ecuador] and we ended up here for several years."[3]

Not only did Bach never intend to arrive in Costa Rica, he attests that he did not even know, or at least did not consciously remember, that the country existed until he found himself at its border. However, the vagaries of nature (the Darién gap in Panama turned out to be inaccessible to motorcycles), political unrest in Panama, and love (for a U.S. American woman whom Bach met in Costa Rica) ultimately kept him in Costa Rica for much more than "several years." He ended up settling in the country, working as a geologist and raising a family. The family later left Costa Rica for Mexico, where Bach took a job in the metal mining industry in 1994, and then lived in Turkey for a period of time. In 2009 Bach returned to Costa Rica, joining his daughter, who had married a Costa Rican childhood friend and was taking her first steps in the tourist industry.

These two radically different stories testify to the wide range of backgrounds and motivations that led U.S. Americans to Costa Rica, as well as to the variety of their migratory experiences and identity work as represented in their retrospective migratory stories.[4] Immigration, as Massey and his colleagues remind us, stands at the intersection of the individual's decision and large-scale national and international processes and historical events.[5] The individual's decision to migrate is often influenced by issues of class, race, sexuality, ethnicity, nationality, and gender. These personal parameters then intersect with the large-scale national and international processes and historical events. It is this intersection that creates the desire or the need to immigrate, determines its realization, and shapes life in the new country of residence.

This chapter examines the background of U.S. Americans who moved to Costa Rica between the 1950s and the late 1970s along parameters of class, ethnicity, gender, lifestyle, and ideology and their intersection with broader national and international trends and events. In addition to those who arrived in the country as representatives of the U.S. government or U.S. American businesses and their dependents, there were several distinct groups of U.S. Americans who chose to move to Costa Rica. These include women who married Costa Rican men, a phenomenon that peaked in the decade after World War II; Quakers and other dissidents, who left the United States in response, firstly, to the Korean and secondly, and in even greater numbers, to the Vietnam War; and finally, in the early 1970s, U.S. American retirees enticed by favorable legislation into retiring there. In this chapter I review each type of immigrant and analyze the factors of both push and pull—what led them to leave the United States and what drew them to seek out what they thought would be a better life for themselves in Costa Rica. I trace the process through which Costa Rica became for these U.S. Americans what O'Reilly and Benson have termed a "geography of meaning;" a place which, beyond economic and political improvement, held "certain meanings for the migrants in terms of their potential for self-realization."[6] These associations between places and the imagined potentiality of life there were neither inherent nor natural. Rather, they stemmed from the histories of colonialism and imperialism that were not a bygone phenomenon but rather a manifestation of what Aníbal Quijano refers to as the ingoing coloniality of power.[7] These cultural imageries were also the result of wider associations that shaped the image of both countries, with the United States perceived as a powerful modern nation tainted with materialism and decay (among many other associations) and Costa Rica seen as tropical, beautiful, temperate, and lush with a simple, somewhat primitive or backward lifestyle. To these were added more practical factors such as Costa Rica's proximity to the United States, the good relations between the two countries (making it a "safe" choice for immigration relative to destinations in South America, Asia, or Africa), and the highly asymmetrical economic power relations between the two countries, which effectively enabled U.S. Americans to drop out of the rat race of U.S. American social and economic constraints and live financially comfortable lives in Costa Rica.[8]

Turning Away from Ms. Liberty's Torch: U.S. Emigration in a Historical Context

The perception of immigration in the United States as a one-directional flow of the "tired, poor, huddled masses" into the country was so deeply rooted in public opinion, the perceptions of the U.S. government, and the observations of scholars of immigration that for many decades the phenomenon of emigration *from* the United States was simply overlooked. While data regarding immigration to the United States has been continuously gathered from as early as 1819, data about emigration from the country only began to be collected following the Immigration Act of 1907.[9] Even after this date, scholars have tended to focus more on return immigration (immigrants who, after a certain period, opt to return to their country of origin) and not on emigration by U.S.-born citizens.

Yet, as the data shows, immigration in the United States is a bidirectional phenomenon, and while considerably smaller in scope than immigration to the country as well as in relation to international migration trends, emigration has still in no way been insignificant.[10] A phenomenon since the founding of the republic, sometimes consisting of a mere trickle of individuals and at other times a larger current, such emigration reflects not so much economic distress, as is the case for many of those who immigrate to the United States—though economic factors do play a role—but rather individual discontent and dissident collective trends that could not find a place within U.S. American society. These trends reflect profound political, social, and cultural changes and schisms that have led to the creation of U.S. American diasporas throughout the Americas and beyond.[11] Significant waves of such emigration include Confederates who left the country following the South's defeat in the Civil War and settled in Brazil, Mexico, Nicaragua, and British Honduras;[12] the post–World War I "Lost Generation," including many authors, artists, and musicians, who, suffering from cultural and intellectual distress, chose to relocate to France or Mexico;[13] Black artists and writers who emigrated to Mexico and Europe seeking a life free of racial discrimination after World War II (Richard Wright, an African American writer who emigrated to Paris in 1947, stated, "There is more freedom in one block in Paris than in the whole of the United States");[14] and members of the Hollywood elite and New York union trades activists, who, during the McCarthy era, chose to flee to Mexico to avoid charges of communist affiliation.[15]

The rate of emigration from the United States rose consistently after World War II. In response to the question in a Gallop poll from 1946: "If you were free to do so, would you like to live / settle consistently in another country?" only 2 percent responded "yes"; by 1971 this response rose to 12 percent.[16] The data regarding the number of U.S. Americans who actually acted on this wish is scant and inconsistent, as the Truman administration halted the collection of data regarding U.S. citizens abroad in 1951, and moreover, because the precise definition of who counts as an "immigrant" was never fixed or clear-cut. In 1959, 1.59 million U.S. Americans lived outside the United States, a third of whom were civilians and the others military personnel and their dependents.[17] In the first half of the 1960s, the annual rate of emigration from the United States was sixty-six thousand people. Between 1965 and 1969 this figure rose to 150,000 and in 1971–72 it reached a height of 280,000 emigrants a year.[18] This peak is attributable to the effects of the Vietnam War, with those seeking to evade the draft fleeing to Canada and elsewhere, as well as to the war's broader shockwaves.[19] In subsequent years the rate of emigration gradually declined.[20] Robert Warren and Ellen Percy Kraly estimated that some 789,000 U.S. Americans emigrated between 1975 and 1990.[21] Although outside the scope of this research, it is important to note the phenomenon of late twentieth-century and early twenty-first-century U.S. emigration, framed mostly as a lifestyle emigration, to countries in the Americas such as Mexico, Panama, Costa Rica, and Ecuador, as well as to countries outside the hemisphere and even as far as New Zealand.[22]

When considering the growing phenomenon of emigration following World War II, diplomat and scholar Harlen Cleveland argued, in his 1960 study on U.S. Americans abroad, that "the overseas American is the average American."[23] It might be more accurate to say that the U.S. emigrant of those years fit the "All-American" profile, that is, was perceived as part of the backbone of U.S. society: most were white, middle-class, and typically younger and more well-educated than the U.S. average, a profile that created what sociologist Ada Finifter called "psychological mobility" toward emigration.[24] In her 1976 research on the topic, Finifter claimed, rather anxiously (and somewhat prematurely), that the result of this trend was a possible "brain drain" from the United States.[25]

After the mid-1960s, the U.S. emigrant could also be described as a baby boomer—part of the largest generation in U.S. history.[26] Their childhood was characterized by abundance, especially in comparison to that of their parents, who grew up during the Great Depression and came of age during the World War II. Yet alongside material affluence, the rise of the suburbs, and the introduction of television—to name just a few of the attributes of this postwar period—the baby boomer generation was also shaped by the ever-looming shadow of the Cold War, the threat of communism, and nuclear anxiety. They experienced the political upheavals of the 1960s and the emergence of such transformative social crusades as the civil rights movement, the women's liberation movement, the antiwar movement, and the broadly defined counterculture. The ethnic and socioeconomic profile of U.S. American emigrants following World War II testified to feelings of estrangement and exclusion among those who were supposedly the central beneficiaries of a strong and prosperous society. It is these feelings that are expressed by many U.S. Americans who immigrated to Costa Rica, regarding both the impulses that led them to leave the United States and gravitate to Costa Rica and the factors that shaped their lives there.

National Identity Work on the Move: Do Immigrants Beget Immigrants?

The intersections between individual biographies—affected by factors of class, gender, ethnicity, place of origin, and family histories—with the political, economic, and cultural circumstances in the United States and globally recur as motivations for the move of many U.S. Americans to Costa Rica. These intersections further shaped life in Costa Rica and the identity talk of the U.S. Americans.[27] Indeed, in tracing these push-and-pull factors in the accounts given by U.S. Americans in Costa Rica, it is important to bear in mind the retrospective nature of these passage stories. Related some forty to sixty years after the act of immigration, they were inevitably shaped and reshaped over the course of the ensuing lifetime in Costa Rica. We should also be attentive to the hierarchy of values implicit in these accounts: some—primarily ideological ones—are regarded as more legitimate and worthy and are therefore explicitly told, while others, like personal distress or economic difficulties, are suppressed or downplayed.

Interestingly, a study carried out by Harlen Cleveland, who queried over three hundred U.S. Americans living outside the United States in the 1950s, found out that one-fifth of the participants had parents who were not born in the United States, while more than half had at least one grandparent who was born outside the country.[28] Considering that the United States was a migrant society, the findings are not surprising, yet they attest to the existence of a familial "migratory repertoire," as Massey et al. have termed it, or a "rite of passage," in José Moya's words—a willingness and even eagerness to immigrate, along with shared experiences and practices related to immigration and the maintaining of family ties across countries and continents.[29] This type of familial background, transmitted through the parents' recounting of childhood memories, a material culture with rich allusions to foreign places, and a sensory memory of flavors and odors, can help explain the alienation felt by some children and grandchildren of immigrants to the United States, a sentiment that in turn facilitated their own emigration.

Kathrin Morales was born in 1929 in a small town in Ohio. In 1957 she was a young mother and a widow whose husband had recently died in a car accident. She was taking a cosmetics course in the evening and working as a waitress at a diner, which is where she met a Costa Rican man, a World War II veteran who was studying at the University of Pittsburgh as part of the GI Bill. When he returned to Costa Rica after graduating, the couple continued to correspond, and two years later Morales moved with her daughter to Costa Rica, where the couple later married. When I asked her if in considering immigration she had not worried about being an outsider in Costa Rican society, she replied that as a second-generation Russian-American, alienation had been a familiar experience throughout her life in the United States: "I felt foreign, because my grandparents spoke Russian."[30] A talented cook and a professional in the catering business, Morales associated the sense of foreignness with the smell of foods: "When I was little the house smelled European, there is that smell of European houses. I don't know if it's the way they cook or what they do." The Cold War further intensified Morales's sense of alienation because it created an explicit clash between her family's cultural identifications and the U.S. anti-communism crusade: "During World War II the Russian church in Cleveland asked for donations so my mother and father sent a donation and guess what came out in the newspaper [a few years] later? That they were communists . . . When I moved to Costa Rica my cousin asked, 'How can you go to a foreign country?' I said, 'Phyllis, I've always been foreign, it doesn't bother me.'"[31]

Morales's personal history as a young widow and single parent pursuing a better life for herself and her daughter by leaving their small town and tight family circle and embarking on an independent and indeed adventurous life, her familial history of immigration, and the anti-Russian atmosphere in the McCarthy–era United States all intersected in her decision to leave the country. For her, as for many other U.S. Americans in Costa Rica who were second- and third-generation immigrants in the United States, the familial history of immigration made their own emigration easier because they lacked a strong sense of attachment or belonging to the country and many of them saw their move to Costa Rica as one more link in a chain of family migrations in search of new opportunities. Ironically, whereas in the United States Morales felt alien and was indeed often denounced for her Russian background, in Costa Rica she saw herself as a U.S. American, as exemplified by her devoted membership in the U.S. Women's Club and her strong objection to the inclusion of non-U.S. American women in it.

Unlike Morales, whose identity work in Costa Rica revolved around her U.S. American origin, others were driven to question their identification as U.S. Americans. Doris Stam, a missionary of the Latin America Mission, was originally from Connecticut, a descendant of Swedish immigrants; her husband, John, was born in the United States to a Dutch immigrant family. The couple met at Wheaton College and moved to Costa Rica in 1952. In our talk in Guadalupe, a suburb of San José, John, a well-known theologian, presented himself, in English, as Dutch rather than U.S. American and delighted in yet another non-U.S. identity—the nickname "Don Juan" that his Costa Rican friends had given him. Doris mentioned that their children, growing up in Costa Rica, used to identify themselves as Dutch and Swedish, ignoring their U.S. background.[32] In a similar way, relating to a question about his adaption to the heat in southern Costa Rica, Richard Erikson, who was born in Minnesota to Norwegian immigrants, admitted that it was very difficult for him, "since I am a Nordic."[33]

Other U.S. Americans living in Costa Rica testified that their migratory family history had had a contradictory effect on their move. They recounted that while their foreign background had made them more open to foreigners and therefore inclined toward immigration, in leaving the United States they nonetheless felt that they had betrayed their parents who had endured hardships in order to become U.S. citizens. In 1947 Anna Fredrikson was a secretary in a Hollywood film studio when she met a Costa Rican man, who she later married. She attributed her openness toward him to the fact that her father had been a Norwegian immigrant, so she was not "prejudiced" against foreigners. She recounted that although her father had not objected to her marriage, "he made me hold up my hand and swear I'll never give up my U.S. citizenship, because he had attained it, you see, being Norwegian."[34]

Global Wars and Individual Openings:
World War II and the Korean War as Migratory Triggers

Wars are a significant push-and-pull factor and in many cases create substantial migratory influxes. World War II was indirectly responsible for the arrival in Costa Rica of U.S. American women who married Costa Rican men they had met when the latter were studying in the United States after their military service with the Allies. I could not trace statistics regarding the number of such wives, but out of thirty-nine women interviewed for this study, ten arrived in Costa Rica as a result of such a marriage. Seven of them did so in the 1950s, two in the late 1960s, and one in the early 1970s. They all said that there had been no question that they would follow their husbands back to Costa Rica, both because the men could not legally stay in the United States and also, perhaps even more compellingly, because it was customary for the woman to follow her husband. In any case, none of the women I interviewed had been reluctant to move to Costa Rica. On the contrary, post–civil war Costa Rica had seemed to them like a prosperous place, and its Central American location gave it a tropical charm. Mary Thompson met her future husband, Pat, in her hometown in Massachusetts after he graduated from MIT. "Everybody was charmed by Pat because like so many Latino Costa Ricans he was charming. His father is from Kansas, a corporation lawyer I guess, and the mother was [from a family of] coffee heirs from Costa Rica. Well, the whole thing was very glamorous to me." Regarding the move to Costa Rica, Thompson said she "didn't mind [it] a bit": "I knew it was going to be for my whole life and it was fine, it was a great adventure."[35]

For many of those interviewed the move to Costa Rica was perceived as a way to overcome constraining gendered roles and perceptions.[36] Many of the women came from small towns and felt they were embarking on an adventure that would rescue them from provincial life, as did Morales, for example. They expected that the crossing of geographical borders would enable them to cross gendered ones as well, in other words, that they would be liberated from the restricted role assigned to women in the United States in the 1950s. This expectation was fulfilled to a certain degree, but not through a transformation of gender perceptions and roles in Costa Rica so much as through the economic mobility they experienced following the move, especially the greater availability of domestic help that freed them from the burden of homemaking tasks. In this regard, as Sheila Croucher suggests with respect to the general phenomenon of Western women who settled in the Third World, since "gender intertwines closely with the privilege they enjoy in terms of race, class, and nationality," these women "traded" on their constructed racial, national, and economic superiority to compensate for their assigned sexual inferiority, which had not changed with their move.[37] Moreover, many of them were sorely disappointed to discover that the predicament of women, which, following immigration was imposed on them as well, was much worse in the macho culture of Costa Rica, in both the domestic and the public sphere, such as their inability to work outside the home, for example, their relations with men, and the more conservative dress codes.

The impact of World War II on U.S. American men should also be considered. Richard Johnson, for example, was born in 1923 to a family of simple farmers in South Dakota. He studied electricity at the Michigan School of Technology, from where he was drafted soon after the attack on Pearl Harbor and subsequently served four years as a captain in U.S. naval bases in the Pacific. It was the first time he had ever traveled outside northern United States and his first experience of life in the tropics. When the war ended, he opted not to return to Michigan, enrolling instead at the University of Southern California in Los Angeles, where he encountered and became enchanted with Hispanic culture. In his interview he remembered that by the time he finished school he had still made no plans for the future, so when, at his graduation party, a Costa Rican man offered him a job on his banana plantation in Costa Rica, he jumped at the offer and soon moved to that country with his new bride. Two years later, backed by U.S. financiers, Johnson established the first margarine brand in Costa Rica, Numar, which was later bought by the UFC. Johnson was a vice president at UFC for several years before going out on his own.[38] While his story is no doubt exceptional in terms of material success, it does demonstrate the extent to which the symbolic capital of U.S. nationality facilitated a rapid social and economic mobility even for U.S. emigrants of modest backgrounds.

The Korean War is not, on the whole, regarded as a historical event that resulted in mass emigration from the United States.[39] This macro perspective, however, conceals the significance of the micro history of the Quakers who established Monteverde. While numerically insignificant, the Quaker immigrants had a profound influence on their immediate surroundings and on the larger picture of immigration to the country.[40] The resulting media exposure about the settlement as the first, and only, successful U.S. agriculture community in Costa Rica served, together with word of mouth, to raise the profile of Costa Rica and ultimately inspired other U.S. Americans to move there—agriculturists, entrepreneurs, and those such as draft dodgers and counterculturists who left the United States as a response to the Vietnam War.

"A Cultural Tide That Swept Us All Away": U.S. Counterculturists in Costa Rica

In writing about the flow of U.S. Americans to Canada during the Vietnam War, John Hagan beautifully depicted it as "a tidal wave of social and political protest that swept across the United States in the late 1960s, cresting at the close of the decade and spilling across the border."[41] A smattering of drops from this wave traveled south instead and reached as far as Costa Rica.

John Foulks, who was a student at the University of Chicago between 1967 and 1971, starved himself in order to be declared underweight and therefore unfit for the draft. He recounted his ongoing sense of alienation and distrust toward the Nixon administration as being even more of a disillusionment than the 1968 Chicago Riots, which he had personally witnessed, and these combined factors led to his decision to leave the United States, infused with an anger that not even forty years in Costa Rica has diminished: "The unbelievable lie . . . the fact that everybody knew that what these people said was completely false and yet the lie continued and continued and continued both under the Johnson administration and the Nixon administration and people just . . . Do I have to go through everything that was happening back then?!"[42]

In 1974 Foulks, accompanied by three friends, two men and a woman, moved to Mexico. They later discovered they could not buy land there because of regulations prohibiting land ownership by non-Mexicans but were nonetheless determined not to return to the United States. In 1977 they embarked on a canoe trip along the Atlantic coast of Central America, heading south to Costa Rica, where, as they had previously learned from other U.S. American travelers, foreigners could easily buy land. Foulks and his friends anchored in Puerto Limón and soon established a cacao farm in Punta Uva, farther south on the Atlantic coast.

Like the draft dodgers and conscientious objectors, U.S. American veterans of the Vietnam War also found a refuge in Costa Rica—both from the trauma of war and occasionally from the tedium of going back to their familiar life back home. Thomas Dent, born in California's San Joaquin Valley to a farming family of Italian origin, served as a paratrooper in Vietnam. While he was overseas, his family lost their land, and Dent had no place to go back to and in any case no desire to reintegrate himself into his former life. Instead, he was drawn to what he described in the interview as the drug culture of the West Coast and essentially became what he called a hippie biker: "Obviously, the army was a little bit more than what I had expected . . . and I had seen the world—even though it was war and Vietnam, I was aware of the fact that there was more to the world than the San Joaquin Valley. And so I really didn't want to go and get a job."[43]

In lieu of "getting a job," Dent joined the Peace Corps and was sent to Costa Rica. Despite this, in his interview Dent shaped his narrative as a classic immigration story: he recounted arriving in Costa Rica with a hundred dollars in his pocket and no ties to his former life ("I had no money, no family"). He also said he had not originally planned to stay in Costa Rica: "Thinking that it's halfway to the Equator, [I thought] I'll go to Costa Rica [and] if I don't like it—I'll quit."[44] But not long after he arrived, Dent married a Costa Rican woman. After working for the Peace Corps for several years, he left the organization but stayed in Costa Rica, working in agriculture. Whereas in the United States, according to his account, he could not have afforded to own his own land, in Costa Rica he was able to buy a small farm in the Central Valley.

The indignation, disillusion, and estrangement triggered by the political and social turmoil of the 1960s and 1970s, alongside the real fear of being drafted to fight in Vietnam, or the traumatic experience of those who served there, all intersected with the counterculture mindset, which highlighted movement and drifting as part of the international culture of youth (described by Dent as "just keep going").[45] Foulks recounted that the political events of those years enhanced his sense of living through a unique time in history: "These were very tremulous years as you know, and they had a tremendous effect on everybody who lived there and everybody who lived through them. It's more than likely that if I had been born, say, five years earlier or five years later I probably never would have left the United States. I think a lot of the reasons why I left the United States were because I happened to be at that particular point in history."[46]

He further remarked that the political and social upheavals in the United States intersected during the late 1960s with a new psychological and existential experience of young people across the world, which was shaped to a large extent by what he depicted as the widespread use of mind-altering drugs: "Let's be very frank.... That was when it [drugs] became a big part of the culture and everybody I knew, and myself, were involved in it at that time. And people just tended to have ideas, they were thinking about alternative ways of living.... They actually took these ideas seriously. This was the thing at that moment. I always say, it was a cultural tide that swept us all away."[47]

The tide was an international one. U.S. American anthropologist Jacqueline Waldren, who had herself arrived in the late 1950s to the small village of Deià on the Spanish island of Palma de Mallorca and witnessed the numerous U.S. and European counterculturists who settled there in later years, sees this generation's strong impulse for travel as connected to contemporary philosophical trends: "Inspired by French Existentialism, each was seeking to realize himself through free choice between alternatives, through self-commitment. To exist, therefore, meant becoming more and more an individual and less and less a mere member of a group." This realization, she noted, in many cases involved immigration, as "these individuals felt 'truth' lay outside their home countries."[48] In writing about U.S. American dropouts who moved to Hawaii from the late 1960s onward, Lucy Pickering uses the term *existential mobility* to depict a type of relocation in space that is related to a sense of self as developing and moving. She quotes an informant as saying that "we engage in the kind of physical mobility that defines us as migrants because we feel another geographical space is a better launching pad for our existential selves."[49]

Catherine Trundle underscores the gendered subtexts of this counterculture's existential migratory narratives. In writing about young Anglo-American women who arrived in Tuscany during this period, Trundle argues that the experimental counterculture of the 1960s, which encouraged young people to challenge the social conventions of the day, was a strong motivating force for immigration, especially for women who were escaping patriarchal frameworks and perceived the journey itself to be a liberating act. She notes that these immigrants tended to construct themselves as inherently "different" and an "odd fit" in their home societies. "Immigration, as a natural and inevitable decision, was often retrospectively and reflexively built into the narratives."[50]

In a similar vein, emigration from the United States was in many cases the last stage in a transformation in the emigrant's lifestyle and mindset. As Dent's experience illustrates, many emigrants crossed cultural borders before eventually crossing geographical ones. A similar process led Sharon Hage to Costa Rica. She was born in 1946 in Philadelphia, into what she described as a "typical American middle-class family."

> At a certain point I felt like I was living in a library full of books I'd already read. . . . The Sixties fascinated me, and I started having questions in my mind about what I want to do in my life and I looked around me and what I saw around me just wasn't interesting to me. I wanted adventures, so that's why I moved to California, and the adventure began. . . . This may have something to do with being an expatriate eventually, although I had no idea at that point that I was going to be an expatriate.[51]

In 1971, after living for two years in an artists' commune in Los Angeles, Hage and her partner, the leader of the group, decided to go to Costa Rica to find a new location for the commune. While the search for different ways of life involved a conscious rejection of the United States, which was perceived as a decadent place where spiritual redemption was impossible, the search itself was rooted in U.S. American culture and even in a traditional U.S. American "pioneer" terminology involving the creation of a spiritual utopia: "We wanted to change our reality, to be different than the kind of reality we were living in the United States, and we thought that living in a country like Costa Rica, where it was so beautiful, and we could be free there, that [it] would be a beautiful place to create Utopia."[52]

The proclaimed push factor of the United States was its inability to provide spiritual redemption. But the pull factors of Costa Rica, as Hage and her fellow commune members recorded them, were revealing insofar as they encompassed not just the tropical romance of the country and its nonmilitary policy but also various practical motivations, primarily economic. "I have always had a fascination with the tropics . . . And also, Costa Rica has no army and I thought this was very beautiful, and brave, in this world, to not have an army, and also dollars go a lot further in Costa Rica: we could buy land and settle down and support ourselves while still being free."[53]

Hage listed a mix of tropical romanticism, ideology, and pacifist identification—the 1948 abolishment of the Costa Rican army was idolized by U.S. dissidents—and practical, financial considerations. Even young people such as Hage and her friends could afford to buy a large property in Costa Rica, and thus, as she says repeatedly, to buy their freedom.

Both the commune movement of the late 1960s in the United States (1969 was defined by *Newsweek Magazine* as the "year of the commune") and the onset in 1968 of the second phase of the counterculture,[54] which was less naïve and more radical, even violent, than the first, form a significant part of the social and political construct that led to the desire to leave the United States.[55] Immigration to Costa Rica, among other places, was an outlet for those who rejected mainstream U.S. society, with its voracious demand for material success and achievement, and enabled U.S. Americans to live rel-

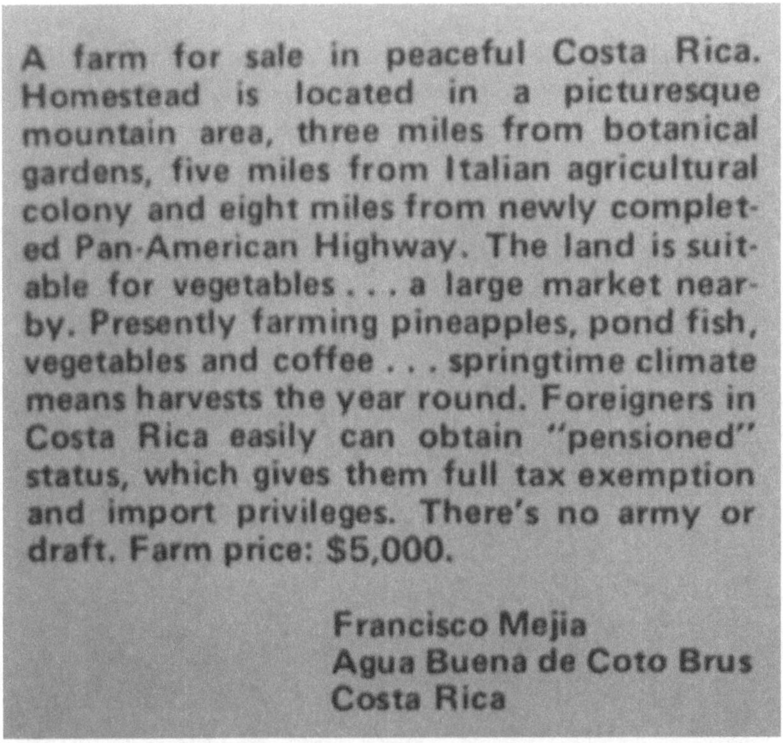

> A farm for sale in peaceful Costa Rica. Homestead is located in a picturesque mountain area, three miles from botanical gardens, five miles from Italian agricultural colony and eight miles from newly completed Pan-American Highway. The land is suitable for vegetables . . . a large market nearby. Presently farming pineapples, pond fish, vegetables and coffee . . . springtime climate means harvests the year round. Foreigners in Costa Rica easily can obtain "pensioned" status, which gives them full tax exemption and import privileges. There's no army or draft. Farm price: $5,000.
>
> Francisco Mejia
> Agua Buena de Coto Brus
> Costa Rica

Fig. 3. Ad offering a property in Costa Rica, early 1970s. Courtesy of *Mother Earth News*.

atively free of economic concerns and social standards. Theodore Bart, a fellow member of Hage's commune and a fashion designer, followed her to Costa Rica. He further analyzed immigration as a means to quit the "rat race" in the United States: "Everything [in Los Angeles] was so rush rush rush, and here and there, and blah blah blah, and Costa Rica was so laid back. You didn't have to worry about anything, you didn't have to do certain things, and you didn't have to meet [any] standards."[56]

Thus, in rejecting what is perceived as the U.S. American values of hard work, efficiency, and material success, the move to Costa Rica was not only a move to a different space but also to a different perception of time, one that was more relaxed and less demanding and which enabled U.S. Americans to achieve peace of mind and create a different version of themselves.[57]

> Homesteading in the central mountains of Costa Rica, we've had fun and success raising vegetables, goats, chickens and our kids (3½ and 2). Now we're looking for neighbors... families who could buy land nearby and perhaps cooperate with us on crops and stuff. We're not a commune, have no religious affiliations and aren't trying to establish a Utopia. We'd just like a few friends around and a few children for ours to play with.
>
> The climate here is mild and healthy, and water is plentiful year around. Just about anything will grow if properly cared for. Residence requirements are easy to meet, and small parcels of land on this mountain cost $200 to $300 per acre.
>
> We'd be happy to hear from people interested in knowing more about the area. We speak Spanish and could help locate land and arrange purchase.
>
> > Dick, Sharon, Trilby and Ethan Maehl
> > Villa Colon
> > Costa Rica
> > Centroamerica

Fig. 4. Ad inviting U.S. Americans to a joint homesteading in Costa Rica, early 1970s. Courtesy of *Mother Earth News*.

Unlike immigration to the United States, emigration from the country was usually perceived as a movement of individuals or nuclear families, rather than of extended families or regional networks.[58] Yet both the Quaker immigration of the early 1950s and the counterculture immigration of the late 1960s and early 1970s did in fact amount to a movement of a network of this sort. In 1973 a U.S. American family residing in the Central Valley published an ad in the Contact section of *Mother Earth*, a counterculture magazine, inviting like-minded U.S. Americans to join them, recommending the climate and the low prices of land (fig. 4). Several similar ads were published in *Mother Earth* in the early 1970s. It was in response to one such advertisement calling readers to join a group looking to purchase land together in Central America and establish self-sufficient communities that Eric White and his wife came to Costa Rica from Hawaii in 1972 with several friends: "I heard about a commune in Costa Rica, like-minded people . . . so that had brought us down here. We went right there and met [them]—there were maybe thirty people living there, and all North Americans."[59]

The counterculturists were disdained by bourgeois U.S. Americans in Costa Rica, who saw them as tarnishing the U.S. image.[60] Joan Stevens, who worked as an English teacher in San José, recounted that they were perceived as "more of curiosity than anything else . . . they were looked down upon by all people."[61] In a letter to the *TT*, a U.S. American retiree named H. Hensel complained:

> As a newly retired construction worker from Chicago, the Mrs. and I arrived in San José hopping to get away from the crowds, smog, and hippies of the U.S . . . Why does the government here allow those hippies to be on the same street as decent people? Their hair is as long as that of their U.S. pot smoking brothers, they act just as uppity, and I think they are just as bad as anything in the United States. We came here to get away from that disgusting scum and it's bad to find them in such a beautiful country as Costa Rica. Can't the government do something?[62]

A response letter the following week from a U.S. American living in the Canal Zone, Panama, dubbed Hensel "Archie Bunker" after the leading character of the popular U.S. American TV sitcom *All in the Family* famous for his conservative, old-fashioned views, and criticized him for benefiting from Costa Rica's economic conditions.[63]

The clashes over what Hayes has termed "the performance of Gringoness" had not affected the ordinary Costa Ricans,[64] who more or less accepted with equanimity the U.S. counterculturists and viewed them as a curiosity or an expression of the international zeitgeist (Jane and Michael Warren, who arrived in 1971, recounted that whenever they drove in their colored Volkswagen, the locals would wave their hands and enthusiastically make the peace sign).[65] However, Costa Rican authorities and some of the local media shared the disdain of the U.S. American bourgeois for the counterculturists' physical appearance and regarded them as unproductive to the Costa Rican state (fig. 5). An article in the *TT* quoted a piece in the local newspaper *La Hora* about the possibility of cleaning up what they dubbed the "malodorous" hippies, and rumors spread among the "longhairs," as the *TT* called them, about an upcoming law that would legalize the shearing and bathing of apprehended hippies. Captain Guillermo Álvarez, head of the local narcotics division, confirmed to the *TT* that the police did occasionally block the entrance to the San José branch of McDonald's in order to "inspect" the counterculturists: "If I could bathe and shave them I'd love to, but it's illegal."[66] The captain further noted that twenty out of a hundred people detained for drug-related allegations were foreigners but did not disclose their national origin.

U.S *Pensionados*: Retiring to Better Lives

For its part, Costa Rica had its own hopes and interests with regards to U.S. American immigration. From the mid-1960s the Costa Rican government actively encouraged the immigration of European and U.S. American individuals by enacting legislation and economic incentives, most notably the 1964 passing of law no. 4812, known as Ley de Pensionados. This was an attempt to attract members of the middle and upper classes to settle in the country by removing barriers

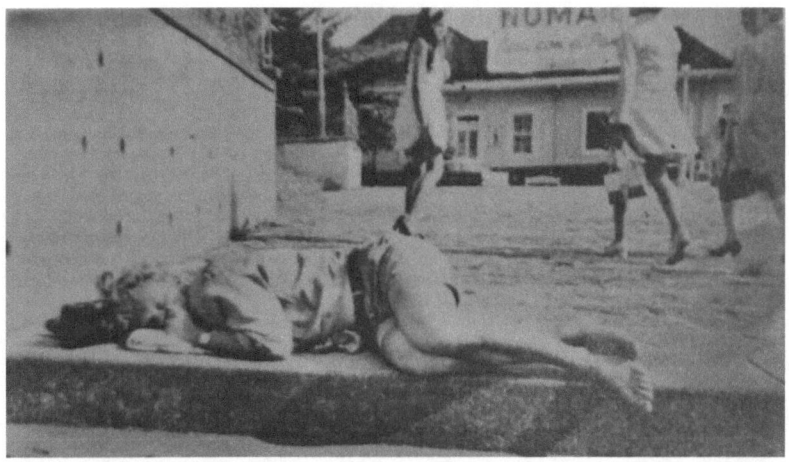

Fig. 5. Ticas observing a U.S. American hippie on the streets of San José, 1974. Courtesy of the TT.

to foreign land purchase and economic activities. The immigrants could obtain residency status in Costa Rica without being required to give up their original nationalities, with the only stipulated requirement being that they deposit a monthly payment into a Costa Rican bank account.[67] The 1971 revised version of the law stated that every foreign immigrant who deposits at least three hundred dollars each month would receive residential status, as long as they commit to not work in Costa Rica, a condition that later facilitated the image of the foreign retirees as wealthy people of leisure who came to take advantage of Costa Rica's economic distress.[68]

The foreign *pensionados* were under the authority of the Instituto Costarricense de Turismo (ICT, the Costa Rican Department of Tourism)—a testament to their precarious status in the country and to the Costa Rican expectation that they would expand the tourist industry by opening hotels and attracting their compatriots to visit Costa Rica. A pensionado club, headed by John Biesanz, a U.S. American sociologist who studied Costa Rica and retired to the country, was established in San José as early as 1968. But it took several years for word to spread about the welcoming conditions for foreigners in Costa Rica, and the great boom in retiree migration started only in the early 1970s, by which time the San José Pensionado Club was receiving no less than three thousand letters a year from U.S. Americans inquiring about retirement in Costa Rica.[69]

It is difficult to determine how many U.S. Americans actually immigrated as a result of the pensionado law, as they were recorded under many subcategories of residency. Writing a series of articles in the Costa Rican daily *La Nación* in 1974, Miguel Salguero estimated that since 1969 several thousand retirees, the majority of them U.S. citizens, had settled in Costa Rica.[70] In 1977 an unpublished report of the ICT estimated their number at 1,340—66 percent of the total population of foreign retirees in the country (2,032)—and further estimated that each retiree had an average of 4.4 dependents, amounting to 7,300 U.S. Americans who benefited from the pensionados law.

In his 1974 articles, Salguero quotes the retirees' proclaimed reasons for moving to Costa Rica, including its fine climate, the kindness of the Costa Rican people and their receptivity to foreign settlement (Salguero adds that the Costa Ricans indeed had no "phobia" of foreigners), and the "imponderable" landscape.[71] Echoing the terminology of nineteenth-century Costa Rican propaganda, the foreign retirees compared the country to Switzerland—but with many Latin advantages. Eric Torres of the ICT depicted the U.S. American retirees as calm people engaged in back-to-the-country settlement: "The North American *pensionado* has traditionally come to Costa Rica to live in peace, to retire to his beach house or farm and raise pigs or whatever."[72]

The U.S. American pensionado was not only a legal and economic status. It was also derived from and responsible for specific practices and discourses that constituted their identity work. The *TT* reported on the daily routine of the pensionados of the San José area—drinking coffee at Cafe La Cueca in downtown San José, crossing the street to the post office to check for mail from the United States, talking about Robert Vesco, about real estate opportunities in Costa Rica's beachfronts, Costa Rica's exhausting bureaucracy, and fishing: "Another day—another hour to relax in San José."[73] Issues of concern to retirees—from handling their taxes back in the United States to finding love during their "golden years" in Costa Rica—were addressed regularly in the paper's advice columns, with personal ads targeting the pensionados directly ("1970 Volvo, ideal for retirees").[74] Relatively older and more affluent than other U.S. Americans in Costa Rica, the retirees were perceived by the other U.S. Americans as more foreign than themselves on an imagined spectrum of integration (even their car plates had an identifying PEN tag that marked them as foreign, while also making them a target for theft). Furthermore, the other U.S. Americans, no less than the Costa Ricans, saw the pensionados as an economic opportunity ripe for exploitation. So, for example, Jim Coleman, a U.S. American artist living in Costa Rica, described the U.S. retiree in the country as "someone you could sell stuff to."[75]

However, the allegedly clear classification between young counterculturists and aged retirees is complicated when we consider the fact that the pensionado status was not contingent upon age but rather on economic procedures, and effectively anyone could legally become a pensionado. So while the image was that of an elderly, conservative, business-minded person, in fact many young U.S. Americans took advantage of the law, and the motivations that they provided for immigration were not very far from those of their counterculturist compatriots. An article published in May 1972 in the *TT*, titled "Jerry Wolf Discovered His Shangri-La in Guanacaste," featured the story of the Wolf family, originally from New Jersey, who, following a holiday in Costa Rica, decided to take advantage of the retirees' law and move to Costa Rica. Depicting the reasons for the move, Jerry Wolf sounded very much like the counterculturists who decided to opt out of the U.S. rat race: "We lived well, American style in New Jersey. We were well off but not really happy, working twelve hours a day in a world where we were only parts in a big machine and where problems were never-ending."[76] In Costa Rica, Wolf and his family offered fishing excursions on their boat, *Happy J's II*, with an overnight stay at the motel of U.S. American retirees Sophie and Warren Davidson (originally from Oregon).[77] Apparently the ban on pensionados' working was not strictly implemented, while the Costa Rican hopes for the development of tourism infrastructure by the retirees was at least partially accomplished. Another example of the amalgamation of these two allegedly distinct trends of U.S. immigration was the case of the Wilson family, who arrived in

Costa Rica in 1978 following what they perceived as harassment on the part of the U.S. authorities because of their alternative lifestyle. Although in his early forties, Mathew Wilson, the father, acquired the legal status of a pensionado. Reflecting on the advantages of life in Costa Rica, Wilson's widow, Lisa, noted the ability to get by on a monthly pension of only 300 USD.[78]

In the mid-1970s, however, Costa Rican public opinion gradually turned against the retirees, with harsh criticism over the privileges that came with this status, especially after the 1973 Vesco scandal, in which the dubious U.S. businessman was granted retiree status in Costa Rica based on his investments in the country. The title of the aforementioned 1974 series of articles by Salguero—"Costa Rica vende sus tierras a extranjeros" ("Costa Rica sells its lands to foreigners")—leaves no room for doubt regarding his negative view of what he termed the "pacific invasion" of this foreign population, among whom retirees were a prominent segment. It is important to note that Salguero does not rebuke U.S. immigration as a whole, emphasizing that the problems he has focused on were caused by a small minority, whereas 90 percent of U.S. Americans in Costa Rica were fine people. Moreover, he does not call for a moratorium on immigration or even for the annulment of the pensionado law but rather urges the Costa Rican authorities to create strong regulations to eliminate land speculation and protect the local population so that Costa Ricans do not become "peons" of the foreigners.

Over the course of the following years, the terms for receiving pensionado status were hardened.[79] Apparently, some of the U.S. American retirees in Costa Rica supported such changes, seeing it as a way of protecting the benefits of those already living in Costa Rica, while others felt betrayed. One was quoted in the *TT* saying, "They needed us when they had no money, and now when the country is making an international name for itself, we're being shoved aside"; he threatened to move to Spain.[80] A headline in the *TT* read, "Pensionados Bring Millions to Costa Rica" and the subsequent article indicated that since 1965 Costa Rica had received a hundred million *colones* (Costa Rican currency) as a result of the pensionado law.[81] In 1978 the percentage of U.S. Americans among the general pensionado population in Costa Rica declined from 66 percent to 53 percent.

Costa Rica: A Geography of Multiple Meanings

The circumstances and motivations that led U.S. Americans to leave the United States and immigrate to Costa Rica resulted from the intersection between individual background (gender, class, ethnicity, and personal life experience) and broader social, economic, political, and cultural developments and trends, both in the United States, Costa Rica, and the global arena. Prominent among these were the end of World War II and the onset of the Cold War, which on the one hand exposed many U.S. Americans to life outside the United States, as its civic or military representatives, and on the other hand triggered among others a resistance to their government's imperial policies on the global sphere, especially the Vietnam War. Sociopolitical and cultural developments such as the emergence of the protest movements of the 1960s and the rise of the youth culture and counterculture, both of which stressed the breakdown of familiar social frameworks and encouraged a kind of spatial and mental drifting, led in the early 1970s to large waves of emigration from the United States, a percentage of which made its way to Costa Rica.

For its part, Costa Rica was eager to receive wealthy, powerful, northern, "white" immigrants, as a means of improving the country's economic condition and ethnic composition. The passage of the pensionado law in 1964 explicitly attests to the very straightforward economic benefits Costa Rica hoped to gain from these immigrants: not just a general boost to the country's economy, but direct monetary payment.

While the economic factor did play a role in leading U.S. Americans to Costa Rica, the meanings that they have derived from settling in the country are much more diverse. Two of the distinct types of U.S. American immigration to Costa Rica discussed in this chapter were seemingly very different—the young counterculturists on the one hand, and the U.S. American older retirees on the other. However, a closer look reveals that immigrants of both trends were looking for a different way of life that would provide them with both economic well-being and peace of mind. Whereas the counterculturists' identity emphasized a rejection of the United States resulting from a sense of alienation toward its military policies and materialistic values, that of the pensionados stressed the easy life available in Costa Rica. For both groups, the meaning of Costa Rica lay in its ability to provide the opportunity to live peacefully and to withdraw from what some termed the rat race. Members of the counterculture, who usually lacked any economic funds, did not work in Costa Rica, and therefore could not afford a monthly deposit of several hundred U.S. dollars in a Costa Rican bank couched their move in terms of spiritual redemption. Yet for them too, money was a consideration, as is clear when Hage, the founder of the commune in Dominical, uses the word "freedom" to explain the decision to settle in Costa Rica. The freedom being referred to was, among others, a material one, available due to the radical asymmetrical economic and political power relations between the United States and Costa Rica, a dynamic that facilitated this immigration in the first place and was then further intensified as diverse U.S. Americans established themselves in Costa Rica.[82]

What is worth noting is the extent to which a shared national origin has not facilitated a sense of affiliation or solidarity among the different groups of U.S. Americans in Costa Rica, who tended to define themselves not only in contrast to Costa Ricans but also to other types of U.S. American immigrants to the country, as the public debate over the pages of the *TT* between the pensionados and the counterculturists makes clear. It is this identity work, carried out by the various segments of U.S. Americans in Costa Rica through practices of settlement and social organization, that is the subject of the next chapter.

two

Places and Networks
Settlement, Community-Building, and Identity-Making

> We sort of got farther and farther out
> and away from civilization.
> —JOHN FOULKS, author interview

In 1976 the *TT* extolled the publication of an eighty-eight-page-long telephone directory of U.S. Americans in Costa Rica, which "plac[ed] San José, for better or for worse, in the ranks of the world's major capitals."[1] However, the news report also noted, with regret, the fact that since the directory took two years to compile, "quite a few of the people listed are no longer here and a number of newcomers are not included." Beyond the inaccuracies that resulted from the flux in the U.S. American community in Costa Rica, the directory also failed to capture parts of the population that actively resisted the initiative: "Some residents objected to be listed 'with the gringos,' while others said they didn't want anyone to know where they were."[2]

Both this restless flux and the desire to live under the public radar were also reflected in the 1963 Costa Rican census, which recorded the foreign population in Costa Rica according to residents' seniority in the country. Out of 2,051 U.S. Americans included, 37 percent (763 people) had lived in Costa Rica for less than one year and an additional 31 percent (648 people) had lived in Costa Rica for less than three years. Only one-third of the U.S. population in Costa Rica had lived in the country for more than three years. Interestingly, fifty-nine U.S. Americans were categorized as having always lived in Costa Rica—that is, as natives.[3] Karen Hill-Webber, who arrived in Costa Rica in 1953 following her marriage to a Costa Rican man, experienced first-hand the restlessness and short-lived excitement of her compatriots. "The Americans—I would say only about 10 percent of them, or less than that, came and stayed. They were people that would come down, moved by everything, and within two years, five years, at the most ten years, [they] were washed out."[4]

The mapping of U.S. Americans in Costa Rica, then, is an attempt to describe an elusive and highly fluid community. Nonetheless, some of them lived in Costa Rica for years, sometimes decades, and settled in different parts of the country—the metropolis of San José and the larger Central Valley, rainforests, and beachfronts. This choice of geography was neither random nor arbitrary but rather reflected their individual and collective self-perceptions and served as a means of identity work.[5] In the Central Valley, many U.S. Americans took part in developing and sustaining the U.S. clubland—a dense network of social, philanthropic, and business associations that, although lacking a tangible physical space in the form of a U.S. American center, nonetheless served as a social space that anchored distinct U.S. communities.[6] In this respect, this network was a prime tool for community-building and a negotiation of individual and collective identifications.

This chapter considers the dynamics and tensions between these two modes of affiliation—a place and a social network—as a key component of the identity work performed by U.S. Americans in Costa Rica. In recent decades, scholarly discourse on privilege migration highlights the evolution of transnational identities and modes of identifications based, allegedly, on social networks, ideologies, and lifestyle rather than attachment to specific places.[7] The fluidity of U.S. Americans in Costa Rica might appear to align with this line of thought, since their monetary and symbolic fortune allowed them a significant degree of mobility in their transnational practices and habitus (as expressed in their reluctance to become Costa Rican citizens, for example). However, an opposite scholarly discourse stakes out a position precisely for the importance of places in a globalized world and among immigrants whose privilege allows them to avoid a forced attachment to one place.[8] In this chapter I will argue that the U.S. immigration to Costa Rica illuminates the importance of locality among immigrants who are considered fluid and transnational, by taking a close look at where they chose to live and at their identity work through various practices of emplacement.

These two modes of identification—affiliation with a geographical place and affiliation with social networks—are not mutually exclusive. The constant movement of immigrants was shaped by social and family networks, resulting in the creation of a web of places that became an entity in and of itself above and beyond the various locations.[9] In addition, the U.S. clubland, though physically intangible, not only served as a social space but also created a spatial map of the presence of Americans in the Costa Rican Central Valley. Two concepts that are often employed in relation to the space that colonizers, immigrants, and expats occupy are the "bubble" and the "enclave." Both are useful in the analysis of the U.S. settlements and clubland in Costa Rica and the identity work that these entailed, particularly when considering the extent to which these entities were either closed and exclusionary or instead open and inclusionary of various human and cultural elements from the local surroundings.

Place-Making and Self-Making:
The Creation of Place-Based Identities

Writing about the importance of place-making in the construction of migrant identities, Brigitte Bönisch-Brednich and Catherine Trundle have argued that "in a fluid world of movement, place remains a deeply contested and symbolically rich site in which to constitute the self, even for those on the move."[10] This self-constitution is done, practically and discursively, through the transformation of a "space" into a "place," which Andrew Starthern and Pamela Stewart defined as a "socially meaningful and identifiable space."[11] Edward Casey described that process as a "gathering" of "experiences and histories, even languages and thought."[12] Through this process, places come to serve as a critical site of identity work, so much so that we can talk about a place-based identity "as a cognitive sub-structure of self-identity" consisting of "an endless variety of cognitions relating to the past, present, and the anticipated physical settings that define and circumscribe the day-to-day existence of the person."[13] Yet such meanings are neither intrinsic to a specific place nor neutral but are rather socially, culturally, and emotionally constructed (Arjun

Appadurai has argued, quite beautifully, that locality is a "structure of feeling") and are based on a long tradition of representation and of the imagined-self people believe they could potentially develop in a specific place.[14] Places, however, are not only an inventory of histories and practices but also a platform on which people construct memories, formulate meanings from events, and establish rituals.[15] The examination of the different factors that facilitated the settlement of U.S. Americans in Costa Rica should take into consideration the mental baggage they brought with them from the United States, including in particular their concepts of culture and nature, and the imagined selves they aspired to constitute in their new places of residence.

In the 1950s most U.S. Americans in Costa Rica resided in San José and the Central Valley, as did the majority of native Costa Ricans. From this nucleus they gradually spread out and established new settlements, creating a network of U.S. communities across different provinces of Costa Rica, as depicted in table 2.

Table 2. U.S. Americans according to their place of residence in Costa Rica

YEAR / PROVINCE	1950	1963	1973
San José	674	120	2,444
Alajuela	29	11	242
Cartago	81	2	156
Heredia	16	1	123
Guanacaste	12	-	109
Puntarenas	224	2	171
Limón	74	2	122
Other places	1019	1913	72
Total	2129	2051	3,453

Source: Adapted by the author from Costa Rica national censuses for the years 1950, 1963, and 1973.

As the table shows, in the 1950s one out of every three U.S. Americans in Costa Rica lived in the province of San José, mostly in the city itself. Many of them were affiliated with the U.S. administration or were businessmen, either independent or employees of U.S. corporations. The institutions that served them were located near each other in the downtown area: the U.S. embassy and the Costa Rican-North American Cultural Center / Centro Cultural Costarricense Norteamericano were located on Avenida Central; the oldest English-speaking church, the Good Shepherd, which opened in 1864, was on *Calle* (street) 3; the bilingual school, Lincoln, opened in 1945 on *Calle* 21, between Avenida Central and Avenida Primera, while the offices of the TT occupied a picturesque two-story building on Calle 6. This concentration of U.S. American residences in the center of San José was initially due to its adjacency to U.S. American institutions and places of employment, which facilitated a rather comfortable way of living, due to easy access to networks of other U.S. Americans and contact with the United States (including the regular delivery of material goods, newspapers, and so forth from the United States, which made it possible to maintain a semi-U.S. lifestyle). However, there was no distinct *territorial* U.S. colony: the residences of U.S. Americans were not clustered in a particular quarter or neighborhood. This is in contrast, for example, to the two apartment buildings occupied by U.S. political exiles of the McCarthy era on Avenida de los Insurgentes (Insurgents Avenue) in Mexico City, the few streets in which U.S. Americans congregated in 1950s Barcelona, or contemporary enclaves of U.S. American expats in such places as Cuenca, Ecuador.[16]

However, at some point in the early 1950s U.S. Americans started to venture further out. So, for example, Anna Fredrikson, who arrived in 1951, lived first in an apartment on Avenida Central, but two years later she and her Costa Rican husband moved to the burgeoning quarter of Los Yoses in the eastern part of town, near the University of Costa Rica.[17] Two years after that the Costa Rican-North American Cultural Center also moved from Avenida Central to the same barrio. Mary Thompson, who arrived in Costa Rica in the early 1950s following her marriage to a local man, recalled the period of her arrival in San José as infused by a repetitive drumming outside her window, which turned out to be rehearsals in the nearby Parque Central for the Quince, the Costa Rican Independence Day, commemorated on September 15. In 1953 her family bought a property in Escazú and moved there.[18] This was about the same time that the U.S. embassy also moved from Avenida Central to a Monticello-like house on the road that connects Escazú and Santa Ana, as a result of which the area became popular with U.S. Americans.

It is possible that Thompson's and Fredrikson's move to the outskirts of San José was influenced by the fact that they were married to Costa Rican men and thus were more inclined to move into Costa Rican neighborhoods or were following their husbands' wishes. Yet we can still appreciate their experience as U.S. women who were disconnected from the relatively cosmopolitan milieu in downtown San José and entered more local surroundings. These were the years in which the larger metropolitan area of San José took shape by incorporating small towns and villages, such as Guadalupe, Moravia, and Tibás. In the 1950s even San José itself was described by U.S. Americans as a peaceful "garden city," and the towns around it were still completely rural, their landscape dotted with coffee farms and offering very little infrastructure. For U.S. Americans, moving to these Costa Rican "suburbs" meant a change of both practices and self-perceptions: it immersed them in the Costa Rican natural surroundings that they treasured, while at the same time cutting them off from their U.S. networks in Costa Rica and from a relatively urban lifestyle and thus contributing to their sense that the move to Costa Rica was also a journey back in time—a frequent theme in accounts of the experience of immigration to the country.[19]

While in the United States the suburbs were completely new settlements, constructed from scratch (and designed to combine modern living standards with a "traditional" rural appearance) and promising a new, modern lifestyle, in San José suburbanization occurred by the city "swallowing up" existing villages and small towns, which typically retained their municipal status and communal nature. Unlike the U.S. suburbs' demographic homogeneity, consisting as they did of young, mostly white, middle-class nuclear families, the new suburbs of San José were in fact old towns, whose communities were held together by kinship and other long-standing ties.[20] When

U.S. Americans migrated to these communities, many found that the new environments highlighted their alienation and foreignness and contributed to their isolation. Moreover, even though the San José metropolitan area was not big, once they began to spread out the poor infrastructure and a lack of transportation restricted the ability of U.S. Americans to keep in touch with each other. In the 1963 bulletin of the U.S.A. Women's Club, members wishing to buy tickets to the club's annual luncheon were directed to contact one of the club executives. The list attached to the bulletin, providing the names and places of residence of the various executives, highlights the geographical spread of U.S. Americans: three lived in Escazú, two in Los Yoses, and one in each of the following quarters: Escalante, La Granja, La Guaria, González-Lehaman, and Barrio Gimenez.[21]

The English-speaking or bilingual schools both reflected and shaped the process by which U.S. Americans spread throughout the San José metropole. In 1953 Lincoln School moved from downtown San José to Moravia, in the northeast part of the city. In 1972 Country Day School, owned by a U.S. American named Woodson Brown and popular among U.S. Americans who wanted their children to study according to the U.S. curriculum, moved from downtown Parque Morazán to Escazú, west of the city, close to the U.S. embassy and to where many U.S. Americans who were affiliated with U.S. institutions resided. The third English-speaking school, Costa Rica Academy, favored by the counterculture parents, operated in the town of San Antonio de Belén, northwest of central San José, in the scenic property of a Jesuit mission, surrounded by streams and vegetation that met the counterculturist desire for an idyllic rural lifestyle.

Many factors came into play in choosing the place of residence, including work, economic status, and so forth. But in addition, the various quarters and neighborhoods, and in particular their distinct climates and natural environments, were chosen as a result of the U.S. Americans' internal perceptions about themselves. As such they constituted a significant component of their identity work and their creation of new, desired selves or the maintaining of older, fixed ones. In reflecting on their choice of where to live, interviewees often saw it as related to their level of adjustment to life in the tropics in general and level of integration in Costa Rica in particular, as well as to the way in which they perceived themselves as "tropical" versus "temperate" or "U.S. American" people. The settlements west of San José, such as Escazú, Santa Ana, and Ciudad Colón, were known for their warm climate and some of the U.S. Americans who resided there developed a place-based identity in which their place of residence came to symbolize their larger integration into the local way of living and their endorsement of a "tropical" lifestyle. This was also reflected, for instance, in their choice of clothing and architecture as well as in practices such as gardening. Conversely, the cooler weather of the mountainous neighborhoods to the south, east, and north of San José, such as Moravia, San Pedro, and Curridabat, was perceived as familiar to the immigrants from back home in the United States and therefore as enabling the preservation of their former selves. "I need to have the opportunity to wear a sweater," stated one interviewee, originally from Minnesota.[22]

Settling the Beachfronts and Rain Forests: New Spirits and Old Habits

While in the 1950s most of the U.S. Americans resided and worked in the San José metropolitan area or the Central Valley, a minority had already begun to settle outside of it, in the rain forests and beaches of Costa Rica. Living in such places distanced these immigrants not only from other North Americans and their networks but also from the local society of the Central Valley, which was considered the core of "Costa Ricanness" and as such, despite being mostly mestizo in its ethnic composition, perceived of itself as "white."[23] The areas outside the Central Valley were therefore not only a different geographical space but also a different racial one—the site of indigeneity and Blackness, which contrasted with the image most U.S. Americans had of Costa Rica and entailed a very different experience in terms of integration and cultural and social identifications.[24] Living in these places therefore had far-reaching implications on the identity work of the U.S. Americans who resided there, both with regards to the U.S. Americans in the Central Valley and to the Costa Rican population in their places of residence.

The Quakers who left the United States due to their objection to the Korean War established the colony of Monteverde in 1953 near the village of Santa Elena in the province of Puntarenas. Their writings express their desire to fully integrate into Costa Rican society so as not to be considered foreigners.[25] Their emplacement and localization were done through their experience with the Costa Rican land and relations with locals, who functioned as agricultural and cultural mentors. Lucille Guindon, one of the founders of the colony, wrote, "From our neighbors we learned when to plant different things, not only seasonably but by the time of the moon."[26] U.S. American agriculturists in Costa Rica, who came from a very different natural environment in the United States, repeatedly depicted their struggle with the difficult conditions of the heavy soil and dense vegetation of the rainforest, stressing their engagement with the land as evidence of their shared experience with the local *campesinos* (farmers)—despite the great division in economic and technological terms—and their consequent belonging to the place. Several U.S. American settlers joined the massive Costa Rican colonization of the country's south, an area known as *frontera sur*, which became accessible following the progression of the Inter-American Highway.[27] The Cole-Christensen family established its farm, Finca Loma Linda (beautiful hill farm), in this new area, near the town of Buenos Aires. In his memoir, *A Place in the Rain Forest: Settling the Costa Rican Frontier*, Daryl Cole-Christensen describes the hardships that his family went through, yet consistently conceptualizes his experience as a reenactment of the conquest of the North American frontier, with the latter's ideology and practices applied here in the context of the Costa Rican frontier, and elaborates on his role as a U.S. settler in mid-twentieth-century Costa Rica. His place-identity combines gendered, national, and cultural perceptions to portray him as a "masculine" U.S. American pioneer conquering "feminine" Costa Rican nature, bringing civilization and progress.[28] Elsie Mae Fiala and Walter Fiala and their two young children, originally from Iowa, settled in 1956 near the village of Potrero Grande in southern Costa Rica and ran an agricultural farm for a company backed by U.S. American and Costa Rican investors. They were the only U.S. American family in this vast region. In letters to her family back home, Elsie Fiala reflected on her self-realization as a U.S. American woman among indigenous people in the Costa Rican rainforest:

Fig. 6. John Stam, missionary from the United States, in Santa Cruz, Guanacaste, 1956. Courtesy of the Stam family.

"I get aggravated at the people sometimes but maybe there would be less ulcers in the States if they lived like they do here. They just don't worry!!!"[29] Missionaries from the Latin America Mission served in remote settlements in Costa Rica. Following a year of language training in San José, Doris and John Stam were stationed in Santa Cruz in the Guanacaste province, where they lived for two years, trying to convert Costa Ricans to Protestantism and in turn being converted themselves to what they described as the campesino way of life (fig. 6).[30]

Alongside these agricultural settlements of U.S. Americans in the 1950s, and in many ways antithetical to them in spirit, colonies of beach dwellers began to gather along Costa Rica's remote and isolated beachfronts, a phenomenon that illustrates the connection between social trends in the United States and immigration to Costa Rica and which presented a new model of identity work and new cultural practices of emplacement among U.S. Americans in the country. Whereas U.S. Americans who settled in the rain forests largely tracked Costa Rican patterns of settlement, this alternative settlement trend's fascination with and hunger for the beachfronts bore the influences of U.S. culture, and in particular its counterculture.

Looking out through the windows of his United Fruit Company cottage in Golfito on the Osa Peninsula, agronomist Clyde Stephens, a UFC employee, was captivated by the sight of all the "beatniks, draft-dodgers, hippies, flower children, and drug cultists." Stephens, whose only U.S. American acquaintances in the area until then had been fellow UFC employees, recounted that "for only a few Costa Ricans colones they bought squatters rights to exotic little parcels of tropical paradise along the rugged shorelines of the beaches, bays and rivers."[31] A prominent figure among these squatters and one of the first to arrive in this remote area was Tom Clairmont, a native of Akron, Ohio (fig. 7). A former U.S. Marine and World War II veteran, Clairmont had lost a leg in the war and used his compensation money from the army to purchase a decommissioned military submarine chaser. Captain Tom, as he was known, spent several years traveling the coast between Panama and Costa Rica engaging in semilegal commerce. In 1950 he docked his ship on the shore of Playa Cacao in the Osa Peninsula, where he soon bought a plot of beach for 125 colones—about 16 U.S. dollars at the time. Clairmont lived in the ruins of his ship and later built several ranchos around it and opened a bar. Living in this extremely remote and beautiful spot, Clairmont transformed from an ex-U.S. marine into a symbol of the counterculture and the free life that rejected all attributes of "respectable" appearance and behavior. Accessible primarily from the ocean, his place turned its back on the land and could barely be reached from it. As such, it facilitated a "lawless" lifestyle outside the social norms of both Costa Rica and the United States and attracted travelers and expats from the latter and from Europe as well as a few Costa Ricans. Stephens, the enchanted corporation employee, described the lifestyle on Clairmont's beach as "simple, friendly, and liberal," but concerned local residents depicted it as a scandalous cult where young female Costa Rican runaways had sexual relations and smoked pot with U.S. Americans.[32]

In the 1950s, this kind of settlement was a novelty for both Costa Ricans and the U.S. Americans living in the country, but over the course of the two decades that followed it was joined by several other communes of a similar spirit. The communal settlements often began back in the United States, established as a result of their members' rejection of the modern urban way of life in favor of a simpler, more natural existence. These immigrants then left

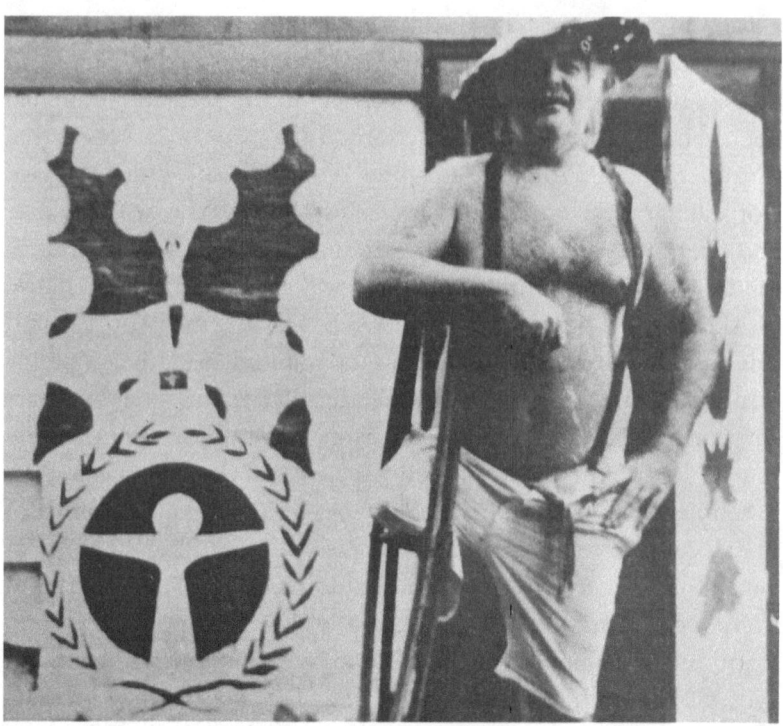

Fig. 7. Tom Clairmont, known as "Captain Tom," in Playa Cacao, 1972. Photograph by Rick Berg. Courtesy of the TT.

their homeland, which in interviews they tended to portray as overindustrialized and even rotten and decaying, in favor of Costa Rica, which they described as pure and pristine and therefore enabling an individual and collective transformation.[33] One such commune was established in 1968 in the valley of Orosi, east of San José. Eileen Steinberg, originally from Chicago and later a student in New York, recounted that she "had to leave the concrete" and live in nature.[34] The commune later moved further south to Copey de Dota, where it continued to exist in one form or another until the late 1970s. Eric White, who arrived there in 1972, recounted that it was "very isolated at the time. It was access[ible] by four-wheel drive and just beautiful, I mean, the climate, everything."[35]

White highlights three important components of these settlements and the identity work they facilitated. The first was the beautiful landscape in which they were situated and its natural amenities, which was a commodity in and of itself, desired and consumed by people who saw themselves as antimaterialistic;[36] the second was their isolation, which attested to the residents' wish to withdraw from mainstream society and congregate together (Joan Stevens, the U.S. American teacher living in San José, testified that "you could hardly meet hippies in the Central Valley, they were in the forests and the beachfronts").[37] For some, like John Foulks, the counterculturist from Chicago who fled the United States in 1974 and ended up on a forested property above Punta Uva with several U.S. American friends in 1977, living in the rain forest was part of a gradual, conscious process. "It wasn't like we were in Chicago one day and 'Oh, let's go and live in the rain forest.' It was a slow process in which we got sort of farther and farther and farther out and away from civilization."[38] Finally, the third component involved in the settling of these isolated communities was the monetary and technological advantages of U.S. Americans, who could afford, for example, the Land Rovers that were the only way to reach their habitations.

A somewhat similar settlement was established in 1972 by Sharon Hage and her group of ten, mostly male, friends in Uvita, near the village of Dominical, on the southern Pacific coast. Its members engaged in what Hage described as the study of comparative religions and amateur gardening.[39] Contrary to the Quaker engagement with the Costa Rican land, the U.S. American counterculturists were interested in what one of these settlers defined as "gardening and hanging out."[40] They were neither looking to emplace themselves through sustainable agriculture in Costa Rica nor dependent on its products for their survival, but rather inclined more toward the ideas of the Back to the Land movement in the United States and the transformation from urbanites to people of nature. Although commune members romanticized the campesino way of life, they were in actuality focused on their personal self-quests. Sensitive to the mental, cultural, and class gap between themselves and the Costa Ricans, they neither aspired nor believed it possible to integrate into the local culture.[41]

Due to poor infrastructure and long-held prejudices in Costa Rica about the "Blackness" of the area and its "otherness" vis-à-vis the

Costa Rican core, the Atlantic coast was less populated than other parts of the country. Those U.S. Americans who settled here, such as Foulks, were drawn to this region precisely because of its wild nature and exoticism. In the early 1970s, a handful of U.S. Americans settled in Cahuita, north of Puerto Viejo, and attracted visitors who tended to stay for only short periods. Following a scandal involving public nudity and possession of marijuana by a group of U.S. American counterculturists, the *TT* cited a U.S. American observer as saying, "It's a pity. They're a little late. They would fit right into Haight-Ashbury in the mid-1960s." A fellow U.S. American resident of Cahuita went as far as asserting that the leader of the group seemed to have "Manson-like power" over his followers, in a clear reference to Charles Manson's 1969 massacre in Los Angeles. Always concerned about the image of U.S. Americans in Costa Rica and trying to police them, the *TT* lamented, "Must Paradise Be Full of Poison Ivy?"[42] Rather than cultivating a local place-identity, the U.S American counterculturists' settlements were therefore perceived as an extension—in both time and space—of the U.S. counterculture and a chance to carry on this lifestyle and identities after the latter had faded in the United States. Moreover, contrary to the rain forest settlements, the beachfronts were seen as more of a borderland, the "fringes of the rug," as Mary Louise Pratt described the eighteenth-century European colonization of the beachfronts of the Americas.[43] The U.S. American's counterculture settlements hosted cultural practices, discourses and references that were imported from the sending society but often clashed with those of the host society and did not penetrate into the mainstream. In this respect, the U.S. Americans who lived in the beachfronts perceived themselves—and were perceived by other U.S Americans and Costa Ricans—as removed from Costa Rican norms and society and living in somewhat of a foreign bubble that itself comprised multiple shifting and various agendas. Foulks, though he was part of the counterculture in the United States, disdained its representation and practices in Costa Rica. He portrayed the U.S. counterculture settlements in Costa Rica of the time as "little enclaves" that were part of a network extending from the United States southward: "People coming down in their Volkswagens busses or whatever and they all get together, doing a lot of drugs. . . . We really wanted to get out into the local [surrounding] and be in the local culture. We wanted to get away from the whole American experience from back home, both the counterculture and the established culture."[44]

Snow and Anderson refer to mechanisms of association or distancing as another component of identity work.[45] When Hage and her friends lived in the commune near Dominical, there were at least two other U.S. settlers in the area—Richard Erikson in nearby Uvita and Jim Brown, who owned a *finca* (farm) south of Dominical. Both of them were agriculturists who opted not to interact with the commune members, scorning their loose lifestyle and particularly antagonistic to the mostly male composition of the group, which aroused suspicions (and hostility) regarding the group's possible homosexual orientation.[46] The commune members, for their part, formed close relations with the members of the Copey de Dota commune and together constituted a popular stop on Costa Rica's so-called "Gringo Trail." Theodor Bart, who lived in the Dominical commune, was aware of its status as another tourist attraction in Costa Rica and the internalizing of that perception by the commune members: "[We were] one of the attractions of Costa Rica, to see the guys of Dominical, look at the peacocks."[47]

Settlement in the Central Valley versus that in the rain forests and beachfronts also both reflected and constituted explicitly gendered identifications and practices. While there were some U.S. American women who lived on the Costa Rican periphery with their families and saw it as a significant component of their identity work, in many cases the rain forests and beachfronts were considered unfit for them, and families split, with the U.S. American wives staying in the San José area and the husbands working on a farm outside the Central Valley and retuning home on weekends. Sometimes this was because the women themselves were reluctant to live on the farm. Henrietta Boggs recalled in her memoir that as an urbanite Southern girl visiting a Costa Rican finca for the first time, she had expected something out of *Gone with the Wind*, envisioning her upward mobility from a working-class girl into the "lady of the manor." But the Costa Rican farm was nothing like Tara, the fictional Georgian plantation, and she could not imagine herself living in such a place.[48] Jane Mora, the young bride of a Costa Rican man, recounted her first tour to the family dairy farm, located a forty-five-minute drive up a dirt road, where her husband dreamed they would live together. Mora admitted that it was exciting and new ("I do not think I ever saw a cow, we didn't have much of them in Los Angeles"), but "there were no flushing toilets. I said, I can't live here."[49] Contrary to these stories, Karen Hill-Webber, who had grown up on a Texas ranch and arrived in Costa Rica in 1951, was thrilled to live on the cattle farm of her husband's family, but her father-in-law objected to the idea and she was placed in a San José apartment, while her husband spent the weekdays on the farm.[50] Adam Klee, who had a vast farm in the Nicoya Peninsula, "at the end of the road," said that his wife lived in Santa Ana rather than on the farm because that "was customary here."[51] In this respect, adhering to this gender division was another form of acculturation into Costa Rican society through the adaptation of place-based norms.[52]

A Paradise with an Eighteen-Hole Golf Course: The "Pacific Invasion" of the Gringos

Alongside the counterculture U.S. American settlements along the coasts, a different pattern of U.S. American colonization began to emerge in the 1970s. This wave reflected a more financially established lifestyle and a vision of Costa Rica's natural surroundings as a good investment rather than a simpler way of life or a path to spiritual redemption. These settlements were the result of the growing Costa Rican national debt and the instability of the coffee market, which impoverished Costa Rica and its farmers. The state could not afford to carry out its welfare policies, and many farmers sold their land and migrated to the cities.[53] This predicament converged with the rise in U.S. American immigration to Costa Rica, many of whose participants gradually took interest in real estate investment in the beachfronts and rain forests. In this respect, U.S. immigration was part of what several scholars have termed "planetary gentrification," in which the flow of individuals from the Global North into the Global South went hand in hand with processes of rural gentrification.[54]

The lifestyle of these people entailed a different self-identification with and through place. So, for example, Nosara, established in 1970 on the west coast of the Nicoya Peninsula, was designed as a Florida-style golf community for U.S. citizens. U.S. American entrepreneurs promised to sell their compatriots large properties for the price of a condominium apartment in Florida (hence establishing Costa Rica, as in the case of the counterculturists' settlement in Cahuita, as an extension of a specific way of living in the United States) and flew them over from New York to tour the place. William Russell, who lived in the Central Valley in the early 1970s, remembered that in the marketing material of the project U.S. Americans were invited to imagine the beautiful tropical beachfronts made even more perfect by an eighteen-hole golf course and a twenty-story hotel (they were asked to imagine this because nothing had yet been constructed and would not be for years to come, and the marketing brochures in fact depicted images of condos in Florida.).[55] Smaller-scale gated communities of U.S. Americans, such as Flamingo Beach and Playa Hermosa, popped up all along the coast of the Nicoya Peninsula. These communities functioned as U.S. American enclaves, ensuring that their residents could preserve their U.S. American lifestyle and identifications and avoid any significant contact with the Costa Rican people, who they encountered mainly in the guise of employees.

These settlements, and the U.S. American real estate entrepreneurs behind them, became the target of criticism in Costa Rica. In his previously mentioned, widely read 1974 series of reports in *La Nación* journalist Miguel Salguero compellingly identified Nosara as the first case of unbridled land speculation (*desenfrenada especulación*) by U.S. Americans in Costa Rica.[56] The method, which was then reproduced on other beachfronts and in the Central Valley, consisted of buying cheap agricultural land used for raising cattle and parceling it into small plots on which residential units were constructed and then sold at enormous profit. Salguero documented such developments in many places in Costa Rica, which together amounted to what he called "a general sale of Costa Rican lands." In the 1970s the new U.S. American developments began to gain a bad reputation. "Wherever I see a tractor working through a farm, I smell a gringo," a Costa Rican man was cited as saying in Salguero's article.[57] In several places, such as Piedades de Santa Ana in the Central Valley, the U.S. American presence had become so dominant that Salguero described them as a "U.S. colony" and called on Costa Rican authorities to intervene in order to halt this frantic land speculation before it precipitated major negative economic and social changes in the country.

The public debate on U.S. Americans purchasing Costa Rican land interfaced with two critical discourses in Costa Rica. The first was the old debate about U.S. influence in Costa Rica and the latter's fear of subjugation. This originated in the late nineteenth century, when the establishment of the UFC's enclaves along the Atlantic coast resulted in Costa Rica becoming the first banana republic, and continued with the growing influence of the United States in the country during World War II, which in 1943 led political thinker Rodrigo Facio Brenes to claim that Costa Rica had become a semicolony of the United States.[58] The land purchasing, which Salguero described as a "pacific invasion," was yet another manifestation of U.S. influence, this time from the bottom up by individuals who were not part of the U.S. administration but many of whom in fact, like the counterculturists, had arrived in Costa Rica partly due to their objection to it.

The fact that Costa Ricans, whom Salguero characterized as naïve in comparison to the sophisticated U.S. Americans, were eager to sell their land only made things worse in his view, because it confirmed broader fears about the diminishing of lands in the Central Valley—the second Costa Rican discourse of which the U.S. land purchasing ran afoul. While it is true that this diminishing was also caused by squandering cultivation methods, it led to a real fear that in the future Costa Ricans would be landless in their own country, with U.S. Americans holding most of the beautiful or fertile properties.[59] Salguero claimed that this was because the U.S. buyers were raising land prices way above the average Costa Ricans' financial means, thus forcing them to become city paupers or subordinated to U.S. American land owners.[60] A letter in the TT by Carlos Jinesta, a Costa Rican who resided in California, reflected the confusion and growing fear of Costa Ricans in face of the estate boom. "Let's face it, Costa Rica is a piece of real estate with a big FOR SALE sign on it. And the Costa Ricans are so happy about the so-called boom of the economy that they are selling out. America has the money to buy any country, any day, and it is happening."[61] The writer went on to warn about the political implications of such land purchasing (to this the editor wrote in response, "This is something we worry about too").[62] This process, which took place throughout the 1970s, escalating even further during the economic crisis at the close of the decade, facilitated both the identity work of U.S. Americans in Costa Rica as real estate people and practices of emplacement that emphasized profit making out of the land, which led to the portrayal of "the gringo" as a greedy entrepreneur.

Membership: Identity Work in the U.S. Clubland

So far, I have dealt with place-based identification as one form of individual and collective identity work among U.S. Americans. In what follows I consider individual identity work and community-building through the establishment of and membership in social networks.

The U.S. clubland in the Central Valley of Costa Rica was a dense network of social, philanthropic, and business associations, which, as the logic of inclusion and exclusion of clubbing dictates, both reflected and shaped the characters of the diverse U.S. American populations, who while they might not have congregated together in their homeland were, in Costa Rica, brought together by their common foreignness and more particularly by their shared national origin. Although divided along lines of gender, wealth and class, lifestyle, and ideologies, taken as a whole, the U.S. clubland served as a key tool for creating individual identifications based on association—or disassociation—either by choice or by exclusion. It also facilitated a collective identity based on shared experiences and identifications of U.S. Americans, which was further translated into claims for physical and symbolic space by this population in the Central Valley and the local surroundings.

Unlike immigrants of other nationalities and ethnicities in Costa Rica who established communal institutions that boasted fancy venues, such as the German Club and the Italian Club, or the Centro Israelita of the Ashkenazi Jewish community, U.S. Americans formed no general organization or representative body based on strictly national lines; nor did they create any physical space to serve as a permanent, tangible home for their entire national community.[63] An ad hoc body dubbed "the American Colony" was elected annually to organize the Fourth of July picnic, whose location wandered over the years from the garden of the U.S. embassy to various parks in San José area. This lack of communal institutions and physical markers can perhaps be attributed to the community's relative lack of financial means or to the sense of transience that was common among U.S. Americans in Costa Rica. In any case, it was an absence that further enhanced the role that the U.S. clubland came to play in shaping the visibility and representation of U.S. Americans as a group and their individual identity work through affiliation with a social network. For example, in the telephone directory I mentioned earlier, each U.S. American was identified not only by his or her address and phone number but also by the social organizations to which they belonged. The clubs were an anchor of stability for the U.S. American community, evidence of its continued existence beyond the presence of any particular individual. Moreover, these clubs were also the main arena in which the contours of the community were drawn, and where various types of U.S. "Americanness" in Costa Rica were affirmed and negotiated. As the body of members frequently changed, with newcomers constantly joining and the recently arrived quickly becoming senior members and experts, the social organizations themselves, and any move between them, became a significant locus of identity work. It was in these clubs that the process of acculturation took place, wherein newcomers were educated about the "correct" way of being a certain type of U.S. American in Costa Rica—whether a compassionate U.S. club woman or a U.S. American member of the business milieu—on both the practical and the mental levels. The club members, for their part, saw it as their role to assure that their fellow expatriates would not turn into "Tarzan" and withdraw into the jungle, to paraphrase Paul Theroux's famous remark about white expats in Africa, but rather stayed part of an organized, monitored social organization, with a U.S. orientation claiming a shared identity, interests, and power in the Costa Rican surroundings.[64]

The social and physical aspects of the U.S. clubs in the Central Valley were mutually constituted. Tracing the different locations of the clubs enables us to sketch the meticulous identity work carried out in them and the relations of such identification to the creation of physical spaces, in terms of the U.S. immigrants' assimilation or alienation. In her writing about the social spaces of expats in Jakarta, Meike Fechter rejects the image of these spaces as a kind of bubble that hovers above the city, a sealed space of societies of foreigners, and proposes the more complex image of membranes: "Although it implies a clear division between the inside and outside, the bubble also has a membrane—like a cell's membrane, which can be permeable and allow outside fluids to enter the cell's inside [and] there are flows and exchanges of substances, ideas, and people across their boundaries."[65] In this respect, the clubs should be considered as contact zones between the foreign population and the local surroundings, in which encounters between the local and the foreign took place in changing dynamics of power relations.[66]

Another term to consider with regards to the different locations that U.S. Americans turned into their social spaces, even for ad hoc meetings, is the Spanish notion of *querencia*, borrowed from Dennison Nash's writing about U.S. Americans in Barcelona in the 1960s. The multiple meanings of querencia refer to a place where one feels at home, as well as the longing for such a place. In bullfighting jargon, for instance, querencia indicates those spots in the ring where the bull feels safe.[67] Without suggesting that U.S. Americans in Costa Rica necessarily felt intimidated, the use of this term to describe the shifting spots of the clubs captures the sense in which these places shaped a migratory spatial sphere where U.S. Americans, especially women, felt at home, or safe. Since these places were, in many cases, not exclusively U.S. American, for example the lobbies of local hotels, or local restaurants and churches, they manifest the fragile nature of the U.S. presence and the accommodation of various U.S. Americans to distinct Costa Rican public surroundings, in which the choice of location was based on the social, class, gender, and age stratifications among them.

Club Life in Costa Rica:
Transnational Spaces and Social Networks

While the U.S. clubland in Costa Rica—which began to emerge after World War II in tandem with a rise in U.S. influence in the region and the correlative growth in the number of U.S. American immigrants—was inspired by similar social clubs in the United States, it also reflected the influence of expat and colonial heritage.[68] Yet the clubs were not a mere replication of U.S. American or colonial clubs; rather, they were shaped and reshaped in response to the changing needs, interests, and predicaments of various segments of the U.S. American population in Costa Rica. In this respect the U.S. clubland should be considered a transnational physical and mental space in which the identity work of U.S. Americans, both individual and collective, took place vis-à-vis the United States, Costa Rica, and, to a lesser extent, other patterns and practices of expatriatism and colonialism.

Several scholars have maintained that clubbing is embedded in the U.S. American nature and is a fundamental tenet of U.S. political and civil society.[69] Others have argued that this impulse of association was constrained by the individualism inherent in the U.S. American character, which became even more pronounced in the twentieth century.[70] This, and fragmentation of U.S. society, was expressed in part through immigration and the reluctance of some immigrants to be associated with other U.S. Americans, while at the same time the impulse to associate brought others to search for more solidarity by creating a home away from their homeland.

On the transnational level, scholars have stressed the significance of civil organizations in the formation of an expat civil society and their practical as well as symbolic value. The clubs created a physical and mental space that was in-between homeland and adoptive country and served as a dynamic framework that functioned on the borderland between the heritage and practices of the homeland and those of the adoptive country.[71] In some cases, U.S. American social clubs in Costa Rica functioned also as a borderland between formal and informal U.S. power and as an instrument for advancing the U.S. agenda and image in Cold–War Central America through unofficial channels. In this respect, they accorded with one of the distinguishing features of U.S. imperialism from its earliest days, namely the lack of a strong core of civil servants and the consequent reliance on semiformal agents, who were asked or took it upon themselves to represent U.S. agendas, as they interpreted them, and made this activity a critical factor of their identity.[72]

National, Gendered, and Economic Contours of the U.S. Clubland

In his seminal work on expatriate communities, Eric Cohen suggested that a community builds itself by constructing sets of "us against Others." Leo Spitzer maintained that it does so, sometimes, in response to a view that "others" them and pushes them to create separatist community organizations.[73] This is certainly true for U.S. Americans in Costa Rica. The lack of actual walls and guards at the club's door did not mean that there were no gatekeepers protecting the boundary between them and "others." Rather, these gatekeepers simply became more subtle and elusive. The clubland was the main arena in which "others" were defined, both for the U.S. expat population and those outside it. Borders were drawn between different groups based on criteria such as gender, profession, or class, in a manner that Snow and Anderson defined as "associational distancing."[74]

Roland Barthes makes the point that boundaries themselves should be the site of investigation, rather than the "cultural stuff" they enclose.[75] In the case of the social organizations of U.S. Americans in Costa Rica, as with similar organizations of other nationalities in Costa Rica and other countries, it is useful to remember that these boundaries had a dual purpose. They served to both distinguish the foreign population from the local one and to unify the expat population itself in order to overcome internal differences of gender, ethnicity, class, ideology, and lifestyle. At the same time, the very logic of clubbing, with its implicit and explicit criteria for membership, dictated that these clubs also generate and expose differences. The simultaneous movement of inclusion and exclusion that characterizes the clubbing sphere also determined and reflected individual and collective identity work with regard to changing levels of integration and contact with the local population. Thus, by deciding who could associate with whom, on what terms, for what purpose, and in which spaces, members of the U.S. clubland constantly defined and redefined themselves and their relationship to "others"—whether Costa Ricans, other foreign nationals, or their compatriots.

The U.S. clubs provided a sense of the familiar ("I could say something and they knew what I meant," recalled one of the members of the women's club who dubbed it her "lifeline") while at the same time helping U.S. Americans reach out beyond the foreign enclave to engage with their Costa Rican surroundings through excursions, encounters with locals, and charitable activities.[76] The clubs, whose members carried out all these activities under their protective wings, sometimes adopted a patronizing point of view toward the local population and environment. Furthermore, these activities gave U.S. Americans visibility and enabled them to define their role in Costa Rica as contributing both to Costa Rican welfare and to the image of the United States during the Cold War era.

Patterns of engagement and exclusion with regards to the Costa Rican public sphere and population varied, of course, from one club to another, but can be found in most of them. The first U.S. organization in San José, Post 10 of the American Legion (AL), was established in 1920. It was followed, after World War II, by Post 11 in Heredia, a small town in the Central Valley, and Post 16 in Golfito, on the southern Pacific coast. All three were affiliates of the Panama division of the organization. The posts were professional, binational (because the Costa Rican army was an American ally during World War II their veterans were given membership in the AL), and single-gender organizations that brought together male U.S. and Costa Rican veterans based on a shared experience in the U.S. Army. The AL aimed to strengthen the shared identity and unity of its members, who met once a month at the Hotel Centroamericano in the center of San José, as well as to promote the public image of the United States abroad through charity activities (the organization was defined as an American patriotic society). In 1979, for example, the Costa Rican AL posts financed the construction of a swimming pool in San José and donated two hundred and fifty swim suits for children.[77] The AL had a women's auxiliary unit in San José for the wives, widows, and sisters of U.S. American and Costa Rican veterans, which focused mainly on charity and less on social gatherings.

The second organization of U.S. Americans, the U.S.A. Women's Club, was established during World War II and in direct response to that conflict. The members, wives of Costa Rican men and U.S. Americans, participated in the digging of shelters in San José and raised some $125,000 for the United States' war effort. The club goals, as set down in its three constitutions, were to unify U.S. American (and later English-speaking) women in Costa Rica, to further the interests and image of the United States in the Americas, and to work for the benefit of Costa Rica through charitable activities.

The criteria for membership were gender-based, of course, but also, and in contrast to other U.S. clubs in Costa Rica, strictly national, at least at first: only U.S. American citizens or women who were first-degree relatives of U.S. Americans were eligible. This intersection of gender and nationality expressed the U.S. women's need to carve out a space for themselves both within Costa Rican society, as many of the members were married to Costa Rican men and the club helped them maintain their U.S. American identity, and the foreign community. Several other organizations in San José, such as the International Club, offered a social framework for non–Costa Rican women, yet the U.S. American women insisted on a national criterion and emphasized their role in serving the U.S. cause in Costa Rica.[78] This changed in 1959, when, in an effort to improve the image of the United States and in particular that of the "Ugly American" who refuses to integrate, the U.S. ambassador to Costa Rica ordered the club to open its gate to all English-speaking women in Costa Rica. The mandate attests to the perceived importance of the women's club as the largest, most established civic association of U.S. Americans in Costa Rica, but also to the gendered aspects of U.S. hegemony during the Cold War. The members, torn between their wish to keep their linguistic and cultural querencia and their self-perception as working in service of the United States, reluctantly obeyed, and over the years the club eventually became more binational. In 1965 it changed its name to the Women's Club of

Costa Rica / Club de Mujeres de Costa Rica (WCCR), but English remained its lingua franca.

Despite being open to all U.S. women in Costa Rica, not all chose to join, a choice that often reflected the social stratification of U.S. Americans in the country along axes of class and age. Many of the members of the women's club were not financially wealthy, particularly not the U.S. American wives of Costa Rican men and those whose husbands worked for Costa Rican firms. Yet, the nature and style of the querencia that the club provided gave it in some eyes a negative image of an upper-class U.S. enclave. It was, moreover, seen as an extension of the conservative United States and closely associated with the U.S. administration and its policies. This image of the club alienated many U.S. American women in Costa Rica whose age, economic status, profession, language skills, lifestyle, or acculturation into Costa Rican society set them apart from such affiliations. Doris Green, who married a Costa Rican man and arrived in Costa Rica in 1967, knew about the U.S. Women's Club, "but I really wasn't interested in joining a group that I perceived as a sort of separate club."[79] For many of the young women who arrived in the country in the early 1970s, the club represented an old-fashioned and patriotic extension of the United States—in other words, precisely what they had hoped to get away from. In 1972 Diane Abrahams was living in Santa Ana near San José, where she worked as a teacher in English-speaking schools and associated with like-minded artists in counterculture circles. Asked if she had considered joining the club, she replied, "Oh no, it was for the wealthy old ladies."[80]

For many members, the U.S. Women's Club mitigated the culture shock that attended their arrival in Costa Rica but became redundant or indeed incongruous over time, following their deeper integration into Costa Rican society or a change in their lifestyle. For others it served as a way back into the U.S. American milieu. Joan Stevens, who has been living in Costa Rica since the late 1960s, working first as an agricultural instructor in rural communities and then (as already mentioned) as an English teacher in San José, joined the WCCR only in the early 2000s, after her marriage to a U.S. American: "That's when I began to really become maybe a little more American than I had been before."[81]

Despite consisting of a network of several hundred women, the largest such association in the U.S. clubland in Costa Rica, the WCCR had no physical space (the 1975 inventory of the Club's possessions lists only several paper tablecloths, two samovars, some one hundred paper cups, and a handful of other items).[82] As early as 1959 the club's president called for the establishment of a physical center to serve not only the club's needs but be available for the use of other U.S. clubs as well.[83] However, the necessary funds never materialized and the club members were left without the proverbial "room of one's own." While the emphasis on the nationality and gender of club members was supposed to promote unity among the women, the club's choices of space for its meetings sometimes brought the differences between the members to the surface. So, for example, its annual luncheon was always held in San José's most lavish hotel, the Grand Hotel, or at the aristocratic Union Club, establishments frequented by the club's upper-class members, typically the wives of diplomats and businessmen, but unfamiliar and uncertain terrain for the less affluent members.[84] Regular meetings were held, inter alia, in the U.S.-Costa Rican Cultural Center and in the lobby of the U.S. embassy—the latter signifying the women's familiarity with this institution (in 1960 four out of nine new members gave the U.S. embassy as their contact address in Costa Rica) but also their marginalization insofar as they were relegated to the lobby rather than receiving a proper meeting room. In the mid-1950s, the club began using space in the English-speaking schools and churches and for a short period in the 1960s, for lack of a public place that could host the growing number of attendees, also the private homes of members. This last practice highlighted the social and economic gaps between those members who gladly opened their homes and happily boasted of their lifestyle and those who were less affluent and thus reluctant or even unable to do so. The meetings in private homes also splintered the club into numerous local neighborhood clubs, each taking on the characteristics and status of the particular San José barrio in which its meetings took place, rather than a large, general, and inclusive U.S. American network. It was perhaps for this reason that the club soon resumed its gatherings in public U.S.-associated spaces, including a branch of the U.S. American Pizza Hut chain, which opened in the city in 1974.

In 1945, following the end of World War II and the growing importance of soft power in U.S. foreign relations, the Costa Rican-North American Cultural Center was established in San José, part of a chain of similar centers opened by the United States Information Service (USIS) in several countries during this period. Although it was a formal U.S. government institution and not a civic organization, and despite being intended more as a means of propaganda geared toward the local population, the center attracted U.S. Americans to its activities and constituted another social network.

The Centro Cultural, as it was known among both U.S. Americans and Costa Ricans, offered English classes and cultural activities, such as dances and screenings of Hollywood films, as a means of promoting U.S. culture and lifestyle. As such it was a prime arena for encounters between U.S. Americans and Costa Ricans.[85] Mark Bach, who it will be recalled arrived in Costa Rica in 1968, related that the weekly square dances were an opportunity for himself and his fellow single U.S. American men to meet single Costa Rican women, who in turn came to meet U.S. American men.[86] However, the Centro Cultural also served to connect those within the U.S. American expat community, many of whom were involved with it either as consumers or as employees. The Centro Cultural offered Spanish classes, a library of books and recent magazines from the United States, a cafeteria with U.S. American style cuisine, and, during the 1950s, an English-speaking nursery. So while from the point of view of the U.S. administration the Centro Cultural was a tool of the U.S. Cold-War era propaganda, U.S. Americans in Costa Rica appropriated it as another social network for their community and a means of maintaining contact with their homeland and with fellow compatriots.

The 1964 passage of the Ley de Pensionado prompted the formation of the Pensionados Club. Established in 1968 by U.S. sociologist John Biesanz, the club was naturally aimed at the foreign population, of which U.S. Americans were of course a prominent part, and was open to both sexes. Though being one of the most explicit expressions of a U.S. American bubble, the club also strove to help U.S.

American pensionados venture beyond the retirees' network. In its monthly meetings, the club usually sponsored lectures by Costa Rican officials and people from the business sector with the aim of mediating between newly arrived retirees and the Costa Rican bureaucracy and creating a business hub for the club's members. In this respect, the "U.S. Americanness" shaped and promoted in this club was that of the small-scale entrepreneurs and people of leisure who came to Costa Rica to live peacefully but were not necessarily interested in acculturation in the country. A symbolic expression of this attitude is found in the club's venues, which were usually various hotels and golf clubs that catered to the needs of U.S. Americans. In an attempt to improve the negative image of U.S. American retirees, the Pensionados Club encouraged its members to take part in philanthropic activities and volunteer work—but with little success. In the mid-1970s, following the public criticism over the foreign retirees' privileges and the toughening of the criteria for gaining retiree status, the club's membership, which stood at around one hundred in its first years of operation, declined steadily, and in 1975 the club closed.[87]

Contrary to the bubble-like Pensionado Club, the Costa Rican branch of the Hash House Harriers (sometimes dubbed House Harriers Club, or HHH), which opened in the Central Valley of Costa Rica in the early 1970s, was the perfect example of the intangible character of the U.S. clubland. It also reflected the craving of U.S. Americans to engage with their Costa Rican surroundings, both human and natural, and their tendency to borrow from colonial traditions and practices of clubbing, in this case the running clubs of the 1930s British empire.[88] The Costa Rican HHH maps another contour of the U.S. American population's engagement with the Costa Ricans and other nationalities, based on criteria of culture (primarily fluency in English) and class, reflected through the professional status of the members, and therefore, ipso facto, also gender. Although membership was nominally open to all nationalities and both genders, the lingua franca was English and women did not partake in the club's activities, which took place in the woods on the outskirts of San José. The club's goals were engagement in physical activities, familiarization with the Costa Rican natural environment, and social gathering; the latter also being perceived as an opportunity to do business in an informal setting. The members of the HHH therefore tended to be businessmen, and its activities—exercising in the Costa Rican nature—took on a very masculine character, as a means of regenerating U.S. manhood in the Costa Rican nature. Bill Barbie, a U.S. American businessman who was among the founders of the club, recounted that the HHH meetings gained such popularity that no business meetings were scheduled for the first Monday of the month.[89]

The Little Theatre Group (LTG), an English-speaking amateur theater group, functioned as a social organization no less than as an artistic institution. It was established in 1949 by Albert Williams, a British military man who had been transferred to San José from the Panama Canal. Williams depicted the establishment of the theater as a pioneering act: "If you knew you were coming to Costa Rica, you came with the knowledge that you had to settle down somewhat and make your own entertainment."[90] The LTG began its operation in the most lavish building in San José, the National Theater, which was built in the late nineteenth century and whose design was inspired by the royal palace in Versailles. Taking advantage of the National Theater's suspension of operation in 1948 due to the civil war in Costa Rica, Williams used his contacts with people highly placed in the government to secure permission for the LTG to temporarily move its operations into the building. At a time when many other buildings in San José were doubtless similarly empty, their insistence on installing themselves in the highly prestigious National Theater building attests to the LTG's sense of their own significance despite being a small and marginal organization in the Costa Rican artistic sphere. When the war was over and the Costa Rican National Theater resumed operation, the LTG moved to other, inevitably more modest, U.S.-affiliated spaces, such as English-speaking churches and (like the women's club) the lobby of the U.S. embassy.

The LTG accepted every English-speaking person in Costa Rica, and in this regard aspired to create a bi- or even multinational sphere that revolved around artistic interest and an affiliation with Anglo-American culture. Despite this aspiration and Williams's insistence on the British spelling of the word "theatre," the LTG was dominated by U.S. Americans. The fact that it operated in English and that its repertoire was based on adaptations of Broadway, off-Broadway, and West-End hits kept it a mainly foreign social space. Even though the 1970s were considered a golden age for Costa Rican theater, the LTG never staged a play by a Costa Rican (or indeed any non-English-speaking) writer.[91]

Yet the LTG was a transnational space in the sense that it performed adaptations of the cultural products of one country, mainly the United States, into the context of a different one. Most LTG productions were revivals of mainstream Broadway and off-Broadway hits, such as Neil Simon's *Barefoot in the Park* (1973) and Frank Loesser and Abe Burrows's *Guys and Dolls* (1972). But other productions reflected new trends of U.S. American culture and granted physical and symbolic space to a more alternative segment of the U.S. American population in early 1970s San José. Such was the revival of *Alice in Wonderland*, a production that involved the creative work of several counterculture expat artists influenced by the Manhattan Project's celebrated 1970 stage adaptation of Lewis Caroll's classic. While the program text billed the show as a family-friendly dramatic fantasy, the production's psychedelic illustrations were explicit in their references to drug culture (fig. 8). And unlike the usual ads in the LTG programs, which tended to feature local businesses, an advertisement in the *Alice* program promoted a gallery of psychedelic art in San Francisco—further evidence of the transnational nature of the staff involved in the production and the audience of this specific show.

If *Alice in Wonderland* was an attempt to celebrate and revive the artistic spirit of the U.S. counterculture in Costa Rica, other productions took a more critical tone, reflecting the unique perspective of the expat, who observes his/her homeland from the outside. In May 1969 the LTG put on an evening of two plays by Edward Albee, *The American Dream* and *The Zoo Story*, the latter a play that had been banned in the United States because of its explicit treatment of homosexuality. The program's texts emphasized the opportunity that the LTG's staging of the play provided to consider the homeland from the outside: "Our directors have chosen these plays because they feel that they are unusually challenging, especially for Amer-

Fig. 8. Poster for the San José LTG production of *Alice in Wonderland*, 1973. Designed by Marg Wells, Tom Jackson, and Millie Jackson. Courtesy of the Little Theatre Group of Costa Rica.

icans living abroad. To be able to look at American society from a detached point of view, which is essentially what Albee himself is doing, should provide an exciting evening of theater."[92]

Much like Albee's revival at the LTG, the U.S. American clubland in Costa Rica enabled U.S. Americans to stay in touch with their cultural heritage but also to observe it from a distance, creating a perspective that was both adoring and critical. Through an intricate selection of U.S. American and Costa Rican cultural practices and members, these clubs shaped the complex identifications of their members as people who were at once a part of the United States and apart from it. U.S. American clubs were thus engaged in the creation of identifications and spaces that were neither entirely U.S. American nor Costa Rican; they provided their members with a familiar framework that also enabled them to venture out into and be influenced by the Costa Rican human and physical environment. With regards to the U.S. American clubland in San José, these boundaries were sometimes more penetrable, as in the case of the HHH and the LTG, and at other times more solid, like those of the women's club and the Pensionado Club.

Elusive Communities and Identifications

In this chapter I considered the choice of place of residence and affiliation with a U.S. American club as forms of individual and collective identity work. These choices were made by individuals, yet had a cumulative and collective effect. Taken together, they provide a shape to the map of the elusive communities and identifications of U.S. Americans in Costa Rica. Membership in these clubs and the choice to live in a specific place, whether the Central Valley or a rain forest or beachfront, or even the decision of where to live within the relatively small San José metropolitan area, in the cooler northeast sections or the warmer west and south, all were expressions of the intricate identity work that shaped individual identifications toward both the Costa Rican surroundings and the U.S. American population in the country. In this respect, as with any process of identity-making, these choices were fluid and changeable, functioning as a litmus test for an individual's national and cultural identification at various phases of his or her life in Costa Rica.

While there is a distinction between an identification based on a specific place and one based on affiliation with an intangible social network, these categories also overlap: settlement in particular places is influenced by social networks. This is especially evident in the case of those U.S. American counterculturists who arrived together in Costa Rica or came there following in the footsteps of their like-minded compatriots. At the same time, although the U.S. American clubs in Costa Rica lacked a dedicated concrete location, yet their various places of operation and the movement between them created a physical U.S. American presence in the Central Valley. This articulation of places gives form to the changing U.S. querencias expressive of the shifting identifications of the people who frequented them. Taken together, places and social networks were crucial modes of identity work for U.S. Americans in Costa Rica.

three

From Cowboys to the Guardians of Eden
Identity Work in Costa Rican Nature

> I got nature inside me. I had absorbed so much nature.
> —EILEEN STEINBERG, author interview

I felt as close to paradise as anywhere I'd ever been. I had never seen a place like this on any coast—virgin forest sloping down to the sea, fast-running, clear, fresh water flowing over boulders into the ocean, abundant wildlife—and all of it for sale, cheap! I could actually own this if I wanted. Well, not really, not land and trees, rocks and streams and living things—these were not things any human could truly own—but I could have a temporary human authority over them if I desired.[1]

Echoing Christopher Columbus, who described the landscapes of the Americas as a "terrestrial paradise," this description by Jon Marañón's depicts the impact the landscape had on him as a newly arrived immigrant from the United States in the early 1970s.[2] It shows not only his appreciation of the beauty of the property he considered purchasing on the southern Pacific coast of Costa Rica but also gives a sense of the future he envisioned for himself in this place. Marañón's enchantment with the land's magnificence and its abundant fauna and flora was accompanied by an assessment of its potential value and instantaneous commodification through the possibility of buying it for cheap (throughout the years Marañón did indeed purchase many tracts of this earthly paradise), followed immediately by a sense of ambivalence about the ethical propriety and practical feasibility of this commodification. All these themes reappear in the discourse of U.S. American settlers reflecting on their lives in the two principal forms of Costa Rican nature: the rain forests and beachfronts.

This chapter considers the extent to which the Costa Rican natural surroundings—always depicted as powerful and inspiring—were a crucial site, literally and figuratively, in the identity work performed by U.S. Americans in the country. I examine discourses, practices of emplacement, and representations employed by these U.S. American settlers—who were farmers (either independent or employees of agricultural firms), entrepreneurs, naturalists, and people who withdrew from civilization in search of a quiet life, often in fact being some sort of combination of all of the above—in order to appreciate the means through which nature became a decisive factor in their identity-making as U.S. American men and women in Costa Rica.

Encountering Tropical American Nature: The Mental Baggage of the U.S. Settlers

The choice of a destination for immigration, especially if not compelled by economic considerations, is often driven by the desire to find places that are aesthetically speaking "beautiful landscapes," which the immigrant considers the required setting for his or her intended lifestyle and desired self.[3] This beauty, however, is not innate. Simon Schama argued that "landscapes are culture before they are nature; constructs of the imagination projected onto wood and water and rock."[4] Roland Barthes has pointed out that landscapes are neither "neutral" nor "natural;" rather they are a construct of our systems of signs, a social construction shaped by mental attitudes and ideologies in a process that takes place both consciously and unconsciously. To properly understand them, we need to decipher this system of signs and situate any given "landscape" within its own natural and cultural history.[5]

In choosing to come to the rain forests and beachfronts of Costa Rica, and continuously throughout their lives there, U.S. Americans deciphered the meanings of these landscapes and at the same time created new meanings as part of their practical and discursive process of emplacement in their new habitats. Marañón and other U.S. American settlers in Costa Rica were very "belated travelers," to borrow Ali Behadad's description of travel writers who came after the first wave of European colonialism. As such, their impressions and representations of Costa Rican nature, the consequent practices of emplacement, and the construction of identities in relation to these places relied on hundreds of years of accumulated botanical, geographical, and ethnographic knowledge, as well as historical experiences and ideologies forged over the course of several centuries throughout the Americas.[6] Sometimes it was precisely as a result of this knowledge that they learned about these places and were attracted to them in the first place.

Beyond this preexisting knowledge, the identity work of U.S. Americans in the Costa Rican natural surroundings was shaped by interconnected hierarchies of class, race, sexuality, ethnicity, nationality, and gender that created a unique reaction when they came into contact with the Costa Rican environment. U.S. Americans settlers brought with them their own background and experience with nature, whether as urbanites seeking to reinvent themselves in nature or as North American country folks adapting themselves to the tropics. In establishing their lives in the Costa Rican countryside they relied on familiar cultural tropes—such as the North American frontier experience, scientific exploration, the counterculture quest for the ideal life, and the Californian beach culture, as well as others—and combined these with new models, specifically and primarily that of the Costa Rican farmer, the campesino. In this way they established new individual and collective identifications.

In the writings and oral testimonies of these immigrants one finds echoes of earlier representations that had been handed down over the centuries and adapted to fit changing needs and interests. The very words Marañón chooses (and which recur in the accounts of many of his compatriots)—wildlife, forest, sea, as well as the image of paradise—carry distinct and time-specific cultural associations. Candace Slater has stressed that new representations often rework and integrate older images for diverse strategic ends, such as progress or conservation, and that images—especially those of nature and particularly ones fashioned by outsiders such as travelers, colonizers, and immigrants—are never innocent.[7]

Prominent among these images, and crucial to the identity work of U.S. Americans in the wilds of Costa Rica, is the dual perception of the tropical American Rain Forest as a paradise or "green cathedral," on the one hand, and, conversely, as the Jungle—a "green hell."[8] This dichotomy dictated practices of life and also shaped the role that U.S. Americans saw for themselves as agents of progress and capitalist entrepreneurs, aiming to subjugate the rain forest and transform it into an economic enterprise, or, conversely, as guardians of a romanticized ahistorical state of pristine nature. U.S. Americans' stories thus relate to the richness of Costa Rican nature in terms of material goods, with allusions to the myth of Eldorado, and also as sites for a spiritual quest. Also notable are references to earlier narratives of conquest and settlement, such as that of the nineteenth-century North American frontier. This narrative was transplanted into the practices and discourse of the settlement of the Costa Rican southern region, *la frontera sur*, and facilitated the construction of a pioneer identity on the part of the U.S. Americans who settled there. This self-perception was also explicitly gendered, offering an affirmation of the perceived gendered regimes of masculinities and femininities stemming from the "Wild West" but at the same time also undermining these regimes through gender role reversals driven and enabled by the act of immigration.

The image of paradise, evoked in Marañón's depiction, is of particular interest on several levels. While many lifestyle immigrants refer to their new homes as "paradise," in order to enhance the dichotomy between their past and current lives,[9] among immigrants to Costa Rica this use of the paradise trope is ubiquitous. For example, U.S. naturalist Alexander Skutch wrote, "Of the many parts of the earth to which the term 'a naturalist paradise' has been applied by enthusiastic naturalists, none deserve this praise more than Costa Rica as it then was."[10] Indeed, nowhere in Central America is the concentration of biodiversity higher than in Costa Rica. And despite the dubious distinction of having the world's highest rate of deforestation during the first two-thirds of the twentieth century, Costa Rica's image as a paradise on earth has only increased thanks to the combination of its outstanding natural beauty and conservation policies (some of which were the result of the economic crisis of the 1980s and geopolitical circumstances) implemented from the latter half of the twentieth century onward.[11] However, William Denevan has convincingly demonstrated the extent to which the view of the Latin American nature as a pristine, and moreover *empty*, paradise was enhanced at critical points in time, one of which was the mid-twentieth century, as part of the need to legitimize foreign political and economic action (either European or U.S. American) in the allegedly unpopulated Americas, constructed as a free, empty land ready for development and control. Indeed, Costa Rica's international tourism campaign branded the country as an empty paradise, anticipating foreign penetration and development.[12] Besides implying richness and abundance, the use of the Edenic trope is of course a critical component of individual identity work, due to its allusion to the Creation myth, which facilitates rebirth and salvation. Marañón and many others represented themselves as an Adam or Eve of sorts arriving in a pristine, empty paradise where they were reborn as new (and improved) people.

In short, the settlers' perceptions, practices, and representations regarding Costa Rican landscapes reflect their familiarity with earlier myths and images, as well as their awareness of contemporary geopolitical power relations and ideologies. These perceptions, in turn, shape individual and collective identity work regarding landscape and its use, as reflected in Marañón's uncertainty about his own place, as a human being but also as a U.S. American immigrant, in this earthly paradise. Could he integrate into it? Or, thanks to his economic and symbolic fortune, could he become its owner? And if so, at what cost?

Frontier/*Frontera*: From the Wild West to the Wild South

In both the United States and Costa Rica, the notion of the frontier was fundamental in shaping ideas about historical progress and the role of the nation, policies and practices of settlements, and individual and collective identities. In both countries the frontier functioned as a territorial and symbolic outlet that mediated social pressures by providing nonhegemonic social actors with the possibility—either practical or imagined—of owning a piece of land and thus seeing themselves as partaking in the national ethos of agricultural settlement.[13] However, whereas in nineteenth-century United States the frontier was associated with a specific geographical space, in Costa Rica the notion of *frontera* was employed to describe any public land that was a reserve for agricultural use in case of a land shortage in the Central Valley due either to aggregation of lands or their exhaustion as a result of harmful farming methods such as "slash-and-burn" (*tala y quema*). Furthermore, whereas in the United States, according to prominent historical theories, the frontier was believed to be "closed" as such by the late nineteenth century, in Costa Rica the *frontera* felt open-ended. As Costa Rican anthropologist María Bozzoli de Wille observed, "It was a common belief that the Costa Ricans will never lack land . . . for the agriculturalists whose land lost its fertility, and for the agriculturalists' sons who could not inherit land, there was always the mountain area over the horizon, the primary forest."[14]

The Costa Rican frontier that lay beyond the Central Valley was not only a new geographical space but also a distinct racial one—the site of indigeneity and Blackness. Elsie Mae Fiala, for example, wrote to her family in the United States that contrary to what she had read about "Spanish Costa Rica" in an article in *Reader's Digest*, in the area in the south of Costa Rica where she resides 85 percent of the population was native.[15] As Giovanna Giglioli, Magen Rivers-Moor, and others have demonstrated, the tendency to reduce Costa Rican society to the Central Valley, thereby overlooking the rest of the country, was fundamental to the facilitation of the homogenization of Costa Rica as a racially white society. However, beyond the boundaries of the Central Valley lived the racially others, that is, the nonwhite populations of Costa Rica: the indigenous people and the Black immigrants from the Caribbean islands and their descendants, who occupied mainly the Atlantic coast and the south of Costa Rica.[16] The presence of unacculturated populations in these regions both strengthened the perception of these lands as a "frontier" lying beyond civilization, and therefore "savage," and served as "proof" that they were such. For the U.S. Americans who resided there, usually one family in a remote farm among mestizo and indigenous Costa Ricans, this entailed a distinct self-perception vis-à-vis both the history of the United States frontier and their present position in Costa Rica.

The notion of the Costa Rican frontier was embedded mostly in one specific landform—the rain forest. While on the North American frontier the call was to "Go West," in the Costa Rican case it was to head "*más adentro,*" deep into the heart of the forest, where one would encounter dense flora, wild animals, and indigenous people. The campesino who strides bravely into the rain forest, machete in hand, to clear a piece of land and make a home for his family was among the country's most emblematic national figures.[17] This perception both grew out of and encouraged the practice of squatting, a phenomenon common since the colonial era that held a special significance in the Costa Rican collective consciousness beyond its function as a practical housing solution. Under legislation known as *denuncio*, squatters could claim up to fifty acres of public land (*tierra baldía*) subject to proof of improvement of the land, that is, deforestation.[18] While squatting did not eliminate the concentration of large tracts of land in the hands of Costa Rican businessmen and international firms, it did serve as way to relieve social and economic pressure, thereby avoiding the need to enforce agrarian reform. It also contributed to the creation of the myth of Costa Rica as an egalitarian society of small landholders with unlimited access to land, a feature that both Costa Rican propagandists and U.S. American writers alike depicted as the backbone of Costa Rican society and a key to its stability.[19] On the practical and individual levels, this method resulted in a relatively free dispersal of land. And even though U.S. Americans usually bought their properties, this practice of squatting, coupled with the lack of restrictions on foreign land ownership, strengthened their perception of Costa Rica as a place where land is free for the taking, much like the North American frontier used to be.

The settlement of the Costa Rican frontier (i.e., the lands beyond the Central Valley) was, however, ultimately contingent upon the development of infrastructure, a task in which the United States and U.S. Americans were deeply involved. In 1945 the Inter-American highway, whose construction was largely sponsored by the United States, reached the town of San Isidro de El General, across the Cerro de la Muerte.[20] The construction of the highway marked a new phase in the settlement of the Costa Rican frontier, as it enabled many poor or landless peasants from the Central Valley and Guanacaste, as well as a handful of U.S. American settlers, to move into the southern region. The writings of these U.S. American settlers clearly suggest the extent to which they combined the Costa Rican ethos regarding the opening of new frontiers with their perception of this site and themselves through the historical and cultural prism of the nineteenth-century U.S. frontier, as it was developed in the U.S. educational system and elaborated in popular culture. They also highlight the important role played by their family histories, which typically involved settlement in the North American frontier, pertaining to the frontier and its iconic representations.

As some of these settlers drew explicit links between their own experience in mid-twentieth-century Costa Rica and that of the North American frontier settlers a hundred years earlier, they regarded their move in space as also a passage in time. This view not only made their settlement in Costa Rica a more familiar process but also legitimized and even glorified it. It also shaped the various roles in which they cast themselves as frontier men and women, including the mission they sought for themselves in the development of the Costa Rican frontier and its accompanying potential for monetary profit and personal self-realization.

The language with which Daryl Cole-Christensen chose to portray the odyssey of his family, who in 1952 established the Finca Loma Linda farm in Coto Brus, an area of thick rain forest in the south of Costa Rica, calls to mind the opening scene of a Western: "One afternoon in June, several weeks after the beginning of the wet season, when the rain had been falling for hours over much of southeastern Costa Rica, several horseback riders were making their way over a narrow trail toward the close of the day."[21]

Cole-Christensen gives little detail about his life in the United States, enhancing the sense that he saw himself as being born, or rather reborn, on the Costa Rican frontier in a manner that renders his past life irrelevant. He does reveal that his family were farmers, originally in Connecticut and later in California, and recounts that when he had reached "the right age," his father presented him with a choice: to earn an academic degree or "the chance to come to Central America, preferably Costa Rica, and look about for a piece of land where they could *start in again*" (my emphasis).[22] His move to the Costa Rican frontier was therefore a choice between two very different lifestyles and identities, which can also be seen as a choice between culture, always attributed, in the U.S. American settlers' life stories, to the United States, and nature—the essence of Costa Rica.[23]

Cole-Christensen embraced nature: Finca Loma Linda was spread over an area of 130 square acres of partially deforested virgin rain forest. They farmed a variety of crops, including corn and beans, and raised cattle. In his memoir, *A Place in the Rain Forest: Settling the Costa Rican Frontier*, Cole-Christensen exalted what he saw as the opportunity to experience the nineteenth-century U.S. frontier on that of twentieth-century Costa Rica: "Here we have immediate relationships with natural forces and, as individuals, we have remarkable freedom to act without many of the restraints of social convention. Phrases that have been used in the past to describe such freedom are 'rugged individualism' and 'the pioneering spirit.'"[24]

Néstor Gracía Canclini has observed, with respect to U.S. tourists in Tijuana, Mexico, that "North Americans bring with them [a myth] that has something to do with *crossing the border into the past, into the wilderness*" (my emphasis).[25] Yet such a retreat in time is also a broader convention of travel writing and imperial discourse, used to depict the colonial encounter as a journey of the white man from civilization, through liminal spaces (such as an ocean, a desert, or a jungle), into the past.[26] Moreover, this travel back in time as a result of the travel in space was part of a narrative that viewed non-European territories or those outside North America as situated in an earlier stage of development. As Matthew Hayes observed, following Quijano, "This diachronism (or simultaneous experience of time as both past and present) understands objective cultural differences in Eurocentric terms that assign 'underdevelopment' to a temporal field of sociohistorical stages and thus racializes, ethnicizes, or culturalizes sociospatial differences in wealth."[27] This narrative therefore served to facilitate the civilizing role of U.S. Americans who went there as well as their sense of the potential for self-realization and new self-identity.[28]

Insofar as this regeneration was viewed as a kind of rebirth, it is no wonder that the move was also sometimes depicted as a return to childhood. An article published in the *TT* about Cole-Christensen and his wife notes that they are living in a thatched-roof house, yet unlike descriptions of the lives of lower-class mestizos or indigenous people, here this simple lifestyle is associated with the innocence of childhood rather than class and ethnic degeneration: "Indigeneous? Cholos? Poor white trash? Far from it! Just a couple of nice kids."[29] The representation of whites in the jungle as children "adopted" by the forest is one that was popularized by the character of Mowgli in Rudyard Kipling's *The Jungle Book* and has persisted ever since. In the context of the U.S. American settlement in Costa Rica, this representation was a means of blurring the asymmetrical power relations that existed on the geopolitical level through the use of romantic images and the reduction of global power relations to the individual level. Such representation was intended to minimize the agency of the U.S. American settlers and their economic and symbolic fortune by representing them as innocent and harmless; they are, after all, just nice kids (Marañón maintained that he was "still a boy" when he arrived on the southern frontier, though he was twenty-one at the time.)[30]

In both the United States and Costa Rica, the frontier was a wellspring of youth for U.S. Americans, a place where they could shed their past and become regenerated.[31] Conquering the frontier was therefore simultaneously a move backward and forward: the settlers moved "backward" to a simpler, even primitive, way of life that was no longer available in the United States but also moved "forward" into new, improved selves (by living close to nature instead of, for instance, becoming an academic).

A crucial icon that traveled from the Wild West to the Costa Rican rain forest as an object of identification was that of the cowboy. In the 1970s Marañón's family invested in land along the future route of the Inter-American highway in the southern Pacific region, and in the meantime, until the highway was constructed, the Costa Rican land became a prominent feature in Marañón's childhood fantasy: "Instead of pursuing the life of a tropical explorer, researcher, ecologist, photographer, sustenance farmer, surfer or spiritual seeker, all of which I had at times envisioned, I was going to become a *cowboy*? Yahoo!"[32] The Costa Rican practice of raising cattle contributed to the sense among U.S. Americans that Costa Rica in the second half of the twentieth century could serve as a large playground for reenacting the experience of the Wild West of a century earlier. In one of its patriotic Fourth of July supplements, the *TT* drew an explicit analogy between late twentieth-century Costa Rica and the mid-nineteenth-century United States: "A trip to Guanacaste is like going back to the days of the 'Wild West' in the United States. Cowboys, cattle, boots, 10-gallon hats greet the visitor as he arrives in this hot, dry part of Costa Rica. . . . For the adventurous, or those who just want to get away from it all, Guanacaste is full of opportunities."[33] The article thus links the withdrawal from civilization into the frontier with the notion of "getting away from it all," an impulse that indeed characterized many U.S. Americans in Costa Rica. Like its North American predecessor, which offered land for free or cheap along with the excitement of something new and pristine, the Costa Rican frontier was also, as the *TT* article promised, "full of opportunities"—professional, financial, and emotional.[34]

The conceptualization of life in the Costa Rican rain forest as a reenactment of the Wild West and the effect this had on the settlers' identity work as white, U.S. Americans was further articulated in their writings and oral testimonies through references borrowed from U.S. American popular culture. Fiala wrote to her in-laws back home that a man on a horse who had chased her in the forest seemed like Roy Rogers pursuing Dale Evans. After an incident in which she and her husband took care of a wounded indigenous man, she commented, "Well, like it is around here it is never dull and we have really been like the Wild West only I guess you call it the Wild South."[35] Fiala has therefore cast herself in the dual role of the protagonist of a TV Western and a resourceful U.S. American woman, an agent of both compassion and civilization who extends help to the natives.

Cole-Christensen and other U.S. American settlers in the Costa Rican frontier were the products of a U.S. American educational system in which Fredrick Jackson Turner's theory of the frontier was the official narrative.[36] They adopted this narrative of a free and empty land waiting to be allocated according to their needs and saw themselves as pioneers reenacting the "peaceful conquest" of the frontier in order to civilize it.[37] But the land was not in fact vacant, as Fiala noted in her letters to her Iowan family. The remnant of the indigenous population of Costa Rica, those who had survived the extermination of the colonial era and the hardships of life in a republic that thought of itself as a "white nation," were pushed into the rain forests, especially in the south.[38] The existence of an indigenous population aligned perfectly with the view U.S. Americans held of Costa Rica as a frontier, and their presence in the Costa Rican rain forests was perceived as yet another indication of the country's primordial nature. It was a presence, however, that also complicated the U.S. settlers' identity work and self-assurance regarding the legitimacy of their settlement, as it echoed the precedent of the Anglo-American conquest and colonization of indigenous lands in North America.[39]

Beyond the actual living indigenous peoples, U.S. Americans also had to deal with their dead and their ghosts. A U.S. woman who had settled in the Orisí Valley claimed that the ghost of an "Indian" was living in the bed of the river passing through her property; Fiala remarked that a sudden spark in the dark of night was proof of "Indian supernatural power," or a sign of "Indian gold" glowing through a grave.[40] These remarks echo the myth of Eldorado about hidden treasures buried in the ground and reflect both the U.S. American settlers' sense of themselves as extraordinary people living in a remarkable place and their fantasies of potential profit.

The Costa Rican indigenous population was a source of both opportunity and misgiving. When the Fialases found it difficult to make a living from agriculture, they planned to plunder pre-Columbian graves and sell the artifacts in the shops of San José. They also considered sponsoring tourist excursions into the jungle that would consist both of hunting of wildlife and searching for treasure in local pre-Columbian graves. Other settlers firmly objected to this practice and were deeply ambivalent about their lives on formerly tribal land, taken from a population that was marginalized, stripped of most of its land, and made the subject of folklore. Skutch, the U.S. naturalist who bought a property of 130 acres in the Valle del General in southern Costa Rica and turned it into a nature reserve, tried to cope with this ambivalence and take a moral stand by prioritizing conservation, advocating a vague concept of "love" and "appreciation" for the land as justification for his ownership as opposed to the discourse of the historical rights of indigenous people:

> Sometimes, in a meditative mood, I ask myself whether, from the moral standpoint, my title to this land is as valid as that of the men whose dust lies here beneath the red clay. Perhaps the only answer to this perplexing question is that he most deserves to have the land who makes the best use of it. If my love of the mountains and the rivers and the forests is greater than theirs; if these things speak more meaningfully to me and I am more keenly appreciative of their beauty; if I strive harder to preserve this natural setting in its pristine splendor and to conserve the soil's fertility—then, perhaps, I can justify my possession of this land that once belonged to them.[41]

The question of the legitimacy of settling the Costa Rican land was raised also vis-à-vis the greater indigenous and mestizo Costa Rican population, highlighting the contrast between two distinct perceptions of land ownership: the right to private property, advocated by those U.S. American settlers who purchased their land, and the Costa Rican practice of squatting. The clash between these views was exacerbated by the unequal economic status of the U.S. American settlers, on the one hand, and the Costa Rican peasants and squatters on the other. So, for example, in his memoir, in a chapter titled "The People Who Needed the Land," Cole-Christensen describes a meeting of landowners, U.S. Americans and other nationals, to discuss ways of handling squatters. Like Skutch, Cole-Christensen wonders who most deserves to own the land—the one who legally owns it? The one who farms it? The one who, allegedly, appreciates it most? Though he embraces the view that the de facto practice of cultivating the land gives the right of ownership, when faced with squatters on his own uncultivated land he, like many other U.S. American settlers, including Marañón and Fiala, demanded that the police evict them (usually without success).[42]

The reenactment of the conquest of the Wild West, which stirred such excitement among U.S. settlers, brought to the surface a familiar conflict between contending practices of land use and ethical questions regarding land ownership that echoed the historical experience in North America. Conceptualized within the framework of the nineteenth-century U.S. West but enacted in the context of the Cold-War era U.S. American settlement in Costa Rica, these conflicts were a key factor in the identity work of U.S. Americans settlers on the Costa Rican frontier with respect to their distinct roles there.

A Green Cathedral or a Green Hell: Discourses and Practices in Costa Rican Amazonia

The Costa Rican rain forest evoked a mixture of ambivalent responses among U.S. American settlers with respect not only to its function as a new frontier but also to its very essence. On the one hand it represented an emerald forest filled with marvels, a site of adventure and discovery and, above all, of self-discovery. On the other hand, it constituted a jungle, a source of danger whose dense vegetation was inimical to human life. These conflicting discourses were translated into place-based rituals and practices of emplacement, broadly divided between deforestation and agricultural development on the one hand and preservation of the natural world on the other. In both views, however, the rain forest retained its aura of mystery, established during the earliest days of European expansion, with conventions of representation characterized by a rhetoric of superlatives and excess. In his memoir, for example, Marañón advocated the idea that "symbiosis, adaptation, metamorphosis, evolution, sustainability—personal, biological, social, global life-and-death processes seem so accelerated in the tropics, more obvious, more spectacular, more diverse, more interconnected."[43]

Writing about the rain forests, as Neil Whitehead suggests, is replete with a rhetoric of mystery: "the discovery of the fantastic, the survival of the anachronistic, and the promise of marvelous monstrosity."[44] U.S. American settlers in the Costa Rican rain forest adhered to this tradition when they documented not just what they saw but also what they believed to exist but could not see. Cole-Christensen, recounting the arduous journey to his farm, described his anticipation of the arrival: "as though there, just beyond the trees ahead of the trail, a sentient creature waited."[45] Skutch wrote that nowhere except for the bottom of the ocean are more secrets waiting to be explored than in the rain forest "that has most stubbornly withheld its secrets from the prying gaze of men."[46] This mysteriousness generated among the settlers a sense that they were living in a majestic, wondrous place, and a sense of themselves as unique and exposed to extraordinary and even supernatural realms. Some of them invoked religious and spiritual terminology in their descriptions of the rain forest and their interactions with it. Skutch wrote, for example, "I rarely entered it without a feeling of awe, without a reverential, meditative pause, as though I passed through the portals of some magnificent temple, pervaded with delicate incense, illuminated by a dim, religious light."[47] He described a sense of a mission, even grandeur, as he "yearned to live in peace with all creatures in the rainforest" but at the same time "desired to do something even more difficult: to penetrate, as far as possible, to the secret springs of this multiplex phenomenon called life, to understand its significance in the whole vast drama of cosmic evolution."[48]

Echoing the notion of returning to a primal, pristine world, Marañón suggested that life in the Costa Rican rain forest enabled "close relations between the ancient and the modern world, between the fantastic and the realistic." This perception led some settlers to adopt practices grounded in the forces and cycles of nature and to replace modern technologies with traditional ones, as Marañón testified:

> When to plant, when to harvest, when to travel, when to fish, when and where to hang drying fish at night, when to haul cargo, when to marry, when to party—the moon was consulted for everything. Everyone "knew the moon" and sought it out for orientation. "How is the moon" was a more common question than "What time is it?"[49]

Jack Ewing was another settler who testified that as part of his identity work he was converted to the methods of the moon. Originally from Colorado, Ewing arrived in Costa Rica in 1972 and later became the owner of Hacienda Barú near Dominical on the southern Pacific coast. He admitted that initially he "used to doubt much of the campesino wisdom regarding the moon, writing it off as superstition, but my curiosity stimulated me to listen and observe." Over time he came to adopt the local beliefs in the power of the moon and became a conveyor of that knowledge to other U.S. Americans, as well as an enthusiastic participant in the local *fiestas de la luna llena* (full moon parties).[50]

These testimonies are a clear manifestation of what Nigel Rapport identified as localization as a cultural technique.[51] The adoption of local agricultural and cultural practices, first perceived as "superstitious" but later replacing the more modern U.S. American methods, and the endorsement of local concepts of time and its measurement (or at least what U.S. American settlers understood these to be) were powerful expressions of cultural identification through place-making and the development of a place-based identity.[52]

The close proximity to nature was also a crucial component of identification that shaped the everyday lives of those U.S. American settlers who were not farmers but engaged in what they termed spiritual work. A member of a commune in southern Costa Rica maintained that in their new country, unlike back home in Los Angeles, members did not feel the need to use psychoactive drugs, as nature was a strong enough consciousness-altering force: "The nature was very present. . . . The sounds that you hear, it's a never-ending thing, so calm and so part of what the planet is doing. It changes your head a little bit, it really does."[53] It is interesting to note that while the rites of the moon are often associated with feminine rituals and practice, the majority of testimonies regarding these rites are from male U.S. Americans, while female U.S. American settlers often described the sun as a more significant force.[54] Eileen Steinberg, a member of a commune in rainy Copey de Dota, southeast of San José, described the course of a typical day on the farm, the tempo of which, due to the farm's lack of running water and electricity, was determined not by technology but by the cycles of nature: "The sun came over our head for one hour at noon. That's when we swam in the river. It was icy cold . . . [Then] dusk would go around, and I'd get everybody [to] 'prepare for the dark, prepare for dark' and we got our candles ready." A former urbanite who had lived in Chicago and New York, she recounted how these natural rhythms utterly transformed not only her daily life but her inner self: "When you live by the sun, the rhythm slows down towards natural being. Life is slow. [It] slowly slows down. Away from the franchise of the city, away from the cars. The best thing was not to come to town for as long as possible, for like two months, and then you really got used to the rhythm. I have nature inside me, I had absorbed so much nature in those eight years in the farm."[55]

Linda Sheinin, who lived in Dominical in the mid-1970s, recalled that the sunset was "the high point" of the day: "The whole community [of U.S. Americans] used to just go out to the beach at sunset and just sit on the logs. . . . We just watched the sunset every night, like King Kong did."[56]

This allusion to the iconic scene from the movie *King Kong* suggests that the tropical landscapes and rhythm invoked not only excitement and admiration but also a sense of danger and fear, and over time led to a gradual decay and growing inertia in the minds of the U.S. American settlers. In the beginning, as Sharon Hage of the commune in Uvita recounted, life in the Costa Rican rain forest had a positive effect on the urbanites, and they all became "thinner and healthier."[57] However, another member noted both the aggressive aspects of the tropical climate, particularly the rainy season that cut off the remote community for months at a time, and the deceptive, tempting nature of the slow rhythms of tropical life, which eventually took its toll on many of the members, recounting: "You get into that southern tropical lingering and everything is just drifting into nothing."[58]

The danger of everything transforming into nothing that was perceived to be a consequence of life in the jungle was the mirror image of the view of the rain forest as marvelous. The photograph on the cover of Cole-Christensen's memoir shows him from the back, a small figure vanishing into the woods, and adheres to the tradition of eighteenth-century naturalists who depicted the American rain forest as something dramatic, potent, constantly in motion, controlled by mysterious powers, and overwhelming for human beings:[59] "[The forest is] the domain of amphibians and reptiles, epiphytic plants, insect and birds. Lianas drooped from many of these trees, the vines themselves encrusted with epiphytic life; and in the forest understory were many ferns, palms, philodendrons, and delicate, shade loving plants."[60]

The destructive power of the rain forest was quite clear to those who tried to make a living by farming it. It quickly became apparent that the soil of the forest was saturated with water and therefore less fertile than expected. However, rather than accepting this as part of the natural order, the settlers, products of the United States of the 1950s with its firm belief in progress and technology who furthermore perceived themselves as promoters of these values in Costa Rica, regarded the rain forests as an enemy to be vanquished. This was necessary not only in order to sustain their lives and even become prosperous but also in order to overcome the danger to their state of minds and productivity. Cole-Christensen describes the cleared land as a place where one can settle, establish a community, and overcome loneliness, whereas the forest was "restricted, enclosed, almost suffocated one upon weeks and months within it. It allowed no light . . . *no one had demonstrated that anything useful could be done with the forest*" (my emphasis).[61] The rain forest, in other words, was seen as useless and indeed dangerous in its natural state, both economically and mentally; the wonder, salvation, and profit occurred only once it was subjugated and transformed. A key tool in this process was a technology that was novel in 1950s Costa Rica—the chainsaw.

> There is the swished, mellow sound of the steel disks cutting through the surface soil into the fine roots below; and, as we look down, a marvelous thing is happening: this virgin ground is turning, and a rich, dark furrow following behind each disk, the black loam curled and turned up. Ages unfold behind us . . . Now this land is released from its bondage to the forest. The earth is free and loose; the earth crumbles easily; the earth smells vaguely of mold and yet virile too; this earth retains the power, the character of an earlier time.[62]

Cole-Christensen's explicitly gendered description is grounded in several levels of discourse: it echoes European imperial and colonial discourses about the feminization of the "empty land," hemispheric discourses that depicted transnational relations in the Americas in gendered terms as encounters between the masculine United States and feminine Latin America, and finally, Costa Rican national discourses that constructed Costa Rican nature as feminine and the mostly foreign agents of progress as masculine.[63] Cole-Christensen perceived the land as a maiden released from hundreds of years of subjugation to the dark forces of the rain forest, a site where he, as a U.S. American man, can regain his masculinity by fertilizing it. The narrative is almost erotic—in response to his touch, the virgin land is freed and loosened, crumbling easily and spreading an aromatic scent. Like the frontier ethos elaborated earlier, so too deforestation is a two-directional movement, at once backward and forward: when Cole-Christensen used the chainsaw, he saw not only shifting clods of earth but also "ages unfold behind us." The change in space—this time not horizontal but vertical, into the depths of the earth—is once again a change in time. Unlike Skutch and Marañón, who found meaning and even sanctity in untouched nature, Cole-Christensen aimed to bring light into the jungle, literally and metaphorically, by cutting trees: "There is a cathedral-like effect because we have made long, crisscrossing corridors of space within it [the forest]."[64]

The practice of deforestation was by no means exclusively U.S. American. "I used to love to cut trees with my chainsaw. I loved to hear them fall," recalled a peasant leader from the Osa Peninsula.[65] U.S. American settlers in Costa Rica adopted common patterns of land management and bolstered them with new technologies, resources, and ideologies of progress and U.S. technological superiority, a view that helped them legitimize and glorify their presence in Costa Rica. Even Wilford (Wolf) Guindon, one of the founders of the Quaker colony of Monteverde in the early 1950s who left the United States during the Korean War, held similar views about his role in contributing to the development of Costa Rica. As one of the first salesmen of chainsaws in Costa Rica, he explicitly linked the practice of deforestation there to his identity work as a U.S. American citizen in the country: "From the very first I wanted to have a forested property that I could clear and turn into a productive family farm. By coming to what was called an 'undeveloped' country I saw this as a way to contribute to its development, converting forest jungle into pasture."[66]

Fig. 9. Walter Fiala, a U.S. farmer pictured here with a tiger hunted and brought down on his farm in southern Costa Rica. Courtesy of Elsie Fiala, David Fiala, and Jean Birkland.

Tigers in the Backyard:
Gender Work in the Costa Rican Rainforest

Insofar as both nature and gender are cultural constructs, it is important to examine how they intersected in the construction of the identities of U.S. American women and men who lived in the Costa Rican rain forests. At first glance, it seems that the discourses and practices of U.S. Americans of both sexes who settled in the Costa Rican hinterland reproduced the same gendered division that prevailed in both countries. Specifically, they appear to reaffirm the perception of nature as the outdoor domain of men, from which women, whose place is indoors, are alienated.[67] Moreover, they also reaffirm perceptions that evolve out of the intersection of gender and other categories of identity, mainly ethnicity. The naturalist Skutch depicted his own world in Costa Rica as one of exclusively masculine associations, a world into which no woman penetrated up until his late marriage. Skutch portrayed himself as sort of a Robinson Crusoe exploring his vast property accompanied by indigenous male helpers who functioned as research assistants and also, in the tradition of viewing indigenous men as less masculine than white men, as housekeepers—a role otherwise reserved for women.[68] Cole-Christensen also underscored the "traditional" labor division that prevailed on the Costa Rican frontier: "Sons will work with fathers, brothers and uncles in the field; mothers and daughters will work in the homes."[69] This division was needed, he argued, not only to uphold tradition but also because nature posed a danger to women and womanhood. In a subchapter of his book, titled "Three Flights for Survival," Cole-Christensen describes three cases of death and loss involving women and children on the southern frontier: a pregnant woman who was killed and another who lost her baby (in two separate aviation accidents) and the ten-year-old daughter of local settlers who was killed in a wagon accident.[70] Emergencies and accidents were not uncommon on the southern frontier, but by focusing on cases involving pregnant women and a young girl, Cole-Christensen contends that the frontier was particularly hazardous to femininity and reproduction (echoing his views described above that the rain forest is antithetical to production). For him, women on the frontier were at the mercy of the men who made the decision to live in the rain forest; furthermore, being confined to the home, women had only the negative and none of the positive constitutive experiences of life on the frontier, namely, life in nature. He maintains, "I cannot speak for my wife and our girls, waiting at home as they did each Tuesday and Friday; each trip during these severe months of the wet season was a view beyond the empty window where the rain fell, and the darkness and the sound of the years were lost in waiting and stillness."[71]

A depiction of the muted woman sacrificed for the sake of the man's life in nature appears also in Guindon's narrative of his transformation from a farmer to an ecological activist. Guindon and his wife, Lucille (Lucky), were among the founders of the Quaker colony Monteverde. In the first two decades of their lives there, Wolf Guindon worked in Monteverde's dairy, located inside the colony compound. But in the early 1970s, following an encounter with U.S. American scientists George and Harriett Powell, who arrived at Monteverde to conduct research on the cloud forest, Wolf became interested in nature preservation and gradually abandoned the dairy. He began spending much of his time with George Powell in the forest, creating the cloud forest nature reserve of the colony. As for Powell's wife, Harriett, despite being a scientist in her own right, in both Guindon's and George Powell's memoirs she is depicted as a schoolteacher (a common occupation of women on the North American frontier) and associated with the Quaker women who stayed home.[72]

The Quaker women dubbed themselves "the widows of Peña Blancas," after the remote area of the forest in which their husbands spent their days. In Wolf Guindon's memoir there is a distinction made between the wife, an emblem of domesticity and family in the home, and the "mistress," by which he means the rain forest. Thus the U.S. American settler in Costa Rican nature saw himself not only as a pioneer and a farmer but also as a lover: "All around him was the emerald jungle, the mistress he had been carrying on with for decades while his wife took care of their family and home in Monteverde."[73] For her part, Lucky Guindon wrote that "it's at night, when I'm lying in bed, that I start thinking and wondering why he's not back yet," adding, "As far as I was concerned Wolf sacrificed his family for the Reserve."[74] In her husband's memoir, Lucky is portrayed primarily as a mother of eight and is mentioned mainly in the context of pregnancies that went wrong—that is, in the context of the threat that nature poses to reproduction. She and other women of the colony did not enter the forest or partake in the creation of the reserve, which became the hallmark of Monteverde, but instead cultivated orchids on the margins of the jungle. Although in later years Lucky Guindon became renowned for

Fig. 10. *Roots*, drawing by Lucille (Lucky) Guindon of Monteverde, Costa Rica. Courtesy of Lucille (Lucky) Guindon.

her detailed drawings of the forest, this practice, although perhaps constituting an appropriation of nature, functioned entirely within two distinctly feminine traditions of relating to nature—that of the botanical drawing, done by women who were typically at a remove from nature itself and created their work inside buildings, and that of the home garden, which in this case existed on the edge of the rainforest, that is, on the margins of the main experience of life in Costa Rican nature (fig. 10).[75]

The picture that emerges from these patterns of representation is complicated, however, when we turn from the narratives written by men to those written, or told, by the women themselves. Both Fiala's weekly letters to her in-laws in Iowa and her written memories describe a daily struggle to maintain a household in the rain forest but also her own process of falling in love with the forest and the extent to which her identity work was based on equal participation in the experience. Contrary to Cole-Christensen's and Guindon's depictions of their wives as alienated from nature and even victimized by living within it, Fiala's writing echoes the idea of nature as the "Greater Household of Earth," with no division or contradiction between outdoor and indoor spaces.[76] The wife of her husband's employer, a U.S. American woman named Bea whose home is decorated with the sloughs of poisonous snakes, serves as her model for the rugged life of women in the jungle: "One day she said there was a tiger at the back of the house and a snake at the front. In between running from front to back she threw a piece of wood in the stove to keep the fire going."[77]

The rain forest is Fiala's symbolic capital, and in her writing she glorifies her life there and creates her identity as an adventurous woman of nature. Not only is she unafraid of nature, she looks for every opportunity to encounter animals, both the small ones that are either pets or foodstuff and the wild ones, with a tiger being the ultimate accomplishment.

> Well we got our tiger . . . Anyhow he [one of their workers] brought it up on Sat. He come a tearing up the road like a Lone Ranger and demanded where Don Walter is. Walt happened to be in Potrero and as he said he had a tiger skin in his sack, I [was] about to die . . . So I helped the man skin out the head and the feet which he left in it. It was so exciting, and of all of the things to be doing I was baking bread that day so I was skinning the feet out with the man and then I remembered the bread so I had to run in and punch down the bread and it took forever to get the tiger meat off my hands. Then back out to help the man . . . I took so many pictures. Its teeth were just huge and its skin is really pretty. They have a place in San José that will tan it and so I'll have a rug out of it. Walt said it over the radio that Elsie claims the skin because she skinned it, which I didn't do all of, just the feet.[78]

Though her letter opens with the first-person plural pronoun "we," Fiala makes it clear that this was *her* tiger; she skinned it with her own hands, working side by side with the local employee, crossing gender, ethnic, and class barriers alike. In her writing there is no division between the domestic sphere and wild nature—she bakes the bread and skins the tiger at the same time. Nature is her asset, both monetary and symbolic. Whereas Cole-Christensen depicted the southern frontier as a dangerous place for women and children, in Fiala's portrayal nature gradually became a haven for herself and her children, while culture is perceived as threatening: "We've been lucky as the kids are hardly ever sick. But I imagine if they were out among civilization, they would have something all the time [*sic*]."[79] Despite financial and other hardships, she insisted on remaining on the farm that had become her home and the core of her identity, saying, "I don't want to leave, I hate to think that I will have to leave."[80] When her husband Walter took a job in the Osa Peninsula, she stayed on the farm, where she was one of just a handful of women and the only foreign one. In 1973, after twenty-six years, financial difficulties forced her to leave the farm and move to a small apartment in San José. When I met her in 2009, she was still known among her peers at the women's club as "the woman from the jungle," a label that pleased her very much as it set her apart from the rest of the urbanite club members.

Joyce Brown made the opposite journey. In 1978, after six years of living in San José, she and her children moved to a farm on the southern Pacific coast, to join her husband, Jim. She recalled that while at first she had been ambivalent about the move because her earlier experience of traveling to the Costa Rican periphery had been traumatic, their relocation to the rain forest actually turned out to be highly positive one because she felt freed from the constraints she had felt in San José, moving for example from a small, closed house with barred windows to one with many openings to the outdoors and no constrictions on the windows and doors. Moreover, the move, which was so radical that it could almost be considered a second immigration, also provided a form of closure for Brown, since life in the Costa Rican forest reminded her of her childhood in Colorado: "I had the forest, the wildlife, flowers, I could get on the horses and ride."[81] After moving to the farm, Brown, as the manager's wife, was given the traditional female role of being in charge of the well-being of the local workers, but, as she emphasized, she also took on roles beyond that of the compassionate care giver who stays indoors: "My husband would send me out with the cowboys to check the cattle. I was *out*." Brown further emplaced herself in the rain forest through her dedication to the rescue and care of wild animals, becoming a sort of amateur veterinarian and bridging the alleged gap between femininity and nature by dubbing herself a "jungle mom."[82]

Unlike Fiala and Brown, who had both grown up on farms in the Midwest, Linda Sheinin was born and raised in a middle-class family in Baltimore and later immersed herself in the artistic scene of the early 1970s counterculture in Los Angeles. She arrived in Costa Rica in 1975 with her young daughter and settled in the village of Dominical on the southern Pacific coast, later marrying a Costa Rican man. However, as she recalled, she was the one who decided to buy land and establish a cattle farm, which she perceived as a good investment but also a way to cross national and gender barriers and to emplace herself in the local culture through the regional practice of cattle raising. As she recounted, her role model was a local Costa Rican woman who was the only female ranch owner in the region, and she partnered with her. "I love to ride horses and I like cattle and, I don't know, that was the big thing that was happening in our area, cattle ranches and cattlemen."[83] Since cattle was both the hallmark of the southern Pacific area and also a masculine profession, choosing to become the owner of a cattle ranch made Sheinin (one of the very few U.S. Americans I interviewed who assumed Costa Rican nationality) at once an integral part of her local environment and at odds with it. Her foreignness, though, mediated this deviation of the local norms.

While Fiala, Brown, and Sheinin were not the norm, since most U.S. American women—like most Costa Rican women—lived in the Central Valley, their accounts suggest that rather than being afraid of or estranged from nature they in fact found in it multiple forms of freedom and security that were not always available to them in the cities and towns. Moreover, the rain forest became their arena for constructing a place-based identity that was embedded in practices related to life on the "frontier"—horse riding, cattle breeding, encounters with wild animals—in a way that took them outside the confines of both their gender and their foreign nationality.

Reinvention and Environmental Exploitation along Costa Rica's Beachfronts

Antithetical to the intensity of the rain forest, the beachfronts were associated above all with emptiness and a pristine quality, and as such, facilitated a different place-based identity for U.S. Americans, one grounded in the potential for purification and rebirth. Marañón's "arrival scene" at a small bay in Uvita, on the southern Pacific coast, after several days of hiking in the dense jungle, is typical: "Mesmerized by the gently swaying greens and blue of the beautiful, mountainous coast, assimilating the massaging energy of the friendly sea, I felt a tremendous sense of well-being."[84] The healing powers of the Costa Rican beachfronts and the potential for a new start are evoked in many immigration stories and attest to the strong attachment they formed with this place, which was portrayed as a sharp contrast to their former lives. Michelle White, a young college graduate who arrived at Manuel Antonio on the Pacific coast in 1974, remembered her encounter there with a U.S. Marine veteran who was paralyzed from the waist down from polio: "His dream, after he retired, was to move to a tropical island and live real simple right on the beach, in a beautiful paradise with his wife and some teenage daughters. And so they moved down and at that time there was no electricity and the road was not paved."[85] White herself was due to stay in Manuel Antonio for a month but ended up staying a full year. "It was gorgeous, it was just gorgeous . . . it was pretty much like paradise those days." (At this, Michelle's husband, Eric, interrupted the talk and remarked bitterly—"not like today.")[86]

In the U.S. American settlers' memories and stories, the persistent perception of the beachfronts as undeveloped places is related to archetype narratives and myths about creation and renewal, which in turn generated their perceptions of themselves as innocents seeking purer lives, away from civilization. But the empty beachfronts also inspired fantasies of lost islands, pirates, and quick fortunes and harked back to stories about the white man's arrival in the Americas, in which U.S. Americans cast themselves as entrepreneurs or the creators of new entities. Cocos Island, some 365 miles off the shore of Costa Rica but part of its national territory, was among Ferdinand Magellan's landing sites, and many believed that some of his treasure was buried there.[87] The island was also a site for making new fortunes: in 1964 a Costa Rican official warned against a group of U.S. Americans who were looking to turn Cocos Island into a haven for drug trafficking. He also warned that a group of entrepreneurs from Las Vegas was intending to use Costa Rican strawmen to establish the island as a center for recreation and gambling.[88] Another fantasy triggered by the island was expressed in a manifesto sent to *La Nación* and reprinted in the *TT* in August 1973, titled "Declaration of Independence of the Independent Free Republic of Cocos Island." The newspaper was careful to note that the letter could well be a prank but nonetheless remarked that "cultists and hippies" were living on the island in spite of its status as a nature reserve.[89]

In 1974–75 the *TT* published several articles about the "rape" of Costa Rican beachfronts by U.S. Americans. In an article about Tamarindo on the Nicoya Peninsula, the author draws a direct link between the greed of the Spanish conquest and that of U.S. Americans, exemplified in the character of businessman Robert Vesco: "Once upon a time, only Indians visited Tamarindo Beach [and] legend says that burial grounds rich in gold lie underneath the pastures of Cabo Velas, the northern tip of the bay, and now the Robert Vesco family *finca*."[90] But greed was not the exclusive purview of financiers. In 1974 two U.S. counterculturists, or "beachcombers" as they were called, came up with an idea for turning a quick profit. They decided to export conches, collected on the beach by native residents (the *TT* article described them as indigenous), to the United States. The initiative's overnight success had the additional effect of raising awareness of Tamarindo among a growing number of U.S. counterculturists. "Overnight, Tamarindo hosted a cast of characters as freaky as any Southern California beach scene."[91] But within several weeks the population of conches in Tamarindo was exhausted and the flock of foreigners moved on to the next place.

Patronizing Eden: From Developers to Conservationists

The two main characters of U.S. Americans who settled the Costa Rican rain forest were that of the developer taming the "green hell" for profit and progress and that of the guardian of the marvelous "green cathedral." These partially merged together in the 1970s when the Costa Rican forests were reevaluated as a new type of commodity—an ecological one. Following massive uncontrolled deforestation, which accelerated after World War II, Costa Rica reached the point that it was losing five hundred square kilometers of its primary forest annually, 1 percent of the country's woods.[92] In the 1970s, a growing awareness of the severity of this assault on Costa Rica's natural environment, along with a deterioration in the profits from agriculture, led to a change in the country's economic and environmental policies as well as some of its long-standing practices and public discourse. From the 1970s on, the Costa Rican frontier, no longer perceived as eternal, came to be imagined in other terms. Its monetary and symbolic fortune now hinged on the preservation of the rain forest, that is, safeguarding its natural state rather than developing it. This shift was accompanied by new economic policies that set monetary incentives for reforestation.[93]

U.S. Americans who had become part of the development and exploitation of the Costa Rican rain forest and beachfronts, perceiving themselves as pioneers bringing progress to Costa Rica and developing place-based identifications and practices that relied on the clearing of the forest, gradually conformed to these new winds. The change was no doubt affected by economic factors, but memoirs and oral histories of U.S. American settlers reveal the extent to which this shift served, yet again, as a site for their identity work vis-à-vis both the United States and Costa Rica.

Referring to the changes that this new mindset triggered in their relation to the rain forest and practices of land management, U.S. American farmers in Costa Rica described a spiritual, religious journey, underplaying the financial incentives behind it. Jack Ewing, the owner of Hacienda Barú, a vast cattle farm on the southern Pacific coast, recounted a 1972 excursion to an area of mangrove soil that he was considering turning into pastureland. It was the first time he had ever encountered a group of Capuchin monkeys: "I was hooked. Never again would I entertain the idea of converting this bubbling caldron of life into a cattle pasture. . . . That day I began a journey of discovery that, over the next twenty years, transformed me from a cattle man into a naturalist and environmentalist."[94]

In the late 1970s the Hacienda Barú was converted into a nature reserve, and in the early 1990s became part of Costa Rica's fast-growing ecotourism industry.[95] Cole-Christensen, who had seen the rain forest as an enemy to be vanquished, expressed retrospective remorse over his role in its destruction: "Who could possibly be more destructive than those of us who propose to open up such a frontier? . . . We believed, we tried, we failed, we recovered and tried again, and we learned."[96] In 1979 the Cole-Christensen family returned to the United States but the farm stayed in foreign hands, functioning as a research station for universities from the U.S.

In the 1950s and 1960s, some of the U.S. American settlers were equipped not only with new technologies such as the chainsaw but also with ideas about the superiority of progress and development that helped define their view of themselves and their role in Costa Rica. From the 1970s on, their identity work with respect to their lives in the Costa Rican nature resulted in the same patronizing perspective, but toward different goals that provided them with a distinct mark of identity as the country's guardians. The *TT* endorsed the idea that precisely because of the mistreatment of nature in their own homeland, U.S. Americans should be careful not to repeat the same mistakes in Costa Rica. "We have seen the damage that has been wrought to natural beauty in the United States, in the name of progress development . . . that these mistakes were made in the United States by Americans is certainly no reason for them to be copied in other lands by other peoples. That they should be repeated in other lands by Americans is even less excusable."[97]

The United States, in other words, was no longer the model for the conquest of the frontier or for developing a nation's natural resources, and U.S. Americans no longer perceived themselves as agents of agricultural progress. Instead, they saw themselves as agents of an ecological mission, endorsing the preservation of nature, which they saw themselves as appreciating more than the Costa Ricans. The *TT* endorsed the idea that Costa Rica could still be rescued from the ecological disaster that the United States was going through, yet again with the help of U.S. Americans. Nature preservation became a goal in its own right, but for U.S. Americans who lived in the rain forests and beachfronts it was also a key component in their politics of identity, a means of legitimizing their presence in Costa Rica and imbuing it with meaning. Reflecting on his life journey, Marañón, who had originally come to Costa Rica to avoid the Vietnam draft and went on to become a farmer and later an ecological activist, wrote, "It seemed interesting to me that, while across the ocean my countrymen were sacrificing limbs and lives in the Vietnam War, I was getting all worked up about saving some trees . . . [T]hey needed a human like me to protect them from other humans who didn't care for trees."[98]

Once a practice reserved for naturalists like Skutch, nature preservation became a key component of identity work and a practice of emplacement that legitimized the gradually contested presence of U.S. Americans who had taken over large tracts of Costa Rican land. It enabled them to perceive themselves not as foreign settlers but as the altruistic guardians of Eden.[99] Practices of emplacement connected to nature preservation also enabled veteran U.S. immigrants to distinguish themselves from the newcomers, by casting the latter as harmful to the natural environment. So, for example, Barbara Williams, who arrived in the Osa Peninsula in the early 1970s, described the purchase of a long strip of beachfront several decades later by a U.S. American as a negative intrusion: "Then they came with motorcycles and the equipment and the whole atmosphere had totally changed from very *tranquilo* into a nightmare."[100] The distinction is given linguistic expression in her choice to use a Spanish word to describe the local status quo (*tranquilo*) and an English one (nightmare) to describe the change. As they separated themselves from both U.S. Americans and Costa Ricans, the identity work of some of the U.S. American ecological activists eventually resulted in an a-national identification—neither U.S. American nor Costa Rican—but rather one based on their relation to nature. When I asked the man behind the pseudonym Marañón how he regards himself in terms of national identity, he replied, "Oh, just a citizen of planet Earth."

four

Becoming a U.S. Woman in Costa Rica
Gender, Immigration, and Transnationalism

> While flower arrangements and dances are still welcome, activities at a higher intellectual level are much desired.
> —FAY DRESNER, U.S.A. International Women's Club of Costa Rica, 1959

Boarding the train from Puerto Limón to San José in the fall of 1941, and still dizzy from the eight-day-long journey on a United Fruit Company vessel from the United States, young college graduate Henrietta Boggs, an Alabama native, made a commitment to herself: "Watching the breath-taking sunset, I told myself I would never go back, never return to Alabama and that suffocating Presbyterian world."[1] As the train climbed up from the Atlantic coast to San José, winding through the mountainous twists and turns, Boggs, who had come to Costa Rica for an extended family visit, dreamed of a new life as a free woman in the "Land of Eternal Spring," as Costa Rica was described in postcards she had received from her aunt. When at last they met, however, that same aunt was quick to crush her fantasies: "You'll find it different from what you're used to in the States . . . more formal, and girls have less freedom." "Even American girls?" Boggs recalls asking. "Yes. Their reputation can be so easily ruined."[2]

Boggs ended up staying in Costa Rica, where she married the young José (Pepe) Figueras, who would go on to become the most prominent political figure in post–World War II Costa Rica. They had three children together but ultimately ended up divorcing. Her reconstructed reflections, related some fifty years after her arrival in Costa Rica, were no doubt shaped by her subsequent life experiences in the country and by the processes of memory and attest to the critical role of gender as a factor throughout all phases of immigration. Whether consciously or not, gender comes into play in motivations for the move from one's country of origin and shapes the immigrant experience and practices in the receiving country as well as the retrospective recounting of them.

This is especially true of noneconomic immigrants, who are looking for a "better way of life" and are, in Greg Madison's terms, "existential immigrants" insofar as they seek self-discovery, a process in which gender is a significant factor.[3] Sheila Croucher has rightly criticized works on life-style immigration for being blind to the issue of gender, stressing the need for a more articulate analysis of gender as a set of socially constructed norms and expectations, especially among life-style immigrants: "The roles and constraints from which they seek emancipation frequently relate to gender and this is particularly true for women."[4] Based on her research on Anglo-American women in Florence, Catherine Trundle further argues that "migration and especially affluent migration, is often the search for an improved life that promises freedom and the enactment of a new ideal self. In this respect, gender plays a critical role."[5]

In dreaming of gender emancipation in Costa Rica, Boggs was following a long tradition of female travelers and immigrants who associated geographical mobility with class and gender emancipation.[6] As corporate and administrative expatriatism came to substitute colonialism, scholarly attention turned to the experiences of women living outside their country due to their spouse's job and struggling to find their way through the different "roles" assigned to them by different agents, such as the homeland administration or the foreign community itself.[7] These women, many of whom often lacked a sense of agency at home, found life abroad to be an opportunity for empowerment and control over themselves, as well as over the locals with whom they interacted, who were typically either domestic workers or the recipients of their charitable work. They were granted such power due to their privileged status as the wives of Western businessmen or representatives of Western administrations, and in some cases through the symbolic attributes of whiteness. However, this kind of emancipation or upward mobility usually failed to include all the domains in the life of an expat woman. For example, she could experience class mobility and a life of leisure unavailable to her in her country of origin, but on the other hand be unable to work outside the home or be restrained in her dress code or social interaction with men.

The model "gendered geographies of power," developed by Sarah Mahler and Patricia Pessar, enables us to examine the changes in gender regimes across transnational spaces, mapping the extent to which they are reaffirmed or reconfigured, or perhaps a combination of both processes, and at what level (individual, organizational, state, and so on).[8] Considering U.S. American immigrants to Costa Rica through this lens, this chapter looks at the ways in which the crossing of geographical borders affected gender roles; enabled, or promised, the crossing of gender boundaries; and created new ones. It also looks at instances in which it in fact consolidated familiar gender roles—at the individual, organizational, and communal levels. The chapter focuses on the gender-specific opportunities and challenges U.S. American women in Costa Rica encountered and how sex and gender intersected with other identities and social markers, such as ethnicity, nation, and class, as well as on the implications of these intersections for the immigrants' experiences, practices, and identity-making.

Simon de Beauvoir famously stated that one is not born a woman but rather becomes one.[9] In the spirit of this notion of "becoming," Pessar and Mahler defined gender as a process, in which "people do 'gender work' using practices and discourses to negotiate relationships, notions of 'masculinity' and 'femininity,' and conflicting interests."[10] Here, too, I do not assume the existence of an inherent, monolithic, or fixed model of the U.S American woman in Costa Rica; rather, I am interested in the way gender work becomes part of identity work and identity talk.[11] Therefore, in the discussion below I examine the various strategies, institutions, practices, and discourses through which diverse models of U.S. American femininity in Costa Rica were negotiated, contested, and came to be culturally established. As Meike Fechter suggests, being a woman abroad, on the continuum between an expat and an immigrant, is a kind of profession.¹² And indeed, as we will see, special institutions were established in order to create, and monitor, this process of becoming a U.S. American woman in Costa Rica.

The chapter examines the gender-specific repertoires that U.S. American women brought over with them from their lives in the United States, which varied greatly depending on their individual background (in terms of ethnicity, education, religion, economic status, and so forth) as well as the different periods, places, and societies from which these women came, and the ways in which they adapted these repertoires to fit their lives in Costa Rica. Its focus is on U.S. American women who lived in the San José area and who were, in many cases, the wives of U.S. American administrators or businessmen. These women maintained contact with the United States, visiting there annually as well as importing an ongoing supply of U.S. American products, from food and clothes to magazines. In this regard, their gendered identifications were transnational in nature, as they were anchored in and transcended one or more nation-states, and involved political, economic, social, and cultural processes.¹³

Two main institutions played a significant role in these processes of gender work—the U.S. American women's club and the *TT*. It was in these arenas that contested ideas and practices regarding the role of the women looked at here were publicly negotiated, confirmed, or rejected and then represented through practices and texts. The articulation of gender perception and practices of both the United States and Costa Rica that took place in the U.S. Women's Club and the *TT* enable us to examine them as gendered "transnational cognitive spaces."¹⁴

In what follows, I will first examine the members of the U.S. American women's club during the late 1950s. These women constructed their gendered identities as "club women" through a notion of service directed at two occasionally conflicting aims: U.S. interests in Cold-War Costa Rica and their own aspirations and needs. I will then explore the opportunities and challenges occasioned by immigration for the U.S. American housewife and mother of the 1950s in light of the availability and widespread use of inexpensive and readily available domestic help in Costa Rica. Finally, I will consider the transnational gendered discourse and practices among U.S. American women who arrived in Costa Rica during the early 1970s and who aspired to adapt the ideas of the U.S. women's liberation movement to their lives in Costa Rica.

In the Service of Their Homeland and Themselves: The U.S. American Women's Club

Many of the U.S. American women who lived in the Central Valley, wives of U.S. Americans administrators and businessmen or Costa Rican men, used the U.S. Women's Club as the main arena through which they constructed their identifications vis-à-vis both the United States and their Costa Rican surroundings. This dual process of identity work was performed mainly through the notion and practices of *service*—whether to U.S. American women in need, to the Costa Rican people, or to what they perceived as the interests of the United States in the Americas in the first decades of the Cold War. It was primarily through this service, with its explicit gendered dimensions, that these women confronted and overcame their liminality and marginalization as both women and foreigners and constructed a physical and symbolic space for themselves within the U.S. American community and the Costa Rican public sphere.

Established in 1940 by a former teacher from Pennsylvania, Elizabeth Robinson Settle de Oreamuno Flores (the wife of Costa Rican politician Alberto Settle de Oreamuno Flores) and several of her friends, all wives of Costa Ricans or U.S. American businessmen and governmental officials, the U.S.A. Women's Club, as it was first called, was modeled after women's clubs that the members had known in the United States. It was shaped, however, in response to the realities of the women's lives as U.S. American women in Costa Rica and the role they sought for themselves as U.S. American women abroad during the Cold War.[15] The United States and Costa Rica were not, however, the only points of reference. The club was molded by and formed part of a long tradition of colonial and expat women throughout the world who advocated for the needs of women abroad and who in most cases carried the status of "dependents," that is, had come to live abroad because of their husbands' work.[16]

While the couples may have arrived together, once in Costa Rica the men and the women led very different lives. The men typically held a job outside the home and assimilated into the social milieu of their work, which in many cases kept them in a U.S. American atmosphere; their wives, nonetheless, coped with more radical changes, both in and outside the home. For many, immigration signified a decline in their lifestyle and perception of themselves as modern women. In the United States, many had been professionals, who had benefited from the rise in women's participation in the work force during World War II.[17] Their professional lives had been an important aspect of their self-identification back home, and many of my informants described themselves as career women, even if on a modest scale—secretaries, saleswomen, and teachers. In Costa Rica, however, they were frustrated by their inability to obtain a job due to language barriers and various legal and cultural obstacles.[18] Costa Rican women usually did not work outside the home, and of those who did, almost 40 percent were maids. This figure explains somewhat the prevalent perception of women's labor in Costa Rica as low class,[19] and sometimes even as morally repugnant, as another main occupation for women was prostitution.[20] The Costa Rican tourist industry was not developed in the early 1950s and jobs for English-speaking women were scarce and limited almost exclusively to teaching in U.S. American schools.

The intersection of gender, nationality, ethnicity, and class in the context of working outside the home was even more explicit in the case of U.S. American women who were married to Costa Rican men. Some of these women recounted bitterly that for a woman to work outside the home, even if economically necessary, was considered an insult to the husband's masculine role as provider, or to the family's social status. One such wife recalled that her insistence on working as an English teacher caused a scandal within her husband's Costa Rican family, where no woman had ever worked outside the home before, and undermined their perception of the strict divide between a "lady" and a laborer, to the extent that her mother-in-law refused to send her maid to the young couple's home, on the grounds that "if she [the U.S. American wife] can work *outside* the home she can also work *inside* the home."[21]

Struggling with culture shock, isolation, and loneliness, many U.S. American women in San José (and its immediate surroundings) in the 1950s retreated, or were pushed back, to more gender-segregated spaces than the ones they had left behind in the United States and assumed more traditional "feminine" activities and roles.[22] Seeking out venues beyond their domestic and familial sphere, they, like many expat women across the world, used the women's club as a transitional space, a home away from both their personal home and their national home, which provided them with a sense of belonging and sometimes also a semiprofessional outlet as secretaries, treasurers, heads of various committees, and managers of clubs: a partial compensation for their inability to work outside the home. The club not only filled their days, which were relatively free as a result of affordable live-in maids and childcare, but also came to be a key factor in their self-identification as U.S. American women providing an essential service.

The women's club focused on two core targets of service, U.S. American women in Costa Rica and Costa Rican society, particularly its poor. For U.S. American women the club helped alleviate the difficulties associated with their immigration. A member who only heard about the club after her first lonely year as a young mother in Costa Rica remembered how relieved she was to discover it, dubbing the club her "lifeline."[23] Club members (themselves often only recently arrived) helped the newcomers and empowered themselves, as the holders of specific and crucial knowledge regarding the correct way to be a U.S. American woman in Costa Rica. The actual activities carried out at the club revolved around raising money and supporting local organizations and communities in need. However, the overreaching target of service, and what guided the members of the club in terms of both their rhetoric and actions, was always the perception of themselves as advocates of U.S. American interests in Cold War Central America. This service to U.S. interests was bound up with the other two targets of service and imbued them with greater meaning: the members helped each other not only to shore up their spirits as individuals but also to strengthen and unite the community of U.S. American women in Costa Rica by enabling them to retain a sense of being part of U.S. American culture; they helped Costa Ricans in part because they believed this would benefit U.S. interests on the geopolitical level. The members sought to function as human emblems of a compassionate United States, participating in the introduction and distribution of U.S. American lifestyles, material objects, and ideologies through which they propagated a positive image of the United States as philanthropic, and, more fundamentally, as feminine—with its attendant notions of glamour, compassion, and soft, nurturing nature—but also as representing progress and modernity. Club members thus saw themselves in effect as goodwill ambassadors. Harlan Cleveland, a scholar and diplomat who conducted research about U.S. Americans stationed abroad in the service of the United States, dubbed the wives of these diplomats "the Pretty American," as opposed to the depiction of their husbands, who were perceived as "the Ugly American."[24] In shaping and promoting such a model of the compassionate and politically informed U.S. American woman, the club members played a role in a greater scheme to wield U.S. American femininity as a political tool. As historian Emily Rosenberg has noted, following World War II and particularly in the first years of the Cold War, women were accorded enormous significance in the project of spreading the U.S. way of life and casting it as superior to the Soviet one, and various models of U.S. femininity became a crucial component in the Cold War and an emblem of such superiority.[25]

The negotiation of members' identifications and roles took place in the women's social meetings and oral conversations but was consolidated in the club's extensive textual realm, which included, inter alia, the monthly bulletin and the annual report, New Year greeting cards, and cookbooks, but was most clearly expressed in the club's three constitutions, composed respectively in 1958, 1965, and 1975. A comparative reading of these documents reveals the women's responses to the changing political and social conditions in which they lived, their needs and aspirations, and their ongoing process of identity work vis-à-vis the United States and Costa Rica. The various products of the club's writings should not be read, however, as a single authoritative voice, but rather as the contesting ideas of multiple women who were engaged in the collective negotiation of their role as U.S. American women in Costa Rica.[26]

These writings, moreover, were often in sharp conflict with everyday realities, thereby complicating the women's ideas about themselves and their practices.

Although the club was founded in 1940, its first constitution was signed on October 5, 1958. Article 2 described the club's two aims as follows: "To unite U.S.A. women in order to further fellowship and understanding, and to promote good relations among the Americas."[27] In other words, the members perceived themselves as having a mission which is extended beyond social gathering and self-help to play a significant role in inter-American relations. Note that Costa Rica is not mentioned at all, a fact that may imply that this goal was seen as applying to the role of *all* U.S. American women abroad and not only in Costa Rica. As many of the club members had already lived in several other countries as the wives of career diplomats and businessmen, we can assume that this wording was influenced by their life experience in other countries or even borrowed directly from the constitutions of other women's clubs.

Charitable work was the backbone of the women's club and I will elaborate on it later, but this expressed tendency toward diplomacy is intriguing.[28] It is the result, perhaps, of the affiliation of many members with the administrative and business sector of U.S. Americans in Costa Rica. In 1960, for example, four out of nine new members listed the U.S. embassy as their contact address in Costa Rica, and the first collection of recipes published by the club was titled *Embassy Row Specialties*.[29] For the wives of diplomats and other official U.S. envoys, membership in the women's club was perceived as crucial and almost mandatory (albeit not explicitly so). In his article from 1959, Cleveland wrote about the wives of diplomats who, through their behavior, "often make or break their husband's careers and U.S. foreign policy as well," implying that they should be kept satisfied—and monitored—so that they do not become a problem for their husband or the expat U.S. community in which they live, and by extension damage the broader U.S. cause.[30] Fechter uses the rather benign metaphor of a bubble to describe the expat social spaces, including women's clubs, in late twentieth-century Jakarta, but reading Cleveland's words, written some fifty years earlier, the women's club seems to take on more of the aspects of a cage in which the U.S. American women were contained and kept at bay. "The idea [of the club] is to enhance the morale of the men at the office: by making sure of an adequate ration of 'belonging' for their wives."[31] The club was therefore a means both of keeping the women busy and of giving them a sense of purpose.

One such purpose in the Costa Rican context was community-building. Starting from the end of World War II, U.S. Americans in Costa Rica gradually came to define themselves as a unique group, distinct from the broader British dominated English-speaking community. The members of the women's club, through both written and oral testimonies, essentially credited themselves, and the club, with inventing a U.S. American national and cultural tradition in Costa Rica. As early as 1944 the members organized the first Halloween ball, whose success prompted other "service clubs" in the country to adopt the custom in the following year.[32] In 1949 club members initiated the tradition of a Memorial Day ceremony for U.S. soldiers. Two years later, they held the first Fourth of July picnic. The *TT* later claimed that it was in fact the U.S. embassy staff, composed of U.S. men, who initiated the picnic, but the women's club professed pride in these initiatives forms part of their gendered identity work, which glorified and legitimized the participants within the U.S. American community and consolidated their self-perceptions as mothers of the community and guardians of the U.S. American heritage and values.[33]

In later years, the club took a greater part in promoting U.S. interests and diplomacy, and actively involved itself, either directly or indirectly, in this process. Shortly before U.S. president Kennedy's 1963 trip to Costa Rica, the club sent a letter to Costa Rican president Francisco Orlich expressing their wish to be involved in the visit: "It would be of extreme interest for us to have you tell us the plans your government has made for President Kennedy's visit and what our organization can do to make it a complete success. As always, you will find us ready and willing to cooperate in any way."[34] While the club archive holds no mention of how or if President Orlich responded to the letter, or if the women's club took an active role in the visit, we do know that at least some of the members met

Kennedy at a reception in his honor organized by the American embassy in San José.

However, an inherent conflict existed between the rhetoric of promoting good relations among the Americas, or at least in Costa Rica, and the club members' wish to keep it an exclusive U.S. haven, practiced through the admission of U.S. American women or first-degree relatives of U.S. citizens only, and challenges soon arose. In the fall of 1959, a year after the first constitution of the club was formulated, Whiting Willauer, U.S. ambassador to Costa Rica at the time, approached the club members and informed them, as Anna Fredrikson, who served as the club's correspondence secretary, later recalled, that "President Eisenhower has asked that we open these clubs" to all English-speaking women in Costa Rica.[35] The ambassador assured the members that the same request had been made to all U.S. social clubs across the globe, hence attesting to the weight they had attained as a tool of U.S. propaganda during the Cold War. "He said we cannot keep on with this Ugly American, that we can't be exclusive."[36] Kathrin Morales, another member, remembered that the ambassador expressed his firm belief that an exclusionary U.S. club, even if philanthropic and social in nature, caused resentment among the local population and thus was harmful both to the image and to the strategic interests of the United States. "He thought it was kind of pushing Costa Ricans away, and that we should invite them," Morales said.[37]

Ambassador Willauer requested that the club's name be changed from the U.S.A. Women's Club to the San José Women's Club and that it change its criteria for membership so that every English-speaking Costa Rican woman could be eligible for membership, thus replacing the strict national criterion for membership with vague cultural ones. It stood to change not only the Club's national composition but also its class and ethnic makeup, potentially opening its doors to every English-speaking *tica*, including even the Black Costa Ricans—the mostly lower-class descendants of Caribbean immigrants—many of whom worked as cooks in the homes of U.S. Americans in Costa Rica. The ambassador's appeal caused turmoil within the club's ranks, exposing its stratification along axes of age and class, with the older women primarily objecting to the inclusion of Costa Ricans and the younger ones generally supporting it.[38] Following an impassioned debate, the club voted to change its name—but to the U.S.A. International Women's Club, not the San José Women's Club as the ambassador had requested. The club members were therefore willing to see themselves as international, but not as Costa Rican. Despite this, in the 1965 constitution they did tailor article 2 to accord with the ambassador's demand, writing, "The object of the club shall be to unite English-speaking women in a club to further the understanding and fellowship among themselves and the people of Costa Rica."[39] Following a mass registration of both English-speaking and non-English-speaking Costa Rican women to the club, efforts were made to restrict their numbers. These efforts were perceived, or presented, ironically, as a way to promote good relations between the club's U.S. American and Costa Rican members. In 1962 the club president took advantage of the club's English-only annual report to argue that "an effort should be made (discrete manipulation of membership drive?) to maintain this balance, as an imbalance either way could cause discontent and interfere with at least one of the club's purposes which is surely amity between the two groups."[40]

The ambassador's request and the club members' delicate manipulation of it attest to the intersection of gender with other categories such as nationality, class, and ethnicity that were part of the identity work of members in constructing their entities as U.S. American women in Costa Rica. Morales, a long-time member, recalled that the U.S. American women covertly agreed to stick to English so that the Costa Rican members would feel like outsiders and that this conflict over language, which reflected broader cultural gaps, lasted about two years, until the U.S. American women felt that "we got it back again."[41]

The 1965 constitution reiterates the club's goals as they appeared in the earlier constitution, but this time, instead of the general term "Americas," Costa Rica is mentioned specifically. The first article read, "To further fellowship and understanding among club members and the people of Costa Rica, to undertake projects of benefit to Costa Rica and to promote international good will."[42] To this was added a new clause, stipulating that in order "to maintain the character of the club and preserve its heritage, the president and the first vice-president shall always be United States citizens."[43] In that same year, the club took several steps that manifested its hybrid identity and its transnational position. On the one hand, its name was changed to the Women's Club of Costa Rica (WCCR), with records explaining the decision as designed to make it easier for non-U.S. women to join. It was also registered for the first time in the Costa Rican *Registro Civil.* On the other hand, the club joined the U.S.-based Federation of U.S. Women's Clubs, paying an annual membership fee of $10.[44] U.S. American women in Costa Rica were thus concerned with their position vis-à-vis Costa Rican women and their influence on the club and their own identifications. They accepted Costa Rican women but under the stipulation that they could not serve as its leadership. Such a clause was grounded in the perception of the inherent U.S. American "character" of the club and the members themselves, which they were determined to maintain.

However, ten years later, the 1975 constitution reflected the changes in members' practices and identifications, as they no longer talked about U.S. American women, the United States, or the Americas. Their club had become bilingual and was now called the Women's Club of Costa Rica / Club de Mujeres de Costa Rica, whose goals were: "To promote the union of women who speak English in order to establish comradeship between them and the people of Costa Rica, thus to develop international links of friendship" and "to generate a creative attitude in public affairs by means of analyzing and investigating the social and economic development processes."[45] While the club allegedly substituted its national criteria of U.S. American origin and first degree family relations with cultural ones, namely fluency in English, the phrasing suggests that the members still maintained a certain distance between "women who speak English" and "the people of Costa Rica" and still constructed their identities around the notion of service to the latter. This service, however, was no longer depicted as charity but as "social investigation," which imparted to it a professional, even scholarly, aura.

Between Philanthropy and Self-Fulfillment:
The Feminine Mystique of the Expat Woman

Philanthropic work was the backbone of women's clubs both within the United States and outside it. "No meeting shall pass in which the club has not done something for the benefit of others," announced a speaker at a 1906 conference of (mostly male) women's club supporters that took place in the United States.[46] But in clubs outside the United States, philanthropy was perceived even more strongly as the *obligation* of expat U.S. American women in the service of their homeland. In writing about the charitable activities of Anglo-American women in Tuscany, Trundle reveals the individual and collective identity work that charity activities facilitated as "a central means through which participants navigate a sense of place, craft a space for collective action, negotiate moral personhood, [and] come to understand their own agency and class position."[47] In the Central Valley of Costa Rica in the 1950s, charity became a crucial means by which U.S. American women, marginalized and constrained both as women and as foreigners, could carve a space for themselves in the expat community and the Costa Rican public sphere. It brought them into contact with Costa Ricans beyond those of their family circles or domestic help and enabled them to advance what they regarded, with a sense of superiority, as their values and norms. Lacking employment, they sought self-worth by transplanting an ethic of work and achievements into the sphere of volunteering, which also enabled them to overcome class and seniority distinctions among themselves and provided them with the opportunity to gain positions of influence and prestige within the club and in the various U.S. networks.[48] As they strove for deeper involvement with and recognition from their host society, the women found a sense of purpose and belonging to local life through their ability to participate in and support local systems of charity, constructing an image of themselves as efficient and compassionate U.S. American women.

The women's club in Costa Rica's first service activities took place during World War II and attest to the double targets—both Costa Rica and the United States, who were, at the time, united in the Allied cause. Club members aided the construction of shelters in San José but also raised and sent home $125,000, asserting their affiliation with the United States and their patriotism.[49] In 1948, during the Costa Rican civil war, club members, careful to take no side in the conflict, sewed dolls for Costa Rican children. A year later they handed out 576 pairs of socks to the poor. The club's logo featured the motto "Service-Friendship-*Servicio-Amistad*," and its texts repeatedly urged its members to make philanthropy a crucial component of their identity as U.S. American women abroad. "The main purpose of the club is to help Costa Rican charitable institutions . . . doesn't it give each of you a feeling of gratification?" inquired the president in her 1950/51 annual report.[50]

In 1960 the members decided to establish a social service group. The club president noted that "there are quite a few women here who would like to learn more of the social problems here and means of taking care of them." This group soon became one of the club's most important institutions. The admission of English-speaking Costa Ricans the year before enhanced the club's integration, with the Costa Rican members serving as mediators between the U.S. American women and the local environment. The social work enabled the former to enter private and public spaces that had previously been inaccessible to them, bringing them into close contact with locals and giving them a chance to see "the real" Costa Rica, specifically of course the particular sphere of the poor and needy, while still remaining under the club's protective wings and its patronizing gaze. So, for example, spirited individual members conducted "social welfare visits to underprivileged people," a phrasing that combined anthropological and charitable perspectives; provided transportation for sick children to hospitals; and organized for them visits to the theater.[51] Other activities included Christmas bazaars and bake sales, but also large-scale initiatives that involved feminine U.S. American know-how and values, sponsored by U.S. organizations, both governmental and nongovernmental. In 1963, for example, the members attempted to establish a nutrition center in Escazú that would provide meals for poor children and sewing classes for their mothers, as well as daycare for the children of working mothers, a vocational center, a vegetable garden, and a room for the meetings of the Costa Rican Anti-Alcohol League (noting that "alcohol is a problem here").[52] The project's committee asserted, "Self-help is our motto. We feel that by teaching them to sew and letting them use our sewing machines (donated to us by CARE) we are helping them to better themselves."[53] The municipality of Escazú set aside a piece of municipal property for the nutrition center, but due to lack of funds it never materialized. Special events, like bingo nights, dance balls, and fashion shows, were open to nonmembers and even publicized in the Costa Rican press, and proceeds from their ticket sales went toward the club's philanthropy, mainly the support of hospitals and educational programs. These activities rendered the U.S. American women visible within wider relational realms and public spheres, U.S. American and Costa Rican alike.

The women's club members connected themselves to diverse segments of Costa Rican society and at the same time advanced U.S. American culture and ideology, positioning themselves as its presenters. A look at their activities in 1963 reflects this dual function and the symbolic value of the members' activities. In January members were photographed in the Costa Rican press donating blood as part of a national campaign, with the accompanying text hailing them for their contribution and casting it as evidence that they were part of Costa Rica, sharing their blood with its people.[54] They later collaborated on a literacy project sponsored by the first lady of Costa Rica, collecting a thousand second-hand books and distributing them in schools and hospitals. In April the club sponsored the Costa Rican tour of the All Florida Fashion Show, a commercial enterprise that dispatched beauty pageant winners from Florida to Central America. The tour, which received significant coverage in the local press, presented young U.S. models dressed in the latest U.S. fashions, celebrating—with the endorsement of the U.S. women's club—the glamorous and liberated lifestyle of young U.S. women.[55] That same month members were active in the "Thrift and Gift" shop, a charity store that sold second-hand domestic items, such as clothing and electronic appliances donated by the members, that operated out of the American Legion office in San José and whose profits all went to the city's children's hospital. The final meeting of the year consisted of the much-anticipated and by now traditional tea with the first lady of Costa Rica at the Casa Presidencial.

But charity was a double-edged sword. While serving to establish the cultural identity of U.S. American women in Costa Rica as efficient, cosmopolitan, and compassionate it also entrenched their

Fig. 11. WCCR's president handing a check to Costa Rica's minister of culture, 1978. Courtesy of *La Nación*.

role as primary care-givers on the familial, communal, and national levels. In 1958 club member Fay Dresner submitted to the club's general assembly a document titled "Thoughts about Our Program," in which, contrary to the determinedly chipper tone of the monthly bulletins and annual reports, she portrayed a merciless picture of the life of the U.S. housewife in San José. Dresner argued that the club's activities perpetuated and even exacerbated the cultural stagnation and boredom that were the main characteristics of the lives of these women, particularly those of a certain social milieu, in San José. "By language barriers, indifference, or the actual absence of such activities in the life of San José, American women withdraw from what stimulating activity is available," she wrote.[56] While not dismissing the importance of the role of homemaker, Dresner called for self-fulfillment through other activities as well, saying, "In addition to their *obligation* to support local charities and contribute to the well-being of the Costa Ricans among whom they are living, the American women here have personal needs that the club could help fill [my emphasis]." Dresner urged her fellow members to venture beyond their dual obligation, in her words, as both women and U.S. expats and start paying attention to their own intellectual and emotional needs: "While flower arrangements and dances are still welcome, activities at a higher intellectual level are much desired . . . the Club should therefore provide its members with the opportunity to get out of the routine of their homes, small circle of friends, and business social life to flex their own muscles and minds and engage in some stimulating and energetic activities."[57]

Dresner called for the establishment of interest groups that would strengthen the friendship among women who share hobbies and agendas and suggested that these groups, which she proposed to call *juntitas*, be available to both members and nonmembers, thus serving as an effective means of breaking the club's exclusion of local women and the contours of the U.S. bubble. The invitation to come up with ideas for groups that reflected their world, ambitions, and desires resulted in the social service group discussed above, which was aligned with established club goals and image and was immediately approved. The request for a Latin American dance group, however, "the cha-cha, mambo, meringue etc. which always intrigue newcomers from the States," proved more problematic.[58] Whereas the club offered regular ballroom and square dancing as part of its promotion and preservation of U.S. cultural heritage, Latin dances were practiced and presented by U.S. American women mostly as part of a folklore show, or in a private forum.[59] The club's executives considered them too sensational and recoiled at their affiliation with the lower class and with native or Black ethnicities. No less significantly, Latin dance raised fears of an opening for intimacy with local men.[60] The long negotiations over the launching of such a group, including an unfruitful search for a female dance teacher, attest both to the U.S. American women's desire to get to know the local culture and experience its exoticism and to the club's role as a gatekeeper of the "appropriate" manner of their acculturation into local society and culture. The Latin dance class was eventually offered in the evenings, so that husbands of the members could take part in it but was discontinued after only a short while.

The 1965 application form of the club (fig.12) reveals the interests of U.S. American women and their identity work through the organization: on the one hand, their steadfast foreignness, and, on the other, their interest in integrating into the local culture at least to a certain extent, as evidenced by the two Spanish classes on offer. In addition, an English class was also offered to *ticas* (the colloquial name for Costa Rican women), and some of the interest groups were assembled as English-Spanish endeavors. The members' interest

> **APPLICATION FOR MEMBERSHIP
> IN THE
> U. S. A. INTERNATIONAL WOMEN'S CLUB**
>
> Name: _____
> Mailing Address: _____
> Barrio: _____ Telephone: _____
> Nationality: _____
> Husband's Occupation: _____
> Which of these groups would you be interested in joining?
>
> Book Club_____   Bridge Beginners_____
> World Affairs_____   Canasta Beginners_____
> Spanish Beginners_____   Explorers_____
> Spanish Advanced_____   Flower Arranging_____
> English Conversation_____ Social Service_____
> Name other interests: _____

Fig. 12. An application form for the U.S.A. International Women's Club, circa 1965. Courtesy of the Women's Club of Costa Rica.

in such domestic activities as cooking and handicrafts is evidenced by the assortment of groups devoted to these practices. The three dimensions—national, transnational, and international—of the club are manifested in some of the interest groups. The Explorers, for example, aimed "to acquaint the foreign colony with the sights and places of interest in and around San José," thus enabling the women to venture out of their homes. Five brave explorers even took a road trip to Panama.[61] The transnational and international interests can be seen in programming such as occurred in May 1969, when a special meeting of the World Affairs group was held in the evening, so that husbands could attend, and the participants watched movies about marijuana and LSD consumption in the United States.[62] Another meeting was dedicated to topics such as decolonization in Africa. In the late 1970s, along with stitchery, bridge, and a book club, members were interested in yoga and comparative religions, thus reflecting the influence of trends from the United States.

Ladies of Leisure and "Bad Mothers": Refashioning the Roles of U.S. American Women

The question of service as a key component of identity work was addressed not only in the public sphere of U.S. American women in Costa Rica, that is, in their club and charity activities, but also in the domestic sphere, inside their homes and as part of their self-negotiation. Most men and women who moved to Costa Rica during the 1950s brought with them ideas and practices that held that men were the breadwinners and women were homemakers and mothers. Such ideas were shaped by Cold War anxieties and the compulsion that saw in the unification and strengthening of the U.S. family a crucial tool in the fight against communist subversion. Eileen Tylor May stresses that the family was perceived as the most significant protection against the Russian threat, as exemplified by a 1959 issue of *Life Magazine* that featured a couple spending its honeymoon in an atomic bomb shelter.[63] She further shows how the revival of domesticity in the post–World War II United States and the attempted containment of women, both professionally and sexually, during this period was directly linked to fears regarding the encroachment of communism during the Cold War and the efforts to ward off this threat.[64]

Immigration challenged these self-perceptions and practices. However, part of the pressure the U.S. American woman in Costa Rica endured was due to the demands of various agents that she maintain the practices and values of the U.S. American home under very different circumstances. For example, she was expected to run the house without "electronic servants," as electronic appliances were dubbed in the United States; rather, she should employ a maid (*china*) who also took care of the children. The china, a Costa Rican term derived from *Quechua*, was a young indigenous or mestiza girl who lived in the house and was available to the lady throughout the whole day.[65] While the norm in mid-twentieth-century Costa Rica, as in other Latin American countries, live-in maids were rare in the United States of the time.[66] This domestic arrangement, which both accorded with the local custom and compensated for the lack of electronic appliances on which the U.S. American housewives had come to depend back home (see chapter 5), imparted greater leisure time and a sense of upward mobility unfamiliar to these working- and middle-class women from the United States. They were part of the intangible commodities enjoyed by affluent immigrants in their countries of destination and had a significant impact on both the everyday practices and the identity work of U.S. American women in Costa Rica.[67] In a letter to the *TT* in 1959, a writer calling him or herself "Observer" suggested examining "the effect of servants upon households and the utilization of the new leisure time by wives."[68]

Mary Thompson, who arrived in Costa Rica in 1951, was one such wife. Growing up in a working-class family in a small town in Massachusetts, she met her Costa Rican husband when he came to study in the United States after World War II as part of the benefits provided by the GI Bill (see chapter 1). In her interview, she lamented her husband's machoistic behavior but noted that this had not led to more traditional expectations of her as a wife and mother. She in fact felt that she experienced greater freedom in Costa Rica than she would have had in the United States thanks to the presence of affordable domestic help. Thompson recounted her afternoons in the Central Valley in the early 1950s driving around with her older son while the china took care of the baby: "I drove around to meet other American women . . . that's what I did in the afternoon. I was very lucky . . . I was a lady of leisure. I was very lucky."[69]

Thus Thompson, who in our talk stressed her working-class background and her job as a teacher prior to her marriage, redefined herself in Costa Rica as a "lady of leisure," a phrase normally associated with the upper class but here employed by Thompson to describe her lifestyle as a middle-class woman in Costa Rica who enjoyed privileges she could not have had in the United States. Throughout our talk, she referred to two activities that symbolized freedom and modern U.S. American femininity: driving, which at the time would have made her stand out in terms of both gender and status as there were not many cars in the Central Valley in the 1950s, and hardly any Costa Rican women drivers; and smoking in public.

On the one hand, then, immigration brought about a regression to more traditional gender relations insofar as U.S. American women were unable to work outside the home and those who were married to local men also experienced more explicitly machoistic attitudes. One U.S. American who arrived in Costa Rica in the 1950s with her Costa Rican husband said that while women in the United States at that time were "curtailed," in Costa Rica it was like "the stone age."[70] On the other hand, however, in their everyday practices, especially their domestic arrangements, many U.S. American women actually experienced greater freedom, leisure time, and emancipation from domestic tasks. The issue of domestic help in particular demonstrates the intersection of gender with other sociocultural and political identities, such as class and ethnicity. As Croucher argues, even when expat or immigrant women were granted a certain measure of liberty as women, this was in many cases not due to a change in gender roles per se but to the fact that "gender intertwines closely with the privilege they enjoy in terms of race, class, and nationality."[71] In other words, in cases like that of the U.S. American women in Costa Rica and other immigrant and colonizing Western women, some of them "traded on their constructed racial, national, and economic superiority to compensate for their assigned sexual inferiority."[72]

U.S. American women were expected to adjust as naturally to their role as the "ladies" of a household with domestic help as their Costa Rican middle- and upper-class peers did but at the same time to also maintain their U.S. values and practices, especially with respect to motherhood. In practice this change was fraught with challenges. The power relation between the women and their maids was complicated by the former's foreignness and unfamiliarity with the Latin American institution of domestic help. Many women told me that their maids would call them *niña* (girl) instead of *señora* or *doña* (lady) or exploit the language barrier to "play dumb" so that the U.S. housewife ended up doing the housework herself. They recounted this with a sense of shame over their failure to adequately enforce the running of their household and their humiliation at the hands of these domestic workers; at the same time, this was mixed with a sense of pride, as they linked this failure to their supposedly egalitarian U.S. American nature that made them unqualified to assume the authoritative stances required.[73] In a 1960 column in the *TT*, Marge Durant, a woman who had previously lived in San José but at the time of writing was stationed with her husband in Caracas, depicted herself as a women's club lady who spent her days at the club. As in Thompson's narrative, the word "leisure" recurs in her description. In the column, titled "Maids I Have Known," she described hiring a succession of maids and referred to her household as "queer" (an interesting choice of word in the context of gender, given that she might have used many less loaded adjectives, such as "odd," "weird," or "different") because she was helpless at retaining them.[74] Even more interesting is her confession, toward the end of the piece, about her lack of interest in house management: "I am really one of those rare women who admit right out loud that I HATE housework. I dislike the kitchen and women's magazines full of page after page of beautiful ten-tone color cuts of new dishes and arrangements leave me cold."[75]

Living abroad therefore enabled some of the U.S women to reconsider the gendered domestic roles characteristic of the United States. However, this was not a simple story of gender emancipation due to class mobility and privileges that were the consequence of the immigration process. Along with this new freedom and potential emancipation from traditional domestic tasks there arose a new set of constraints and new gatekeepers who found such freedom threatening. One such influential gatekeeper was "Your Child's Health," a weekly column written by Migel Ortiz, a Costa Rican pediatrician educated in the United States, and published in the *TT* between 1956 and 1959 (and for a short period in 1972). In his column Ortiz instructed U.S. American mothers on child-rearing in Costa Rica, providing advice on issues such as nutrition and tropical diseases and often bringing his point home by using anecdotes and insights purportedly based on his encounters with these mothers and their children in his clinic. These columns are a clear example of the means by which U.S. American women in Costa Rica were kept in line, via a warning—made by a pediatrician—of the hazardous consequences that their new-found freedom could result in.[76]

In one of his columns Ortiz stated that "American families lead a different life here than they do in the States. There is, for example, a less intimate contact between mother and child here due to the fact that mothers transfer many of their duties to the servants."[77]

He advises the mothers, indeed exhorts them, to allow the maids to replace them in the tasks of cleaning and cooking but not in childcare. In one of his most relentless pieces he recounts the story of a young U.S. American mother who brought her little girl to his clinic but could provide no relevant information about her, as she had transferred all responsibilities to the china: "The point in this story is that too many mothers depend altogether too much on *chinas* (nursemaids) for the care of their children . . . Frequently I am forced to ask mothers: 'Do you think your *china* is as *good a mother* as you are?' . . . the answer to these questions is always 'no' . . . Yet, many mothers who come to Central America from other countries see in the availability of a low cost [*sic*] nursemaid the opportunity to relinquish entirely the care of their children."[78]

Ortiz draws a link between the economic advantages afforded by immigration from the United States to Costa Rica and what he sees as a deterioration in the emotional and moral values of the U.S. American mothers. In the United States of the 1950s mothers were perceived as responsible for the home and the family, a role seen as imperative to the U.S. American way of life; any diminution of it was perceived as a risk to the core of U.S. American culture.[79] In Costa Rica this danger was embodied by the china, the lower class, ethnically different maid. In this narrative the china is allegedly jealous of the mother and tries to alienate her children from her. She does so through drawing them closer to the local culture by speaking to them in Spanish, of which many U.S. American parents were ignorant, and exposing them to local folklore ("Another common practice among *chinas* is to frighten the child into going to bed by threatening him with witches, hones and other horrors").[80] The china's perceived hypersexuality, derived from her nonwhite ethnicity and low class status, led Ortiz to advise mothers to request their chinas renew their medical certificate every year, as prostitutes were required to do. In some cases it even brought him to deliberately accuse them of sexually abusing children and babies: "Some *chinas* have been known to indulge with their small charges. These cases have even involved small babies who, as a result, have suffered physical injury." Ortiz summed it up by stating, "What all this adds up to, is that you cannot, if you want a healthy happy child, depend on the *china* for the love and care which is, and should be, your responsibility. . . . [The *china*] cannot take the place of the mother."[81]

The columns were published in the widely read English-speaking newspaper, the arena par excellence for collective U.S. American identity work, but, as they were written by a Costa Rican pediatrician, they enable us to examine the double perspective directed at U.S. American women: that of the Costa Rican elite and of the U.S. establishment in the country. On the face of it, Ortiz writes about practices of U.S. child-rearing in Costa Rica and provides a cruel portrait of the china. Nonetheless, his writing is more of an indictment of the U.S. American mothers, who are not that morally superior to the despised china. They are portrayed as exploiting the privileges of their new lifestyle in order to desert their duties and indulge in leisure and freedom. Ortiz's writing echoes prevalent Costa Rican perceptions of U.S. American women as loose and immoral (Anna Fredrickson, wife of a Costa Rican man, reflected bitterly on this, saying, "my maid has five kids from five different men, but I was considered the loose American." Asked why, in her opinion, such an image prevailed, she shrugged: "I don't know, maybe because of the movies").[82] However, considering its arena of publishing, the *TT*, "Your Child's Health" can therefore be read as a call for U.S. American mothers to return to their traditional roles and for the reestablishment of the norms of the middle-class U.S. American home as practiced in the United States. It is a cautionary voice, warning against the adoption of Costa Rican norms of child-rearing, which are perceived as threatening to the integrity and strength of the U.S. American home abroad.

Tarantula in the Airmail:
Bringing the Word of *Ms.* Magazine to San José

So far I have described the "gender work" performed by U.S. American women who arrived in Costa Rica in the late 1950s. These women carried with them gender perceptions that were typical of white, middle-class women of that particular decade and proceeded to adapt them to their lives in Costa Rica. Those who arrived in the early 1970s, despite coming from similar milieus (i.e., middle-class, white communities), had very different gender perceptions. Many

Fig. 13. Elizabeth Dyer (*right*), first editor of the *TT*, with fellow staff members Elenor Hamer (*left*) and Shirley Harris and an unidentified printshop worker, reviewing proofs at Imprenta Borrasé, late 1950s. Photograph by Foto Solanov. Courtesy of the *TT*.

of them were familiar with or had directly experienced the social protest movement of the 1970s and were especially influenced by the women's liberation movement. Indeed, for these women, coming to Costa Rica was in some cases a deliberate act of liberation that involved withdrawing from familiar, patriarchal frameworks and reflected the "drifter" ethos of the youth generation. While many arrived either as independent travelers, or as part of a commune, some, like their 1950s compatriots, followed spouses whose work took them to Costa Rica. However, the society they encountered did not necessarily seem to offer them the freedom they were looking for. For many of them Costa Rica appeared to be a regressive culture, in which women's rights and status were curtailed. Still, once there, they sought to carve out a space for themselves and pursue the ideals they espoused. They did so primarily in two complementary ways. The first was by joining consciousness-raising groups (which had been popularized by U.S. feminists beginning in the 1960s), and the second was by writing columns in the *TT*. These activities make an interesting case study for the gendered identity work on both the individual and the collective levels through the examination of transnational gendered practices and the creation of gendered transnational spaces as part of the immigration process.

Just as in the late 1950s Ortiz's column (along with similar columns, such as "Fashion" and "Lady Talk") was a call for the preservation of U.S. American family patterns and traditional gender relations, so the *TT* columns of the 1970s expressed the gender-related values popular in the United States and their negotiation in the Costa Rican context. These changes were personally exemplified in the family that owned the newspaper, the Dyers. Founded in 1956 by Elizabeth Dyer, who was also its first editor, the *TT* went on hiatus for twelve years and resumed publication in 1972 with Dery Dyer, the daughter of Elizabeth and Richard Dyer, as editor. Dery was born in 1952 and lived in Costa Rica until the age of eight. She spent her high-school years at a boarding school in the United States and then attended Wellesley College. In the early 1970s she was called back to Costa Rica to take care of her sick mother; when the latter passed away, Dery and her father decided to reopen the paper. Dery was thus a kind of transitional figure in the annals of the U.S. immigration to Costa Rica. On the one hand, her early childhood experience was connected to the older generation of U.S. Americans in Costa Rica; on the other, she was affiliated with the new generation of U.S. Americans who arrived in the country—young college graduates who were politically and socially informed.

The changes Dery introduced into the *TT* reflect the new winds that were blowing in the United States regarding gender. Several weeks after she reopened the paper, Ortiz's columns and "Lady Talk" were discontinued, and in their place appeared two new columns—"Women Here and Now," which featured profiles of young U.S. American women living in Costa Rica, and the more radical "Women's Lib and You." Contrary to Ortiz's "Your Child's Health," which had been an authoritative instructional column, written by a man and focusing on children (positioning the women readers exclusively and entirely within their role as mothers), "Women's Lib and You" was a self-help text, written by women and focused on women and their needs. "Women's Lib and You" aspired to bring the word of the second wave of white liberal U.S. feminism to U.S. American women in Costa Rica in ways that were applicable to their lives there. In our interview, held in the old newsroom of the *TT* in downtown San José, Dyer, who not only edited the paper but also wrote some of the "Women's Lib" columns, acknowledged a profound sense of mission: "We tried always to look at how it [feminism] would apply here, and of course we were at that point so *converted*, we were so pro, so we figured everybody needs this, *it was definitely a missionary zeal*" (my emphasis).[83] The columns were signed by Anne Eliot, the (misspelled) name of the protagonist of Jane Austen's *Persuasion*, a pseudonym of Dyer and several other female staff members, which enabled them to avoid direct identification but also expressed a group spirit: "It was like a group effort, so we kind of came together with an Anne Eliot idea of an entrapped feminist who could bring the words to the ladies of Central America."[84]

Seeing herself as a U.S. American woman with a mission in Central America, Dyer perhaps was not that different from the older generation of women's club members. She did not specify whether these women were U.S. Americans or Costa Rican, but the fact is that the columns were written in English and inspired by *Ms.*, a feminist magazine first published in the United States in 1972, the same year that the *TT* resumed publication. Many columns of "Women's Lib and You" were based on direct quotes or close paraphrases of texts and ideas that appeared in *Ms.* The *TT* frequently urged its readers to subscribe to *Ms.* by reminding them that a subscription would cost only a mere two dollars above its price in the United States (while noting the caveat that each issue would take up to three months to arrive in Costa Rica). Dyer and her cowriters sometimes bought *Ms.* on their visits to the United States or received it from U.S. friends and then offered their readers a delayed and somewhat softened version of the magazine's U.S. liberal feminism.

Onka Dekkers, a writer with the contemporary feminist periodical *off our backs*, coined the famous image of *Ms.* as a "female mindset on those glossy pages slipping into American homes concealed in bags of groceries, like a tarantula on banana boats."[85] What kind of tarantulas did Dyer and her staff intended to slip into the homes of the *TT* readers, most of whom were older and more conservative? While some of the columns addressed issues of gender relations in general, others related specifically to gender in the context of the immigration process and the lives of U.S. American women in Costa Rica. Thus they allowed for a certain comparative examination of what the writers perceived as the meaning of being a woman in the United States versus being a U.S. American woman abroad. Published in April 1972, the column "Machismo and Marriage," for example, considers the concept of machoism and the gendered expectations for young boys. It opens with a harsh criticism of the way Costa Rican males are reared and educated, describing such stereotypical themes as the "traditional" visit to a prostitute when the Costa Rican boy is fifteen or the Costa Rican husband hanging out in dark nightclubs with his mistress who is "a symbol of [his] affluence."[86] The mistress, a well-established figure in Costa Rican society as in other Latin societies, was a sore point for many U.S. American women, especially the older generation. Yet this description of dark bars and cheap hotels was closer to North American moral standards, or fantasy, than to Costa Rican reality and attests to the writers' disconnection from Costa Rican norms, in which longtime relations of the husband with a woman other than his wife, and even the existence of simultaneous households, prevailed. A U.S. American wife of a Costa Rican man told me that the mistresses and infidelity of Costa Rican men were among the most commonly discussed topics of conversation among women in social gatherings and the reason for many breakups. Another U.S. American woman married to a Costa Rican man stated proudly that her mother-in-law had threatened her son that she would break his neck if he ever betrayed his wife. The woman stressed that this kind of "hard line" was the exception to the rule.[87]

"Women's Lib and You" was therefore novel not only in its feminist ideology but also in its open condemnation of Costa Rican society, something that the *TT* had until then been careful to avoid, believing that as "privileged guests" in the country U.S. Americans should not criticize Costa Rican social institutions. The gendered perspective enabled a more critical view of Costa Rica but also an assessment of gender relations in the United States. As "Anne Eliot" wrote in the column about machismo and mistresses, "Does this sort of thing happen in other cultures? Sure! In the U.S., though not an 'accepted' part of society, it happens all the time. And perhaps it is even worse there because it is not accepted but occurs underhandedly, with tactic approval."[88]

The writer then concludes that "machismo is everywhere" and should not be condemned any more severely in Costa Rica than in the United States, urging women everywhere to fight against its manifestations. The examination of machismo and the problem of the mistress was a topic that united older and younger U.S. American women in Costa Rica, with the younger women typically seeking to raise the feminist consciousness of their older peers. It is interesting to note that the article did not seek to assert the superiority of the United States over Costa Rica but rather highlighted the universality of gender relations. This attitude was in the spirit of sisterhood that characterized white U.S. American feminism, but with a significant difference: whereas *Ms.* adamantly prescribed feminism as the answer to Latin machismo, and indeed came under criticism for turning feminism into yet another U.S. commodity to be exported to the rest of the world, the *TT* was careful not to provide U.S.-made prescriptions but rather to acknowledge the worldwide prevalence of gender inequality.[89]

The "Women's Lib and You" columns were self-help texts aimed at providing a practical guide for gender emancipation. In many cases they did so through self-testimony, a common convention in women's magazines. One column, titled "One Woman's Moment of Truth," paraphrased the title of Jane O'Reilly's famous article "The Housewife's Moment of Truth," with a feminist modification.[90] By paraphrasing O'Reilly, the *TT* text acknowledged its authors' familiarity with current U.S. American feminist ideas, and by changing "The Housewife" to "One Woman" the title signifies the idea that the writers (and by implication the readers) refused to define themselves as housewives. It also conveyed the inclusive message that every, and any, woman could experience "a moment of truth." "Anne Eliot" encouraged her readers to look for life-changing points in their lives, with immigration being one of these moments. The imagined readers were U.S. American women in Costa Rica who were undergoing a process of change and awakening and learning to acknowledge their physical and mental strengths. So, for example, the issue of harassment in the street, a frequent complaint among young U.S. American women who considered it part of the machoistic culture in Costa Rica, was addressed through a call for women to practice judo or karate.

On a more philosophical level, "Women's Lib" argued that liberation sometimes required leaving the past behind, and in this respect immigration to Costa Rica was perceived as an opportunity, not a setback, if met with conscious awareness and taken as an occasion to do "gender work." Yet the column did not acknowledge the significant intersections of gender with other categories, most notably ethnicity and class. So, for example, there was no acknowledgement that traveling was usually the prerogative of the nationally, economically, and ethnically privileged, and that the lives of U.S. American women in Costa Rica were shaped by such privileges. In a column titled "Exploding Some Myths about Men and Women," the writer challenged the traditional division of labor in the family, asking, "Is 'domesticity' really a woman's domain, by nature? . . . Is there any reason why domesticity—care of the house your man inhabits with you—can't be shared too?"[91] This column received offensive responses from U.S. American male readers. What was missing, however, is the acknowledgment of the prevalence of domestic help in the homes of U.S. Americans in Costa Rica, which allowed these women to free themselves of domestic tasks by employing other women of a lower class and different ethnicity. This use of domestic help was emancipating but also challenged their call for sisterhood and equality, a fundamental tension that the "Women's Lib" columns did not address. Unlike Ortiz's columns, which at least acknowledged the means by which U.S. American women in Costa Rica gained their domestic emancipation, the 1970s writing in the *TT* turned a blind eye to this dynamic.[92]

The importance of immigration and travel in the process of women's emancipation was another recurring theme in the *TT* columns and articles. Such pieces had also been common in the paper's first period of publication, when it featured, for example, the travelogue "Central America on a Shoe String," written by a Canadian couple who crossed the Americas on bicycles in the late 1950s. But whereas the travel writing of that decade had invariably depicted the travelers as ultimately returning to their home and familiar routines, and whereas 1950s columns like Ortiz's had stressed the hazards that immigration posed to the U.S. American family and especially to motherhood, the articles of the 1970s presented immigration and travel as a crucial component of the hoped-for female emancipation.[93] The story of Linda Vaccariello, a young single mother from California traveling in Central America with a fellow single mother and their toddlers, was featured in a *TT* article titled "Young Moms Find Adventure on Trip" (it is unclear if the double meaning of this wording was intended). The two women depicted their adventures in the Mexican desert and among the indigenous population in Guatemala, where they described an incident in which they rescued a peasant from the hands of a robber. "Everybody was afraid of him [the robber]," Vaccariello recounted, "nobody wanted to do anything, so we did." Her description suggests both a challenging of traditional gender roles, insofar as it is the young women who boldly take action in a situation of physical menace, but also a confirmation of gender roles insofar as Vaccariello depicts herself and her friend as empathic and compassionate U.S. American women and mothers who rushed to the help of the weak in Central America. In a special column of "Women's Lib and You," Vaccariello stated, "We left, more determined than ever to break the chains of society that bind women to home and hearth, depriving them of even the smallest adventures so common to men . . . We have taken a peek and there is no turning back. Women can argue for those things that were rightly ours for centuries, but it is only by our actions, bold as they may seem at the time, that we are able to change the world. And we will."[94]

Such rousing texts in the *TT* were read in the context of other U.S. American feminist activities that were adapted to Costa Rica, such as the consciousness-raising groups that sprang up in the Central Valley in the early 1970s. Although inspired by similar groups in the United States, the gender work performed in them focused on the adoption of the ideas of the U.S. women's liberation movement within the context of the everyday lives of expat women in Costa

Rica.⁹⁵ Barbara Eigen and her husband, Eric, former New York artists who left the United States in 1970 because of their objection to U.S. foreign policies, ran two such consciousness-raising groups, she for women and he for men, in the San José area. Barbara taught pottery at the University of Costa Rica, worked in her studio in Escazú, and penned the column "Women Here and Now" in the *TT*. In a 1974 interview with her in the *TT*, she said that she was highly familiar with feminist activities in the United States and with U.S. legislation regarding women, despite living abroad for several years. She described herself as a member of the women's liberation movement and talked about her consciousness-raising group, which consisted of twelve women, of whom ten were U.S. American, one was British, and one Australian.⁹⁶ In our correspondence, Eigen recalled that the discussions were a kind of general gender work with a special emphasis on the intersection of gender and immigration, with the women discussing their feelings regarding life in Costa Rica. "One woman in the group was in Costa Rica because of her husband's job. She had left her job in the United States for him. She felt directionless in Costa Rica. We talked about what role she could find for herself."⁹⁷

Another member of the group, Leila Khan, was a U.S. American woman who arrived in Costa Rica with her husband in 1972. She vividly recalled that Eigen "pushed and pushed the idea that our husbands could take care of themselves and that we should take care of our own selves and have our own work and own income. Topics included sex, cooking, child-raising, money, and each person told her own story. It was the most amazing thing to learn that I was responsible for my own life. What a concept!"⁹⁸ Khan testified that the group triggered profound changes in the lives of its members: several of them got divorced, others, including herself, went back to school, or got a job.⁹⁹

Eigen, Khan, and Dyer described a feminist discourse and range of feminist activities directed at U.S. American women, or in any case at English-speaking women. They had no contact with Costa Rican women's or feminist organizations, such as the older La Liga Feminista Costarricense or the Movimiento para Liberación de la Mujer, established in 1974.¹⁰⁰ When the *TT* covered a feminist parade in San José, the tone was nostalgic and subtly patronizing, in another manifestation of the narrative of transition that viewed non-European territories or those outside North America as situated in an earlier stage of development: "For observers who remember the dawn of the women's liberation movement in the U.S in the late 60s, a recent rally by the Movimiento para Liberación de la Mujer had a familiar air."[101] Dyer stressed that while they did believe that U.S. American feminist ideas suited Costa Rican women as well, their "missionary zeal" was directed not at them but rather at the English-speaking milieu. Freed from, or even objecting to, Cold War rhetoric, the U.S. American feminists of the 1970s in Costa Rica saw no need to serve Costa Rican society or even affiliate themselves with it.

From Women's Club to Women's Lib: Transnational Gendered Spaces in Costa Rica

The identity work of U.S. American women in Costa Rica, which to a large extent was gender work, was considered in this chapter through two lenses—the transnational one, namely the importation of discourses and practices of femininity from the United States and their implementation and adaptation to the lives of U.S. American women in Costa Rica; and the notion of service to various agents and purposes. These two perspectives bring into clear focus the evolution of various models of the cultural entity of U.S. American women in Costa Rica.

As I emphasized at the beginning of the chapter, this cultural entity was neither fixed nor singular. U.S. American women who arrived in Costa Rica from the 1950s to the 1970s brought with them diverse gendered repertoires, shaped by their ethnicity and class and inspired by the radical changes in the status of women and the gendered role assigned to them in the United States during this period. These repertoires then encountered the various modes of life available to U.S. American women in Costa Rica. While initially perceived by many of these women as a chance to break free of the patriarchal frameworks of home, immigration proved to be a more complex experience, and the reality of their new lives often forced them to find means to preserve their sense of self in the face of these changes.

It is interesting to note the dominant place that the United States occupied in the gender work of U.S. American women, even after several decades of living in Costa Rica. The women's club members constructed their identities as U.S. American women abroad around the notion of service to the interests of their homeland, which also enabled them to carve a significant space for themselves in the Costa Rican public sphere and the U.S. American community of the Central Valley. The persona of the "Pretty American" assumed by many of these women attests to the critical role gender came to play in the enactment of U.S. power in the Cold War era as well as the way in which the gendered identifications of U.S. Americans in Costa Rica, both individual and collective, were shaped by this power. However, it was this very notion of service, the "obligation" of the U.S. American woman abroad, as club member Fay Dresner described it in 1959, that carried the seeds of resistance and enabled the development of the struggle against the local version of the U.S. feminine mystique. The changes in domestic arrangements, most notably the leisure granted by the availability of domestic help, compensated in some respects for the inability to work outside the home and created the cultural identity of the U.S. American woman of leisure, which drew harsh backlash in the public arena of the local U.S. American community, as expressed in the widely read *TT*.

The United States, and the *TT*, also played a critical role in the feminist thinking of U.S. American women in 1970s Costa Rica, the metaphorical (and in the case of *TT* editor Dery Dyer also biological) daughters of the women's club generation. While many of them opted to leave the United States due to their resistance to its policies and mainstream society values, their social and cultural spaces, both the refashioned *TT* and the various consciousness-raising groups, were similar to the women's club in their creation of transnational gendered spaces in which the U.S. American mentality and values could be adapted to the Costa Rican reality, and in which the ongoing negotiation of the correct way of "becoming" a U.S. American women in Costa Rica took place.

five

Material Culture on the Move
Things and Meanings between the United States and Costa Rica

> We have all the luxuries of life—orchards, roses-moonlight-quiet and such—we just don't have the necessities.
> —ELSIE MAE FIALA, letter to her family in the United States, 1956

"Look at this house—can you make it out?" Larry Washington pointed toward the darkness on a night drive through Escazú, a small village near San José that, ever since the 1950s, has been popular among U.S. Americans in Costa Rica. Washington, the son of U.S. Americans who arrived in Costa Rica in the 1960s, has lived in the country on and off since childhood and knew many of the U.S. Americans who passed through it. "It was constructed in the 1950s by a U.S. American missionary from Colorado, who built himself an Aspen-style ski chalet," he explained. "Rumor has it that upon his return to Colorado he built a Costa Rican hacienda over there."[1]

The night was too dark to glimpse the chalet constructed by the homesick Coloradan missionary in temperate-zone Costa Rica, let alone to inspect its interior, filled with furniture and ornaments imported from Colorado, or the U.S. American dishes being prepared in the kitchen at the time the missionary lived there. But I could nonetheless grasp the tension inherent between the house, the place in which it was situated, and the place it was supposed to resemble or represent, because it was a friction common in the dwellings and household possessions of many U.S. Americans in

Costa Rica. In this respect, the dwellings of U.S. Americans in Costa Rica were, as Alison Blunt and Robyn Dowling described dwellings of immigrants in another context, "a lived place and a spatial imaginary," which represented, shaped, and reproduced the discourses, everyday practices, and material cultures of individuals, nation, and empire.[2]

"In a commodified world," argues Leora Auslander, "people may understand themselves to be more truly represented by their things than by their elected representatives. People exist through their things."[3] Benson and O'Reilly further suggest that "the physical building, the interior design, the furnishing, the objects that make home are significant in understanding belonging in that they draw attention to the ways in which consumption, identity, and belonging are co-constructed."[4] This tendency is even more pronounced in the material cultures of people on the move. Tracing the "social life" of the things and objects that U.S. American immigrants brought with them from home, imported later on, adopted in Costa Rica, or constantly longed for will thus enable us to examine such processes of identity work as they were performed and communicated.[5] Through the houses in which they lived, the things that filled these homes, and the foods they produced and consumed, U.S. Americans in Costa Rica both constituted and represented their identifications vis-à-vis the United States and Costa Rica alike.[6] In this regard, practices related to homemaking were transnational in nature, as they were anchored in and transcended one or more nation-states and involved political, economic, social, and cultural processes. Originating in the United States and adapted to life in Costa Rica, these practices formed a crucial component of the U.S. Americans' emplacement in their new country of residence, a means by which they created a place-based identity as well as the "production of locality," which Erin Tylor defined as "the development of a relatively bounded material environment and the objectification of social relations within it."[7]

For most U.S. Americans, the move from the United States to Costa Rica was perceived as one from an affluent society to a place of shortage and lack and, in another manifestation of the narrative of transition, these immigrants often depicted Costa Rica as a place lagging anywhere from fifty to several hundred years behind the

United States in terms of its material culture. However, what Costa Rica supposedly lacked in "culture" it more than made up for in its abundance of "nature." In this respect, material culture served as another manifestation of the mapping of the culture/nature dichotomy onto the perceived differences between the United States versus Costa Rica. The natural beauty and lush surroundings of Costa Rica, as Michael Janoschka and Heiko Haas argued in respect to the significance of the beauty of natural surroundings, was, among lifestyle or affluent immigrants, yet another commodity consumed as part of their identity-making.[8]

The distinct material cultures created by U.S. Americans in Costa Rica were the result of the encounter between their personal background, period of immigration, and place of residence in Costa Rica. Differentiated by class, gender, ethnicities, and other biographical aspects, they all brought with them various repertoires of material culture and habitus related to the value of things in general and U.S. American things in particular. For instance, many of those who arrived during the 1950s were born in the 1920s and 1930s. Their childhood was overshadowed by the Great Depression and their young adulthood by World War II; many of them thus cherished the material affluence of postwar United States and were reluctant to leave it behind. For some of these immigrants, who were mostly white, middle-class, and young, the lack of domestic appliances and relative modesty of material objects in Costa Rica was experienced as a threat to self-perceptions that had been shaped by their class, gender, and ethnic identifications.[9] However, from the late 1960s on, this material lack was experienced by many U.S. American immigrants to Costa Rica as a welcome emancipation from the burden and even constraints of U.S. American consumer society and as an appreciated return to a more simple, primal lifestyle. Once in Costa Rica, the immigrants' choice of where to settle—particularly the Central Valley versus the rain forests and beachfronts—also expressed a particular positioning along the spectrum of nature versus culture and created distinct practices and self-perceptions that were further embedded in the choice of the things they acquired, used, and cherished.

The notions and practices related to domestic material culture also had an explicit gendered dimension insofar as they occupy a significant place in the interviews given by women, while male informants paid it little to no attention. The design of the home and consumption for the home were generally constructed as the responsibility of the (house)wife. In the context of the 1950s and 1960s affluent U.S. society, some scholars view the design of home and consumption of articles for domestic use as signifiers of the Feminine Mystique, as women were restricted to the domestic sphere, as well as a way to overcome the housewife's marginality and discontent.[10] Based on the writings and oral histories of U.S. American women in Costa Rica, it appears that they were intensely preoccupied with issues of clothes and cooking—as a practical necessity but also as a key component in their identity work with respect to the intersecting categories of nationality, class, gender, and ethnicity.

Bricolages: New People in Makeshift Homes

In the folklore of many cultures, the home serves as a metaphor for the human body and analogies are drawn between its various parts and the body's organs.[11] Indeed, serving as a sort of a larger, second body, the home is modified over time to reflect the changes in one's own identity. In many cases, architecture and patterns of dwelling not only reflect the perceived nature of the individuals who inhabit these spaces but are extended to include their larger society and culture as a whole. Early in the Cold War, an article in *House Beautiful* noted, somewhat myopically, that "our houses are all on one level, like our class structure."[12] Following World War II, the suburban U.S. American house became a symbol of the quintessential U.S. American dream and the fortress of the U.S. American family against the threats of communism and nuclear war, as well as serving as the material emblem of the virtues of capitalism.[13]

For immigrants, the home might carry special significance, as it becomes one of the main arenas in which processes of identity-making vis-à-vis both the homeland and the new country of residence take place, both cognitively and materially. Ahmed et al. suggest that "affective qualities of home, and the work of memory in their making cannot be divorced from the more concrete materialities of rooms, objects, rituals, borders and forms of transport that are bound up in so many processes of uprooting and regrouping."[14] The dislocation of the home involved in immigration is therefore dual: in addition to the physical translocation of material objects—furniture, artifacts, and food stuff—the process of creating new homes in a new country also involves a transformation of the immigrant's *ideas* regarding houses and domesticity, which undergo a process of reevaluation in the new country of residence and adaptation to the their new circumstances.

Contrary to the importance accorded in the United States to stable homes, a certain type of dwelling of U.S. Americans in Costa Rica reflected a preference for transience and precariousness. This preference goes beyond the natural conditions of immigration and attests to a deeper reasoning in respect to the importance of a permanent home, thus reflecting the U.S. American's identity work through homemaking (or refraining from it). Such was the inclination, for instance, of U.S. Americans who chose to retire in Costa Rica. For example, Ben Burnett was the author of the popular TT column "On Jungle Trails and Tropical Tales," in which he recounted his many adventures working for the United Fruit Company in early twentieth-century Central America. Despite living in Costa Rica for several decades, Burnett chose to reside permanently in Pensión Morazán, a three-story guesthouse in the center of San José favored by U.S. American travelers. In doing so he was hearkening back to the romantic figure of the post–World War I U.S. expats, such as Ernest Hemingway, who resided in pensions throughout Europe and whose legendary lifestyle invested this choice with a bohemian aura. In a 1956 column titled "Peace and Plenty Found in Pensión," Burnett applied the notion of plenty, which played a key role in shaping the postwar U.S. American society and national character, to his own transient dwelling in Costa Rica. He argued that it is precisely the transitory nature of his lifestyle and the lack of material possessions, especially the lack of home ownership and his consequent guest status both in the pension and in Costa Rica, that provided him with the sense of plenty, both materially and spiritually. Following a description of Costa Rica's many charms, he concluded by stressing the economic gap between the United States and Costa Rica that facilitated his sense of relative luxury in a country where the strong U.S. dollar went a much longer way than back home: "Add it all, and in my book it spells mighty pleasant living. And I get it all for just $60 a month. Can you beat it up there in Texas or in Nebraska?"[15]

Another transient lifestyle evolved in the early 1950s as U.S. Americans and other nationalities arrived by their boats and anchored along the beachfronts of the Pacific Ocean, living on and off the water. Among the first of these was Tom Clairmont (mentioned in chapter 2, as one of the first foreign settlers in the Osa Peninsula), a native of Akron, Ohio, and a former U.S. Marine and World War II veteran. In 1951, after no longer being able to finance repairs on his ship, Clairmont "revved up his engines full speed and made a spectacular permanent beach landing at Playa Cacao, where he staked his claim to fame."[16] Clairmont built a hamlet from the ship's debris and lived in the ruins of his former shattered U.S. military world, like Christopher Columbus's sailors taking shelter in the remains of their ruined *Santa María*. Later on, he surrounded his new compound with thatched-roof ranchos, a dwelling common to Costa Rica's rural areas, creating a material bricolage that reflected a mental one. In the coming decades, this compound was home to Clairmont, his Costa Rican wife, their children, and various transient Costa Ricans and foreigners, most of whom were U.S. American runaways and dropouts who were attracted to this hybrid dwelling and lifestyle (fig. 14).

Another style of housing imported, literally and culturally, from the United States, was the trailer home, a reflection of the culture of transience of many young U.S. Americans. In 1974 there were eight trailer parks in San José, and their residents were mostly U.S. Americans whom the *TT* described as "in flight from [a] civilized scene"—a scene that included, inter alia, permanent, fixed housing.[17] The presence of so many trailers and their inhabitants was bemoaned by some U.S. Americans in Costa Rica as a symptom of the excessive "Americanization" of the country.[18] Even these trailers, however, the hallmark of the U.S. American fixation with driving in general and its youth culture of drifting in particular, were combined in Costa Rica with local materials and cultures of dwelling, creating hybrid patterns of living.

Jane and Michael Warren, originally from Boston, arrived in Costa Rica in 1971. They first rented a trailer from another U.S. American,

Fig. 14. The compound of Tom Clairmont (Captain Tom) in Playa Cacao, 1973, built from the wreck of his submarine chaser and palm branches. Photograph by Rick Berg. Courtesy of the TT.

which they parked in his backyard, and eventually bought a coffee farm that included a large rancho (a wooden hut or an open-sided shelter, with a thatched roof) in the Central Valley. Under the rancho the Warrens put up a large U.S. military tent they had brought with them from the United States, under which they and their two small children then lived for two years.[19] Sometimes hybrid dwellings of this type made use of the remains of earlier layers of U.S. presence in the country as well as their colonial influence in other places. June Eliot, for example, was a graduate student in the Department of Anthropology at Berkeley University; while in Manuel Antonio in 1974 to conduct fieldwork on pre-Columbian cultures in the region, she was housed in a bungalow in Quepos that had previously belonged to the United Fruit Company, which had already abandoned its activity in the region. The typical UFC bungalow was built according to the pattern of the living quarters of U.S. American officials in the Panama Canal, a style that in turn resembled the British living quarters in Bengal.[20] Eliot and her husband moved into this bungalow, parking the trailer they had driven down from the United States in the yard. There it stood, perhaps serving as a reminder of their origin and a mark of their cultural identification as former 1960s young West Coast U.S. Americans, and maybe also a symbol of the fact that they could always go back home (though they never did return to the United States).[21]

U.S. Americans in Casas Ticas:
Space and Identity in Permanent Housing

Still, transient and makeshift dwelling, whether in a boat, a pension, a trailer, or a tent, was in most cases a passing phase in the annals of the U.S. Americans in Costa Rica. Most of them eventually built or rented permanent homes. In this shift to stable housing, they again combined their U.S. American preconceptions regarding domesticity and material culture with local materials and conceptions to create a hybrid dwelling and equally hybrid identifications.

The most common type of housing in Costa Rican towns and established villages, known as a *Casa Tica* (Tico House), was a single-family one-story structure that usually consisted of a hallway, two bedrooms, and a kitchen. The windows were small and few, and the exterior was painted in bright colors.[22] In much the same way that U.S. Americans viewed Costa Rica and the Costa Ricans as small in size ("It was a Liliputian [*sic*] city, it seemed to us, and we, the Gullivers in red flannel shirts, riding it down," remarked the U.S. general and politician Thomas Francis Meagher upon his entrance to San José in 1859), they regarded the traditional Casa Tica as unsuited to their cultural habits and perceptions of individual space.[23] Joan Stevens arrived in Costa Rica in 1967 as an agricultural instructor. Working in agrarian communities to the southeast of San José, she boarded with local families, often sharing a room with their daughters. Even though Stevens had herself grown up in modest circumstances in a rural Mid-Western community, she was startled by the tightness of space in the tico houses, which she attributed not only to local families' economic status but also to "their concept of space [that] was much different from what we in the States have."[24]

The houses that U.S. Americans built or rented were much bigger, reflecting both their economic status and their cultural perceptions about what constitutes an appropriate standard of living. These latter included, for example, the division of living quarters according to age, gender, and status in the family and the inclusion of electrical appliances as an integral part of modern living. A typical ad in the monthly bulletin of the U.S. American women's club offered "beautiful, modern house in Piedades, Santa Ana. Large, split-level living-dining, three bedrooms, two bathrooms, kitchen with icebox, servants' quarter with bath. Good water (hot-cold). Swimming pool—garden. $150 a month," thus highlighting the standards that these women required in a home—aesthetics, modernity, sanitation, various amenities (hot water was rare in Costa Rican homes at the time), and luxuries.[25] Housing for the live-in maid was also a common feature in the homes of many U.S. Americans regardless of their economic status, reflecting their upward mobility in Costa Rica due to the low cost of living, whereas among Costa Ricans it was found only in the homes of the well-to-do.[26]

U.S. Americans who settled the rain forests and the beachfronts lived closer to the locals in term of their lifestyle and houses. In many cases their first house in Costa Rica was a rancho that served for living and cooking. Toilets and showers were constructed outside the rancho. Yet for most of these U.S. Americans the rancho was only a temporary phase, which they disdained and from which they were careful to distinguish themselves. Darryl Cole Christensen, who in 1953 established his farm in southern Costa Rica, first lived in a small grass-thatched shack but soon constructed a home—and stressed the difference between the two dwellings: "We have made a structure upon the land. This is not a rancho; it is a dirt-floor, aluminum-sided cabin with corrugated aluminum roofing."[27] The Quakers who in 1953 established Monteverde first lived in tents they had brought over from the United States, and later in thatched-roof "shacks," as they called them, which were similar to ranchos. The different patterns of living that prevailed in the colony reflected the settlers' economic status—the wealthier they were, the more their homes resembled houses in the United States. Though they rejected the United States politically and ideologically to the point of exiling themselves from it, they continued to subscribe to the hierarchies and conceptions of U.S. material culture regarding what counts as modern and appropriate living. A U.S. American visitor to Costa Rica confirmed this inclination: "They lived in comfortable modern surroundings in their former homes and they are determined to have them in Monteverde ... Some of the homes are finished to the point of entirely modern living ... Others are still in the 'first unit' stage, and a few of the families continue in the patched-up native houses that were on hand when they bought it."[28]

The narrative of bringing civilization and modernization to Costa Rica, which prevailed among U.S. Americans in other fields, also applied to their attitude toward the local material culture and was a significant part of their identity work as agents of such progress.[29] Describing their changing living arrangements, the Quakers themselves identified a process of evolution from "first unit" Costa Rican style homes to "entirely modern living" in the U.S. American sense, and in the same spirit of their material civilizing mission they took credit for the region's broader shift from the thatched roof to corrugated iron.[30] Elsie Fiala—who, to recall, settled on a farm in southern Costa Rica in 1956—wrote in a letter home that her family was living in a log hut (emblematic of the homes constructed by the early settlers of the American West) and not a rancho, thereby attributing to herself the iconic habitat of the U.S. frontier and casting herself as a pioneer rather than a U.S. American "going native." Her bedroom was so tiny that she and her husband had to sleep in a bunk bed. The toilets and shower were located outside the house, as in the houses of the local campesinos. But Fiala wrote to her family in Iowa that the house was "cute," especially since she had put up her pink café curtains, to which her brother-in-law responded, "Civilization has arrived, pink curtains in the jungle."[31]

Yet many of the U.S. Americans who arrived in Costa Rica during the 1960s and 1970s aspired neither to recreate their U.S. American houses nor to bring civilization to the jungle. On the contrary, a critical part of their identity work through the process of homemaking was to take a communal way of life, which some of them had already experienced in the United States, to another level of simplicity, by adopting the Costa Rican campesino style of dwelling and therefore ostensibly recreating themselves as modest and native. Eileen Steinberg, who was among the founders of a commune in Orosí, southwest of the Central Valley, recalled that in 1969, the commune's first year in Costa Rica, "we lived, all of us, twelve people, in a tiny, tiny shack. There was no electricity, no running water. This house was so old, they sealed the walls by using cow shit between the cracks."[32] The commune later moved to another location, in Copey de Dota, south of San José, where the members built seven ranchos. The houses resembled the style of the campesinos, but in addition to the ranchos the commune members put up various other types of structures reflecting their personal histories, so that the compound as a whole looked like a veritable bricolage of items. So, for example, a Vietnamese mud hut was put up by a commune member who, according to Steinberg, had returned from the Vietnam War "eternally defeated." In between the ranchos and the Vietnamese hut, the members built a steam bath, in which they bathed naked, combining a hippie way of life with the practical need to keep warm in the cold weather of Costa Rica's Cerro de Muerte.

The members of another U.S. commune, who in Los Angeles had lived together in a big house, bought property in Uvita, on the southern Pacific coast, and created their own version of the local rancho. Sharon Hage, who was among the founders of the commune, recalled that they constructed five A-frame structures with a thatched roof and sleeping platforms up on stilts ("It was 35 dollars, complete, including materials and labor [per house]"), but "with no back and no front."[33] The huts were a replica of the rancho, but more sophisticated in their shape and aesthetic. In addition, the members also built a large thatched-roof communal building. Theodor Roszak has argued that these counterculture communes represented a pioneering type of utopia that aspired to create a new way of life, including new family patterns, living arrangements, sexual codes, and moral values.[34] The two communes, in Copey de Dota and in Uvita, indeed challenged the norms of privacy and the division of the housework according to gender and class roles that were significant characteristics of the bourgeois home. They also challenged the notion of the home as a reflection of social hierarchy: while both communes had a leader, all the houses, including those of the leaders, were identical. They also emphasized, especially in Uvita, direct access to the natural surroundings. The A-frame ranchos had no walls, affording direct contact with the outside world. This closeness was a critical aspect of the members' identity work as urbanite U.S. Americans who were purified and born again in Costa Rican nature.

Going back to the metaphor of the home as a large, second body that is repeatedly modified to reflect changes in one's economic, cultural, and mental situation, U.S. Americans in Costa Rica often moved from one house to another. These changes reflected the shifting identity work over the course of their lives and makes manifest that the process of homemaking was not necessarily a statement of belonging and engagement but could also be understood as a declaration of total alienation. Jon Marañón, who settled on the southern Pacific coast of Costa Rica in 1971, lived first in a *choza*—a dirt floor hut, with bamboo walls and a corrugate iron roof—together with a local family who owned the property that he would later purchase; he then moved to a nearby town, where he lived in a typical tico house; and, finally, having grown to become a wealthy property owner, he built his own house on his farm. The house reflected his lack of integration and sense of alienation from both the United States and Costa Rica, as Marañón remarked: "I failed to adapt or keep up with modern Western civilization, and that was fine with me," adding, however, that he was also "no longer so bothered by the idea of living in a house much nicer than those of the employees' families and neighbors, no longer burdened with so much gringo-in-the-Third World guilt."[35]

Memory-Based Inventories: What U.S. Americans Brought, Adopted, and Yearned For

Objects and things, as Amanda Vickery has pointed out, create a landscape.[36] The creation of such landscape is a dialectic process: moving from the United States to Costa Rica, U.S. American immigrants brought with them things that would remind them of their former surroundings, habits, and mindsets and enable them to sustain such identifications in Costa Rica while also choosing those habits and things that they opted to leave behind. Long after the actual move, I tried to trace these things through memory-based inventories recounted by the immigrants. Yet given the reconstructed nature of memory, and the significance of objects as a means for self-representation, these inventories must be treated with caution.

Specifically, they are to be read as attesting not to the actual possessions of the people recalling the inventories but to the things these people remembered having brought from the United States and to those things they chose to mention in discussing their possessions, thus serving as markers of their identity.

Mary Thompson, a native of Massachusetts, arrived in Costa Rica in 1951 with her Costa Rican husband. Almost sixty years later, she clearly recalled the day they uploaded a Swedish sofa and chairs onto a UFC vessel that traveled from Boston to Puerto Limón, Costa Rica. Swedish design was considered modern and sophisticated, and by emphasizing the pedigree of the furniture Thompson was seeking to market herself as modern and sophisticated as well. It also shows her desire to sustain this characterization and self-representation in her adoptive country.

However, the difference in material culture between the United States and Costa Rica challenged the immigrants' self-perceptions with regards to lifestyle, gender, and class. When Anna Fredrikson, who had worked as a secretary in a Hollywood film studio, arrived in San José in 1951 with her Costa Rican husband whom she had met in the United States, she brought along a cutting-edge wardrobe, including several suits from Christian Dior's New Look that was famous for its long skirts. But the San José apartment that her husband's family had rented for the couple could not accommodate such a style of dressing. In her interview, Fredrikson, like Stevens before her, stressed the narrowness of the Costa Rican houses and their lack of amenities, which she thus felt were inappropriate for the lifestyle of U.S. Americans. "They have rented a little house for us and they didn't have closets, they had wardrobes. My height—I'm five foot seven and a quarter. . . . So I put my clothes in the wardrobe and they all doubled up at the bottom."[37] Comment's like Fredrikson's about her height, suggesting that she was "too big" or "too much" for Costa Rica, recurred often in the narratives of U.S. Americans in Costa Rica. Moreover, Fredrikson's frustration at her inability to properly store her Christian Dior sets, designed for the "new woman," attests to a sense shared by many U.S. American women that they could not be themselves in Costa Rica, that is, they could not be the modern woman they had been in the United States.[38]

Closets, then, possessed what Auslander termed a "communicative capacity," that is, the ability to generate meaning through their use; in this case, to encapsulate a difference between being a woman in the United States and being one in Costa Rica.[39] As such, they became one of the "things that matter" for U.S. Americans in Costa Rica, in the sense described by Daniel Miller: objects whose symbolic value surpassed their practical use not just on the individual level, where many personal objects carry symbolic meaning, but in their ability to express a broader difference between cultures and hence to mark an identity.[40]

The sense of traveling back in time due to the differences in material culture was felt most explicitly through the absence of electrical home appliances. These "white appliances," as they were called after their color, were sometimes also dubbed "electric servants" due to their ability to substitute human labor.[41] In U.S. households, the ownership of refrigerators soared from 44 percent in 1940 to 80 percent in 1950 and was associated closely with such individual and collective identity markers as modernity, capitalism, and patriotism. Commercials urging U.S. Americans to buy washing machines, electric irons, refrigerators, and electric stoves cast these home appliances as constitutive of the way of life for which the country's soldiers had fought. In postwar United States, consumption for the family home was defined as a patriotic and even socially responsible act. "Family status must improve: It should buy more for itself to better the living of others," stated *Life Magazine* in 1947.[42] The houses in Levittown, a suburb constructed in New York in the late 1940s that became the model for all those to follow, were all equipped with a refrigerator, an electric stove, and a washing machine. This soon became the new standard and in the process altered long-held practices of consumption by creating new possibilities for cooking and eating and thus new practices and markers of identity for U.S. American men and especially women.[43] The new appliances were imbued, moreover, with political significance and symbolic meaning vis-à-vis the Cold War, in which the electronically outfitted home overseen by its expert female homemaker became a key marker of U.S. superiority.[44]

The material culture of post–World War II Costa Rica, however, could not sustain this identity work. John Campbell, a Quaker who arrived in San José in 1950, noted that due to low voltage, even those houses that had a refrigerator were required to use a generator to operate it, and most still made due with just an ice box.[45] As late as 1973, only 30 percent of Costa Rican households owned a refrigerator.[46] These appliances thus came to represent the difference between the modern United States and backward Costa Rica, and moreover, the difference between the housewife and the practices of homemaking in the two countries. Upon realizing that these appliances were absent in 1950s Costa Rica, one U.S. American woman recalled feeling as if she had been cast back to the Stone Age and, refusing to be romantic about this retreat in time, she said, "It was primitive, not pristine."[47] The prevalence of domestic help compensated somewhat for the lack of appliances, so that in practice it was usually the local help who did most of the manual work in the home.[48] Nevertheless, for many the sense of being denied the advantages of modern housekeeping along with the difficulties of managing domestic staff ended up generating not a sense of upward mobility but rather of frustration, negatively affecting the self-perception of many U.S. American women in Costa Rica as modern, affluent, and professional.

But the significance of the home appliances was not just symbolic. They provided a physical distancing of human beings from nature by enabling the sterilization of foods and the maintenance of body hygiene. For the U.S. Americans in Costa Rica they provided a buffer against a way of life they perceived as too close to nature and ensured what they considered as a higher degree of civilization, which facilitated their self-perception as civilized, modern people and enabled them to approximate the lives they had led in the United States. It is not surprising, then, that owning a refrigerator, often by buying surpluses from the UFC compounds, became an obsession among U.S. Americans in Costa Rica, as in many other countries.[49] Conversely, learning to manage without one enabled U.S. American women to reflect on the way of life they had left behind and assert their evolution into a new self. Fiala wrote to her family that she was doing "surprisingly well" without a refrigerator and described how she sanitized her food stuff by hanging it all on a hook next to her open-fire stove, as the locals did.[50] This sense of accomplishment notwithstanding, sixteen months later she proudly reported in a letter that she was now the owner of a refrigerator.[51]

Washing machines were similarly embedded with both practical and symbolic significance. Just as the refrigerator maintains the hygiene of the food that enters the body, so the washing machine promotes the hygiene of its surface. Concerning the cleanliness of clothes, including intimate items such as underwear and bedding, laundry has traditionally been positioned at the intersection of the public and private spheres, embedded with perceptions about dignity, cleanliness, purity, and morality.[52] Unlike the work of the refrigerator, the labor of the washing machine could be executed manually, but such work was demanding, and many U.S. American women considered it beneath someone of their social class and indeed of their ethnicity.[53] Even Fiala, who was quite comfortable without a refrigerator, complained about her "sore hands" and drew the line of manual work at hand-laundering, "because washing clothes on the rock—no, no." The practical hardship of washing clothes by hand and the consequential symbolic threat to a significant symbol of her femininity—soft hands—led Fiala to expend enormous effort to transfer her washing machine from Iowa to her Costa Rican farm.[54]

Jane Mora, originally from a small town in California, arrived in San José in 1967. She was the young bride of a Costa Rican man from an elite family. But despite the couple's financial stability, their apartment in San José was not equipped with a washing machine, evidence of the difference between the standards of middle-class homes in the United States versus those of elite Costa Rican homes.

> I said, "Let's go to a laundromat," because we couldn't afford the washing machine, which for me was unbelievable because a washing machine in LA was just like having a napkin. . . . And he [her husband] said, "We don't have laundromats." I said, "What do you mean you don't have laundromats?" He said, "Look, you have the *pila de lavar*" [Spanish for big cement sinks, used in both private homes and public sites near rivers and streams to do laundry by hand]. I said, "No, you've got to be kidding . . . I can't wash like that." So I put all the clothes

in a bag and I said, "Take me to the laundromat, enough with this, I need to do the laundry, it's just not funny." ... So he drove me to a place near Desamparados on the side of the road where there were hundreds of *pila de lavash* and that was where the people wash, and I remember sitting there crying, thinking what have I got myself into.[55]

Mora's husband may not have known that laundromats actually did operate in San José at the time. An ad in the *TT* encouraged the U.S. American housewives: "Don't let the rain dampen your spirits or your clothes. Bring both to the automatic laundry."[56] Nonetheless, experiences of the kind described by Mora, Fiala, and Fredrikson further confirmed the women's view that Costa Rica was a backward place in which they could not sustain their gender- and class-related self-perceptions as professional homemakers with soft hands and machines to do their manual labor. They could not be themselves without their "things" and had to develop new selves—to keep the new women's look in the closet or become a woman of nature.

The television was another item that became a symbol of U.S. consumer society and an identity marker for U.S. Americans in Costa Rica. While some enthusiastically endorsed television in order to affiliate themselves with the prime medium of U.S. popular culture, technology, and modernity, there were also those who rejected it for the very same reasons. Elizabeth Harris, a U.S. American woman who has lived in Costa Rica since 1944, recalled her first encounter with a television set during a visit to the United States in the early 1950s. "I remember going to Milwaukee and being in the living room and all of a sudden I saw a television. It was the first time I had seen a television, and my son, of course, was absolutely fascinated with it."[57] She immediately bought the appliance, which President Nixon had depicted in the famous Kitchen Debate as the U.S. answer to the Soviet space race, and brought it back to Costa Rica, where she was able to watch a single Costa Rican channel.[58] Joyce Brown remembered that her parents brought a TV on one of their visits from the United States, and the family, which owned a farm on the South Atlantic coast, used to plug it into the tractor engine and watch the Costa Rican channel.[59] By contrast, in an 1973 article in the *TT* about Jerry Wolf, a U.S retiree, he stated that his home is fully equipped "U.S. style," except for a TV, which the family "detest[s]."[60] Eric White, who led an alternative counterculture lifestyle in a small village in the Central Valley, recalled that in the 1970s theirs was the only house on their street that did not have a TV.[61] The absence of a television was described by Lisa Wilson, who arrived in Costa Rica in 1978 and lived in a remote farm in Santa Maria de Dota, as one of her motivations for living in Costa Rica and not in the United States.[62]

Libraries and Pianos: The Longing for and Disenchantment with U.S. Things

Beyond furniture and home appliances, it was the various small items that U.S. Americans remembered bringing with them, or asked relatives to send to them, that were constitutive for their identity work and creation of their new selves. The parents of young Jane Mora sent her, at her request, ten packages of toilet paper as a birthday present because, as she said, it was "very hard here, very rough," leaving it unclear if by these words she referred to the toilet paper or to life in general in Costa Rica.[63] But when the package arrived she could not afford to pay the ten dollar duty and had to forgo the delivery—evidence of the high price, both monetary and symbolic, of the attempt to maintain a U.S. material lifestyle in Costa Rica. Joyce Brown, who arrived in the early 1970s, remembered that when she returned from her annual visits to the United States she used to bring as many as thirteen suitcases, filled with "everything"—clothes, food, and even things that in her homeland were considered disposable, like her mother-in-law's old rugs, which she rescued from the garbage.[64]

Brown's remarks attest to her sense of shortage and lack in Costa Rica but also to her growing ambivalence about U.S. consumer society. Like other U.S. Americans, she testified that after spending several years in Costa Rica she experienced a kind of culture shock during visits to the United States: "Who needs so many types of toothpaste and biscuits?" she recalled wondering to herself.[65] The move to Costa Rica, especially from the 1970s onward, was experienced by many U.S. Americans as a liberation from U.S. consumerism and materialism. Alongside those who tried to bring "everything" to Costa Rica, and thus maintain their former selves, others tried to leave "everything," material and otherwise, behind. The latter group can be regarded in a sense as expats of U.S. consumer society. Many of these immigrants were affiliated, at least in spirit, with the counterculture movement, and in particular purported to reject U.S. material culture. Their passage stories typically begin with a scene of getting rid of their belongings in the United States, including selling houses, cars, and other material objects, an act that was partly a purification of sorts, designed to signify that they were leaving their materialistic selves behind. In the same spirit of ambivalence that characterized the move from the United States to Costa Rica, however, this act was itself also economically beneficial, with the sales providing the financial means for the immigrants' future life in Costa Rica as nonmaterialistic people. In fact it often made the already existing economic gap between them and the Costa Ricans even bigger. Tracing the memory-based inventories of immigrants of this type, who portrayed themselves as antimaterialists, reveals what was in fact an explicitly material culture—only of a different type. These immigrants typically traveled to Costa Rica by car or minivan, packed with what they perceived as their cultural necessities—not the "white appliances" of the U.S. bourgeois suburban home but "books and tapes . . . the music that was going on, . . . a stereo system," as Sharon Hage recalled.[66] Theodor Bart, another member of the Uvita commune, recalled bringing his "books, art supplies—papers, paints, colored pencils, typewriter, paper to write with, fabrics, that was about it."[67] The commune members used the battery of their Land Rover to operate their stereo and play classical music. Strewn with statues and other art objects made by its members, the rain forest commune came to look, in the words of a visitor many years later, "like some bizarre Fellini set stuck in the middle of the jungle."[68]

Books, serving both as a cultural object capable of expressing self-perceptions and cultural hierarchies, as well as being highly sentimental objects, were mentioned in almost every personal and institutional inventory of U.S. Americans in Costa Rica. U.S. social clubs, churches, and schools served as arenas for the exchange of books, alongside the U.S.-Costa Rican Cultural Center and several

English-speaking bookstores in San José. Still, the constant sense of want for English-language books prevailed, especially outside the Central Valley. One woman who arrived in 1977 stated that the only things she missed throughout her life in the Costa Rican rain forests were "libraries and pianos."[69] Books also served to educate the local population, as part of the role that U.S. individuals and organizations saw for themselves in Costa Rica and as a way to legitimize their presence and gain acceptance. U.S. Americans were engaged in the distribution of English-language books through organizations such as the U.S. Women's Club and through individual initiatives like the library that Jon Marañón hosted in his Uvita farm, which held books and issues of *National Geographic*. The women's club, however, did not keep a library because of the club's lack of a permanent residence, and Marañón closed his after twelve years, disappointed by the lack of interest on the part of his local employees and disillusioned about his ability to serve as a cultural agent.[70]

Two other items that played a significant role in the identity work through material objects of U.S. Americans in Costa Rica were typewriters and sewing machines. Clothes in Costa Rica were perceived by U.S. American women as either too small for their size or unsuited to their style. This drove many of them to sew their own clothes and sometimes also that of their children. Sewing class was among the most popular activities at the women's club, and the widespread use of this practice was yet another manifestation of the differences between the United States and Costa Rica. Whereas in the States clothes were mass produced, branded, and purchased readymade, in Costa Rica they often had to be made from scratch, a difference in cultural practices that impacted self-perceptions and echoed the sense that life in Costa Rica, and the country itself, was unmodern, lagging years behind the United States. Dery Dyer remembered that one of the first things her mother did when Dery enrolled in a boarding school in the United States was to take her shopping at a department store in New York, where she asked the salesperson to "give her all the latest clothes," because, as Dyer recounted, "we were just about five years behind the trend . . . we were wearing clothes that they stopped wearing five years ago."[71]

Whereas sewing machines were associated mostly with women, typewriters were used by both sexes. Their popularity was due partly to the migratory status of the U.S. Americans, which prompted them to write letters to the United States regularly, but also to their self-perception as living extraordinary, even bohemian, lives that were worth writing about. Connected to art rather than to administration, typewriters prevailed in the homes of counterculture U.S. Americans such as Theodor Bart, who had personally carried his typewriter over from the United States when he moved to the beach commune of Uvita, or a woman who lived in a rancho in the remote settlement of Nosara, who declared that her complete possessions amounted to four Arab horses, a lamp, and a typewriter.[72]

The only local artifacts mentioned in the textual realm and oral testimonies of U.S. Americans in Costa Rica are related to natural sources and to the pre-Columbian past, not to modern Costa Rican material culture. U.S. American settlers in the rain forests boasted about turning parts of the local natural environment into symbolic and monetary commodities that they then sent to the United States as evidence of their "exotic" lives or tamed and brought into the home as an ornament. Fiala sent to her Iowan family slides of wild animals found on her farm, and for her own home she had a rug made of the skin of a tiger hunted on her property and skinned by her, boasting in her letter that "its teeth were just huge and its skin is really pretty."[73] Pre-Columbian ceramics, which were widely discovered and excavated in the properties of U.S. American settlers in southern Costa Rica, served both as yet more proof of the exotic life they were living and as a source of income. The Fialases, for example, offered grave-digging safaris for tourists and sold pre-Columbian relics in antiquity stores in San José.[74]

From Hamburgers to Iguanas:
Creating Hybrid Culinary Repertoires

An entire world, Roland Barthes argued, is presented in and signified by food.[75] In the case of immigration, food is even more significant, not only on the proclaimed or symbolic level but also thanks to its sensual capacity. Food links taste, smell, and memory and both recalled for the immigrants their relationship to the memory of home and helped them to either reestablish a sense of being "at home" or constitute new homes in their new countries.[76] Trundle argues that "cooking and eating became a metaphor for individual and community transformation, from unknowing and unconnected outsiders into knowledgeable and relationally embedded people."[77] Like immigrants in other places, U.S. Americans in Costa Rica used food as a key component in their identity work, a means by which individual and collective identities were constituted and represented. Through food-related practices, moreover, they marked power relations between their homeland and adoptive country, signified social, cultural, and economic hierarchies between themselves and Costa Ricans and between different types of U.S. Americans, confirmed as well as undermined gender roles, and expressed their position vis-à-vis such notions as modernity and nature, progress, and health.

The term "food" as I use it here designates many things. It has to do with practices of gathering food, whether by buying or through agriculture; with repertoires of cooking and specific dishes; with the creation of a cuisine and the definition of taste; and with practices of preparation and eating embedded in cultural, socioeconomic, and religious circumstances. It also has to do with the products and dishes themselves, some of which became—to paraphrase Miller's term—"foodstuff that matters": foodstuff and dishes that took on sentimental value and became a symbol of hierarchies of power that originated in the geopolitical realm but were expressed in terms of taste.[78]

The hybrid culinary repertoires that U.S. Americans forged in Costa Rica were the result of the encounter between their version of various U.S. kitchens and Costa Rican cuisine—the local foodstuffs, methods of preparation, and dishes. Culinarily, the passage to Costa Rica was experienced as yet another manifestation of the reversal—whether welcome or unwelcome—from modernity to an earlier period. Broadly defined, post–World War II U.S. cuisine included more and more processed food, such as frozen or canned meat and vegetables, which at the time was imbued with a modern and scientific aura.[79] By contrast, the Costa Rican cuisine in those years was still based largely on raw, unprocessed, and nonbranded products. In this respect, food represented another continuum of difference and hierarchies of power between the United States, which represented Culture (since its food was processed, hence not "natural," and formed part of a system of mass production, marketing, advertising, and branding) and Costa Rica, the locus of Nature (with positive connotations, such as purity, and negative ones, such as uncleanliness and a lack of sophistication). A U.S. American woman who lived in a small village on the southern Pacific coast depicted these differences as the passage from branded hamburgers to fried iguanas.[80] This sense of going back to nature, back, in other words, to basic, was expressed repeatedly in the interviews with U.S. Americans, primarily the women (given that the crossing of national borders was not generally accompanied by a change in the gendered role of food preparation), who recounted—either with grumbling, astonishment, and even occasionally joy—how in Costa Rica they had to cook "everything from scratch."

As with other aspects of the material culture of U.S. Americans in Costa Rica, the particular nature of the culinary repertoire they created was the result of many factors, including their ethnic background and former lifestyle in the United States, their economic status, the period of their arrival, and their place of residence in Costa Rica, which on a practical level determined their access to the U.S. market (either because they brought it back with them from the United States or had it imported), versus proximity to local markets and people.

In the first year of its establishment in the early 1950s, the Quaker colony in Monteverde was rather isolated and thus reliant on the Costa Ricans from nearby communities, from whom the U.S. American newcomers learned and adopted culinary practices. The colony subsisted on the produce the settlers grew in their vegetable gardens and whatever they collected from the natural surroundings. In "What Did We Find to Feed the family," Dorothy Rockwell, who was among the founders of the colony, described how she and the other women "adapted" the recipes they knew from their homes in the U.S. American Deep South to what they could grow in Costa Rica. This included, for instance, the root vegetable aricache (which Rockwell mistakenly dubbed artichoke) and chamol, a root the Quakers used as a substitute for potato, which the heavy ground of the rain forest could not produce. Each family had several hens (an important livestock in the Costa Rican household and one that was typically the domain of women, in contrast to the masculine task of herding cattle) as the main source of meat.[81] Lucille (Lucky) Guindon, another founder of Monteverde, wrote under the title "Frugality" that hens' eggs were too expensive to buy, so if her hens did not provide enough eggs she would often substitute with eggs of wild jungle birds. Taking her diet further and further away from the cultural products to the natural ones, she described herself as "a woman of nature."[82] But old tastes die hard, and as apples were not native in Costa Rica, the Quaker women yearned for substitutes for their applesauce and cakes, especially around Christmas time. After experimenting with guavas and green mangos, they eventually used the most common vegetable in the Costa Rican kitchen, chayote, to make a "mock apple pie." In 1954 the Quakers opened a milk plant and cheese factory, which became so famous it was touted by the Costa Rican Tourist Institute (ICT) as one of Costa Rican's national symbols, next to the ornamented oxcart. Yet in their accounts, none of the Quaker women relate to milk or milk products as important ingredients in their kitchen.[83] "With green things in our freezer and lard in our kettle we do very well. Luxury items are things like peanut butter or crackers," concluded Guindon.[84] Additionally, the food served in the Quakers' public sphere was a culinary hybridization that expressed the merging of the U.S. and Costa Rican simple, peasant cuisine. New Year's Eve dinner was the most important meal of the year, and in 1954 the menu included "fixed roast turkey & chicken (neither very big), cloverleaf rolls, cottage cheese & salad (cabbage) & dill pickles, a big pan of Mashed chamol & furnished raisins for the pie. Janice took green beans & made 4 mince-meat pies which were delicious [sic]."[85]

Fiala, whose farm was in southern Costa Rica, combined products grown on the farm with supplies from the remote capital, which she exchanged with her "Indian neighbors." Although stating "Oh I'm really going native" when writing to her family in Iowa about the food she buys and eats, she clearly drew the line at making tortillas, which she claimed was too exhausting and was perhaps also associated too closely with indigenous food and culture.[86] Instead she baked yeast bread and cakes and reported that hers was the only family in the region that ate such pastries. She recounted how when she brought the fresh pastry to the farm's commissary, "the little thin children of the employees" would chase her and cry in Spanish "*pan, pan*" (bread), a description that reflects her self-perception of cultural hierarchies of taste as well as her alienation from the local culture.[87] Gradually, as the Fialases' economic situation declined and they could no longer afford to keep back their cattle for their own use, and as they became increasingly comfortable in their new surroundings, the family came to depend more and more on game meat from animals they hunted in the forest, such as wild turkeys and tepezcuintle (lowland paca), a large rodent whose white meat was considered a luxury. Fiala then combined that meat with canned macaroni and cheese and canned tuna that she received from her family in the United States.

Rather than a constraint, as it was experienced in the 1950s, self-sustainment and back-to-nature culinary repertoires were perceived as an ideal by the U.S. Americans who settled in Costa Rica's beachfronts and rain forests some twenty years later. Some of them were familiar with this disposition from their lives in communes back in the United States. Barbara Williams, who lived on an isolated farm on the remote Costa Rican Osa Peninsula, ordered plant seeds via mail from the *Whole Earth Catalog*, which was published in the United States and popular among counterculturists all over the world.[88] In addition to the seeds that were imported from the United States and planted in Costa Rica, the recipes for dishes made from these products were brought along as well. The menu of a commune of U.S. Americans in southern Costa Rica in the early 1970s reflected their incorporation of native ingredients into 1970s Californian counterculture cuisine.[89] Just as the huts they built were a refashioning of the local rancho, so their cuisine was a refashioning of the rural Costa Rican kitchen, which they perceived as dull, with the counterculture's taste for Asian exoticism and return to traditional cooking methods. The local ingredients, especially the quest to obtain them in the rain forest under the guidance of locals, as well as the process of transforming them from their raw state into sophisticated dishes, were part of their practices of emplacement in their new place of residence and a crucial part of their identity work as people who are reborn in nature. Sharon Hage explained how searching for the natural ingredients in the rain forest (rather than buying them) and cooking them became part of their self-forging, connecting them to the local environment and people but at the same time also setting them apart:

> We cooked more exotically, we liked to make curries and Chinese cooking and salads and nice desserts made with coconuts and cacao and fish and the roots and stews . . . Learning *how* to cook by going out and digging up roots and picking fruits from the trees and opening up a coconut and making coconut cream out of it and learning how to process cacao into chocolate and learning all the different leaves and things that live in the jungle and making a beautiful meal out of it, well, we were very creative . . . It was back to basics but it was also very magical, very very magical.[90]

Liquor and Brown Rice: Food Stuff That Matters

Contrary to the U.S. Americans in the rain forests and on the beachfronts, those in the metropolitan area of San José obtained their food from the local shops and markets, which were however very different from the shops and markets they knew in the United States. By the late 1950s, supermarkets had achieved hegemonic status in the U.S. American consumer culture and become yet another symbol of the superiority of this lifestyle over the Soviet one. The supermarket was a large, open-spaced building detached from its surroundings, whose interior featured bright lighting, background music, and air conditioning that eliminated odors and all noise from the outdoors. It offered a great variety of products, most of them packaged and prepped to some extent: even meat was presliced and, in many cases, frozen, and the fresh produce came packed. The supermarket's fixed prices and method of self-service also minimized contact with employees, while the use of credit cards minimized the visibility of money. The shift from daily shopping to a big weekly supermarket shop entailed long-term planning, which became, in its regularity, yet another component in the identity-making of the U.S. American housewife as a professional and efficient homemaker.[91]

The shopping experience in Costa Rica was very different and entailed a new type of identity work for the transported U.S. American housewife. An indoor market was established in San José as early as 1880, but its method of shopping and density were those of an open market, and since the closed space held pungent odors from the food stalls, the experience of shopping there was in some respects even more odorous than an open-air market. The purchase of fruits and vegetables was done in special outdoor markets, *ferias*, which operated on Saturdays. For small purchases there was the *pulpería*, a cross between a stall and a grocery store, which Costa Rican writers have described as the heart of Costa Rican national culture but also as a space that encouraged the consumption of alcohol and idleness.[92] The shopping experience in Costa Rica, then, was much more dispersed and involved direct contact with local settings that were otherwise off the beaten path of many U.S. American women. It also brought them into contact with people—both sellers and fellow shoppers—that were outside their regular social milieu. Like laundry, for U.S. Americans in Costa Rica buying food for their families became an activity that moved from the indoors to the outdoors and brought them into contact with their new surroundings that was not always welcomed.

Furthermore, for many U.S. American women the markets were seen as primitive, dirty, carnal places that were diametrically opposed to the sterile environment of the U.S. American supermarket. Instead of reaching for aesthetic and neatly packaged portions of meat, they were thrust into close contact with freshly slaughtered, or soon to be slaughtered, animals. The Costa Rican market was thus not only an old-fashioned method of shopping but also called to mind hunting and the primal struggle for food-gathering. U.S. American anthropologist Dennison Nash, who wrote about a similar experience among U.S. American female shoppers in 1960s Barcelona, pointed to the anxiety that local markets aroused among the women, who felt that they were already far distant from such a struggle.[93] The crowds and the noise, the rubbing of bodies against each other, and the experience of coming in direct contact with the carcasses were all perceived by the women as deviations from their familiar gender and class codes and thus were indeed a source of stress.

Anna Fredrikson, who arrived in Costa Rica in 1951 with her Costa Rican husband, used to go to the market with her sister-in-law, who tutored her on becoming a Costa Rican homemaker. "I hated all the crowds, I hated all the people, I hated everything, and one woman was going to hit me because I let my umbrella drip on her neck. And I said, this is it, no more market for me."[94] After that incident, Fredrikson, like many of her compatriots, began sending her maid to the market, though she reported that she constantly suspected that the maid was cheating her.

In addition to shopping in the local shops and markets, U.S. Americans imported desired products from the United States. Items mentioned frequently in their writings and oral histories were the desired peanut butter and chocolate chips cookies, as well as gefilte fish, a staple of the Jewish-Polish kitchen, thus attesting to the diverse identifications and ethnicities of U.S. Americans in Costa Rica. Traditional holiday foods, such as apples at Christmas and turkeys at Thanksgiving, were also sought after. In the days leading up to the Thanksgiving holiday of 1956, the *TT* reported that six hundred turkeys were flown in from the United States.[95] Some brought the turkeys in themselves to make sure they could keep up with the U.S. tradition outside of the United States. Sue Pardo, who arrived in Costa Rica in 1969, recounted, "At that time you couldn't, you really couldn't get turkeys here . . . So I carried my turkey in my carry-on bag, and only once did I have a problem when the plane was diverted because of Hurricane Mitch and we had to spend the night in a hotel in Panama and I said I need a big bucket full of ice for my turkey and I got it and it was fine."[96]

Another type of "foodstuff that matters" for U.S. Americans was alcohol, which was embedded with national and gendered meanings. From 1850 the Costa Rican government has exercised a monopoly over both locally made and imported liquor.[97] Thus, significantly, the fact that the U.S. embassy's commissary was selling duty-free U.S. branded liquor to a certain social milieu during the 1950s and 1960s served to both reflect and create a gap between U.S. Americans and locals, while enhancing the stratification among U.S. Americans in Costa Rica. An anonymous letter to the editor (signed "Observer") published in the *TT* in 1956 called for an examination of several aspects of the lives of U.S. Americans in San José, including "the complex of the commissary; low priced liquor and the physical, moral, and social effect of its increased consumption."[98] A U.S. American man who had been in Costa Rica since the early 1970s suddenly declared toward the end of our interview, "Of course, I'm a recovering alcoholic," adding that "most of the gringos who come to Costa Rica are heavy drinkers, or become ones the longer they live here." He also related that following his rehabilitation he felt compelled to protect his sobriety by changing his social milieu.[99]

The consumption of liquor by U.S. Americans in Costa Rica also carried gendered implications. A humoristic feuilleton, published in 1959 in the *TT*'s "Lady Talk" and signed "Lili," depicted the inner monologue of a U.S. American woman during a miserable dinner party:

Just one more drink will help me drown the memory
Of the pudding that was laced with pink cement
Though nothing can dispel the dark suspicion
That the thing was made with criminal intent.

It was, the author noted, only thanks to the drinking that she "didn't shoot while Billy wiped his sticky fingers / On me and the Christian Dior I bought last week"; and more broadly it was only the drinking that got her through the social obligations of the U.S. American expat society. She concluded:

What to say! Well—their whisky was my life-line
So before they realize that I'm a louse
Just a line to tell you both deeply
I admire the lovely SPIRIT of this house.[100]

Intentionally or by chance, the recipe published alongside the feuilleton in the "Lady Talk" section was for "Chicken with Brandy," accompanied, as always, by a Spanish translation so that the maid could prepare the dish.[101] U.S. American women's habit of social drinking, an accepted and acceptable practice in the United States as well as a coping strategy in their transition to their new country of residence, was perceived differently outside their homeland and set them apart from the local culture, where women were not allowed in the local cantinas and women drinking in public was socially taboo until as late as the closing decades of the twentieth century.[102] As a result, although U.S. American women were accorded more freedom in this respect than their Costa Rican peers, they, and their compatriots in other countries, were sometimes stigmatized as drinkers and even alcoholics.[103]

Another foodstuff that mattered, albeit very differently, to the self-perception of a certain segment of U.S. Americans in Costa Rica was "health food." The sense of deficiency and privation caused by a lack of canned, processed, or branded food in the 1950s was, in the 1970s, felt with respect to items and ingredients associated with the new craze for health-conscious cuisine. While Costa Rican food was considered natural, it was different from the dishes and brands of U.S. counterculture cuisine. Some U.S. Americans started to make these foods themselves. The Tussey family, who lived in San Ramón de Tres Ríos on the outskirts of San José, opened a granola factory called The Stuff of Life, and the smell of baking granola gave the street the colloquial name "La calle de la granola" (the street of granola).[104] Other U.S. counterculturists futilely sought soybeans in the market of Cartago and brown rice in the *pulperías* as a way of maintaining their habits and, more importantly, their self-perceptions. Julie Woodman, who arrived in Costa Rica in 1972, remembers thinking, "It was like, 'There's no brown rice in this country, what are we doing here?'" and recounts a trip she and her partner took to obtain a bag of brown rice directly from a rice factory: "They told us, 'But that's just for the pigs.' We said, 'We don't care, we want it.' So he sold us a huge sack of brown rice, with all of the hard shell. It was a nightmare trying to clean and cook that rice and it was very poor quality, so you know, we started getting a little looser with our standards and cooperating with white rice and beans."[105] Woodman depicts the process of gradually relaxing her alternative U.S. American diet and surrendering to the local diet of rice and beans, or *gallo pinto*, which is considered a Costa Rican national dish, as evidence of cultural adaptation.[106]

Enclaves of Cream Cakes and Apples: The Preservation of Cultural Identification

Alongside the hybrid repertoires that combined U.S. American and Costa Rican foods and methods of preparation, there were also more defined spaces in which U.S. American food was consumed as part of the participants' identity work. One such culinary enclave was the Fourth of July picnic, held annually in San José from 1951 on. While the event's entertainment included a ride in an ornamented Costa Rican oxcart handled by two Costa Rican men in traditional costume, the menu was based on iconic U.S. American dishes such as hotdogs, hamburgers, ice cream, soft drinks, and beer. In 1975 donuts, cotton candy, peanuts, and popcorn were added. Mary Thompson, who arrived in Costa Rica in 1951, testified that while she normally distanced herself from her compatriots because she perceived them as too "Republican," at the Fourth of July picnic she could be found behind the counter, "being one with them and serving hot dogs with them."[107]

Despite her aversion to the United States and the U.S. American community in Costa Rica, in her own home Thompson kept to the culinary repertoire she had grown up on in the northeastern United States during the Great Depression. "I had *The Joy of Cooking* and I wrote all the recipes out in Spanish . . . They [the cooks] had to read the recipes and learn to do it on their own."[108] Bilingual recipes were published in the *TT*—the only text in the paper that appeared in Spanish—so that the maids could learn how to make macaroni and cheese or brownies for the U.S. American families. The recipes were typically sent in by the readers, but in 1956 a special column was dedicated to recipes from Pan American Airways, reflecting the cosmopolitanism of a specific segment of U.S. Americans in San José at that time.

U.S. American institutions for children and women usually had a typical U.S. American menu. So, for example, the cafeterias in the English-speaking schools in the Central Valley served milkshakes, hamburgers, and fries, and no Costa Rican dishes.[109] Among the members of the U.S. Women's Club, rituals concerning food were a significant part of their identity work and a means of both self-constitution and self-representation. Since the club was perceived, like many similar women's clubs abroad, as a home away from both the national and individual home, intense debates over refreshments revealed conflicting traditions of hospitality, and in particular the conflict between the preservation of culinary repertoires from home versus assimilation in the new country of residence. In this particular conflict, preservation effectively prevailed when the members chose to keep the menu at the monthly "business meetings" and the annual luncheon purely U.S. American (though this cuisine itself is a mixture of the many traditions that make up the migrant society of the United States) mixed together with the ingredients and products available in Costa Rica. Thus, at the annual luncheon of 1978 the menu included "Russian Salad, Mixed Salad, Vegetable Salad, Roast Chicken, Veal Goulash, Cake Bread, Roast Pork, Roast Beef, Ham, Stuffed Fish, Rice, Coffee, Wine."[110]

The club's public events were not the only arena of food preparation and eating, as the organization published several collections of recipes, contributed by the members. The purpose was to raise funds for charity, but the books also tightened contacts between the members through the exchange of recipes and cooking methods, and in addition, by articulating norms for "correct" cooking and home management. They also functioned as a means for the club members' self-expression and representation both as individuals and as a collective.[111] The recipe collections of the U.S. Women's Club reflect the members' varied culinary backgrounds and their attempt to preserve this diverse U.S. American cuisine in Costa Rica; here too the recipes appeared in Spanish so as to be accessible to Costa Rican members of the club, thereby including them in the culinary culture of the U.S. American members, as well as to the member's maids. This allowed the women to impart their knowledge and assure the preparation of the desired cuisine in their homes, without crossing national, ethnic, and cultural boundaries.[112] Published from the 1960s onward, the women's club collections of recipes also reflect the club members' aspiration to see themselves as part of changing trends in U.S. American and international cooking, as well as of international perceptions of femininity.

The first book published by the club was *Embassy Row Specialties* (1963), which reflected the culinary repertoires of the wives of diplomats, women who followed their husbands' careers across the globe and cooked U.S. food in various geographies—or, more commonly, supervised its cooking. The second book, titled *Postres / Desserts* (note that Spanish precedes English), was dedicated to sweets, a culinary domain that has been historically gendered as feminine (fig. 15).[113] The members of the women's club expressed a strong attachment to sweets and complained when the cream cakes, which were not common in Costa Rican cuisine but had been the hallmark of the meetings' refreshments, and a highly gendered dish, were discontinued after the club's president chided its members for their "sticky fingers" and "not enough help to clean the mess."[114] The book's inclusion of a recipe for Steamed Apple Pudding / *Pudín de manzana al vapor* is intriguing, as apples were rare in Costa Rica. It implies that the women had access to imported ingredients, or rather attests to their longing for the flavors of home and the book's role in the preservation of these culinary traditions rather than being simply a practical cooking guide. The next book (1975), which was filled with salad recipes, further highlighted the alienation of U.S. American women from Costa Rican cuisine, which made very little use of fresh vegetables. The fourth book was also published in 1975 and dedicated to casseroles (fig 16). Its opening text, in English and Spanish, informed the readers of the changes taking place in the United States with respect to household management, in particular the decline in domestic help and the rise in women's participation in the work force that had generated new modes of home management and models of femininity. While the readers did not necessarily experience these changes, they were made to feel part of these trends through the club's cookbooks. In 2007 the club published a retrospective collection of member recipes since its establishment in 1940 (fig. 17).[115] The book features typical U.S. American ingredients and dishes, such as broccoli and chicken salad, but unlike the club's previous books it does offer a nod to the local cuisine, perhaps due to the increased number of English-speaking Costa Rican members. Yet there is no chayote or other Costa Rican roots here, as there was in the culinary repertoire of the Quaker women

Fig. 15. Cover of WCCR recipe book, *Postres / Desserts*. Courtesy of the Women's Club of Costa Rica.

Fig. 16. Cover of WCCR recipe book, *Casseroles*. Courtesy of the Women's Club of Costa Rica.

Fig. 17. Cover of WCCR recipe book, *Kitchen Pleasures*. Courtesy of the Women's Club of Costa Rica.

in the 1950s, and the one recipe that is based on black beans is accompanied by saffron rice, a kind of sophisticated version of the *gallo pinto*. Not only is Costa Rican cuisine largely absent from the book but so are trends in U.S. American cuisine, such as the Asian influence on counterculture cooking or the embrace of French cooking in the 1970s. Read as both a personal and cultural text, the cookbooks of the women's club seem like a time capsule of sorts, storing rich information about what was perceived as classic U.S. American taste and cooking—and the longing for U.S. American foods—in Costa Rica.

Identity-Making and Self-Representation through Things

Through the "things that matter" to them, whether large (such as houses and furniture) or small (such as books, typewriters, and even toilet paper), and the practices related to such things, U.S. Americans in Costa Rica constituted and represented their identifications in that country and emplaced themselves in it. The daily choices that U.S. Americans made, whether by choice or through a lack of choice, of which things to use and which foods and beverages to consume, expressed the meticulous fashioning of identity that marked the coordinates of their hybrid identities along the continuum between the United States and Costa Rica and their affiliation with U.S. Americans or engagement with Costa Ricans. No less important are the things that years later they chose to depict as having been used and been significant. Such objects and things are evidence of transnational belonging, recording past, present, and future lives.[116]

Specific values were attributed to the two poles of this continuum by various populations of U.S. Americans in Costa Rica, but in general the things and foods brought from the United States or resembling those in the United States were considered more modern and representative of a more advanced way of life, whether these things were Christian Dior clothes, refrigerators, or granola. Using them also marked U.S. Americans as tending more strongly to maintain their attachment to the United States. Costa Rican things, on the other hand, were typically perceived as less valuable: the local cuisine was viewed as dull, and the houses small and crowded. The

Costa Rican things considered valuable by U.S. Americans were those associated with nature rather than culture, like fruits or tiger skins. In this respect, material culture represented another domain in which the nature/culture dichotomy was superimposed on that of Costa Rica/United States and employed in the identity work of U.S. Americans in the country.

For some however, the distance and difference from the United States was perceived not as a constraint but as a relief—an opportunity to get away from its material culture and consumer society, and to make "everything from scratch," both materially and mentally. In this process, U.S. Americans in Costa Rica created their own individual and collective identities through their choices regarding material objects by giving up on refrigerators but not washing machines, by constructing sophisticated ranchos, and by making mock apple pie with chayotes instead of apples.

six

Looking Back in Amazement
Negotiating Identities as Privileged Immigrants

> We were really on a spiritual quest;
> this is really what we were here for.
> —SHARON HAGE, author interview

During one of the rainy seasons of the early 1980s, Linda Sheinin and Theodore (Theo) Bart were walking from Sheinin's farm on the southern Pacific shore of Costa Rica to the nearest village, Dominical. Bart, a former fashion designer who had moved from California to Costa Rica with his fellow commune members in 1972, and Sheinin, a former singer from Los Angeles who had arrived there three years later, walked for hours under "big, gigantic rain."[1] After crossing fourteen mud slides, they finally arrived at the beach of Dominical, and Sheinin recalled, "We just sat down on a rock and watched the ocean coming, and the sun was going down. I said, 'Wow, Theo, we weren't kidding, were we? We made that our life. This is not a lark; this is our life.' And he said, 'Yes, this is not a lark; this is life.' That was when I really really really realized. This was years later—maybe, like, ten years later. I said, 'How did this happen? We took off in Hollywood Boulevard and here we are on the beach. Interesting.'"[2]

In this closing chapter I focus on the identity talk of U.S. Americans in Costa Rica—namely, the verbal construction and assertion of personal identities that forms part of the identity work, in order to unpack the discursive and rhetorical means employed by these immigrants, primarily those who were part of or identified with the U.S. American counterculture of the 1960s and 1970s.[3] In considering the ways in which these immigrants retrospectively constructed and gave meaning to their immigration and their lives in the adoptive country, I argue that at the core of their stories lies a narrative of coincidence and happenstance, which in turn supports a sense of innocence and lack of agency on their part. The discrepancy between the widespread image of U.S. Americans in Costa Rica as privileged and indeed their de facto monetary privilege, on the one hand, and their self-depiction as marginal and powerless on the other is at least partly a consequence of the narrators' backgrounds: the formative years of many of them were the 1960s, when some of them had identified with the civil rights and antiwar movements. Many had arrived in Costa Rica because of their opposition to U.S. militarism and the materialist way of life. As Mattew Hayes, who encountered similar narration of passage stories and identity constructions among U.S. Americans in early twenty-first-century Ecuador, argues, it is crucial to understand the extent to which such imaginaries regarding immigration and its narration "reflect North American cultural codes, as well as global social positions."[4] These ethics and practices, combined with the informants' attraction to and submersion in mysticism as part of the counterculture, contributed to the shaping of a narrative of coincidental, unintentional, even magical immigration and settlement. The informants constructed their story as one of embarking on a personal and spiritual quest in search of harmony; they did not see theirs as stories about colonization or immigration taking place under profoundly asymmetrical global power relations.[5] As Sharon Hage conceptualized her and her fellow commune members passage story, "we were really on a spiritual journey; this is what we were here for."[6] Through the identity talk they formed their life stories as tales of coincidence and luck, portraying themselves as "accidental immigrants"; these U.S. counterculturists articulated and perpetuated imperialist narratives while nonetheless depicting themselves as people who had neither intended to be colonists nor been rejected by U.S. society in general or by their immediate surroundings or family in particular, but who just happened to walk down Hollywood Boulevard and then, many years later, found themselves on the beach in Costa Rica. This pattern was most explicit in the life stories of this segment of U.S. counterculturists, but it is present to a certain extent in the life stories of many U.S. Americans in Costa Rica of different backgrounds and periods of immigration. It therefore points to a broader and deeper current or tendency of identity work through life stories, which attests to the social construction of memory, the power of what Alessandro Portelli has termed "communal censorship" and the individual circumstances of remembering from the point of view of the present.[7] Such rhetorical patterns also were related to the way in which U.S. Americans portrayed themselves or positioned themselves in the larger scheme of United States–Latin American relations.

Most of the U.S. American counterculture immigrants who arrived in Costa Rica between the 1950s and 1970s fit the profile of the typical U.S. American emigrant of the second half of the twentieth century: young, college graduate, middle class, white. Since they typically arrived in Costa Rica before establishing themselves as professionals in their homeland—in some cases precisely as a means to avoid such establishment, that is, as a way to escape integration into mainstream U.S. lifestyle—most of them were not wealthy.[8] Yet their symbolic capital (including educational, cultural, and social capital) and their access to the U.S. economy nonetheless gave them a position of privilege relative to most of the Costa Ricans among whom they settled, and this imbalance increased further as the Costa Rican economy deteriorated over the course of the late 1970s. Even U.S. Americans who moved to Costa Rica precisely because of their resistance to U.S. imperial policies, militarism, and materialism still enjoyed privilege because of their U.S. origin. Thus, although in their life stories many of the interviewees expressed a sense of marginality of one sort or another—social, economic, ethnic, sexual (as gays and lesbians), or familial, these immigrants' life stories revealed ways in which their lives in their adopted country were shaped by privilege—a status that the immigrants themselves very rarely acknowledged explicitly. In his essay about the patterns of life stories that U.S. Americans tell—and live by—Dan McAdams argues that "it is through stories that we define who we are" and further suggests that these stories are capable of providing "a better understanding of both the people who tell the stories and the culture within which those stories (and those people) are born"—or in which they lived.⁹ This is what makes these stories so illuminative, on both the individual and collective level, and demonstrates why they are a powerful vehicle for exploring the identity work of U.S immigrants vis-à-vis their position in Costa Rica.

"As Luck Would Have It": The Construction of a Coincidental Passage Story

The act of immigration lies at the core of the life stories of U.S. Americans in Costa Rica, but the interpretation of their stories cannot be limited to the move itself. Immigration is a process that is sometimes conceived many years before it actually happens, and in most cases it reverberates throughout the immigrants' lives and life stories.¹⁰ This is especially true of people whose immigration was a post factum realization, or at least was constructed as such, as in the case of many of the life stories of U.S. Americans featured in this book. Their passage stories are therefore biographical stories, which enables me to situate their immigration within the wider context of their own histories and sociopolitical background. Focusing on key moments in the passage stories of the U.S. Americans to Costa Rica enables me to clearly reveal their construction of their immigration as a case of coincidence and happenstance rather than intention and design.

Many of the interviewees declared that they did not know much about Costa Rica prior to their arrival in the country; indeed, several had confused it with Puerto Rico, the unincorporated U.S. territory. Their accounts create the impression of an adventurous journey and of discovery, sometimes spiritual, more so than a migration story, and as such they highlight the unintentional nature of the move and lack of agency on the part of the immigrants. When I asked Jane and Michael Warren why they arrived in Costa Rica in 1971, Jane replied:

> Oh, I'm not sure you wanna hear this because it's too bizarre. We just had a baby, a baby boy, our second child, and we were out eating breakfast one Sunday morning. And I had wanted to travel for a while, and Mike had a very secure job at the university as a department chairman in Boston, and there was

a possibility that he would be dean next ... And as we were driving, and I was sitting next to him, I said, "Why don't we leave the U.S.," because it was snowing, and he said, "Where do you wanna go?" I said, "I don't know where, but let's think about it." And I asked a friend of ours who was in the back seat of the car to hand me a section of the newspaper, the *Boston Globe*, and he pulled a section of the paper and handed it to me, and when he did that, a piece of paper fell down from the paper into my lap, face up, and it said, "Come to Costa Rica." It was an ad for the beaches of Nosara. They were selling land at the time, but the words that caught my eyes were "Come to Costa Rica," and I said, "Costa Rica—let's go to Costa Rica."[11]

Told on the beautiful porch of the Warrens's home in the forested outskirts of Ciudad Colón, this story sounded like a family myth that had been told over and over again.[12] The Warrens tended to portray their decision as sudden, even impulsive, yet also mystical—just as they were asking themselves where they should go next, a piece of paper fell into their lap, as if from on high, and seemed to call on them to "come to Costa Rica." The manner in which their story unfolded concealed, to a large extent, the more rational explanation behind their move, which was elaborated later on in the interview; it involved family disagreements over homeschooling, political discontent with the Nixon administration, and the yearning for a place that was warmer in all respects. Moreover, the story downplayed the role of power relations on both the global and the individual levels: the Warrens were citizens of a global superpower, emigrating to a country that was part of their homeland's sphere of influence. As young, white, educated professionals (Jane clearly implied that Michael was a rising academic at the Massachusetts Institute of Technology; she was a nurse) resettling in a small, agricultural town in Costa Rica, they possessed economic advantages as well as cultural capital deriving from their U.S. origin. While the Warrens had little to do with the construction of these uneven power relations, they nonetheless benefited from them due to their U.S. citizenship (and to a lesser extent also their racialized whiteness in a country that idolized whiteness). Their story should thus be read as one possible version of an immigration story, one that is designed, to a large extent, to accommodate their awareness of the unequal power relations that were at play from the moment of their immigration, and as a means of self-justification in the face of their established position in the country. The choice of Costa Rica as their destination is presented as impulsive, even arbitrary. Moreover, the narrative suggests that Costa Rica invited them—even tempted them, through an ad—to come, implying a kind of personification of the idea that the United States was an "empire by invitation" whose hegemony over other nations was encouraged by those nations and their citizens.[13]

This pattern of portraying the decision to immigrate to Costa Rica as coincidental and even dictated by fate appears in many 1970s passage stories of U.S. Americans counterculturists. Bart, the fashion designer whose story opened this chapter, had been a member of the same L.A. artists commune mentioned in the narratives of several other interviewees. The commune members, aged twenty to forty, congregated around a charismatic guru and immersed themselves in the study of eastern religions. In 1972, after a year of communal life, Bart and his friends concluded that they could not achieve their desired peace of mind in Los Angeles, or anywhere else in the militaristic and materialistic United States: "And then we decided we could never get our head clear of anything because, you know, we were so downtown Los Angeles, practically. It was L.A. So we said, we have to go someplace quieter, and we said, where would we like to go? And then [we] got out a map with the United States and Mexico and Central America and said, why don't we go there, and they [commune members] just pointed at Costa Rica."

Asked if he or his fellow commune members knew anything about Costa Rica at the time, Bart replied, "Absolutely nothing."[14] The construction of the decision to move and the choice of destination as an impulsive, almost arbitrary act was thus embedded in the U.S. and global counterculture, with its spirit of youth rebellion and its emphasis on self-discovery through disengagement with the comforts of life and careers at home (Michael Warren had supposedly forgone deanery at MIT) in favor of movement, travel, and roaming.[15] This lay the groundwork for a passage story that many years later would be described as an adventure and a mystical event rather than a rational process. Like the Warrens's story of their decision to go to Costa Rica, Bart's story refers to an object outside of himself that supposedly dictated his move—this time not an ad but a map. His narrative similarly implies a lack of agency and disguises the rational thinking behind the choice of destination. However, the choice of a particular map—namely, of Central America—defined the potential space for the commune's getaway. Indeed, later on in the interview it became clear that what was first presented as an arbitrary choice was in fact a rather conscious process of selection; as Bart said, "We did want a place where we could get far from civilization, but still within reach."[16]

Arrival Scenes: Falling in Love and Being Rescued

Arrival scenes are a common convention of travel writing. They depict the very first encounter of the traveler with the new place and the local population, and in many cases they set the tone and terms of future relations.[17] Although usually brief in real time, the arrival scene constitutes an important part of the immigrant's story.[18] Yet precisely because of their pivotal status in the passage story, arrival scenes should be read as carefully crafted stories, constructed and reconstructed over time by their narrators as they experienced life in Costa Rica so as to anticipate these experiences and justify them.

Some arrival scenes described by the interviewees focused on the very moment of arrival. Karen Hill-Webber, a Texan, first arrived in Costa Rica in 1951 to meet the family of her Costa Rican fiancé, whom she had met while he was a cadet at the military academy in San Antonio, Texas. Almost sixty years later, she enthusiastically recounted her first impression of Costa Rica: "I remember there was a favorite song of mine from way back in time, 'Somewhere over the Rainbow.' And this is what I felt when I first arrived in Costa Rica, when I was seventeen years old. This is what it looked like, a place over the rainbow . . . I thought it was a paradise, and it was."[19] The constructed nature of this arrival scene is underscored by the way in which Hill-Webber utilized it in order to express her current feelings toward Costa Rica, concluding her arrival scene with the words, "It was very different from what it is now."[20] However, beyond the depiction of Costa Rica as a place that had once been a paradise but was no longer so—a common theme in both Costa Rican and U.S. American narratives about Costa Rica—what is more significant here is the self-representation of Hill-Webber and her reconstruction of an "accidental migration."[21] Hill-Webber made use of a classic product of U.S. popular culture, *The Wizard of Oz*, to portray herself as a young girl arriving at a marvelous—even transcendental—place, located outside the real world. The movie reference also enhanced the sense of the coincidental: like the innocent, childlike Dorothy, Hill-Webber had never intended to go where she ended up (by following her fiancé) but rather found herself there accidentally.[22] It is interesting to note how Hill-Webber misremembered the film, or misinterpreted it for her own rhetorical needs. In *The Wizard of Oz*, Dorothy is quite scared when she first arrives in Oz. In Hill-Webber's retrospective arrival scene, by contrast, she described herself as immediately acknowledging that she had arrived in paradise, but she also recognizes, at the time of the interview, that this paradise has since vanished.

Some of the stories are redemptive; that is, they present a pattern of fleeing from a threat of death and finding salvation in Costa Rica. Many interviewees spoke of the spiritual stagnation of their lives in the Midwest or the suffocating and cold climate—both human and meteorological—of the Northeast's metropolitan areas. However, as young people during the years of the Vietnam War, literal, physical death, and not just spiritual, was very much present in their lives, and some of them had witnessed actual killing on the battlefields. John Arlington Jr. served as a military photographer in Vietnam and Cambodia. After completing his service, he returned to the United States and then quickly left it again, this time for Mexico. In 1973 he was commissioned by a rich U.S. American heir to document the wildlife in the large tracts of land he had purchased in Costa Rica. Despite coming to Costa Rica for a paid assignment, Arlington's arrival scene, like those of the Warrenses and Bart, is constructed around an alleged mystical message directing him there:

> I got out of Mexico as quickly as I could, and when I arrived in Costa Rica, in the first hour, crossing the border, I got down

on my knees and put my hands in the air and thanked the Lord, because I knew I'd found it. . . . I knew that Costa Rica is the gem of the world; he [God] told me this—he told me in Vietnam. [I asked him,] let me live and get out of there. And I'm here . . . . I volunteered for sixty-seven combat missions in Vietnam—combat, okay? Vietnam and Cambodia . . . . [When I arrived in Costa Rica] I put my hands in the air and said, 'Thank you, God.' There was no military, there were no guns, there were no uniforms.[23]

Arrival scenes are often where the stark contrast between the narrators' former lives and their anticipated new lives is most salient.[24] Arlington reconstructed his scene around the dramatic difference between Vietnam and Cambodia, on the one hand, and Costa Rica on the other. Unlike the Warrens's and Bart's allegedly accidental decision to move to Costa Rica, Arlington's was recounted as a fulfilled prophesy: his arrival was the fulfillment of a promise that God gave him in the midst of the hell of war, about a place that was the antithesis of the South-Asian inferno, and when he arrived at Costa Rica it felt like coming to the right place. It is worth noting that the act of raising his hands in the air in thanks to the Lord for saving his life took place neither upon leaving Vietnam and Cambodia nor upon arriving home in the United States (which Arlington was quick to leave again as he did not want to reintegrate himself into a steady job and family life); rather it was performed, allegedly, when he crossed the border into Costa Rica. Recounting his arrival scene in San José almost forty years after the event, Arlington asserted that it was at that moment that he finally felt safe.

Sometimes the arrival scene is constructed around a life-saving moment. Linda Sheinin arrived in Costa Rica in 1975 with her ex-husband to conduct research for a book she was writing, the story of a young woman from Los Angeles who emigrates to a Central American republic and joins a spiritual commune. In recounting this, Sheinin stressed that, at the time, she had had no intention of immigrating—her research trip was scheduled to last two weeks—yet her narrative reveals the extent to which she did already envision herself as the heroine of a migration story.

Upon her arrival in Costa Rica, she was immediately struck by the country's lush greenery, which stood in sharp contrast to the dry and barren landscape of her hometown: "I was very impressed with the greenery. I was living in Los Angeles; it's very dry there, almost desert. I was so impressed with the lushness, the richness of the country."[25] Soon after arriving, Sheinin and her ex-husband got lost. They had left the metropolitan area of San José in order to reach the village of Dominical on the southern Pacific coast but lost their way, and as darkness fell, had to pull over and spend the night in their car, on the edge of the jungle, along with their material baggage—and their mental one. As Sheinin recalled, when she was a child, "There was a *World Book* [*Encyclopedia*] picture with all the snakes in the world in two pages, and all I could think of that night in the jungle was that the car is gonna be crawling with snakes."[26] As in Hill-Webber's impression of Costa Rica as a paradise, so ubiquitous in respect to this country, here too, in Sheinin's description of her first encounter with the country, the theme of the Garden of Eden recurs, through the lushness of the land, anticipating the potential for a fresh start and rebirth—but this time Eden is also conjured through the menacing image of the snake.[27]

Sheinin and her partner survived the night and eventually reached the Pacific Ocean. "I saw, first of all, beaches that were empty," Sheinin recalled. "It was so nice to see that and so not commercialized. Just pristine beaches, pristine jungles, pristine—everything pristine. The people [were] very, very welcoming."[28] There is an interesting discrepancy in Sheinin's description: on the one hand, the beaches were empty; on the other hand, she met friendly, welcoming natives. Costa Rica's southern seashores were indeed sparsely populated at the time. But her portrayal also follows the convention of travel writing on Latin America, which Sheinin had consumed in its popular versions as a child, in which the people were always overshadowed by the overwhelming natural surroundings.[29]

They went on to Dominical, passing through fourteen streams that crisscrossed the rundown road, with Sheinin stepping out of the car each time to check if they could pass with the car. Finally, they faced the very last stream, which appeared to be shallow. By then, Sheinin was too exhausted to get out of the car again:

And I said, we'll pass it. So the car went in, and it was just like this [gesturing with her hands to demonstrate a steep slope]; it just nose-dived—we sank. We had to get out of the car and everything was floating, the clothes and the food; it was a big mess. And there was the car, with the water up to the hood, and we were sitting on top of the car. We were literally sitting on top of the car. We didn't know what to do, like in shock, and somebody from the restaurant, the Parcella, higher up, saw us with binoculars. They saw a car floating in the river and they came to rescue us. They had to bring a tractor. It took hours to bring a tractor from another town, but they finally pulled the car out. But that was my first impression of Dominical—just floating around with the food and sitting on top of a car, and just putting my hands up in the air like this . . . . The car had to be hauled to San Isidro . . . so we had to stay five days more than we thought we were going to in Dominical, and that is when I fell in love with this place.[30]

A poet and a writer, Sheinin appears to have constructed her arrival scene as a combination of many myths and travel writing conventions, which facilitated her identity work as a new, innocent, and welcome immigrant. Her account includes allusions to the Garden of Eden, as we saw, and descriptions of acts involving water that suggest a symbolic rebirth and call to mind several biblical scenes and religious practices: the "great flood" with the rescued couple floating atop their "ark," the repetitive dipping into streams as in a Christian baptism, and the crossing of the water that allows no return to their previous lives and beyond which lies a promised land. The repeated use of the word "pristine" echoes the common convention in travel writing and colonial discourses of describing the travel across territories as a journey back in time. The traveler comes from the peak of civilization, passes through liminal spaces, such as a jungle and an ocean, and arrives at the heart of pristine nature, a world as yet unpopulated and unadulterated.[31] Sheinin traversed rivers that cut her off from her past and functioned as a test of her courage. Finally, she surrendered to the forces of nature: all her material and symbolic privileges—car, clothes, food—floated away in the water, while she and her ex-husband, like the helpless survivors of a shipwreck, raised their hands in the air, begging for help. Sheinin stresses the fact that she was warmly welcomed by the native population—indeed, they rushed to her rescue. It was among these people that she decided to stay, in what sounds like a "going-native" happy ending. After the recounted incident, Sheinin flew back to the United States to pick up her five-year-old daughter and retrieve some money. She then returned to Costa Rica, where she later married a local man and had another child with him.

The motifs embodied in Sheinin's arrival scene recur in other passage stories and reflect the perception of Costa Rica in the eyes of many of the U.S. American newcomers in the early 1970s as well as the consequent identity work that this perception facilitated. No longer viewed as primitive, as it was in the 1950s, Costa Rica is constructed through the identity talk of these later immigrants as a pristine, natural place where people can leave their former lives behind and where they are reborn.

The arrival scene of Lisa and Mathew Wilson, who arrived in Costa Rica in 1978, is similarly formulated as a story of redemption, constructed around a threat of death followed by salvation and rebirth. The Wilsons left the United States after having suffered what they perceived as severe harassment due to their alternative lifestyle. In recounting their decision Lisa portrayed the United States as a cold, hazardous place: "It was cold but there was also coldness with the people. The police stopped us all the time. . . . I don't know why, maybe [it was] our car, because it wasn't brand new, I'm not sure."[32] The family accepted the invitation of U.S. American friends who were living in Costa Rica. They flew to Panama City and took the Tica bus to San José. However, they missed the bus they had originally intended to take, and instead took the next one. Upon arriving in Costa Rica they learned that the bus they missed had been involved in an accident and most of the passengers had been killed. "So when we came to Costa Rica, it was already like a blessing," Lisa said. She recalled that it was just before dawn when they got off the bus at the Central Station in San José: "The Tica bus went on its way and we were sitting and waiting [to be picked up by their friends]. It was beginning to get a little bit light, it was still dark, and all of a sudden the Tica bus was by again and they gave us the baby bottle. We left the baby bottle on the bus! I mean, we were just enchanted by that, because in the States that would never happen."[33]

Several themes emerge from the four arrival scenes analyzed here, and they are typical of many others. The first is the almost immediate acknowledgement of Costa Rica's physical beauty and especially the emphasis on its pristine and virginal state, perceptions that are closely tied to the potential that the immigrants saw in Costa Rica to better their lives and reinvent themselves. Hill-Webber, Arlington, Sheinin, and Wilson all described falling immediately in love with the country, and all likened it to paradise, which is positioned in contrast to the infernal East Asian battlegrounds or the dry and cold United States.

The narrators all share the tendency to underplay their privileged status vis-à-vis the Costa Ricans. Hill-Webber did so by casting herself as the young, unaware Dorothy from *The Wizard of Oz*. Arlington and Sheinin depicted themselves as survivors who were rescued by Costa Rica and the Costa Ricans (note the shared motif of raising their hands in the air, in gratefulness or in despair), rather than as privileged immigrants arriving from the all-powerful United States to rural Costa Rica. These narratives obscure such facts as that Sheinin was arriving by car in a village that did not even have a single tractor at the time, and Arlington was commissioned for a job by a wealthy U.S. American. In Wilson's narrative, the theme of the baby and the lost bottle connotes helplessness and vulnerability, in the face of which the locals once again come to the rescue. Listening to these reconstructed arrival stories many years later, after the narrators had established themselves in Costa Rica, personally, professionally, and financially, I identify them as part of the speakers' identity talk that allows them to stress their own vulnerability and the Costa Rican's warm hospitality, a dynamic that in turn forms part of a larger scheme of relations in which the U.S. Americans cast themselves vulnerable and harmless. Sheinin and Wilson put special emphasis on the warm attitude of the locals, thereby portraying themselves as welcome guests rather than intruders.[34]

Alongside such elated arrival scenes, a small number of immigrants also described experiencing a culture shock and disappointment upon their arrival. Whereas the excited scenes center on Costa Rica's abundance of natural beauty and human kindness, the negative ones portray it as a place of shortage and lack in infrastructure and material culture, stressing in particular its failure to meet the U.S. Americans' expectations of what Latin America *should be* and *feel like* based on their previous experience or fantasies. William Russell, who arrived in 1966 to work in a publishing house, remembers that San José was "extremely boring" compared to Mexico City, where he had previously stayed, and lacked all the familiar "Latin" components such as mariachi musicians, spicy food, and colonial architecture.[35] Bart, who arrived in 1972, recalled a similar disappointment: "I had expected something on the order of Colonial Peru, for some reason, and San José was not that. I was ready to go back to Los Angeles that very same day."[36] Failing to be sufficiently "exotic" or "Latin," Costa Rica did not seem fit to sustain their desired remaking of themselves as U.S. Americans in Central America.

Going Backward, Moving Forward: The Paradox of Identity Work

The movement in time that U.S. Americans reported experiencing when they moved to Costa Rica took them back to the conquest of the North American West and in some cases as far back as the creation of the world. By emphasizing the pristine and in particular unpopulated state of Costa Rica at the time of their arrival they depicted themselves as old-timers, even pioneers, thereby claiming the right of primogeniture, or at least a moral right to live in the country, against the background of mounting criticism over land purchases by gringos and other foreigners. At the same time, they constructed their identity as agents of progress and civilization in various fields and activities.[37]

Richard Erikson was a student of anthropology and a conscientious objector during the Vietnam War who arrived on the southern Pacific coast of Costa Rica in 1971 in order to survey the threat to the local fishermen's way of life from the large oil-drilling project of a European company. He proudly conceived of himself as a kind of "First Man"—he was among the first non-Costa Ricans to inhabit the coast ("The people here could count the foreigners they had seen on one hand") and the first person to dive underwater off that coast.[38] As he recounts, "It was very primitive here, there were no roads to get in here, but it was very exciting. And I'm a real fan of marine ecology, and marine ecology here was really intact. The marine habitat was full of creatures and they [the marine life] had never seen humans in the water, snorkeling or scuba diving, so for me it was fantastic."[39]

The notions of being primary and novel are applied here both to the land and to Erikson himself. Adopting a narrative that views non-European territories or those outside North America as existing in an earlier stage of evolution, Erikson cast Costa Rica's Pacific Sur as a primeval land.[40] But he also inserted himself into this process of creation: a man before there were men, a primordial being among the creatures of the sea, the very origins of life. Erikson attributed to himself a precious status—that of being among the first foreigners to arrive in this remote area and the first human that went under the water surface. Whether or not he was in fact the first or among the first, he managed to acquire for himself this subjective feeling of pioneership despite being a very "belated traveler," to borrow Ali Behadad's phrase, considering that his arrival in Costa Rica took place in the 1970s.[41] As foreigners, U.S. Americans in many cases also stood out from their local surroundings by virtue of one or more physical attributes, for instance their height, light skin, blond hair—or long hair, which for men was a choice that was also a cultural statement. This sense of being a novelty and being different was rewarding. Sharon Hage described how they had become an attraction to the local population: "They would come visit us and we would serve meals and listen to our stereo—we had a stereo—and just get to know each other. We were the first foreigners that they saw; they were pretty intrigued by us. We were pretty strange to them, so they wanted to know us better. We did enjoy that very much."[42]

The ethnographic gaze is reversed here: in Hage's version, the foreigners are the focus of attraction for the locals.[43] Many U.S. Americans enjoyed this attention, and internalized it as part of their identity work, viewing themselves as interesting, important people making a contribution to Costa Rican culture. Whereas in the United States they had been part of the mainstream, even if it was the mainstream of the counterculture, in Costa Rica they were unique and original. This attention created, especially among the 1970s immigrants, a sense of self-spectacle-ization. Jane and Michael Warren recounted that when they toured Costa Rica in their psychedelically painted Volkswagen, the locals would wave at them and sign a V with their fingers (see chapter 1).[44] Hage and the Warrens also implied that they were contributing culturally to Costa Rica: their respective descriptions of the hippie commune on the outskirts of the fishermen's village of Dominical and of the painted Volkswagen driving along the country's backroads bring to mind classic scenes of Latin American literature depicting the introduction of innovations into remote places. The hippies, with their colorful outfits and long hair, were the gypsies who brought the new trends of U.S. youth culture, fashion, and material culture to the heart of the jungle.[45] There is a paradoxical reconstruction here; the introduction of new culture and modern trends to Costa Rica was depicted, in many cases, as the consequence of the search for a simpler, older way of life. This search prevailed also in the counterculture lifestyle in the United States, but in Costa Rica it was expressed specifically in the tendency to embrace and exalt the local campesino lifestyle.

However, admiration for the simple lifestyle of the campesinos and the beauty of Costa Rica did not eliminate or contradict the ambition of U.S. Americans to improve Costa Rica's culture. Rather, this impulse was perceived as part of the U.S. Americans' identity work as new people in a new country, and for some of them, also as a means of fulfilling the role of civilized missionary—this, in some cases, by people who left the United States precisely because of their disapproval of its politics and culture.[46] Jim Coleman, a therapist from New York, arrived in Costa Rica in 1973 following what he described as a dual disillusionment—with the Nixon administration and with psychotherapy. For three weeks he toured the country, trying in vain to find a way to make a living and considering such occupations as cheese making and strawberry farming. As the day of his return flight drew near, he finally had a moment of inspiration, which he later articulated in a fashion typical of other U.S. Americans' revelation stories:

> I realized that everybody was sitting around on their porches with these rocking chairs that had come from Sarchí [a little town that is the cradle of Costa Rican handicraft.] That was sort of an interesting design and I tried to go over in my mind how I would improve it . . . I had no experience at all. I had never made anything with my hands. I had always been in psychology and my first degree was in biology. But, as luck would have it, I was riding on some bus over in Alajuela and I was thinking about it. And about fifteen minutes after I started thinking about it, I said, My God, that's what I'm gonna do; I'm going to become a furniture maker. Because all of the furniture I've seen down here has just been horrible, and I didn't know anything about wood, but it looks like they have pretty nice wood down here. So I said, yeah, I could do that, I guess. *I didn't have any reason*, but I completely, completely convinced myself within half an hour, and after that I never turned back.[47]

In the thirty-five years since that life-changing bus ride, Coleman has become one of the most famous and successful wood artisans in Costa Rica. As in many of the other passage stories of 1970s immigrants, Coleman's is packed with references to luck, God, and fate, rather than reason and geopolitical or economic power relations. Making an almost complete break with his past, he described a moment of rebirth that was at once personal, cultural, and professional—all thanks to a revelation he experienced during a bus ride.[48] Coleman's wording suggests that his dramatic personal shift of lifestyle and occupation served a greater goal outside of himself—improving Costa Rican furniture, which was "just horrible." Although he had no experience with furniture-making, he believed that by leaving his urban way of life and intellectual profession in New York and becoming a carpenter in Costa Rica, and by bringing tools and knowledge from the United States, he could reinvent both Costa Rican furniture design and himself.

The Acquisition of Land: Magic, Kinship, and Charity

Land purchasing and settlement were common practices among U.S. Americans in Costa Rica. The ways in which they constructed them in retrospect, in their interviews, reflect their ambivalence regarding their role in these land acquisitions, which were sometimes large-scale. The U.S. Americans, who tended to portray themselves as marginal and weak with respect to the move to Costa Rica, and who viewed themselves as opponents of materiality and the capitalist ethos of land ownership, constructed their stories in ways that helped them come to terms with the fact that they themselves had become land owners, sometimes wealthy, in a context of highly asymmetrical geopolitical and economic power. Their identity work was directed not only inward, in the form of inner self-negotiation and self-vindication, but also outward, at the Costa Rican public sphere. Until the mid-1970s, Costa Ricans had generally welcomed the U.S. American immigrants' settlement and perceived it as a desired supplement to the country's ethnic composition and economy.[49] This attitude changed following massive land purchasing by U.S. Americans and a series of public scandals involving U.S. American businessmen of dubious intent, most notably Robert Vesco. In an already referenced series of articles in *La Nación* in 1974, journalist Miguel Salguero warned of U.S. colonization and the consequent expulsion of Costa Ricans from their land.[50] By the late 1970s, the personification of U.S. imperialism in the stereotypical character of the greedy gringo was commonplace in Costa Rica. The interviewees' constructed stories of settlement and land purchasing were shaped partly in response to this image.

Eileen Steinberg's story is a case in point. In 1968 Steinberg, originally from Chicago, was among the founders of a commune of U.S. Americans in Copey de Dota, southwest of San José. The commune members experimented with agriculture but mainly immersed themselves in studies of comparative religion and meditation. In our interview, Steinberg reconstructed the story of the purchase of land for the commune as a folkloristic tale of magic and kinship: "So they went there, and Bill [the leader of the commune] had his magic, and he talked to the patriarch of the whole valley, who had 12 kids, 144 grandchildren, and hundreds of illegitimate kids. The wife died and his kids asked, 'What will you do with the property?' And he wouldn't give any of them [the] prize piece of land at the head of the valley."[51]

As Steinberg's story goes, the commune members were the ones who were eventually offered the "prize piece." Steinberg's narrative suggests that Bill, a complete stranger from the United States, was given preference over all the patriarch's biological offspring because he possessed a certain "magic." With this word, Steinberg, who had an ambivalent relationship with Bill, might have been referring to his charismatic and manipulative personality; but the euphemistic terminology of magic and free choice on part of the Costa Rican old man also served her to underplay the unequal power relations that underlay it. Steinberg came from a wealthy background and received a monthly stipend from the United States; the elderly Costa Rican patriarch, like many other locals who sold land to U.S. Americans, wanted to maximize profit from his land by selling it in the best price (Salguero admitted that Costa Ricans were eager to sell, even while he warned about the consequences of such sales). In the same vein, the emphasis on describing a sort of family relations, which recurs also in other life stories of U.S. Americans in Costa Rica, enhanced their image as vulnerable, harmless, and even helpless immigrants, sometimes almost childlike, rather than adults, sometimes of considerable financial means, who are responsible for their actions.[52]

The U.S. American settlers tended to construct themselves as passive in the process of purchasing land. The land was "offered" to them, or else they came "by chance" to know of a property for sale, expressions that echo the role of fate and coincidence that featured prominently in their migratory stories. These references to their passivity as buyers are a significant component in the identity talk designated to highlight the narrators' innocence and undercutting allegations of greed and real estate speculation. It also enabled the U.S. Americans to portray themselves as likable, cherished additions to the Costa Rican family, rather than "rich gringos."[53] For similar reasons, sometimes the purchase was presented as an act of charity (thus acknowledging the asymmetrical power relations between the U.S. American buyer and the Costa Rican seller), or of obedience to a familial obligation, rather than a good monetary deal. All of these themes are evident in Richard Erikson's reconstruction of the way in which he bought his property in Costa Rica. He arrived in the Dominical area in 1972, when he was twenty-one ("but still a boy"), and was soon "adopted," in his words, by a local family. As he recounted, one of the sons of the family became a kind of mentor to him and taught him how to survive in the jungle; thus, Erikson cast himself as the hero of a jungle trope, a sort of Mowgli. Following a short stay in Costa Rica, Erikson left to study at the University of Hawaii. Soon after, he recalled, he received a letter from this friend, saying his father was very ill and in need of money, and asking Erikson to "please come and buy" the family property. Erikson's narrative implies both his innocence and his generosity in buying the property. He admitted that the price of the land was so cheap that even as a young undergraduate student he could afford it, adding, "It was either to buy a car for myself or to buy this property, so I bought this property."[54] Still maintaining the same frame of reference of kinship, he went on to state that following the purchase, he lived with his "adoptive parents" for another year in the property he had bought from them, a time he described as a kind of apprenticeship, until he was mature enough to live there on his own, and they left.[55] The purchase of large tracts of land in later years by Erikson and his parents, who resided in the United States, was depicted by him not as an economic investment (the Inter-American Highway was due to be paved in the region where he lived) but as a means to save the forest from the "primitive" deforestation by Costa Ricans, thus allowing him to cast himself as a protector of the ecological system.

This pattern of presenting land purchases as an act of charity or an obligation resulting from their privilege was common in the life stories the interviewees told. Jane Warren related that she and her husband bought their property in Costa Rica after a neighbor had told them that the owner could not pay the mortgage "and would we *please* go and look at the property."[56] This narrative of an unintentional land purchase and settlement is compatible with the broader narrative of a coincidental migration. Such patterns of representation prevailed not only in retrospective identity talks of U.S. Americans themselves but also in the representation of them, written by other, contemporary U.S. Americans. In an article in the TT about the commune of Captain Tom in Golfito, the journalists stated, "Tom *didn't originally plan* to start a commune, but it wasn't long before young people found out about Tom's tranquil paradise" (my emphasis.)[57] Such patterns enabled U.S. Americans to minimize their role—which took place on the micro level but was nonetheless significant on the macro level—in the striking changes in land possession that Costa Rica experienced as part of its economic decline in the latter years of the 1970s. Some Costa Ricans did make a profit from selling land to U.S. Americans, and in some cases family-like relations were indeed forged. Yet by telling stories about magic, family romances, and charity, U.S. Americans masked their privileged economic status in a time of crisis in Costa Rica and tried to come to terms with their role in the changes in land ownership in the country.

The Craft of Constructing a Life Story

While the identity talk in the form of life stories of U.S. American immigrants in Costa Rica contains much empirical data, these stories are first and foremost cultural constructs that draw on particular public discourses. A close analysis of them reveals multilayered, even contradictory self-perceptions and identifications of both individuals and collectives.[58] The narrators made use of a wide spectrum of possible roles, self-representations, and available narratives.[59] Listening to their stories, one can hear echoes of the biblical myth of the Garden of Eden, of the history of the United States as one in which pilgrims left the Old World in the hope of establishing a utopia in the new one, and of the conquest of the North American frontier. Images of twentieth-century U.S. popular culture are also frequently presented in their narratives, alluding to the informants' historical and cultural references and revealing their self-perception and role models. The immigrants' stories integrate and paraphrase colonial narratives of the Spanish conquest in the Americas, featuring the anticipated white man who is welcomed by the native population.[60]

The interviews I conducted took place between forty to sixty years after the actual immigration. The passage of time shapes memories and allows us to evaluate the impact of multiple layers of individual experience and social, collective impact on the construction of memory and identifications. Moreover, it enables us to contextualize these individual representations within the broader picture of national, regional, and international developments, along with cultural and ideological trends. Spoken language played a critical role in the narration of immigration, settlement, and individual and collective identity work among U.S. Americans, who articulated and perpetuated imperialist narratives. The significance of this pattern was clarified and enhanced as it was repeated in many life stories of U.S. Americans who arrived in Costa Rica, especially during the late 1960s and 1970s. Over the years it has grown into a form of communal censorship that conveys the "appropriate" pattern for telling their passage story. Listening to these identity talks reveal the immigrants' hidden struggles and their commitment to youthful ideologies, even many years later in a vastly different set of national, political, and cultural circumstances—this time not as young counterculture U.S. Americans who took an adventurous trip to Costa Rica but as privileged immigrants coming to term with their life in early twenty-first-century Costa Rica.

Epilogue

The United States had passed me by.
—ANNA FREDRIKSON, author interview

The preceding pages have told the stories of U.S. Americans who moved to Costa Rica after World War II and stayed there, becoming immigrants either by intention or by retrospective fact, though not necessarily in their self-perceptions. The main focus of the book was the diverse repertoires of identity work these people applied in constructing their identities: the narration of the decision to leave the United States and the arrival in Costa Rica; the choice of residential status rather than citizenship (which enabled them to keep their U.S. American citizenship); their choices of place of residence and the cultural practices of emplacement that attached them to these places; and the relations they forged with Costa Rica's natural surroundings, in which many first cast themselves as cowboys and pioneers, reenacting the conquest of the North American West, albeit in a different period and geopolitical realm, or, in later years, the emergence of the character of the U.S. American ecologist, guardian of the lost Costa Rican Eden.[1] I considered their habits of association and disassociation, which yielded the creation of transnational social spaces in which various potential models of U.S. Americans and U.S. Americanness in Costa Rica were negotiated; I also examined their affinity with material things—from Dior's New Look to brown rice—as a means to maintain their former selves or alternatively to create new, desired ones.

Considering practices and discourses in diverse fields, the book adds the story of U.S. American immigration to Costa Rica during the Cold War to the burgeoning scholarship on identity formation among immigrants driven not primarily by economic factors but by an existential quest or aspiration for a different lifestyle, and whose country of origin is typically more affluent than their destination country.

While numerically small (totaling only several thousand or, by other estimates, some tens of thousands of people from the 1950s to the 1970s), the consideration of this particular countercurrent of immigration, occurring in the Americas during the heyday of the Cold War and against the background of momentous social and cultural changes in the United States and Central America, brings to the fore new agents and voices—not the formal policymakers of the state, the military, or the economy, though their importance has been acknowledged throughout this study, but those of ordinary U.S. American immigrants and settlers. It thus enables us to gain new insights about human movement and settlement and the distinct dynamics of regional, national, and transnational identity work under specific global power relations.

As we delved into the lives of Anna Fredrikson, Jane Mora, John Foulks, and the many others interviewed for this research, hearing their passage stories as they reconstructed them several decades after their move, and from the point of view of their present life in Costa Rica, we should bear in mind that the arrival of U.S. Americans in Costa Rica and their lives there took place within a broader scheme of highly asymmetrical power relations between the hemispheric superpower and its Central American ally. These global power relations facilitated the arrival of U.S. Americans in Costa Rica and were manifested at the micro level of individuals in the symbolic and often also material fortune that enabled U.S. Americans to live in Costa Rica for many years as privileged guests rather than unwelcome immigrants. Yet we should also bear in mind that these hemispheric power relations, which largely dictated the welcoming attitude toward U.S. Americans in Costa Rica, went hand in hand with the long-standing Costa Rican perception of itself as an exceptional republic, distinct from its Central American neighbors in term of its ethnic composition, national character, and historical experience. The cadre of U.S. Americans in the country was thus both a means to enhance such an imagined Costa Rican character and "evidence" of its validation.

The Cold War not only shaped the minds of the U.S. American immigrants and their life in the United States but often also affected their arrival in Costa Rica, serving as a key component of their identity work throughout their lives there: some of them were formal representatives of U.S. power (diplomatic, military, or economic), the wives of these representatives and others U.S. American individuals who throughout their lives in Costa Rica made the service of U.S. interests a crucial factor of their identity work—like the members of the U.S. Women's Club featured in chapter 4. Conversely, the Cold War was also a factor in the arrival in Costa Rica of U.S. political dissidents, from 1950s southern Quakers who objected to the Korean War, to 1960s and 1970s counterculture hippies fleeing the Vietnam draft and appalled by the Nixon presidency (or else perhaps driven away by conflicts with their own fathers? Some forty years later, the distinction seems to blur). In any case, moving to Costa Rica was of a piece not solely with the latter group's political resistance to U.S. policies but also with their quest, which in many cases began in the United States and was enhanced by the move to Costa Rica, to withdraw from the mainstream society and make a new start in what was perceived as a pristine, natural place.

Indeed, many of the U.S. Americans interviewed for this research, all grownups by the time they arrived in Costa Rica, depicted themselves or were depicted by others as newborns or young children, thus implying that immigration entailed for them a sort of rebirth. In chapter 6 I analyzed such patterns of identity talk as designated to portray the narrators as innocent, harmless people, rather than powerful and privileged immigrants. But the metaphor of birth and rebirth recurred throughout the book (for example in chapter 3, in relation to the Costa Rican beachfronts), and it enabled me to consider such questions as who was born, from which past and into what present and future, and how this process is retrospectively articulated through the interviewees' identity talk.[2]

Methodologically, this book is based heavily on listening, literally, to the voices of U.S. Americans who lived in Costa Rica, and on my interpretation of their identity talk as a way of understanding how they retrospectively constructed their lives and identities in Costa Rica. This research tool, which was chosen partly by default as a result of the dearth of written sources, eventually proved an exceedingly fruitful one, not only for exposing the diverse experiences of a population that has remained largely under the radar of both Costa Rican and U.S. authorities but also for tracing—in a manner that no formal written sources could possibly provide—the nuanced ways in which the individual members of this population reconstructed their identifications. U.S. immigration to Costa Rica provides powerful confirmation of Alessandro Portelli's assertion that in order to fully understand history we cannot only read (about) it but we must hear it.[3] However, relying on the interviewees' voices raises another question that was posed by historian Lara Putnam in the context of an earlier trend of immigration in the Americas, regarding "the degree to which we make actors' self-understanding part of the parameters of study."[4] The question is pertinent to the two fundamental concepts discussed in this book—perception of immigration and what it means to be an immigrant; and the ambivalent relationship with the United States and/or affiliating with any collective U.S. American community in Costa Rica.

As I described in the preceding chapters, many of the U.S. Americans in Costa Rica did not regard themselves as immigrants and objected to their labeling as such. They saw little similarity between their own experience, both mental and practical, and the experiences of their forefathers who immigrated to the United States or to the experiences of contemporary immigrants in either Costa Rica or the United States. Michael Warren, who arrived in Costa Rica in 1971, recounted:

My parents were both born in Germany and immigrated to the United States. They did so as young adults and became fully American. They became citizens as is usually done in the States, but more than that, their thinking process became very Americanized. And maybe in the back of my mind, when we came here, I thought "Oh, this is probably going to happen to me now. I'm going to change my approach, my way of living, whatever, the way my parents did." And that didn't happen to me. And after a little while I realized that wasn't the way I was gonna change.[5]

As the sense of integration and becoming Costa Rican did not happen, Warren gradually came to think of himself as a U.S. American living *in* Costa Rica, rather than a U.S. immigrant. Similarly, many U.S. Americans in Costa Rica tended to see themselves as people who had come there for various reasons—an adventure, an extended holiday, a job, or in search of themselves—and happened to stay for many years, never actually intending to immigrate and sometimes staying on out of inertia or lack of choice. Theodor Bart arrived on the southern Pacific coast of Costa Rica in 1972 with his fellow commune members and stayed in the area many years after the commune split up and the rustic huts of the original settlement were turned into a luxurious yoga retreat. Lacking the financial means and self-motivation to create a new life for himself in his former homeland, Bart no longer felt capable of returning to the United States, a predicament that he depicted metaphorically: "You think that life is a movie and when you step out of the movie, whenever you step back you're still in the same place. But the movie has long gone. It's been over with for a long time."[6] A similar view was expressed by Anna Fredrikson, who followed her Costa Rican husband to Costa Rica in 1951 and remained in the country after they divorced. When I asked her in 2008 if she had considered moving back to the United States after her divorce, or would consider it now, she replied, "The United States had passed me by. In fact, I was still living, frankly, in the fifties."[7]

Thus, to return to Putnam's question, the case of U.S. Americans in Costa Rica makes a strong argument for the importance of taking actors' self-understanding as part of the parameters of study, because it is precisely the gaps between the self-perceptions of the subjects of the present study and the concrete evidence of their lives that has the potential to cultivate new knowledge about their identity work—and by extension to generate this kind of knowledge about similar immigrations during the closing decades of the twentieth century.

Stressing the importance of listening to the voices of people, Portelli has nonetheless called into question the extent to which we can draw from individual stories to a broader history.[8] This movement between the particular and the general is a tension I experienced throughout the research and writing of this book. My assumptions prior to the field work were somewhat monolithic: I had set out looking to analyze "the U.S. American community" and was confident about the significance of the national origin, namely the United States, in the identity work of U.S. Americans in Costa Rica. I soon learned that in some cases, national origin did indeed bring U.S. Americans of very diverse economic, political, and cultural backgrounds together, in ways that could not have happened in the United States, and played an important role in their identity work. Such was the case, for instance, of Eric White, a young counterculturist who arrived in Costa Rica in 1972 and became the jewelry-maker of the established U.S. American milieu in the Central Valley, an affiliation that provided him with a sense of national belonging he had not experienced at home: "They accepted me like in the United States I would never be accepted [by the] classes they have, business or executives, diplomats. It would never happen in California. Because of the class I was, who I was, how I acted. Here they [said] 'Wow, we need to have an artist in our community.' So, everybody just treated me like a normal person. I didn't feel discriminated against."[9]

But others rejected the assumption that their national origin overshadowed class, gender, ideology, or other parameters of identity. "The fact that we are all Americans doesn't mean we are a community," explained to me, with some irritation, a U.S. American woman who had been living in Costa Rica for many years. She went on to stress her affiliation with expats of diverse nationalities and seemed to be insulted by the way she was automatically assumed to be associated with the U.S. American community.[10] Another woman, a missionary for the Latin America Mission, at first declined my request for an interview based on the subject line of my email: "Interview about U.S. community in Costa Rica." "I am sorry," she wrote back in a chilly message, "but I cannot help you. I do not know U.S. Americans and I am not part of the U.S. community."[11] Jane Mora, who arrived in 1967 as the young wife of a Costa Rican man, pointed to another classification among U.S. Americans in Costa Rica, based on class but mainly on affiliations with Costa Ricans. Recalling meeting U.S. Americans in the local market, she described the "in-between" status of those who were married to Costa Ricans, and its attendant sense of isolation:

> I tried to make friends with them, but I was not accepted [. . .] either because they were embassy people or because they were working for Standard Fruits and wanted nothing to do with people who were married to natives. Once you told them you were married to a Costa Rican they would turn around and just leave you there. So it was kind of a difficult position because you weren't accepted by the Costa Ricans and you weren't accepted by the Americans, and I didn't know anybody else who was married to a Costa Rican. I was a novelty, I thought.[12]

I gradually became much more attentive to the individualization of U.S. Americans in Costa Rica. Throughout the book I tried not to talk about a U.S. American community, as there was no such single experience. Like any identity work, the one that took place among U.S. Americans in Costa Rica was the result of each immigrant's specific encounters between interconnected hierarchies of class, race, sexuality, ethnicity, nationality, gender, religion, and other criteria of self-identification, which in turn created a unique reaction when they came into contact with the Costa Rican environments and people, as well as with other U.S. Americans and other nationalities.

Nonetheless, certain common experiences and discourses did surface in the life stories, writings, and other textual sources that illuminate the identity work of U.S. Americans in Costa Rica. One such common theme is the culture/nature dichotomy, in which the United States is represented as culture and Costa Rica as nature. This dichotomy played itself out in the relation to settlement in the natural surroundings (chapters 2 and 3) as well as in relation to material culture (chapter 5) and entailed wide-held assumptions among U.S. Americans regarding the cultural exchanges between Costa Ricans—who were often portrayed as guides for purposes of food gathering and life in the rain forest—and the role U.S. Americans saw for themselves as having a mission to civilize the Costa Rican people and its natural surroundings. Interestingly, such a role was embraced not only by U.S. Americans who made their identification with the United States a clear component of their identity work but also by dissidents. Even a settler like Wolf Guindon, a Quaker who had been imprisoned in the U.S. for a period of time for being a conscientious objector during the Korean War, stated that coming from a more a progressive country (he did not mention the United States by name), he saw himself as having a role in promoting change and modernization in Costa Rica; and even Captain Tom Clairmont of Ohio, one of the first U.S. American counterculturists in Costa Rica who as early as the 1950s established a commune of dropouts in Playa Cacao on the Osa Peninsula and over the years has become highly controversial among both Costa Ricans and U.S. Americans in the country, was depicted in an article in the *TT* as "making a conscious effort to bring culture to Cacao."[13]

At some point, however, such perceptions regarding the association between U.S. and culture became disconnected from the notion of the United States as a relevant frame of reference for identity work. For some immigrants, the many years of living outside the United States eroded its significance as an object of affiliation, and they replaced it with other frames of reference—either local, regional, or a-national. One U.S. American woman living in Costa Rica told me that it is not the United States primarily from which she emigrated; rather, what was significant for her was the fact that at a very young age she had left her small hometown of North Hollywood. Another man, originally from Colorado, described himself as a citizen of the Southwest. A woman who moved to Costa Rica from Texas said that in both places she lived among horse people, and that this was the frame of reference for her identification, rather than nationality. Borrowing Jeffry Lesser and Raanan Rein's useful metaphor of self-representation and identity-making as small change in one's pocket that is used interchangeably for self-fashioning and self-definition,[14] it is possible to say that U.S.

Americans in Costa Rica rarely tended to represent their identity through a single bill of national origin but rather transcended the boundaries of national origin and broke their identity down into many different coins—gender and its stereotypical attributes ("I am a woman who tries to do good"),[15] ecological identifications ("a citizen of planet earth"),[16] professions (horse people), or spiritual and human identifications (like the woman who spoke of her "spiritual heart which has no country").[17] Some of them, especially those who had served in Vietnam or were affiliated with the U.S. counterculture, tied their reluctance to identify with their national origin to their life experience ("The Vietnam War kind of took that out of me").[18] Many expressed dual identifications—with both the United States and Costa Rica, often distinguishing between the state and the people ("I am a U.S. patriot and I'll always will be," stated John Arlington Jr. But, later, when speaking of his relation to the Costa Rican people he said, "I am we, I am not they").[19] The tendency among the U.S. American immigrants to identify with the Costa Ricans but reject Costa Rica as a nation or a state is related to the aforementioned reluctance to identify with nation states, and in some cases due to a lingering U.S. patriotism, but also, more specifically, it reflects their critical view of early twenty-first-century Costa Rica as corrupt and poorly administered. Many of the U.S. Americans who immigrated to Costa Rica had initially idealized it as a kind of heaven on earth, the polar opposite of the depraved and troubled United States. For them, immigrating to Costa Rica was a moral and cultural statement about themselves and their desired selves. As their perspective changed and this idealized picture of Costa Rica—and of their youth—receded, they tended to identify only with their immediate surroundings.

Throughout dozens of interviews I never encountered a hyphenated identification, such as U.S.-American-Costa Rican or vice-versa. They were U.S. Americans *in* Costa Rica, or else neither U.S. American nor Costa Rican. "I'm a North American, I'm not a Costa Rican. I'm a guest in their country," testified Joyce Brown after living in Costa Rica for almost forty years.[20] U.S. Americans who live close to Costa Ricans, through marriage or other circumstances, said they were aware of the fact that they would always be considered foreigners. "Most of my husband's friends probably up to the last ten years did not even know my name," said the wife of a Costa Rican man bitterly. "For them I am '*la gringa de Pablo.*'"[21] Another U.S. American wife of a Costa Rican man related that she feels herself to be a U.S. American woman living in mental exile in Costa Rica.[22] Reflecting the degree of alienation among some U.S. American immigrants, Michael Warren described his realization that he would never become a true tico, with a jab at his fellow U.S. Americans who became enthralled by the local way of life: "So we picked a role that was definitely expatriate—as opposed to pretend ticos."[23] Another U.S. American expressed his sense of alienation by naming his property Terra Extranjera ("foreign land").

Notwithstanding the individualism and patriotism of my interviewees, I suggest that it was also the privileges (monetary and symbolic) entailed by their U.S. American background that account for the nonintegrative nature of U.S. Americans and their identity work as unaffiliated immigrants. Apart from cases of intermarriage, the choice of whether or not to integrate into Costa Rican society was solely theirs, and they had no incentive, aside from their own inclinations, to do so. Their life as privileged guests was facilitated by social and cultural networks, their financial status (itself derived from the asymmetrical power relations between the United States and Costa Rica), and the welcoming attitude of the Costa Rican state. It is in this sense that the case of the U.S. American immigration to Costa Rica during the Cold War, an immigration that chronologically preceded the burgeoning migratory flows and body of research about lifestyle migration and privileged migration, is illuminative, as it enables us to follow the identity work of immigrants who did not perceive themselves as such due to their privileged status and relate it to privilege and power on the geopolitical level.

"Only Death Requires That We Be Precise"

Life stories, which are the main methodology of this research, encompass not only the past and present but also the imagined future. When I asked my informants to reflect on their future, specifically where they thought that they would likely live the rest of their lives, many said the question depended more on their financial and familial situation than on mental and emotional identifications relating to the United States and Costa Rica. However, many of the mostly elderly interviewees expressed great concern regarding the issue of where they wished to be buried, reflections that powerfully express the ambiguous and fluid nature of their identifications.[24] Kathrin Morales, who moved to Costa Rica in 1953 following her acquaintance with a Costa Rican World War II veteran who had come to study in her hometown, could not make up her mind whether to be buried in Costa Rica, where she has lived most of her life, or beside her first husband in the Ohio town where she grew up.[25] Joyce Brown prepared instructions to cremate her body and spread the ashes in her native Colorado.[26] Adam Klee, who arrived as a veterinarian in the late 1960s, said he wanted his body cremated and his ashes scattered in three different places: the New England farm where he was born, his own farm in Costa Rica's Nicoya Peninsula, and the ocean.[27] John Arlington Jr., a Vietnam veteran, said he wanted to be buried in the United States.[28] Anna Fredrikson decided she wished to be buried in the Methodist cemetery in San José.[29] Capturing the complexity of the identifications of U.S. Americans in Costa Rica, as well as the unique power of death to crystallize them, Mary Thompson told me that immediately after her divorce from her Costa Rican husband, she neither acquired Costa Rican citizenship nor returned to the States but bought a burial plot in the old cemetery of the foreigners (*el cementerio de los extranjeros*) in San José.[30] These choices reflect the way that many U.S. Americans lived and continue to live their lives in Costa Rica: de facto immigrants who have never fully embraced this status and whose identities convey foreignness.

Notes

Introduction

1. My use of the term "U.S. Americans" to refer to people of U.S. origin is designed to acknowledge the fact that the United States constitutes only part of the American continent and to avoid the imperialistic tendency to appropriate the term "America" to the United States exclusively. This distinction is especially crucial in research about the United States in the context of the Americas and is common in this literature. See, for example, Merleaux, *Sugar and Civilization*; Renda, *Taking Haiti*.
2. Stephen Schmidt, "Gringos Worried . . . but Staying," *Tico Times*, July 31, 1979 (all *Tico Times* articles—henceforth *TT*—mentioned in this book were obtained at the Biblioteca Nacional Miguel Obregón Lizano, San José, Costa Rica).
3. On the Cold War as a cultural construct, see Appy, *Cold War Constructions*.
4. Tylor May, *Homeward Bound*.
5. Cohen, *Consumers' Republic*.
6. Snow and Anderson, "Identity Work among the Homeless," 1348.
7. Snow and Anderson, "Identity Work among the Homeless," 1347.
8. Sheila Croucher laments the blind spot that fundamental works about contemporary immigration have with respect to gender and calls attention to the significant role of the latter throughout the immigration process (Croucher, "Gendered Spatialities").
9. On the return to locality in migration studies in response to the dominance of the transnational perspective, see Bönisch-Brednich and Trundle, *Local Lives*.
10. On transnational migration, see Glick Schiller, Basch, and Szanton, "From Immigrant to Transmigrant."
11. Janoschka and Haas, "Contested Spatialities," 1.

12. Benson and O'Reilly, *Lifestyle Migration*, 6.
13. In the years of the Cold War, the United States did not execute direct territorial rule in Central America, as it did in the formal age of U.S. imperialism in the three decades following 1898, when it seized control of former Spanish colonies and established an empire of island colonies across the Tropic of Cancer, or in the early decades of the twentieth century when it controlled Caribbean territories such as Haiti and the Dominican Republic. Yet it did exercise indirect influence, through military, economic, and cultural leverage, to achieve and maintain power and sway and therefore can be defined as an informal empire. For a discussion of the application of the terms "imperium" and "hegemony" to the United States, see McCoy, Scarano, and Johnson, "On the Tropic of Cancer." On the nature and scope of twentieth-century U.S. imperialism, see, for example, McGranahan and Collins, *Ethnographies of U.S. Empire*; Bender and Lipman, *Making the Empire Work*; Grandin, *Empire's Workshop*; Joseph, LeGrand, and Salvatore, *Close Encounters of Empire*; and Stoler, *Haunted by Empire*.
14. Putnam, *Radical Moves*, 1.
15. For a deconstruction of the link between economic wealth and privilege among lifestyle migrants, see Benson and O'Reilly, *Lifestyle Migration and Colonial Traces*, Kindle locations 2624–29.
16. Cited in Kordick, *Saints of Progress*, 123.
17. During the economic depression of the 1930s, Mario Sancho Jiménez mocked this image in his book *Costa Rica, Suiza centroamericana*. See also Colby, *Business of Empire*, 63–66.
18. Giovanna Giglioli has aptly argued that Costa Rica's alleged exceptionalism was a tenable narrative only if one narrowed one's prism to the population of the Central Valley alone (Giglioli, "¿Mito o idiosincrasia?"). Yet this view of the country as a whole is found in many textbooks on Latin America. See Skidmore, Smith, and Green's *Modern Latin America*, whose chapter on Costa Rica politics and policy opens with the statement: "Costa Rica has always been unique" (108). These views were represented in Costa Rican textbooks as well. So, for example, a third-grade geography textbook from 1958 maintained that "the white race clearly prevailed. Costa Ricans descend almost entirely, from . . . Spaniards who . . . conserved purely their customs and blood. In this way, a sober, simple, moral, hardworking, robust and sane nation was formed in Costa Rica" (cited in Kordick, *Saints of Progress*, 147). On the construction of this myth and its analysis, see Palmer and Molina, *Costa Rica*

Reader, 9–54; Cortés, La invención de Costa Rica; and Giglioli, "¿Mito o idiosincrasia?"

19. Jane Mora, a U.S. woman married to a Costa Rican man from an elite family, recalled that when she would go out walking with her mother-in-law in early 1970s San José, the latter used to introduce every person in the street as a family member—and "as it turned out, they were all actually relatives" (Jane Mora, interviewed in San José, May 25, 2009).

20. On the imagined nature of Latin American nations and the significant role of race in their construction, see Holt, "First New Nations," i–xiv.

21. On the construction of race and nation in Latin America, see Appelbaum, Macpherson, and Rosenblatt, Race and Nation; Lesser, Immigration, Ethnicity, and National Identity; Baily and Miguez, Mass Migration; Andrews, Blackness in the White Nation; de la Fuente, Nation for All.

22. On Black population and culture in Costa Rica during the colonial period, see Lohse, "Cacao and Slavery in Matina, Costa Rica, 1650–1750"; Cáceres, Negros, mulatos, esclavos y libertos; Meléndez Obando, "Los últimos esclavos de Costa Rica"; and Meléndez Obando and Tatiana Lobo Wiehoff, Negros y blancos.

23. On the revision of the Costa Rican myth of agrarian equality in mid-nineteenth-century Costa Rica, see Gudmundson, Costa Rica before Coffee; on the revision of Costa Rica's ethnic composition after independence and Black immigration from the Caribbean Islands, see Christian, "'Latin America without the Downside'"; Leeds, "Representations of Race, Entanglements of Power"; Putnam, Company They Kept; Chomsky, West Indian Workers; and Meléndez and Duncan, El negro en Costa Rica.

24. In her research about Costa Rican immigrants in twenty-first-century northeastern United States, Carmen Kordick depicts the jolt they experienced at being treated as Mexicans, or Latins in general, "since it places into question the deep-seated belief of most Costa Ricans that they are 'white' or at least 'whiter' than other Latin Americans." Kordick, Saints of Progress, 155.

25. Meagher, "Holidays in Costa Rica," 274. For similar views on the part of U.S. officials and travelers, see Colby, Business of Empire, 63–66.

26. Grandin, Empire's Workshop; Renda, Taking Haiti, 22. For a discussion of the significance and practices in the U.S. empire of island colonies, see McCoy and Scarano, Colonial Crucible.

27. On the United Fruit Company in Costa Rica, see Colby, Business of Empire; Putnam, Company They Kept; Chomsky, West Indian Workers; Fallas, Mamita Yunai.

28. LaFeber, *Inevitable Revolutions*, 57–58.
29. Schifter, "Origins of the Cold War," 76. This unity between his foreign and domestic policies served Calderón's political interests, while at the same time increasing the involvement of the United States in Costa Rican internal politics. Some scholars argue that it was this shift of alliance from Germany to the United States, and the subsequent policy of deportation and property confiscation of German Costa Ricans, that ultimately led to the Costa Rican civil war (see Acuna, *El 48*). On the German coffee oligarchy in Costa Rica and its affiliation with the Nazi regime in Germany, see Nemcik, "Germans, Costa Ricans"; Yashar, *Demanding Democracy*, ch. 1; and Schifter, "Origins of the Cold War," ch. 3.
30. This aid was small compared to the military aid to other Central American republics. Nicaragua, for example, received $300 million in aid. Schifter, "Origins of the Cold War," 92.
31. In the face of mounting criticism of these terms in Costa Rica, the U.S. announced that manufacturing would be transferred to local cooperatives, but as the war ended and rubber was no longer needed, the local farms were all shut down and their employees laid off. Schifter, "Origins of the Cold War," 182.
32. Facio, "Means and Ends," 187.
33. On the highway's construction in Costa Rica, see Kordick, "Constructing Costa Rica's Inter-American Highway"; Rutkow, *Longest Line on the Map*, 255–56, 270–74.
34. On the origins of the Little Theatre Group of Costa Rica, see Bert Williams, "The Little Theatre Story," in *Program of Angel Street (Gaslight)*, 1967, 1, LTG archive; on the establishment of the U.S. women's club, see Gail Stone, *Summary of Activities*, March 1959, WCCR archive.
35. On U.S.-Latin America relations during the Cold War, see Brands, *Latin America's Cold War*; Joseph and Spenser, *In from the Cold*; Smith, *Talons of the Eagle*, sec. 2; and Yashar, *Demanding Democracy*.
36. During Costa Rica's civil war, an estimated one thousand to four thousand people were killed (between one to five percent of the nation's total population). The relatively low impact of the war was partly due to its concentration in only three provinces in the center of Costa Rica (on the civil war see for example Bell, *Crisis in Costa Rica*; Acuña, *El 48*). Recent scholarship has attributed the war to class and regional frictions (Díaz-Arias, "Battle of Memories in Costa Rica"; Kordick, *Saints of Progress*, ch. 3; Solís, "La institucionalidad ajena").

The rise to power of a communist party was not exclusive to Costa Rica, but rather part of the increased popularity of communism throughout post–World War II Latin America; see Skidmore, Smith, and Green, *Modern Latin America*, 448; Longley, "Resistance and Accommodation," 21.

37. Figueres had the far-reaching ambition to unify all Central America, with Costa Rica being merely the first step. See Ameringer, *Don Pepe*, 38–48.
38. Kordick, *Saints of Progress*, 122. On Davis's involvement in the Costa Rican civil war, see Davis, *Few Dull Moments*, 127–36.
39. Ameringer, *Don Pepe*, 69–70.
40. Davis, *Few Dull Moments*, 128.
41. Kordick, *Saints of Progress*, 6.
42. Cited in Longley, *Sparrow and the Hawk*, 53. See also idem, "Resistance and Accommodation."
43. Kantor, "'New Deal' Government," 12.
44. Kennedy, "Address at a White House Reception."
45. Ameringer, *Don Pepe*, 174.
46. Paul P. Kennedy, "Kennedy Meeting 6 Latin Leaders for Talks Today," *New York Times*, March 18, 1963.
47. "Nunca en la historia de Costa Rica hubo tan espontánea manifestación," *La Nación*, March 19, 1963.
48. *La Nación*, March 17, 1963.
49. In an article in *La Nación*, the affair is depicted as a "national degradation" (*envilecimiento nacional*), but Vesco himself is described as a foreign millionaire, rather than specifically identified as a U.S. American, and the harshest criticism is reserved for Figueres and his successor, Daniel Oduber Quirós (*La Nación*, August 30, 1977). U.S. newspapers highlighted Vesco's relations with President Nixon, with headlines contrasting U.S.-based corruption and Costa Rican purity ("Costa Rica: Scandal in Paradise," *Time*, June 11, 1973, 45). The *TT* was concerned over the Vesco affair's possibly negative impact on the image and lives of U.S. Americans in Costa Rica. Numerous articles condemned Vesco and explicitly disassociated him from the rest of the U.S. American population in the country. See, for example, Dery Dyer, "Robert Vesco: The Whale in the Puddle," *TT*, 50th Anniversary Special, May 19, 2006. On Vesco, see Suñol, *Robert Vesco compra una república* and Herzog, *Vesco*.
50. On the first Anglo-American settlers in Costa Rica, see Murchie, *Imported Spices*. On Costa Rican immigration laws, see Venútolo, "La inmigración extranjera."
51. British citizens were among the most prominent of the European immigrants in Costa Rica, followed by Italians and Spaniards

(Venútolo, "La inmigración extranjera.") On the various migratory populations in Costa Rica, see Sandoval-García, *El mito roto*.

52. Boggs, *Married to a Legend*, 49.
53. Adapted by the author from Instituto Nacional de Estadística y Censos, *Censo de población y vivienda*, 1950, 1963, and 1973, ANCR. On British and Britain in Latin America, see Miller, *Britain and Latin America*, 205–54 and Bulmer-Thomas, *Britain and Latin America*.
54. National Archive and Records Administration, RG 59, 137 census files 170–74, boxes 584, 585, 589.
55. See Nelson, *Historia del Protestanismo*.
56. Marriage to a Costa Rican man was viewed by some of these U.S. women as a sort of fantasy. Young U.S. women, especially those of modest backgrounds, imagined a transformation from working-class life in a small town in the United States to a glamorous, colorful life in Latin Costa Rica. On a similar identity-construction among U.S. women who married Italian men, see Trundle, "Romance Tourists."
57. On 1960s and 1970s U.S. counterculture immigration, see Pickering, "Waiting for Chronic"; Waldren, *Insiders and Outsiders*; Rodgers, *Welcome to Resisterville*; and Hagan, *Northern Passage*.
58. Palmer and Molina, *Costa Rica Reader*, ch. 5. For a more critical perspective on the years following the civil war, see Kordick, *Saints of Progress*.
59. On the Ley de Pensionados, see Puga, "Un lugar en el Sol."
60. Harvey Friedlander, a U.S. American, provided the alternative estimations based on his forty years of residency in Costa Rica and his involvement in the community of U.S. Americans in the country (interviewed in Santa Ana, May 14, 2009). On the difficulty of estimating immigration rates and the scope of high-end immigration due to the immigrants' reluctance to be documented and fluid practices of movement, see Janoschka and Haas, "Contested Spatialities," 23; Hayes, "'It Is Hard Being the Different One'"; Benson, "Postcoloniality and Privilege"; and Banks, "Identity Narratives."
61. The self-perception as a receiving society rather than a sending one was shared by the United States and Costa Rica. As late as the twenty-first century, Costa Rica refused to acknowledge or to assist Costa Rican immigrants in the United States. See Kordick, *Saints of Progress*, 157.
62. Finifter argued that in 1970, out of an estimated several hundred thousand U.S. Americans living abroad, only one thousand gave up their U.S. citizenship (Finifter, "American Emigration," 32). Dashefsky and Woodrow-Lafield interviewed U.S. Americans who lived in

Australia for thirty years but still had no intention of applying for Australian citizenship (Dashefsky and Woodrow-Lafield, *Americans Abroad*, 5).

63. Richard Erikson, interviewed in Golfito, May 27, 2009.
64. Mark Bach, interviewed in Alajuela, April 27, 2009.
65. See Hayes, *Gringolandia*; Benson and O'Reilly, *Lifestyle Migration*.
66. *Oxford English Dictionary*, s.v. "immigration," accessed August 15, 2021, https://en.oxforddictionaries.com/definition/immigration; *Merriam-Webster*, s.v. "immigration," accessed August 15, 20201, https://www.merriam-webster.com/dictionary/immigration.
67. Joan Stevens, interviewed in Ciudad Colón, May 22, 2009. Antony Spencer found similar responses among U.S. Americans in early twenty-first-century Costa Rica: "I hadn't thought of myself as an immigrant. I think I always thought of myself as an American living in another country" (Spencer, "Americans Create Hybrid Spaces," 66–67).
68. See Sandoval-García, *El mito roto*; Sandoval-García, *Threatening Others*.
69. Croucher applies the term "privilege migrants" to early twenty-first-century U.S. Americans in Mexico (Croucher, *Other Side of the Fence*). Spencer proposes the term "high-end immigrants" to describe U.S. Americans living in Costa Rica during the same period (Spencer, "Americans Create Hybrid Spaces").
70. See Benson and O'Reilly, "Migration and the Search."
71. Hayes, *Gringolandia*, 25.
72. See Benson, "Class, Race, Privilege"; Benson, "Postcoloniality and Privilege"; Hayes, "'It Is Hard Being the Different One'"; Van Noorloos, "Residential Tourism and Multiple Mobilities"; Janoschka, "Imaginarios del turismo"; Croucher, *Other Side of the Fence*; and Banks, "Identity Narratives."
73. Cohen, "Expatriate Communities," 24. Benson and O'Reilly argue, following Lundström, that the very distinction between "expatriates" and migrants signals the white normativity of this field of research (Benson and O'Reilly, *Lifestyle Migration and Colonial Traces*, Kindle locations 263–78).
74. Cohen, "Expatriate Communities," 14.
75. Backer, "Rootless," 273. O'Reilly similarly encountered the perception that "expatriatism is freedom" in her research on British residents in the Costa del Sol region of Spain, who, in the name of such freedom, were reluctant to be interviewed (O'Reilly, *British on the Costa del Sol*).
76. Thomas Dent, interviewed in Alajuela, April 10, 2009.

77. Bach, interview.
78. O'Reilly, *British on the Costa del Sol*, 44–45.
79. Except where otherwise noted, all interviews cited in this article were conducted by the author, and all interview recordings and transcripts are in the author's possession. Most of the informants' names have been changed, in order to protect their privacy.
80. Thomson, "Anzac Memories," 25; Florencia Mallon has similarly stressed the impossibility and pointlessness of trying to find a representative figure. Mallon, "Introduction," 1.
81. See Squire, "Experience-Centered and Culturally-Oriented Approaches," 48; Perkiss, "Reclaiming the Past." A study concerning Soviet and post-Soviet immigration to Costa Rica in the 1990s was based on three times more female than male interviewees; see Rodriguez and Cohen, "Generations and Motivations."
82. Croucher, "Gendered Spatialities."
83. Mahler and Pessar, "Gendered Geographies."
84. For a comparative perspective on the immigration of U.S. women, see Croucher, "Gendered Spatialities" and Trundle, *Americans in Tuscany*.
85. On the difference between narratives told by men and those told by women in imperial contexts, see Melman, "Under the Western Historian's Eyes."
86. On the snowball technique in oral history–based research in Costa Rica see Rodriguez and Cohen, "Generations and Motivations," 149.
87. Portelli, *Death of Luigi Trastulli*, 74.
88. McAdams, *Redemptive Self*, 13–14.
89. Linde, *Life Stories*, 3. See also Cavarero, *Relating Narratives*.
90. James, *Doña María's Story*, 124.
91. McAdams, *Redemptive Self*, 10.
92. Spitzer, *Hotel Bolivia*, Kindle locations 5798–821.
93. The positionality of the interviewer is an important question in all research and has been discussed extensively. See Rivers-Moore, *Gringo Gulch*, 184–89; Nagar-Ron and Mutzafi-Haller, "'My Life?,'" 1–11; Kikumura, "Family Life History"; Portelli, *Death of Luigi Trastulli*, 29–44.
94. On the term "Clubland," see Cohen, "Networks of Sociability."
95. Geertz, *Interpretation of Cultures*, 9.
96. Massey et al., "Theories of International Migration," 431–32.
97. See, for example, Levitt, DeWind, and Vertovec, "International Perspectives on Transnational Migration"; Glick Schiller, Basch, and Szanton Blanc, "From Immigrant to Transmigrant."

98. On the renewed emphasis on locality in migration studies, see Janoschka and Haas, *Contested Spatialities* and Bönisch-Brednich and Trundle, *Local Lives*.

1. Crossroads

1. On the Quakers' immigration and settlement, see Chornook and Guindon, *Walking with Wolf*; Guindon et al., *Monteverde Jubilee Family Album*; Masing, "Foreign Agricultural Colonies in Costa Rica."
2. "Monteverde Statement of Aims and Ideals, 1959," in *Monteverde Jubilee Family Album*, 101.
3. Mark Bach, interviewed in Alajuela, April 27, 2009.
4. David Snow and Leon Anderson defined identity work as "the range of activities individuals engage in to create, present, and sustain personal identities that are congruent with and supportive of the self-concept" (Snow and Anderson, "Identity Work among the Homeless," 1348).
5. Massey et al., "Theories of International Migration."
6. O'Reilly and Benson, "Lifestyle Migration," 6.
7. Quijano, "Coloniality of Power." See also Hayes, *Gringolandia*, 13–14; Benson and O'Reilly, *Lifestyle Migration*.
8. On the relationship between beautiful landscapes and the economic factor in lifestyle migration, see Janoschka and Haas, "Introduction"; on lifestyle migration as a neoliberal phenomenon, see Benson and O'Reilly, *Lifestyle Migration and Colonial Traces*.
9. Some scholars contend that the overwhelmingly high rate of immigration to the United States simply overshadows the phenomenon of emigration from the country (Dashefsky and Woodrow-Lafield, *Americans Abroad*, vi), yet others have argued that there was a deliberate intention on the part of government authorities and even academics to hide the real figures of U.S. emigration (Axelrod, "Historical Studies of Emigration"). Interestingly, as Carmen Kordick and Carmen Caamaño Morúa have shown, the exact same attitude prevailed in Costa Rica in the second half of the twentieth century, as Costa Rican authorities declined to acknowledge the emigration of lower-class Costa Ricans to the United States because the phenomenon undermined the national ethos of Costa Rica as a prosperous, receiving society (Kordick, *Saints of Progress*, 154–55). See also Caamaño, *Entre "arriba" y "abajo."*
10. Warren and Kraly, "Elusive Exodus." Around the time of World War I and during the economic depression of the 1930s, the rate of emigration was higher than the rate of immigration (Axelrod, "Historical

Studies of Emigration," 44). Studies of specific populations depict a more radical picture. Dino Cinel found, for example, that 60 percent of the Italian immigrants who arrived in the United States between 1908 and 1923 returned to their homeland within a couple of years (Cinel, *From Italy to San Francisco*, 2).

11. For a survey of U.S. emigration and expatriatism and its significance from President Jefferson's time in Paris, see Croucher, "Americans Abroad."
12. Harter, *Lost Colony*; Holdridge, "Toledo."
13. Pizer, *American Expatriate Writing*; Dolan, *Modern Lives*; Gordimer, "Hemingway's Expatriates"; McMahon, "City for Expatriates."
14. Stovall, "The Fire This Time," 186. See also Stovall, *Paris Noir*, and Fabre, *From Harlem to Paris*.
15. Anhalt, *Gathering of Fugitives*; Schreiber, *Cold War Exiles in Mexico*.
16. Finifter, "American Emigration," 32.
17. Cleveland et al., *Overseas Americans*.
18. Bratsberg and Terrell, "Where Do Americans Live Abroad."
19. About 50,000 U.S. Americans crossed the border to Canada (see Rodgers, *Welcome to Resisterville*; Hagan, *Northern Passage*; Kusch, *All American Boys*). Between 1960 and 1976, the following six countries were the top destination for U.S. American emigrants (in descending order): Mexico, Germany, Britain, Canada, Japan, Australia, and Israel. The motivation for moving to these countries varied greatly, and, interestingly, the data chooses to refer to these individuals not as "immigrants" but as "Americans abroad" (Bratsberg and Terrell, "Where Do Americans Live Abroad?").
20. Bratsberg and Terrell, "Where Do Americans Live Abroad?," 788.
21. Warren and Kraly, "Elusive Exodus," 5.
22. On late twentieth-century U.S. emigration, see, for example, Trundle, "Against the Gated Community"; Pickering, "Past Imperfect"; Trundle, *Americans in Tuscany*; Banks, "Identity Narratives"; Benson, "Postcoloniality and Privilege"; Croucher, *The Other Side of the Fence*; Hayes, "'It Is Hard Being the Different One'"; Palma Mora, *Norteamericanos en la Ciudad de México*; Puga, "Un lugar en el Sol"; Spencer, "Americans Create Hybrid Spaces"; Calderón-Steck and Bonilla-Carrión, "Algunos aspectos sociodemográficos."
23. Cleveland et al., *Overseas Americans*, 7.
24. Finifter, "American Emigration," 34.
25. Finifter, "American Emigration," 36.
26. See Brooks, *Boomers*; Light, *Baby Boomers*; Tyler May, *Homeward Bound*; Macunovich, *Birthquake*.

27. Identity talk is part of the broadly defined activities of identity work (Snow and Anderson, "Identity Work among the Homeless," 1348).
28. Cleveland et al., *Overseas Americans*, 72.
29. Massey et al., "Theories of International Migration," 452; Moya, *Cousins and Strangers*.
30. Kathrin Morales, interviewed in San José, April 16, 2009.
31. Morales, interview.
32. Doris and John Stam, interviewed in Guadalupe de San José, April 15, 2009.
33. Richard Erikson, interviewed in Golfito, May 7, 2009.
34. Anna Fredrikson, interviewed in San José, July 18, 2008.
35. Mary Thompson, interviewed in Escazú, July 15, 2008.
36. On similar expectations among European women in European colonies and their negotiation of gender roles, see Grewal, *Home and Harem*; Chaudhuri and Strobel, *Western Women and Imperialism*; Pratt, *Imperial Eyes*, ch. 5; Melman, *Women's Orient*.
37. Croucher, "Gendered Spatialities," 22.
38. Richard Johnson, interviewed in Santa Ana, November 20, 2011.
39. Finifter, "American Emigration," 32.
40. For a similar case of a small-scaled foreign immigration that had a significant impact on the receiving society and served as a focal point for additional flows, see Waldren, *Insiders and Outsiders*.
41. Hagan, *Northern Passage*, 18.
42. John Foulks, interviewed in San Ramón de Tres Ríos, May 14, 2009. On the 1960s social and political protests movements see Chalmers, *And the Crooked Places*; Rosen, *World Split Open*.
43. Thomas Dent, interviewed in La Guácima, April 10, 2009.
44. Dent, interview.
45. Dent, interview.
46. Foulks, interview.
47. Foulks, interview.
48. Waldren, *Insiders and Outsiders*, 162.
49. Pickering, "Past Imperfect." 50.
50. Trundle, *Americans in Tuscany*, 46–47.
51. Sharon Hage, interviewed in Playa Hermosa, April 13, 2009.
52. Hage, interview.
53. Hage, interview.
54. Leech, *Youthquake*, 139.
55. For a review of the evolution of U.S. American counterculture, see Braunstein and Doyle, "Introduction."

56. Theodore Bart, interviewed in San Isidro de El General, May 15, 2009.
57. On the significance of the change in perception of time among U.S. Americans in Hawaii see Pickering "Waiting for Chronic"; on the desire to quit the Western rat race and the demands of the working world among lifestyle migrants in Morocco see Escher and Petermann, "Marrakesh, Medina," 36.
58. Dashefsky and Woodrow-Lafield, *Americans Abroad*, 5.
59. Eric White, interviewed in San Bosco de Alajuela, April 28, 2009.
60. On the quest to be considered a "good gringo" rather than an obnoxious one and the implicit practical consequences of being a "good guest" among U.S. Americans in Cuenca, Ecuador, see Hayes, *Gringolandia*, ch. 3.
61. Joan Stevens, interviewed in Ciudad Colón, May 22, 2009.
62. H. Hensel, letter to the editor, *TT*, July 28, 1972.
63. Cecil High Jr., letter to the editor, *TT*, August 4, 1972.
64. Hayes, *Gringolandia*, 106–7.
65. Jane and Michael Warren, interviewed in Ciudad Colón, March 11, 2009.
66. "Police Denied Illegal Bathing of Hippies," *TT*, March 2, 1973, 3.
67. Asamblea Legislativa de la República de Costa Rica, "Ley no. 4812." On the reluctance of U.S. Americans in Costa Rica, as well as elsewhere, to acquire local citizenship see the introduction to this book.
68. The law defined several categories, including *pensionado* (retiree) and *rentista* (rentier, a property owner of substantial means). Additional benefits stipulated in the law include exemption from import tax on household goods up to $7,000; tax free import of a new car every five years; and the right to be insured by Costa Rican social security for immigrants under the age of fifty-five. On the pensionados law see Puga, "Un lugar en el sol."
69. "Retirees Close Club—Cite Divergent Interests," *TT*, October 10, 1975.
70. Miguel Salguero, "Costa Rica vende sus tierras a extranjeros," *La Nación*, May 6, 1974.
71. Salguero, "Costa Rica vende sus tierras."
72. "The New Pensionado—No Longer the Retiring Type," *TT*, February 6, 1979.
73. Jerry Wolf, "Bull Session Lures Sages," *TT*, June 15, 1973.
74. "Where to Find It," *TT*, April 2, 1975.
75. Jim Coleman, interviewed in Piedades de Santa Ana, April 1, 2009.

76. Yehudi Monestel, "Jerry Wolf Discovered His Shangri-La in Guanacaste," *TT*, May 5, 1972.
77. Monestel, "Jerry Wolf Discovered His Shangri-La."
78. Lisa Wilson, interviewed in Santa María de Dota, May 14, 2009.
79. The 1977 revision of the law stated that only people older than fifty-five could enjoy the pensionado status, and the amount required for the monthly deposit was raised.
80. Stephen Schmidt, "Retirees Oppose New 'Pensionados' Law," *TT*, July 15, 1977.
81. "Pensionados Bring Millions to Costa Rica," *TT*, June 13, 1977.
82. Cleveland et al. argue that in countries in which the income is low, "even an average salary of U.S. Americans positions you in the category of *Gods*, in terms of material, if not spiritual reward." (Cleveland et al., *Overseas Americans*, 16). Matthew Hayes documented such motivation for migration among North Americans in Ecuador, using Timothy Ferriss's early twenty-first-century notion of Geoarbitrage and links it to transnational relocations tied up with global inequalities (Hayes, *Gringolandia*, 60).

2. Places and Networks

1. "Anglo-American Directory Out," *TT*, July 30, 1976.
2. "Anglo-American Directory Out." When I conducted my field work in Costa Rica, in 2009, several potential interviewees declined my request for a meeting on the basis that my research is about U.S. Americans in Costa Rica and they did not define themselves as such, or in any case objected to being included in this category.
3. Adapted by the author from Instituto Nacional de Estadística y Censos, *Censo de población y vivienda 1963*, Cuadro 60, ANCR.
4. Karen Hill-Webber, interviewed in Curridabat, March 8, 2009.
5. See Snow and Anderson, "Identity Work among the Homeless," 1348.
6. The term "clubland" refers to a sphere of social organizations and implies a synergetic effect, both spatial and mental, derived from the accumulation of many such associations. See Cohen, "Networks of Sociability," 171.
7. For classic works on this subject see, for example, Levitt, DeWind, and Vertovec, "International Perspectives on Transnational Migration"; Glick Schiller, Basch, and Szanton Blanc, "From Immigrant to Transmigrant."
8. See Janoschka and Haas, *Contested Spatialities*; Bönisch-Brednich and Trundle, *Local Lives*.

9. In writing about Caribbean immigration to the Central American isthmus, Lara Putnam underscores the creation of a network of places and the way in which movement between these places, rather than settlement in a specific place, becomes the key character of immigration. Putnam, *Company They Kept*, 15, 134–37.
10. Bönisch-Brednich and Trundle, "Introduction," 1.
11. Strathern and Stewart, "Introduction," 4.
12. Edward S. Casey, "How to Get from Space to Place in a Fairly Short Stretch of Time," 24, cited in Bönisch-Brednich and Trundle, "Introduction," 8.
13. Proshansky, Fabian, and Kaminoff, "Place-Identity."
14. Appadurai, *Modernity at Large*, 178. Candace Slater has stressed that new representations of places often rework and integrate older images for diverse strategic ends—such as progress or conservation—and moreover that images, especially those of nature, and particularly those that are fashioned by outsiders such as travelers, colonizers, and immigrants, are never innocent. Slater, "Visions of the Amazon," 3.
15. Strathern and Stewart, "Introduction," 4.
16. Anhalt, *Gathering of Fugitives*, Kindle locations 2103–4. Anhalt states that the choice of place of residency was thoroughly practical and had nothing to do with the street's name; Nash, *Community in Limbo*, 90; Hayes, *Gringolandia*.
17. Anna Fredrikson, interviewed in San José, July 18, 2008.
18. Mary Thompson, interviewed in Escazú, July 15, 2008.
19. Elsie Fiala, interviewed in San José, April 30, 2009.
20. On U.S. suburbia, see Duany, Plater-Zyberk, and Speck, *Suburban Nation*; Jackson, *Crabgrass Frontier*; Fishman, *Bourgeois Utopias*.
21. U.S.A. International Women's Club, *Monthly Bulletin*, March 1963, WCCR archive.
22. Doris Green, interviewed in San José, April 4, 2009.
23. Giglioli, "¿Mito o idiosincrasia?"
24. On Costa Rican spatial and racial geography, see Christian, "'Latin America without the Downside'"; Rivers-Moore, "No Artificial Ingredients?"; on the links between race and land in the Central American isthmus in general and Costa Rica in particular, see Gudmundson and Wolfe, *Blacks and Blackness*.
25. "Monteverde Statement of Aims and Ideals, 1959."
26. Guindon, "We Were Not the First," 51. On emplacement and belonging through agricultural practices among British immigrants in rural France, see Benson, "We Are Not Expats."

27. On the construction of the Inter-American Highway in Costa Rica, see Rutkow, *Longest Line on the Map*, 255–56, 270–74; Kordick, "Constructing Costa Rica's Inter-American Highway."
28. Cole-Christensen, *Place in the Rain Forest*.
29. Elsie Fiala, letter, May 15, 1961. (In Elsie Fiala letters, 1956–73; henceforth EFL).
30. John Stam and Doris Stam, interviewed in Guadalupe de San José, April 15, 2009.
31. Stephens, "The Golfito Boat People," 241.
32. Stephens, "The Golfito Boat People," 242.
33. On the search for an idyllic, rural lifestyle in internal migration within the United States, see Hoey, "From Pi to Pie," 586; On the habit to contrast former places of residence with the new migratory destinations in order to enhance the latter enchantment see O'Reilly and Benson, "Lifestyle Migration," 7.
34. Eileen Steinberg, interviewed in San José, June 15, 2009.
35. Eric White, interviewed in San Bosco de Alajuela, April 28, 2009.
36. Michael Janoschka and Heiko Haas suggest, in respect to the individual construction of identity through practices of consumption, that within late capitalism consumption does not exclusively mean the purchase of manufactured goods. It is also related to intangible services and, particularly in our case, to the consumption of exotic places and natural landscapes ("Introduction," 3).
37. Joan Stevens, interviewed in Ciudad Colón, May 22, 2009.
38. John Foulks, interviewed in San Ramón de Tres Ríos, June 14, 2009.
39. Sharon Hage, interviewed in Playa Hermosa, April 13, 2009.
40. Barbara Williams, interviewed in Santo Domingo de Heredia, March 11, 2009.
41. Hage, interview.
42. S.S., "Must Paradise Be Full of Poison Ivy?," *TT*, February 25, 1977.
43. Pratt, *Imperial Eyes*, 24.
44. Foulks, interview.
45. Snow and Anderson, "Identity Work among the Homeless," 1349.
46. John Erikson, interviewed in Golfito, May 27, 2009; Jim Brown, interviewed in Dominical, April 11, 2009.
47. Theodore Bart, interviewed in San Isidro de El General, May 15, 2009.
48. Boggs, *Married to a Legend*, 21–23.
49. Jane Mora, interviewed in San José, May 25, 2009.
50. Hill-Webber, interview.
51. Adam Klee, interviewed in Heredia, June 10, 2009.

52. Laura Barbas-Rhoden maintains that there is a frequent association in Latin texts between upper-class women and closed, interior spaces, where they are presumably more secure. "Before the advent of the feminist writers, Latin American texts often portrayed bourgeois women in enclosed spaces, most commonly in the home, walled garden, church, or convent. Beyond such spaces roamed only women of questionable morals or lower social classes" (Barbas-Rhoden, *Ecological Imaginations*, 136).

53. On the deterioration of Costa Rica's economy and the process of urbanization in the 1970s, see Marois, "From Economic Crisis"; Trejos, "Costa Rica."

54. Hayes, *Gringolandia*, 21, 37–38. Research concerning the impact created by the purchase of Costa Rican real estate by U.S. Americans began to appear around 2000; see, for example, Janoschka, "Imaginarios del turismo residencial," and Van Noorloos, "Residential Tourism and Multiple Mobilities." But the advance of U.S. Americans from the Central Valley to the periphery in the 1970s can be traced through a systematic reading of the real estate section of the *TT*, which, during this decade, listed properties for sale in the greater vicinity of San José. In 1977, many ads simply stated, for example, "Beaches, Caribbean or Pacific side" in "Where to Find It / Properties," *TT*, April 22, 1977.

55. William Russell, interviewed in Curridabat, April 1, 2009.

56. Salguero, "Costa Rica vende sus tierras," *La Nación*, May 6, 1974.

57. Salguero, "Costa Rica vende sus tierras," *La Nación*, May 20, 1974.

58. Facio, "Means and Ends for a Better Costa Rica," 187.

59. Salguero argued that while in the short term, the Costa Ricans had gained by selling land to the latter because they received a significant sum of money that allowed them to buy a car or send their children to school, in the long run they lost because they were left with no property and without the financial ability to purchase any in the future, thus becoming peons on their former lands ("Costa Rica vende sus tierras").

60. Despite portraying the Costa Ricans as naïve, Salguero himself tells the story of a general in the Costa Rican army who sold tens of thousands of acres to U.S. Americans after a tough negotiation. Salguero, "Costa Rica vende sus tierras," May 21, 1974.

61. Carlos Jinesta, "Letters," *TT*, November 3, 1972.

62. Jinesta, "Letters."

63. The German Club of Costa Rica, financed by wealthy German immigrants and supported by the German government, opened its doors

in 1911 in a spacious building in downtown San José. On German clubs and associations in San José, see Nemcik, "Germans, Costa Ricans"; on Italian immigrants in Costa Rica and their La Casa Italia, which was founded in 1959 in Barrio Francisco Peralta in San José, see Bariatti, "Inmigrantes italianos en Costa Rica"; on Ashkenazi Jewish communal institutions in San Jose see Pérez Navarro, "Construcción de una comunidad."

64. Theroux, "Tarzan Is an Expatriate." On the monitoring role of social clubs in the United Fruit Company compounds, see Shragai, "Do Bananas Have a Culture?"; Eric Cohen suggests that the expat's social clubs enabled the alleviation of social pressures through drinking and gambling, for example, by keeping it behind closed doors (Cohen, "Expatriate Communities," 38).
65. Fechter, "Living in a Bubble," 39, 42.
66. On Contact Zones see Putnam, *Imperial Eyes*, 4.
67. Nash, *Community in Limbo*, 35.
68. On clubs in the United States, see Charles, *Service Clubs in American Society*.
69. Elizabeth S. Clemens and Doug Guthrie, "Of, By, and Instead of Politics," 25, cited in Trundle, *Americans in Tuscany*, 88.
70. Putnam, *Bowling Alone*.
71. On the role of social clubs in colonial and expat communities, see Hollen Lees, "Urban Civil Society"; Cohen, "Networks of Sociability"; Nash, *Community in Limbo*, 109–11; Fechter, "Living in a Bubble"; Trundle, *Americans in Tuscany*; Cohen, "Expatriate Communities," 41–45.
72. McCoy, Scarano, and Johnson, "On the Tropic of Cancer," 24–26.
73. Spitzer, *Hotel Bolivia*, Kindle locations 203–7; Cohen, "Expatriate Communities," 15–20.
74. Snow and Anderson, "Identity Work among the Homeless," 1349.
75. Roland Barthes, *Ethnic Groups and Boundaries*, cited in Fechter, "Living in a Bubble," 35.
76. Joyce Brown, interviewed in Dominical, April 11, 2009.
77. *The American Legion News for Legionaries*, February 1979, 30, Archive of the American Legion, Heredia.
78. Nationality as a criterion for membership was common in U.S. women's clubs throughout the world, such as those in Barcelona and Jakarta, and the Anglo-American charity associations in Tuscany. This was in marked contrast to non-U.S. American women's clubs that tended to be binational or international, such as women's clubs in India in the late 1940s, which were a meeting place for a national

and racial mix of Hindu and British women. See Fechter, "Living in a Bubble"; Trundle, *Americans in Tuscany*; Cohen, "Networks of Sociability"; Nash, *Community in Limbo*, 113–15.
79. Doris Green, interviewed in San José, April 22, 2009.
80. Diane Abrahams, interviewed in Kfar Saba (Israel), June 11, 2012.
81. Joan Stevens, interview.
82. U.S.A. Women's Club, *President Report* (1975), WCCR archive.
83. U.S.A Women's Club, *President Report* (1959), WCCR archive.
84. Fechter depicted the luxurious hotel in Jakarta in which British women met, and especially the private chauffeurs who brought them there in airconditioned cars as more evidence of their bubble-like lifestyle that ensured no connection with the physicality of the local city (Fechter, "Living in a Bubble," 48); Trundle notes that the meetings of the Anglo-American women's charity association were held in a spectacular location that highlighted the charms of Tuscany, calculated to express and enhance the women's enchantment with their lifestyle (Trundle, *Americans in Tuscany*, 95).
85. On USIS in Europe, see Tobia, *Advertising America*; Nash, *Community in Limbo*, 16.
86. Mark Bach, interviewed in Alajuela, April 27, 2009.
87. "Retirees Close Club—Cite Divergent Interests," *Tico Times*, October 10, 1975.
88. The first HHH clubs were established in the late 1930s as orienteering clubs for British colonial officers and expats in Kuala Lumpur, Malaya (now Malaysia). Its members met on Monday afternoons to go running ("hashing") as a way of overcoming the weekend drinking and Monday morning blues, and expanded from there to other destinations around the world. The rules of the Hash House Harrier runs were based loosely on those of the traditional British "paper chase." For the history of the HHH, see https://thehashhouse.org/.
89. Bill Barbie, interviewed in Santa Ana, November 20, 2011.
90. Albert Williams, "The Little Theatre Story," in *Angel Street (Gaslight)*, 1, 1967, LTG archive. On the LTG movement in the United States, see Chansky, *Composing Ourselves*.
91. On Costa Rican theatre in the 1970s, see Solís and Salvador, "El movimiento teatral costarricense (1951–1971)" and Herzfeld and Cajiao Salas, *El teatro de hoy*. On the influence of exiled Chilean artists on the theatre in Costa Rica after the fall of Salvador Allende, see Thomas, "Chilean Theatre in Exile."
92. *The Zoo Story, The American Dream*, May 1969, LTG archive.

3. Cowboys to Guardians

1. Marañón, *Gringo's Hawk*, 56. "Marañón" was the pen name of a U.S. American who settled in the southern Pacific coast of Costa Rica in 1971. The nickname was given to him by the children of his village and is Spanish for cashew nut, as well as being a region in Brazil and a tributary of the Amazon in Peru (*Gringo's Hawk*, xvii).
2. Columbus, *Four Voyages to the New World*, 369.
3. Escher and Pitermann, "Marrakesh, Medina," 32.
4. Schama, *Landscape and Memory*, 61.
5. Barthes, *Empire of Signs*, 10; see also Baker, "Introduction," 2.
6. Behadad, *Belated Travelers*. Alexander Skutch, a well-known U.S. American botanist, naturalist, and ornithologist who arrived in Costa Rica in 1935, wrote somewhat apologetically, "I have not ventured so far beyond the frontiers of what we can call civilization, nor taken such risks as the great pioneer naturalists of the tropics did." *Naturalist in Costa Rica*, 4.
7. Slater, "Visions of the Amazon."
8. In this context, I capitalize "Rain Forest" and its thorny flip side, the "Jungle," to indicate that they designate a geographic entity that is also a particular metaphoric space (Slater, "Visions of the Amazon," 3). Rain Forests are sometimes equated with Jungles, but they are not the same: A rain forest is a wooded area that receives at least one hundred inches of rainfall per year. The term emerged in the 1960s and 1970s and acquired an aura of science (Slater, *Entangled Edens*, 137). The term jungle, on the other hand, derived from the Hindustani *djanghael* or *jangle* and originally designated wasteland or uncultivated ground. With the imposition of British colonialism throughout Asia and Africa, the meaning of the term shifted from the land itself to the vegetation that occupies such untended areas. With the popularization of British imperial writing, such as Rudyard Kipling's *The Jungle Books* (1894–95), the jungle captivated the imagination of readers in the temperate zones (Putz and Holbrook, "Tropical Rainforest Images," 38). The term "green hell" is taken from Brazilian writer Alberto Rangel's novel *Inferno Verde* (1908); "green cathedral" is a much more recent term, borrowed from Juan de Onis, *The Green Cathedral* (1992). On the Novelas de la Selva (novels of the jungle) in the Latin American literature, see Barbas-Rhoden, *Ecological Imaginations*, 132–36.
9. On the perception of the destination of immigration as paradise among lifestyle immigrants in Morocco, see Escher and Petermann,

"Marrakesh, Medina," 33. On the habit to contrast former places of residence with the new migratory destinations in order to enhance the latter enchantment see O'Reilly and Benson, "Lifestyle Migration," 7.
10. Skutch, *Naturalist in Costa Rica*, 8.
11. On Costa Rica's ecological history, see Steinberg, *Environmental Leadership*; Trejos, *Costa Rica*. On the creation of Costa Rica's image as a peaceful ecological paradise, see Barbas-Rhoden, *Ecological Imaginations*.
12. Denevan, "Pristine Myth," 379. Referring to the eighteenth-century European travelers' gaze, which constructed the American landscape as a blank space, Mary Louis Pratt noted that such "visual descriptions presuppose—naturalize—a transformative project." Pratt, *Imperial Eyes*, xx. For a compelling analysis of the early twenty-first-century Costa Rican international tourism campaign, see Rivers-Moore, "No Artificial Ingredients?"
13. Augelli, "Costa Rica's Frontier Legacy," 1.
14. Bozzoli de Wille, "La frontera agrícola de Costa Rica," 226. On the settlement in the Costa Rican frontier from the end of the colonial period, see Sampar, *Generations of Settlers*. For a consideration of the idea of the frontier in U.S. culture and its reinvention following its alleged closure in the late nineteenth century, see Grossman, "Introduction."
15. Elsie Fiala, letter, May 15, 1961, EFL.
16. On the link between race and land on the isthmus in general and Costa Rica in particular, and on the association of the Atlantic coast with black-skinned peoples, see Gudmundson and Wolfe, *Blacks and Blackness in Central America*. On the Costa Rican spatial and racial geography, see Christian, "'Latin America without the Downside'"; Rivers-Moore, "No Artificial Ingredients?"; Giglioli, "¿Mito o idiosincrasia?"
17. Láscaris, "In Defense of the Corner Store"; Barahona Jiménez, *El gran incógnito*, 55.
18. On the *denuncio* legislation, see Salas Víquez, "La búsqueda de soluciones." See also Brockett and Gottfried, "State Policies"; Nygren, "Deforestation in Costa Rica."
19. See, for example, Meagher, "Holidays in Costa Rica," 274. While historians had already demonstrated that the ownership of land and the notion of small households were more of a myth constructed for national purposes in the liberal era than a reality, the myth was nonetheless significant as such. See Gudmundson, *Costa Rica before Coffee*, ch. 4.

20. On the construction of the Inter-American Highway in Cerro de la Muerte and the effect it had on the region, see Kordick, *Saints of Progress*; Kordick, "Constructing Costa Rica's Inter-American Highway"; Rutkow, *Longest Line on the Map*, 255–56, 270–80.
21. Cole-Christensen, *Place in the Rain Forest*, 43.
22. Cole-Christensen, *Place in the Rain Forest*, 43.
23. Marañón recounted, "While my older brothers braved the cold academia of Harvard and Cornell, I felt blessed to wear shorts and a T-shirt and to sit on bamboo" (*Gringo's Hawk*, xv).
24. Cole-Christensen, *Place in the Rain Forest*, 89.
25. García Canclini, *Hybrid Cultures*, 46.
26. McClintock, *Imperial Leather*, 226, 242.
27. Hayes, *GringoIndia*, 89; Quijano, "Coloniality of Power."
28. Melman, "Under the Western Historian's Eyes"; Chakrabaty, "Post-Coloniality and the Artifice of History."
29. Rex R. Benson, "They Took to the Jungle . . . ," *TT*, March 29, 1957.
30. Marañón, *Gringo's Hawk*, xv.
31. Worster, *Under Western Skies*, 6.
32. Marañón's parents financed the purchase of land and he served as the family representative in the country. "The highway and other major developments slated for the area would someday surely bring financial opportunities." (Marañón, *Gringo's Hawk*, 84).
33. Linda Moller, "Guanacaste Like Old Wild West," *TT*, July 4, 1975.
34. For a similar depiction of Costa Rica half a century later, see Rivers-Moore, "No Artificial Ingredients?," 347: "Unpeopled, uncivilized Costa Rica represents the frontier of civilization, waiting to be 'discovered' by rugged tourists from the North."
35. Elsie Fiala, letter, July 7, 1959, EFL. Roy Rogers and Dale Evans were iconic characters in *The Roy Rogers Show* (NBC, 1951–57) where they portrayed a cowboy and a cowgirl respectively.
36. Grossman, "Introduction."
37. On the narrative of peaceful conquest, see White, "Fredrick Jackson Turner."
38. On the indigenous population in Costa Rica, see *Plan nacional de desarollo*.
39. Pike, *United States and Latin America*, 21–40.
40. Eileen Steinberg, interviewed in San José, June 15, 2009; Fiala, letter, December 27, 1959, EFL.
41. Skutch, *Naturalist in Costa Rica*, 223.
42. Cole-Christensen, *Place in the Rain Forest*, 146–62.
43. Marañón, *Gringo's Hawk*, 22.

44. Whitehead, "Amazonia," 127.
45. Cole-Christensen, *Place in the Rain Forest*, 44.
46. H. D. Thoreau wrote in *Walden*, "At the same time that we are earnest to explore and learn all things, we require that all things be mysterious and unexplorable, that land and sea be infinitely wild, unsurveyed and unfathomed by use." Thoreau, *Walden*, cited in Putz and Holbrook, "Tropical Rain-Forest Images," 52.
47. Skutch, *Naturalist in Costa Rica*, 208.
48. Skutch, *Naturalist in Costa Rica*, 139–40, 227–28. Still, the rain forest's potential was material as well as spiritual. In Skutch's case, the numerous new species that could be found in his property late into the twentieth-century turned it into a new type of botanical El Dorado, and by sending these species to the Smithsonian Institution for research purposes he gained both income and fame.
49. Marañón, *Gringo's Hawk*, 201–2. Lucille Guindon, one of the founders of Quaker colony of Monteverde, testified that among the various things they have learned from their local neighbors was the consulting of the moon for agricultural work (Guindon, "We Were Not the First,"51.)
50. Jack Ewing, *Monkeys Are Made of Chocolate*, 137.
51. Rapport, "Epilogue," 184.
52. On time as a cultural construct and the adoption of local concepts of time and its measurement as a form of cultural identification, see Harvey, *Justice, Nature*, 222.
53. Theodore Bart, interviewed in San Isidro de El General, April 15, 2009.
54. On moon rituals and femininity see Norgaard, "Moon Phases."
55. Steinberg, interview. In writing about European immigrants in Marrakesh, Morocco, Escher and Peterman argue that "it is frequently the slow rhythm of life that attracts the migrants," especially those of the middle class, who are looking to escape the feverish pace of life in the West (Escher and Petermann, "Marrkesh, Medina," 36). On "counter temporal culture" among U.S. Americans in Hawaii, see Pickering, "'Waiting for Chronic.'"
56. Linda Sheinin, interviewed in Pavones, May 15, 2009.
57. Sharon Hage, interviewed in Playa Hermosa, April 13, 2009.
58. Bart, interview.
59. Pratt argues that whereas in the Old World the human being lies at the center of the artistic vision, figuratively and metaphorically, in the New World man is lost in nature (Pratt, *Imperial Eyes*, 111–24).

60. Cole-Christensen, *Place in the Rain Forest*, 5–6. The destructive power of the rain forest is enhanced through use of the literal primacy effect, which determines that the order in which information is presented determines the overall impact of the text, in this case the beginning with reptiles and ending with gentle flowers.
61. Cole-Christensen, *Place in the Rain Forest*, 6.
62. Cole-Christensen, *Place in the Rain Forest*, 128, 126.
63. On the colonial discourse of "feminizing the empty land," see McClintock, *Imperial Leather*, 242. Susan Bassnett argues that such sexual overtones became a convention in colonial travel writing about the opening of new territories (Bassnett, "Travel Writing and Gender," 231). On the gendered discourse of U.S.-Latin American relations, see Muñoz-Pogossian, "Gendered Language." On the construction of Costa Rican nature as feminine, see Rivers-Moore, "No Artificial Ingredients?," 344.
64. Cole-Christensen, *Place in the Rain Forest*, 29.
65. Brockett and Gottfried, "State Policies," 14.
66. Guindon, "Homesteading," in Guindon et al., *Monteverde Jubilee Family Album*, 105.
67. On the foundation of eco-feminist criticism regarding the division between women and nature, see Ortner, "Is Female to Male?"
68. On the discourse of "civilized manliness" and "primitive masculinity," which views indigenous men as less masculine because of their alleged "backwardness," and more broadly on the intersection of masculinity, class, and race, see Bederman, *Manliness and Civilization*.
69. Cole Christensen, *Place in the Rain Forest*, 106.
70. Cole-Christensen, *Place in the Rain Forest*, 51–62.
71. Cole-Christensen, *Place in the Rain Forest*, 223. As with other themes, so too in his writing about women Cole-Christensen follows concepts and representations that prevailed in Latin American writings about bourgeois women—who were described as confined to close spaces (see Barbas-Rhoden, *Ecological Imaginations*, 136)—but even more clearly followed tales about women in the North American frontier, emphasizing the travails of life there, especially in the context of reproduction. Patricia Nelson Limerick argues that representations of women in the frontier often portrayed them as isolated from their families and disconnected from civilization, disoriented in the unfamiliar landscape, and exhausted from the hard work, even though this was not necessarily the reality of these women's lives. Limerick, *Legacy of Conquest*, 48–50. See also Armitage and Jameson, *Women's West*; Kolodny, *Land before Her*.

72. Chornook and Guindon, *Walking with Wolf;* Powell, "The Monteverde Preserve's Beginning," 170–72; Wallace, *Quetzal and the Macaw,* 112–15.
73. Chornook and Guindon, *Walking with Wolf,* 1.
74. Chornook and Guindon, *Walking with Wolf,* 179, 187.
75. A similar picture regarding the position of Costa Rican women of a rural community in the Central Valley vis-à-vis the rain forest can be found in Nygren, "Deforestation in Costa Rica," 30.
76. Journalist Wendy Kaminar coined the term "nature's housekeepers" in the late twentieth century, yet the perception of nature as the Greater Household of Earth and of women's role in domesticating it prevailed since the late nineteenth century. See Unger, *Beyond Nature's Housekeepers,* 3; Mann, "Pioneers of U.S. Ecofeminism." See also Schrepfer, *Nature's Altars.*
77. Fiala, letter, July 16, 1958, EFL.
78. Fiala, letter, no date. The employee delivered the tiger to the Fialases because they paid a cow for every hunted tiger.
79. Fiala, letter, October 29, 1961, EFL.
80. Fiala, letter, February 4, 1960, EFL.
81. Joyce Brown, interviewed in Dominical, April 11, 2009.
82. Brown, interview.
83. Sheinin, interview.
84. Marañón, *Gringo's Hawk,* 25. Arrival scenes are a common convention of travel writing. They depict the very first encounter of the traveler with the new place and the local population and in many cases set the tone and terms of future relations (Pratt, *Imperial Eyes,* 80).
85. Michelle White, interviewed in San Bosco de Alajuela, April 28, 2009 (interviewed together with Eric White).
86. Michelle and Eric White, interview.
87. U.S. Americans in Costa Rica may have read about Cocos Island in Truman Capote's *In Cold Blood,* where one of the protagonists tries to persuade his partner to join him on a mission to the island to recover a treasure trove of Peruvian gold, jewelry, and $60 million allegedly hidden there in 1821 (Capote, *In Cold Blood,* 100).
88. "Transmission Memorandum of Conversation with Foreign Office Official Regarding Potential Costa Rican Narcotic Problem, April 27, 1964," National Archives and Records Administration, RG 84, entry 178, box 14.
89. "Cocos Isle Declares Independence with a Mystery Letter," *TT,* August 24, 1973.
90. Lezak Shallat, "Tamarindo: Fast Buck on the Gringo Trail," *TT,* May 18, 1979.

91. Shallat, "Tamarindo."
92. In 1940, 70 percent of the country was covered with forest, down to a mere 25 percent by 1990 (Brockett and Gottfried, "State Policies," 1).
93. On the change in Costa Rican environmental policies and the evolution of the conservation discourse, which were also the result of Costa Rica's economic crisis in the early 1980s, see Isla, *"Greening" of Costa Rica*; Steinberg, *Environmental Leadership*; Barbas-Rhoden, *Ecological Imaginations*; Wallace, *Quetzal and the Macaw*.
94. Ewing, *Monkeys Are Made of Chocolate*, 179.
95. See Ewing, *Monkeys Are Made of Chocolate*, and the website of Hacienda Barú, accessed September 4, 2017, http://www.haciendabaru.com/ii-history-of-hacienda-baru/.
96. Cole-Christensen, *Place in the Rain Forest*, 8, viii.
97. "Public Beaches? Don't Try Flamingo," *TT*, June 9, 1972. It should be noted, though, that the *TT* was inconsistent in its views on nature preservation in Costa Rica, since, as I mentioned earlier in this chapter, as late as 1974 it advocated the idea of Costa Rica as a new frontier filled with development opportunities.
98. Marañón, *Gringo's Hawk*, 62.
99. Ecological initiatives have been springing up in Costa Rica since the 1970s, but the country's rise to the status of ecological superpower occurred in the 1980s and 1990s, a period beyond the scope of this research. The dramatic shift toward conservation came with the election of President Oscar Arias Sánchez (1987 Nobel Peace Prize laureate) and his efforts to promote what he termed "Peace with Nature." But while Costa Rican policies paved the way for this shift, its execution involved numerous foreign individuals, organizations, and governments, to the point that nature conservation and preservation became an explicit manifestation of coloniality-in-the-making. Steven Palmer and Ivan Molina have argued that some of the ecological research stations and environmental projects established in Costa Rica during those decades resemble colonial-era mission posts (Palmer and Molina, *Costa Rican Reader*, 175–76). On coloniality, see Moraña, Dussel, and Jáuregui, *Coloniality at Large*. For a sharp criticism of the foreign involvement in nature conservation and preservation in Costa Rica, see Isla, *"Greening" of Costa Rica*.
100. Barbara Williams, interviewed in Alajuela, May 7, 2009.

4. Becoming a U.S. Woman

1. Boggs, *Married to a Legend*, 18.
2. Boggs, *Married to a Legend*, 46.

3. Madison, "Existential Migration."
4. Croucher, "Gendered Spatialities," 21.
5. Trundle, *Americans in Tuscany*, 3. See also Hayes, *Gringolandia*, 50–52.
6. Pratt, *Imperial Eyes*, ch. 5; Stoler, *Carnal Knowledge and Imperial Power*, ch.3; Melman, *Women's Orient*.
7. Shragai, "In the Service of Their Homeland"; Fechter, "Living in a Bubble"; Callan and Ardener, *Incorporated Wife*.
8. Pessar and Mahler, "Gendered Geographies of Power."
9. de Beauvoir, *Second Sex*, 330.
10. Pessar and Mahler, "Gendered Geographies of Power," 441.
11. Snow and Anderson, "Identity Work among the Homeless."
12. Fechter, "Living in a Bubble,"46.
13. Glick Schiller, Basch, and Szanton Blanc, "From Immigrant to Transmigrant," 96.
14. Pessar and Mahler, "Gendered Geographies of Power," 446.
15. First founded in the late nineteenth century, women's clubs across the United States attracted hundreds of thousands of mostly middle-class women. While public opinion has traditionally considered these clubs to be embodiments of old-fashioned womanhood and class and racial segregation, more recently scholars have seen them as harbingers of second wave of feminism and a locus of women's activism. See for example Mathews-Gardner, "From Woman's Club to NGO"; Meltzer, "'Pulse and Conscience of America'"; Blair, "Dynamic Force"; Morris-Crowther, "Municipal Housekeeping."
16. On foreign women's clubs see Cohen, "Expatriate Communities," 23; on the U.S. American women's club in 1960s Barcelona, see Nash, *Community in Limbo*, 113–15; on the expat women's club in Jakarta, see Fechter, "Living in a Bubble."
17. On the U.S. American female work force during World War II and the early years of the Cold War, see Kessler-Harris, *In Pursuit of Equity*, 12; Kessler-Harris, *Out to Work*, 300–319; Romero, *Maid in the U.S.A*; Rosen, *World Split Open*, 21–25, 42; Chafe, *American Woman*.
18. Frustration caused by their inability to preserve their professional status in their new country of residence was shared by U.S. American expat women in other countries. See, for example, Trundle, *Americans in Tuscany*, 59.
19. Escamilla Gutiérrez and Vargas Mora, "Peasant Women's Autobiographies."
20. Luisa Gonzáles, a Costa Rican social activist and writer, argued that in the lower-class neighborhoods of 1950s San José, women worked

as either domestic help or as prostitutes (Gonzáles, "Women of the Barrio").
21. Karen Hill-Webber, interviewed in Curridabat, March 10, 2009.
22. For a similar process among late twentieth-century expatriate women in Jakarta, see Fechter, "Living in a Bubble," 45.
23. Joyce Brown, interviewed in Dominical, April 11, 2009.
24. Cleveland, "Pretty American," 34. *The Ugly American* was a bestselling political novel written by Eugene Burdick and William Lederer and published in 1958; it severely criticized the foreign policy of the United States and the aggressiveness of its representatives abroad.
25. Rosenberg, "Consuming Women."
26. The club's texts are fragmented. This is partly due to a dearth of documentation and preservation—the club's lack of a physical center meant that its archive was housed in the homes of different members and often moved from one to the other. At the time that I conducted my fieldwork it was housed in the garage of an old-time member. The other reason is that a certain amount of institutional censorship took place. I have tried to overcome these shortcomings through oral histories and textual sources from the English-speaking press in Costa Rica.
27. *U.S.A. Women Club Constitution*, 1958, WCCR archive.
28. In Trundle's writing about charity organizations of Anglo-American women in Tuscany, the motivation of working to further the U.S. agenda or reputation is not mentioned at all. Instead, the purpose is listed as: "To have fun, to be democratic and to raise more money for charities" (*Americans in Tuscany*, 95).
29. U.S.A. International Women's Club, *Monthly Bulletin*, June 30, 1960, WCCR archive.
30. Cleveland, "Pretty American."
31. Cleveland, "Pretty American," 34. See also Cleveland et al., *Overseas Americans*, 46–67.
32. *Silver Anniversary Year History of the Women Club*, San José, no date, 2, WCCR archive. Almost thirty years later, the *TT* reported that Jalowin, or the Día de los Brujas, was a popular festival in Costa Rica. "At This Rate, Halloween May Turn into a Weeklong Celebration," *TT*, November 2, 1973.
33. Peggy Anson, *Annual Report of the U.S.A. Women's Club*, 1951–52, 1, WCCR archive; see also http://wccr.org/about-wccr/history/through-the-decades-1950s. The "official" narrative of the picnic's history was published yearly by *Tico Times*. See, for example, "Picnic's a Tradition," *TT*, July 4, 1979.

34. Gertrude Rehwoldt, letter, WCCR archive.
35. Anna Fredrikson, interviewed in San José, July 18, 2008.
36. Fredrikson, interview.
37. Kathrin Morales, interviewed in San José, May 25, 2009; Cleveland warned in his article in *Harper's* against the tendency of U.S. American wives in foreign countries to isolate themselves in U.S. American enclaves that have "'a distressing effect on U.S. public relations among the surrounding 'aliens'" (Cleveland, "Pretty American," 34).
38. Fredrikson, interview.
39. "U.S. Women's Club to Vote on By-Laws," *TT*, October 9, 1959; the report does not mention that the change was in response to the ambassador's request.
40. Doris Patton, *President Report*, 1964, no page, no date, WCCR archive.
41. Morales, interview. In a similar conflict over the inclusion of Italian women who did not speak English in the charity organization of Anglo-American women in Tuscany, its president used similar phrasing, noting, "We finally took care of that" (Trundle, *Americans in Tuscany*, 37–38).
42. *U.S.A. International Women's Club Constitution*, 1965, article I, 1, WCCR archive.
43. *U.S.A. International Women's Club Constitution*, 1965, article III, 1, WCCR archive.
44. WCCR website, http://wccr.org/through-the-decades-1960s/.
45. *WCCR Constitution*, 1975, articles A and B respectively, WCCR archive.
46. "Men's Views of Women's Clubs," 285.
47. Trundle, *Americans in Tuscany*, 2.
48. I borrowed this analysis from Trundle, *Americans in Tuscany*, 108.
49. Gail Stone, *Summary of Activities over the Years*, March 1959, WCCR archive; the club's sources do not indicate if this substantial sum was raised from individual citizens or was donated by U.S. businesses and corporations in Costa Rica, such as the local branch of the United Fruit Company. A similar initiative to send money to the homeland during World War II was undertaken by women's clubs in India (Cohen, "Networks of Sociability," 180).
50. Peggy Anson, *Annual Report of the U.S.A. Women's Club*, 1950–51, WCCR archive.
51. U.S.A. International Women's Club, *Monthly Bulletin*, March 1964, 4, WCCR archive.
52. *Report of the Work and Future Projects of the Social Welfare Group of Escazú*, February 2, 1963, 1, WCCR archive.

53. *Report of the Work and Future Projects*; CARE was a subcontractor for the U.S. State Department that provided equipment for U.S.-initiated projects in various countries. Following a similar donation by a U.S. women's club in Germany, the club's president there stated that the "German girls" had started to take English classes and do things "in the American way" (Meltzer, "'Pulse and Conscience of America,'" 60).
54. "Responden a campaña en favor de la donacíon de sangre," *La Nación*, January 9, 1978.
55. Norma Loaiza, "International Women Club auspiciará la presentación de 'All Florida Fashion Show,'" *La Nación*, April 25, 1963; Miryam Francis, "Las seis reinas de belleza que presentarán las modas de Florida," *La República*, May 22, 1963.
56. Fay Dresner, *Thoughts about Our Program*, 1958, 53, WCCR archive.
57. Dresner, *Thoughts about Our Program*.
58. Fay Dresner, *Report on Interest Groups for the Year 1959*, no date, WCCR archive.
59. Mary Lou Tussey, a U.S. American dancer and choreographer, led a dance group that performed such dances. Lou Tussey, interviewed in San Ramón de Tres Ríos, June 11, 2009.
60. Fredrikson, interview; on the perception and appropriation of Latin dances by North Americans, see Paynne Daniel, *Rumba*; Moore, "Commercial Rumba."
61. U.S.A. International Women's Club, *Monthly Bulletin*, March 1963, WCCR archive.
62. Women's Club of Costa Rica, *Monthly Bulletin*, May 1969, WCCR archive.
63. May, *Homeward Bound*, 108. In the late 1950s, 95 percent of U.S. Americans, both men and women, were married before the age of twenty-five (May, *Homeward Bound*, 21).
64. May, *Homeward Bound*; Friedan, *The Feminine Mystique*, ch. 1: "The Problem That Has No Name," 15–32; Cohen, *Consumers' Republic*, 134–45. For a critical view of Freidan and May's interpretation, see Horowitz, *Betty Friedan*; Meyerowitz, "Beyond the Feminine Mystique."
65. A late nineteenth-century Uruguayan dictionary described the china as both appealing and intimidating: "She often suffers from anemia, but she is attractive and when she cares to do so she can be hardworking. She is respectful and loyal." Granada, *Del vocabulario rioplatense razonado*, 195.

66. Thirty-eight percent of the women who were defined as economically active in Costa Rica of the 1950s and 1960s worked as domestic help (*Censo de población y vivienda*, 1927, 1950, 1963, Fondo: Instituto Nacional de Estadística y Censos, ANCR). On domestic service in Latin America, see Chaney and Castro, *Muchachas No More*. On domestic service in the United States, see Kessler-Harris, *In Pursuit of Equity*; Kessler-Harris, *Out to Work*, esp. parts 1 and 2; Romero, *Maid in the U.S.A*; Palmer, *Domesticity and Dirt*; and Katzman, *Seven Days a Week*. Interestingly, Romero found that the incidence of live-in maids tended to be higher along the border between the United States and Mexico and can thus be seen as an influence of Latin American practices and domestic culture on the United States (Romero, *Maid in the U.S.A*, 1).
67. See Janoschka and Haas, "Introduction," 3.
68. Observer, "Letters," *TT*, April 30, 1959.
69. Mary Thompson, interviewed in Escazú, July 17, 2008. Janoschka and Haas refer to domestic help as an intangible service that was yet another commodity for consumption as well as a critical tool in the construction of identities among lifestyle immigrants, particularly women as the main and most direct consumers of this commodity (Janoschka and Haas, "Contested Spatialities," 3).
70. Cynthia Price, interviewed in Heredia, March 11, 2009.
71. Croucher, "Gendered Spatialities," 22.
72. Napur Chaudhuri and Margaret Strobel, *Western Women and Imperialism*, 1992, cited in Croucher, "Gendered Spatialities," 20. See also Grewal, *Home and Harem*.
73. Debora Vargas, interviewed in San José, May 25, 2009; Jane Mora, interviewed in San José, May 15, 2009. On the "servant problem" of U.S. Americans abroad, see Harpell, "White Zones," 322–23; Croucher, "They Love Us Here"; Nash, *Community in Limbo*, 45–48, 63; Emery-Waterhouse, *Banana Paradise*, 325. On the relations between the British colonial lady and her domestic help in India, see Blunt, "Imperial Geographies of Home."
74. Marge Durant, "Maids I Have Known," *TT*, February 26, 1960.
75. Durant, "Maids I Have Known."
76. Ortiz's column should be read in the context of two traditions: instruction manuals for young wives and mothers, along the lines of Dr. Spock, popular in the United States during this period (May, *Homeward Bound*, 43) and instruction manuals for white housewives and mothers in their interactions with nonwhite domestic help, such as the 1959 U.S. best seller *Your Maid from Mexico* and similar,

earlier manuals for European women living in European colonies in Asia and Africa (Hawkins, Soper, and Henry, *Your Maid from Mexico*; Flora Annie Steel and Grace Gardiner, *The Complete Indian Housekeeper and Cook*, 1907, cited in Blunt, "Imperial Geographies of Home," 432).

77. Miguel Ortiz, "Your Child's Health," *TT*, no date.
78. Ortiz, "Your Child's Health," *TT*, June 13, 1958.
79. May, *Homeward Bound*, 109.
80. Escazú, the village near San José popular with U.S. Americans, was known as a hub of witches and shamans in the pre-Columbian period, and its inhabitants believed that their ghosts continued to haunt the current population ("Scenes from Another Century—Change Hardly Visible in Escazú Today," *TT*, March 7, 1975).
81. Ortiz's convictions reiterated those of Dr. Spock, who stressed that children needed the constant supervision of their mothers, or else they would become juvenile delinquents (Rosen, *World Split Open*, 18). Similar warnings were published in British guides for mothers in the early twentieth century: "No one can take the mother's place as regards to the loving and constant watchful care of her little ones" (Steel and Gardiner, *The Complete Indian Housekeeper and Cook*, cited in Blunt, "Imperial Geographies of Home," 432). Anxiety regarding the relation between European children and their local nannies was reflected in instructions to local nannies in various European colonies. In Java nannies were ordered to hold European children away from their body, so they would not get attached to their body odor (Stoler, "Intimidation of Empire," 25).
82. Fredrickson, interview.
83. Dery Dyer, interviewed in San José, May 20, 2009.
84. Dyer, interview. One of the senior editors in *Ms.* coined the term "anonymous feminists" to describe the women who participated in consciousness-raising groups. The term is well suited to describe the group of anonymous female writers of this *TT* column. Farrell, *Yours in Sisterhood*, 66.
85. Onka Dekkers, "Periodicals," *off our backs*, September 1972, 19.
86. Anne Eliot, "Machismo and Marriage," *TT*, April 14, 1972.
87. Mora, interview. On Costa Rican familial patterns see Chant, *Men in Crisis?*; on the broader Latin American context see Elizabeth Dore, *Gender Politics*.
88. Eliot, "Machismo and Marriage"
89. For a critical perspective on *Ms.* magazine's writing on Latin machismo, see Reynolds, "'Hispanism.'"

90. Jane O'Reilly, "The Housewife's Moment of Truth," *New York Magazine*, December 20, 1972.
91. Anne Eliot, "Exploding Some Myths about Men and Women," *TT*, no date.
92. Ignoring the intersection between gender, class, and ethnicity was another aspect of U.S. liberal feminism that the *TT* writers followed. For a critique of U.S. American second-wave feminism's singular focus on the "plight" of white, middle-class women, see Meyerowitz, *Not June Cleaver*. For a discussion of the problem that female domestic servants pose for feminists see Chaney and Garcia Castro, "Introduction."
93. On narratives of U.S. American women who traveled in the late 1960s to Italy, see Trundle, *Americans in Tuscany*, 46.
94. Linda Vaccariello, "Climb a Rope Ladder in a Mexican Norther," *TT*, September 8, 1972.
95. On feminist consciousness-raising groups in 1960s and 1970s United States, see Rosen, *World Split Open*, 196–201; Farrel, *Yours in Sisterhood*, 63–64; Ergas, "Feminisms of the 1970s," 540–42; Sarachild, "Consciousness-Raising," 144–50.
96. Veronica Tommins, "Women Here and Now: Barbara Eigen," *TT*, February 22, 1974.
97. Email correspondence between the author and Eigen, May 29, 2013; transcripts are in author's possession.
98. Email correspondence between the author and Khan, September 20, 2011; transcripts are in author's possession.
99. Email correspondence between the author and Khan.
100. Leitinger, *Costa Rica Women's Movement*, 19–23.
101. Lezak Shallat, "MLM: Arming Women to Fight for Their Rights," *TT*, April 27, 1979. On the narrative of transition see Melman, "Under the Western Historian's Eyes"; Chakrabaty, "Post-Coloniality and the Artifice of History."

5. Material Culture

1. Larry Washington, interviewed in Escazú, July 15, 2008.
2. Blunt and Dowling, *Home*, 142.
3. Auslander, *Taste and Power*, 423. On things as social signifiers, see also Cohen, *Household Gods*; Tolia-Kelly, "Mobility/Stability"; Douglas and Isherwood, *World of Goods*; Bourdieu, *Distinction*. On the meaning embedded in commodities in the colonial context, see McClintock, *Imperial Leather*, part 3.
4. Benson and O'Reilly, *Lifestyle Migration and Colonial Traces*, Kindle location 3733.

5. The notion of the social life of things is borrowed from Kopytoff, "Cultural Biography of Things," 64–69. On identity-work, see Snow and Anderson, "Identity Work among the Homeless."
6. Among anthropologists and cultural historians there is an ongoing debate over whether an artifact has an essentialist meaning and is therefore an object, or whether its meaning is always socially conditioned, rendering it a "thing." The essentialists warn against the reduction of artifacts to "merely an illustration," causing them to "become exemplars or reflections of meanings which are produced elsewhere" (Strathern, "Artifacts of History," 38). While acknowledging this risk, in what follows I treat artifacts as "things" and examine them primarily as part of the social, cultural, and economic system in which they function.
7. On the creation of production of locality through material culture see Tylor, "A Reluctant Locality," 101; and Andrews, "Little Anglo-India," 120. Jacqueline Waldern maintained that "living on the local economy, learning how to acquire goods, to cook and heat water for bathing on a charcoal fire in a tiny brazier, to wash clothes in cold water at the local *lavadero* (washstand)" was a crucial act of creating a sense of herself and her fellow U.S. American and British immigrants as locals in Dejà, Palma de Mallorca (Waldren, *Insiders and Outsiders*, 167–68).
8. Janoschka and Haas, "Introduction," 3.
9. David Potter argued that the notion of plenty was the most important factor in the self-definition of U.S. Americans in the years following World War II (Potter, *People of Plenty*). See also Reisman, *Abundance for What?*
10. Rosen, *World Split Open*, 12; May, *Homeward Bound*, 168. Leora Auslander has stressed the extent to which the design of the home was the main arena for the constitution of a woman's place in the family and society, in the relative absence of other sites (Auslander, *Taste and Power*, 420). Victoria de Grazia and other scholars have argued that consumption has been significantly genderized as a feminine endeavor since the early eighteenth century (De Grazia and Furlough, *Sex of Things*).
11. Vickery, *Behind Closed Doors*, 29.
12. *House Beautiful 1953*, cited in Cohen, *Consumers' Republic*, 125. On the social significance embedded in dwelling and architecture, see Wright, *Building the Dream*.
13. On the domestic revival in postwar United States, see May, *Homeward Bound*. For a criticism of May's theory of such a revival, see Meyerow-

itz, *Not June Cleaver*. On the rise of U.S. suburbia, see Cohen, *Consumers' Republic*, 194–256; Duany, Plater-Zyberk, and Speck, *Suburban Nation*; Jackson, *Crabgrass Frontier*; Gans, *The Levittowners*.

14. Ahmed et al., "Introduction" to *Uprootings/Regroundings: Questions of Home and Migration*, 2003, 9, cited in Bönisch-Brednich and Trundle, "Introduction," 8.

15. Ben Burnett, "Peace and Plenty Found in Pensión," *TT*, October 19, 1956. Referring to similar economic motivations for immigration and practices of living in the country of destination among twenty-first-century North Americans in Ecuador, Matthew Hayes has used the term Geoarbitrage to describe a transnational relocation that is tied up with global inequalities (Hayes, *Gringolandia*, 60).

16. Stephens, *Banana People*, 242; Rick Berg, "Captain Tom Defends His Playa Cacao Commune," *TT*, November 11, 1973.

17. Ben Schmidt, "Weary Transients Find Solace in San Pedro Trailer Park," *TT*, February 23, 1973.

18. Schmidt, "Weary Transients Find Solace."

19. Jane and Michael Warren, interviewed in Ciudad Colón, March 5, 2009.

20. June Eliot, interviewed in Quepos, May 23, 2009. On the cultural significance of the bungalow, see King, *The Bungalow*.

21. While the heritage of the UFC was usually condemned in Costa Rica, after the corporation's withdrawal from the country in the mid-to-late twentieth century its architecture and the living quarters of its upper-class employees became desirable (Row and Stagno, *Arquitectura de las ciudades banaeras*).

22. In 1963, 44.5 percent of the houses in Costa Rica had only one room. Biesanz, Zubris Biesanz, and Hiltunen Biesanz, *Costa Ricans*, 72. Traditionally made of adobe bricks, since the mid-twentieth century the Tico House has been constructed out of cement. In the mid-twentieth century the thatched roof was gradually replaced with corrugated iron. On the Tico House, see Gutíerrez, *La casa de adobes costarricense*; Hiltunen Biesanz, Biesanz, and Zubris Biesanz, *The Ticos*, 143–45.

23. Meagher, "Holidays in Costa Rica," 278–79.

24. Joan Stevens, interviewed in Ciudad Colón, May 22, 2009.

25. U.S.A. International Women's Club, *Monthly Bulletin*, August 1962, WCCR archive. On the division of the domestic space into various rooms according to their functionality as a sign of bourgeois refinement, see McKeon, *Secret History of Domesticity*; Vickery, *Behind Closed Doors*, 293–303.

26. Biesanz, Zubris Biesanz, and Hiltunen Biesanz, *Costa Ricans*, 73.
27. Cole-Christensen, *Place in the Rain Forest*, 37.
28. Rex Benson, "Story of the Monteverde Quakers," in Guindon et al., *Monteverde Jubilee Family Album*, 101–2.
29. On the narrative of transition, see Melman, "Under the Western Historian's Eyes"; Chakrabaty, "Post-Coloniality and the Artifice of History."
30. Guindon et al., *Monteverde Jubilee Family Album*, 15.
31. Elsie Fiala, letter, July 16, 1958, EFL.
32. Eileen Steinberg, interviewed in San José, June 15, 2009.
33. Sharon Hage, interviewed in Playa Hermosa, April 13, 2009. A-frame structures were common in the settlements of counterculturists in the United States as well ("Contacts.")
34. Roszak, *Making of a Counter Culture*.
35. Marañón, *Gringo's Hawk*, 284.
36. Vickery, *Behind Closed Doors*, 226.
37. Anna Fredrikson, interviewed in San José, July 18, 2008.
38. Despite its name, Dior's New Look, which opened his fashion show in 1947, was in fact considered a revisionist style designed to resemble an older style of dressing and to express, through fashion, the notion of reinstating women in their traditional roles after their temporary wartime liberation (Palmer, *Dior*).
39. Auslander, *Taste and Power*, 15.
40. Miller stresses that the term "matter," in contrast to "significant" or "important," "puts the burden of mattering clearly on evidence of concern to those being discussed" and not on objective definitions. Miller, "Why Some Things Matter."
41. de Grazia, *Irresistible Empire*, 419.
42. *Life Magazine*, May 5, 1947. Cited in Cohen, *Consumers' Republic*, 112.
43. Levenstein, *Paradox of Plenty*, 101–18.
44. On the "Kitchen Debate" at the 1959 American Exhibition in Moscow, in which President Nixon, standing before a model of a standard U.S. kitchen, articulated U.S. supremacy in terms not of the space race but of domestic technology, see May, *Homeward Bound*, 164. On U.S. imperialism through the lens of consumption during the Cold War, see Oldenziel and Zachmann, *Cold War Kitchen*.
45. Campbell, "Monteverde Memories," in Guindon et al., *Monteverde Jubilee Family Album*, 12.
46. Biesanz, Zubris Biesanz, and Hiltunen Biesanz, *Costa Ricans*, 72.
47. Cynthia Price, interviewed in Heredia, March 11, 2009.
48. Janoschka and Haas refers to the domestic help as an intangible service that served as another commodity for consumption and a

critical tool in the construction of identities among lifestyle migrants (Janoschka and Haas, "Introduction," 3).

49. Writing about U.S. Americans in 1960s Madrid, a Spanish writer noted that more than a mere domestic appliance, the refrigerator had to them become a sacred item (José Luis Castillo Puche, *Paralelo 40*, 1963, 13, cited in Nash, *Community in Limbo*, 51).
50. Fiala, letter, July 16, 1958, EFL.
51. Fiala, letter, February 9, 1960, EFL.
52. On the relations between laundry and class, see Palmer Mohun, *Steam Laundries*.
53. De Grazia dubbed the 1950s and 1960s in the United States the years of the "laundry revolution," when the manual work of laundry was replaced by the washing machine (de Grazia, *Irresistible Empire*, 439).
54. Fiala, letter, July 16, 1958, EFL.
55. Jane Mora, interviewed in San José, May 25, 2009. The site of the public laundry was in a poor neighborhood in San José, as implied by its name—Desamparados (the abandoned, or the hopeless).
56. *TT*, June 22, 1956.
57. Elizabeth Harris, interviewed in Escazú, April 17, 2009.
58. Harris, interview.
59. Joyce Brown, interviewed in Dominical, April 11, 2009.
60. Yehudi Monestel, "Jerry Wolf Discovered His Shangri-La in Guanacaste," *TT*, March 3.
61. Eric White, interviewed in San Bosco de Alajuela, April 28, 2009.
62. Lisa Wilson, interviewed in Santa María de Dota, May 14, 2009.
63. Mora, interview.
64. Brown, interview.
65. Brown, interview.
66. Hage, interview.
67. Theodore Bart, interviewed in San Isidro de El General, May 15, 2009.
68. Linda Sheinin, interviewed in Pavones, May 15, 2009.
69. Wilson, interview.
70. U.S.A. International Women's Club, *Monthly Bulletin*, October 29, 1960, WCCR archive; Marañón, *Gringo's Hawk*, 177.
71. Dery Dyer, interviewed in San José, May 13, 2009.
72. Polly Johnson Fondley, "No Complaints at Nosara," letter to the editor, *TT*, June 25, 1976.
73. Fiala, letter, no date, EFL.
74. Fiala, letter, July 1967, EFL. Pre-Columbian ceramics were not considered a Costa Rican craft unlike, for instance, the miniature orna-

mented oxcart of Sarchí, which was a national symbol; and therefore, as Magen Rivers-Moore argues, ceramics were "significantly described as being sold at roadside stands rather than in shops or in museums" (Rivers-Moore, "No Artificial Ingredients?," 349).

75. Barthes, "Towards a Psychosociology." See also Mintz and Du Bois, "The Anthropology of Food and Eating"; Caplan, *Food, Health and Identity*; Goody, *Cooking, Cuisine, and Class*.
76. Andrews, "Little Anglo-India,"126. On anthropological accounts of food and remembering, see Sutton, *Remembrance of Repasts*.
77. Trundle, *Americans in Tuscany*, 80.
78. Miller, "Why Some Things Matter."
79. Brown and Mussell, *Ethnic and Regional Foodways*.
80. Sheinin, interview.
81. Rockwell, "What Did We Find to Feed the Family," in Guindon et al., *Monteverde Jubilee Family Album*, 207. On the importance of hens and their genderized status in Central America, see Kockelman, *Chicken and the Quetzal*; Marañón, *Gringo's Hawk*, 147.
82. Guindon, "Frugality," 210.
83. On the Monteverde cheese factory, see Guindon et al., *Monteverde Jubilee Family Album*, 185–96.
84. Guindon, "Frugality."
85. Guindon, "A Letter," 209.
86. Elsie Fiala, letter, May 27, 1961, EFL.
87. Elsie Fiala, letter, May 2, 1959, EFL.
88. On the *Whole Earth Catalog*, see Kirk, *Counterculture Green*.
89. Cookbooks of counterculturists in the 1970s rejected the conformity of U.S. corporate products and endorsed slow cooking and the use of whole wheat, along with appropriations from foreign cuisines (Belasco, *Appetite for Change*, 45–67).
90. Hage, interview. Michaela Benson remarked on a similar process of emplacement through the growing of food among British immigrants in rural France (Benson, "We Are Not Expats," 76).
91. On the development of supermarkets and perceptions of the U.S. American consumers, see Longstreth, *The Drive-In, the Supermarket*; Cohen, "From Town Center." On the exporting of the supermarket to post–World War II Europe, see Scarpellini, "Shopping American Style"; Shaw, Curth, and Alexander, "Selling Self Service."
92. Láscaris, "In Defence of the Corner Store," 194; Barahona Jiménez, *El gran incognito*, 55.
93. Nash, *Community in Limbo*, 48–49.
94. Fredrikson, interview.

95. *TT*, November 9, 1956.
96. Sue Pardo, interviewed in San José, April 15, 2009.
97. The duties on imported liquor and fines on those made at home constituted the second largest source of national income in Costa Rica, after the duties on coffee, and as late as the 1960s, the Resguardo Fiscal was still engaged in seeking out "bootleggers" of spirits (Kordick, *Saints of Progress*, 60–61.)
98. Observer, "Letters," *TT*, November 9, 1956. Studies on U.S. Americans in Mexico and British Honduras from the nineteenth century onward describe alcoholism as a clear symptom of the "tropical decadence" that these communities came to embrace (Schell, *Integral Outsiders*, 64; Holdridge, "Toledo," 388).
99. The informant asked to remain anonymous. Transcripts of the interview are in the author's possession.
100. Lili, "Dinner Party," *TT*, April 10, 1959.
101. *TT*, April 10, 1959.
102. Kordick, *Saints of Progress*, 61.
103. Trundle and Nash discuss the image of U.S. American women as heavy drinkers in Tuscany and Barcelona (Trundle, *Americans in Tuscany*, 97; Nash, *Community in Limbo*, 62).
104. Mary Lou Tussey, interviewed in San Ramón de Tres Ríos, June 1, 2009.
105. Julie Woodman, interviewed in Santa Ana, June 3, 2009.
106. Theresa Preston-Werner traces the many transformations of the Costa Rican national cuisine, and in particular the process by which the *gallo pinto* was "whitened" and distanced from its Caribbean origin so that it could serve as the national dish of allegedly white Costa Rica (Preston-Werner, "In the Kitchen"). On the imagined nature of national cuisines, see Mintz and Du Bois, "The Anthropology of Food and Eating"; Appadurai, "How to Make a National Cuisine."
107. Thompson, interview.
108. Thompson, interview. *The Joy of Cooking*, by Irma S. Rombauer, was first published in 1936 and articulated the basic tenets of traditional U.S. American cooking and the ethics of housekeeping at the height of the economic crisis (see Levenstein, *Paradox of Plenty*, 24–39).
109. "English Language Schools Open," *TT*, August 27.
110. Women's Club of Costa Rica, *Monthly Bulletin*, January 1978, WCCR archive.
111. Communal cook books, typically published by women, have been acknowledged as a significant outlet for feminine literacy and as richly revealing products of the social, cultural, and economic sys-

tem in which their authors lived. It is precisely due to their alleged unpretentiousness that such community cook books can attest to the culture and the self-representations of their authors in terms of nationality, class, ethnicity, and so forth. See Theophano, *Eat My Word*.
112. Tutoring the cook by the "lady" of the house was a common practice in colonial and semicolonial regimes, which sometimes created intimacy between the two women and a two-way exchange of culinary traditions (Harpell, "White Zones," 327).
113. On the gendered aspects of sugar and sweets during World War II, see Bentley, *Eating for Victory*, 85–113. On U.S. American imperialism in the Caribbean and the education of the U.S. American palate, see Merleaux, *Sugar and Civilization*.
114. Olive Caffray, WCCR *President Report*, December 5, 1978, WCCR archive.
115. Worin, *Kitchen Pleasures*.
116. On home-making as transnational practice, see Benson and O'Reilly, *Lifestyle Migration*, ch. 7.

6. Looking Back

1. Linda Sheinin, interviewed in Pavones, May 15, 2009.
2. Sheinin, interview.
3. On identity work and identity talk, see Snow and Anderson, "Identity Work among the Homeless."
4. Hayes, *Gringolandia*, 66–67.
5. For a similar rhetorical pattern employed by U.S. Americans immigrants of the same background in Ecuador, see Hayes, "'It Is Hard Being the Different One.'" On the significance of formative years in the narrators' construction of memory, see Walke, "Memories of an Unfulfilled Promise," 279.
6. Sharon Hage, interviewed in Playa Hermosa, March 4, 2009. On the perception of immigration as an existential quest among affluent migrants see Madison, "Existential Migration."
7. Spitzer, *Hotel Bolivia*, Kindle locations 5800–5820. During my fieldwork I was moving in certain social circles of U.S. Americans in Costa Rica. The U.S. American counterculturists I spoke with knew each other and referred me to other potential interviewees, asking me to "say hi." The communal censorship was therefore evident (on communal censorship see Portelli, *Death of Luigi Trastulli*, 74.)
8. On the common profile of U.S. American emigrants during the second half of the twentieth century, see Finifter, "American Emigration"; Cleveland et al., *Overseas Americans*, 7–21.

9. McAdams, *Redemptive Self*, 13–14.
10. Baird, "Constructing Lives," 59.
11. Jane and Michael Warren, interviewed in Ciudad Colón, March 5, 2009.
12. Rosemary Baird suggests that narrators' significant and retold memories reveal what they perceive to be key events in their life histories and are "usually framed as stories and feature dialogue or inner dialogue, humor, sensory description, climactic conclusion, laughter, enthusiasm or sadness" (Baird, "Constructing Lives," 59). Douglas Massey stresses the significance of migration stories in the creation of "repertoires of migration" (Massey et al., "Theories of International Migration.")
13. Lundestad, "'Empire by Invitation' in the American Century."
14. Theodore Bart, interviewed in San Isidro de El General, May 15, 2009. Sharon Hage, another member of the commune, also recalled that the members felt that their spiritual mission could not be fulfilled in the United States because of the cultural environment (Hage, interview). On the transfer of counterculture groups, practices, and spirit outside the United States in the early 1970s, see Braunstein and William, "Introduction."
15. Benson and O'Reilly remark that lifestyle migration was an "inevitable outcome of late modernity in which individuals are constrained to seek their own styles of life yet remain constrained within their own habitus"; see Benson and O'Reilly, "Migration and the Search," 618. On U.S. American and Western counterculture immigrants in the 1960s and 1970s, see, for example, Pickering, "Waiting for Chronic"; Waldren, *Insiders and Outsiders*.
16. Bart, interview.
17. Pratt, *Imperial Eyes*, 80.
18. On the difference between actual time and perceived and narrated time, see Portelli, *Death of Luigi Trastulli*, 66.
19. Karen Hill-Webber, interviewed in Curridabat, March 8, 2009.
20. Hill-Webber, interview.
21. On the discourse of the destruction of human and nonhuman nature in late twentieth and early twenty-first-century Costa Rica, see, for example, Rossi, *La loca de Gandoca*, 105; Barbas-Rhoden, *Ecological Imaginations*.
22. Self-representation as a child is a common theme in the life stories of U.S. Americans in Costa Rica. Most of the interviewees were in their late sixties and seventies at the time of the interview and naturally regarded themselves as very young when they arrived in the country.

However, this perception also served to highlight their lack of agency and intention—and thus the absence of a harmful intention—in the act and course of immigration (see chapter 3 of this book).

23. John Arlington Jr., interviewed in San José, May 10, 2009.
24. O'Reilly and Benson, "Lifestyle Migration," 7.
25. Sheinin, interview.
26. Sheinin, interview. Leo Spitzer argues, with respect to the encounter between Central European Jewish refugees and nature in South America, that "apparently, the 'old geography books' and the 'old school lectures' that many of them recall having informed them in a 'general way' about their New World destination had shaped their perceptions more profoundly than they may have realized" (Spitzer, *Hotel Bolivia*, Kindle locations 3059–64).
27. The comparison of tropical land to paradise goes back to Christopher Columbus's description of his encounter with the land of the Americas as a "terrestrial paradise" (Columbus, *Four Voyages to the New World*). On the construction of Costa Rica as paradise in its international tourism campaign see Rivers-Moore, "No Artificial Ingredients?"
28. Sheinin, interview.
29. Vargas, *Tropical Travel*, xx–xi; Whitehead, "Amazonia," 122–38; Leys Stepan, *Picturing Tropical Nature*; Pike, *United States and Latin America*.
30. Sheinin, interview.
31. On travel in space as travel in time, see McClintock, *Imperial Leather*, 226, 242. And in the specific context of the Americas, see Pike, *United States and Latin America*.
32. Lisa Wilson, interviewed in Santa María de Dota, May 14, 2009.
33. Wilson, interview. Her description of the Tica Bus going "on its way" brings to mind Bronislaw Malinows's arrival scene in his classic *Argonauts of the Western Pacific* (1922): "Imagine yourself suddenly set down surrounded by your gear, alone on a tropical beach close to a native village while the launch or dinghy which has brought you sails away out of sight" (cited in Pratt, "Fieldwork in Common Places," 37).
34. Pratt stresses that colonial narratives constructed by women often include fantasies about binational and cross-racial and class harmony (Pratt, *Imperial Eyes*, 168). For a contemporary construction of welcoming attitudes toward U.S. Americans in Mexico, see Croucher, "They Love Us Here!"
35. William Russell, interviewed in San Ramón de Tres Ríos, April 1, 2009.

36. Bart, interview.
37. The discourse of pioneership and the self-perception as pioneers breaking new ground are common in the narratives of so-called lifestyle immigrants. See O'Reilly and Benson, "Lifestyle Migration," 1.
38. Richard Erikson, interviewed in Golfito, May 27, 2009.
39. Erikson, interview.
40. Melman, "Under the Western Historian's Eyes"; Chakrabaty, "Post-Coloniality and the Artifice of History."
41. Behadad, *Belated Travelers.*
42. Sharon Hage, interview. For a similar view and for the experiences among U.S. Quakers in Monteverde, see Guindon, "We Were Not the First,"51.
43. On the ethnographic gaze and its reversal, see Swancutt and Mazard, "Anthropological Knowledge Making," 4.
44. Jane and Michael Warren, interview.
45. I am referring here to the opening of Gabriel Garcia Marquez's *One Hundred Years of Solitude,* as analyzed by Mary Luis Pratt, "In the Neo-colony," 467.
46. On the colonial spirit of improvement in the new colonies, see Pratt, *Imperial Eyes,* 61–62.
47. Jim Coleman, interviewed in Piedades de Santa Ana, April 1, 2009.
48. It is interesting to note that the revelation in Coleman's story, as in Sheinin's and Wilson's, takes place on the move (in a bus and a car), literally and metaphorically, in keeping with the habitus of the counterculture, that of travel and transition as a way of self-realization. On the basis of oral histories with Fiat workers in Italy, Luisa Passerini provided an analysis of the meaning of cars as a symbol of progress, authority, and prosperity for people who were born prior to the 1950s; Passerini, "Work, Ideology and Consensus," 51.
49. On Costa Rican racial ideology and immigration policies, see Sandoval-Garcia, *El mito roto.*
50. Salguero, "Costa Rica vende sus tierras."
51. Eileen Steinberg, interviewed in San José, June 13, 2009.
52. On the "adoption" of expats by locals in 1950s and 1960s Deiá, Palma de Mallorca, and the transformation to businesslike relations several decades later see Waldren, *Insiders and Outsiders,* 206. The metaphor of family relations is often employed in colonial or class relations in order to impose order, at least literary order, on relations based on hegemony and dependence. See Holt, "First New Nations," xii, 15–16; for a discussion of the kinship metaphor in Lain American literature, see Sommer, *Foundational Fictions.*

53. On U.S. expats' reconstructed narratives of being embraced and received with fondness by the locals in San Miguel de Allende, Mexico, see Croucher, "'They Love Us Here!'"
54. Erikson, interview.
55. Erikson, interview.
56. Warren, interview.
57. Rick Berg, "Captain Tom Defends His Playa Cacao Commune," *TT*, November 2, 1973.
58. Charlotte Linde stresses the extent to which the strength and importance of a life story lies in its position at the crossroad of private experience and public norm: it reveals much about the narrator's self, but it also touches upon the common ground of social structures and groups; Linde, *Life Stories*, 3.
59. James, *Doña María's Story*, 124.
60. Mary Louise Pratt has stressed the extent to which the imperial myth of conquest and the introduction of civilization generates desires, meanings, and activities long after the end of the imperial regime; see Pratt, "In the Neocolony," 460. Luisa Passerini, on the other hand, warns against the overuse of myths as an interpretive tool and the attribution of deep meaning to them. She argues that when myths are used too freely they can appear to be a kind of master key, capable of opening all doors, and as such, risk implying an ahistorical determinism and agents who lack self-motivation and merely translate eternal images into specific circumstances; Passerini, "Mythbiography in Oral History," 55–56.

Epilogue

1. Snow and Anderson, "Identity Work among the Homeless," 1348.
2. Throughout the book I considered immigration as a birth, or a rebirth. Jeffrey Lesser has beautifully analyzed the reversed metaphor, of newborns as immigrants into the future nation of Brazil in the nineteenth century (Lesser, *Immigration, Ethnicity, and National Identity*, 23).
3. Portelli, "What Makes Oral History Different."
4. Putnam, *Radical Moves*, 233.
5. Michael Warren, interviewed in Ciudad Colón, March 11, 2009.
6. Theodore Bart, interviewed in San Isidro de El General, May 15, 2009.
7. Anna Fredrikson, interviewed in San José, July 18, 2008.
8. Alessandro Portelli, lecture at Tel Aviv University, June 4, 2015, YouTube video, https://www.youtube.com/watch?v=89aqJ2y5tb8.

9. Eric White, interviewed in San Bosco de Alajuela, April 28, 2009.
10. Julie Woodman, interviewed in Santa Ana, June 3, 2009.
11. Roberta Green, email correspondence with the author, March 1, 2009. Transcripts are in the author's possession.
12. Jane Mora, interviewed in San José. Note the interesting use of the word "natives" to describe Costa Ricans who were probably of a mestizo origin.
13. Guindon, "Homesteading," 105; Rick Berg, "Captain Tom Defends His Playa Cacao Commune," *TT*, November 2, 1973.
14. Lesser and Rein, "Challenging Particularities."
15. Joyce Brown, interviewed in Dominical, April 11, 2009.
16. Richard Erikson, interviewed in Golfito, May 27, 2009.
17. Sharon Hage, interviewed in Playa Hermosa, April 13, 2009.
18. Thomas Dent, interviewed in Alajuela, April 10, 2009.
19. John Arlington Jr., interviewed in San José, April 29, 2009.
20. Brown, interview.
21. Mora, interview.
22. Doris Green, interviewed in San José, April 4, 2009.
23. Warren, interview.
24. The words in the subheading come from Amichai, "Clouds Are the First Fatalities," 88.
25. Kathrin Morales, interviewed in San José, April 16, 2009.
26. Brown, interview.
27. Adam Klee, interviewed in Heredia, June 10, 2009.
28. John Arlington Jr., interview.
29. Fredrickson, interview.
30. Mary Thompson, interviewed in Escazú, July 15, 2008.

Bibliography

Archival Materials

Archive of the American Legion post 10 and 11, Heredia, Costa Rica.
Archive of the Little Theatre Group, San José, Costa Rica (LTG).
Archive of the Women's Club of Costa Rica, San José, Costa Rica (WCCR).
Archivo Nacional de Costa Rica (ANCR).
Biblioteca Nacional Miguel Obregón Lizano (San José, Costa Rica).
Elsie Fiala letters, 1956–73 (EFL).
Library of Congress, United States (LOC).
National Archives and Records Administration, College Park MD, United States.

Published Works

Acuña, Miguel. *El 48*. San José: Librería Lehmann, 1974.
Ameringer, Charles D. *Don Pepe: A Political Biography of José Figueres of Costa Rica*. Albuquerque: University of New Mexico Press, 1978.
Amichai, Yehuda. "The Clouds Are the First Fatalities" ("Ha'ananim Hem Hametim Harishonim"). In *Poems 1948–1962*. Jerusalem: Schocken, 1977.
Andrews, George Reid. *Blackness in the White Nation: A History of Afro-Uruguay*. Chapel Hill: University of North Carolina Press, 2010.
Andrews, Robyn. "Little Anglo-India: Making Australia 'Local' at St. Joseph's Hostel." In Bönisch-Brednich and Trundle, *Local Lives*, 119–34.
Anhalt, Diana. *A Gathering of Fugitives: American Political Expatriates in Mexico 1948–1965*. Santa Maria CA: Archer Books, 2009.
Appadurai, Arjun. "How to Make a National Cuisine: Cookbooks in Contemporary India." *Comparative Studies in Society and History* 30, no. 1 (January 1988): 3–24.
———. *Modernity at Large: Cultural Dimensions of Globalization*. Minneapolis: University of Minnesota Press, 1996.

Appelbaum, Nancy P., Anne S. Macpherson, and Karin Alejandra Rosenblatt, eds. *Race and Nation in Modern Latin America*. Chapel Hill: University of North Carolina Press, 2003.

Appy, Christian G., ed. *Cold War Constructions: The Political Culture of United States Imperialism, 1945–1966*. Amherst: University of Massachusetts Press, 2000.

Armitage, Susan, and Elizabeth Jameson, eds. *The Women's West*. Norman: University of Oklahoma Press, 1987.

Asamblea Legislativa de la República de Costa Rica. "Ley no. 4812." In *Colección de leyes y decretos*. San José: Asamblea Legislativa de la República de Costa Rica, 1971.

Augelli, John P. "Costa Rica's Frontier Legacy." *Geographical Review* 77, no. 1 (January 1987): 1–16.

Auslander, Leora. *Taste and Power: Furnishing Modern France*. Berkeley: University of California Press, 1996.

Axelrod, Bernard. "Historical Studies of Emigration from the United States." *International Migration Review* 6, no. 1 (March 1972): 32–49.

Backer, Dorothy. "Rootless." *American Scholar* 56, no. 2 (Spring 1987): 269–74.

Baird, Rosemary. "Constructing Lives: A New Approach to Understanding Migrants' Oral History Narratives." *Oral History* 40, no. 1 (Spring 2012): 57–66.

Baily, Samuel L., and Eduardo José Miguez, eds. *Mass Migration to Modern Latin America*. Wilmington DE: Rowman and Littlefield, 2003.

Baker, Alan H. "Introduction: On Ideology and Landscape." In *Ideology and Landscape in Historical Perspective: Essays on the Meaning of Some Places in the Past*, edited by Baker and Gideon Biger, 1–14. Cambridge, UK: Cambridge University Press, 1992.

Banks, Stephen P. "Identity Narratives by Americans and Canadians Retirees in Mexico." *Journal of Cross-Cultural Gerontology* 19, no. 4 (December 2004): 361–81.

Barahona Jiménez, Luis. *El gran incógnito: Visión interna del campesino costarricense*. San José: Editorial Universitaria, 1953.

Barbas-Rhoden, Laura. *Ecological Imaginations in Latin American Fiction*. Gainesville: University Press of Florida, 2012.

Bariatti, Rita L. "Inmigrantes italianos en Costa Rica: Estudio de integración mediante fuentes orales." *Revista de Historia* 20 (1989): 105–31.

Barthes, Roland. *The Empire of Signs*. Translated by Richard Howard. New York: Hill and Wang, 1983.

———. "Towards a Psychosociology of Contemporary Food Consumption." In *Food and Culture: A Reader*, 3rd edition, edited by Carole Counihan and Penny Van Esterik, 28–36. New York: Routledge, 2012.

Bassnett, Susan. "Travel Writing and Gender." In Hulme and Youngs, *Cambridge Companion to Travel Writing*, 225–41.

Beauvoir, Simone de. *The Second Sex*. Translated by Constance Borde and Sheila Malovany-Chevallier. New York: Vintage, 2011.

Bederman, Gail. *Manliness and Civilization: A Cultural History of Gender and Race in the United States, 1880–1917*. Chicago: University of Chicago Press, 1995.

Behadad, Ali. *Belated Travelers: Orientalism in the Age of Colonial Dissolution*. Durham NC: Duke University Press, 1994.

Bell, John Patrick. *Crisis in Costa Rica: The 1948 Revolution*. Austin: University of Texas Press, 1971.

Bender, Daniel E., and Dana Lipman, eds. *Making the Empire Work: Labor and United States Imperialism*. New York: NYU Press, 2015.

Bentley, Amy. *Eating for Victory: Food Rationing and the Politics of Domesticity*. Champaign: University of Illinois Press, 1998.

Benson, Michaela Caroline. "Class, Race, Privilege: Structuring the Lifestyle Migrant Experience in Boquete, Panama." *Journal of Latin American Geography* 14, no. 1 (March 2015): 19–37.

———. "Postcoloniality and Privilege in New Lifestyle Flows: The Case of North Americans in Panama." *Mobilities* 8, no. 3 (2013): 313–30.

———. "'We Are Not Expats; We Are Not Migrants; We Are Sauliacoise.'" In Bönisch-Brednich and Trundle, *Local Lives*.

Benson, Michaela, and Karen O'Reilly. *Lifestyle Migration and Colonial Traces in Malaysia and Panama*. London: Palgrave Macmillan. Kindle Edition, 2017.

———, eds. *Lifestyle Migration: Expectations, Aspirations and Experiences*. London: Routledge, 2016.

———. "Migration and the Search for a Better Way of Life: A Critical Exploration of Lifestyle Migration." *Sociological Review* 57, no. 4 (November 2009): 608–25.

Benson, Rex. "Story of the Monteverde Quakers." In Guindon et al., *Monteverde Jubilee Family Album*, 101–2.

Biesanz, Richard, Karen Zubris Biesanz, and Mavis Hiltunen Biensanz. *The Costa Ricans*. Englewood Cliffs NJ: Prentice-Hall, 1988.

Blair, Melissa Estes. "A Dynamic Force in Our Community: Women's Clubs and Second-Wave Feminism at the Grassroots." *Frontiers: A Journal of Women Studies* 30, no. 3 (2009): 31–50.

Blunt, Alison. "Imperial Geographies of Home: British Domesticity in India, 1886–1925." *Transactions of the Institute of British Geographers*, 24, no. 4 (December 1999): 421–40.

Blunt, Alison, and Robyn Dowling. *Home*. London: Routledge, 2006.

Boggs, Henrietta. *Married to a Legend—Don Pepe*. Self-published, no date.
Bönisch-Brednich, Brigitte, and Catherine Trundle. "Introduction: Local Migrants and the Politics of Being in Place." In Bönisch-Brednich and Trundle, *Local Lives*, 1–16.
Bönisch-Brednich, Brigitte, and Catherine Trundle, eds. *Local Lives: Migration and the Politics of Place*. London: Routledge, 2010.
Bourdieu, Pierre. *Distinction: A Social Critique of the Judgment of Taste*. Translated by Richard Nice. London: Routledge, 1984.
Bozzoli de Wille, María E. "La frontera agrícola de Costa Rica y su relación con el problema agrario en zonas indígenas." *Anuario de Estudios Centroamericanos* 3 (1977): 225–34.
Brands, Hal. *Latin America's Cold War*. Cambridge MA: Harvard University Press, 2010.
Bratsberg, Bernt, and Dek Terrell. "Where Do Americans Live Abroad?" *International Migration Review* 30, no. 3 (Autumn 1996): 788–802.
Braunstein, Peter, and Michael William Doyle. "Introduction: Historicizing the American Counterculture of the 1960's and 70's." In *Imagine Nation: The American Counterculture of the 1960's and 70's*, edited by Michael William Doyle, 5–13. New York: Routledge, 2001.
Brockett, Charles D., and Robert R. Gottfried. "State Policies and the Preservation of Forest Cover: Lessons from Contrasting Public-Policy Regimes in Costa Rica." *Latin American Research Review* 37, no. 1 (2002): 7–40.
Brooks, Victor D. *Boomers: The Cold-War Generation Grows Up*. Chicago: Ivan R. Dee, 2009.
Brown, Linda Keller, and Kay Mussell, eds. *Ethnic and Regional Foodways in the United States: The Performance of Group Identity*. Knoxville: University of Tennessee Press, 1984.
Bulmer-Thomas, Victor, ed. *Britain and Latin America: A Changing Relationship*. Cambridge, UK: Cambridge University Press, 1989.
Caamaño Morúa, Carmen. *Entre "arriba" y "abajo": La experiencia transnacional de la migración de costarricenses hacia Estados Unidos*. San José: Editorial Universidad de Costa Rica, 2010.
Cáceres, Rina. *Negros, mulatos, esclavos y libertos en la Costa Rica del siglo XVII*. Mexico City: Instituto Panmamericano de Geografía e Historia, 2000.
Calderón-Steck, Flora V., and Roger E. Bonilla-Carrión. "Algunos aspectos sociodemográficos de los estadounidenses, canadienses y europeos residentes en Costa Rica." In Sandoval-Garcia, *El mito roto*, 51–88.
Callan, Hilary, and Shirley Ardener. *The Incorporated Wife*. London: Routledge, 1984.

Campbell, John. "Monteverde Memories." In Guindon et al., *Monteverde Jubilee Family Album*, 12.
Caplan, Pat. ed. *Food, Health and Identity*. London: Routledge, 1997.
Capote, Truman. *In Cold Blood*. New York: Vintage, 1994.
Casey, Edward S. "How to Get from Space to Place in a Fairly Short Stretch of Time: Phenomenological Prolegomena." In *Senses of Place*, edited by Steven Feld and Keith H. Basso, 13–51. Santa Fe NM: School of American Research Press, 1996.
Cavarero, Adriana. *Relating Narratives: Storytelling and Selfhood*. London: Routledge, 2000.
Chafe, William. *The American Woman: Her Changing Social, Economic and Political Roles, 1920–1970*. New York: Oxford University Press, 1972.
Chakrabaty, Dipesh. "Postcoloniality and the Artifice of History: Who Speaks for the 'Indian' Pasts?" *Representations* 37 (Winter 1992): 1–26.
Chalmers, David. *And the Crooked Places Made Straight: The Struggle for Social Change in the 1960s*. Baltimore: Johns Hopkins University Press, 1996.
Chaney, Elsa M., and Mary Garcia Castro. "Introduction: A New Field for Research and Action." In Chaney and Garcia, *Muchachas No More*, 3–15.
Chaney, Elsa M., and Mary Garcia Castro, eds. *Muchachas No More: Household Workers in Latin America and the Caribbean*. Philadelphia: Temple University Press, 1989.
Chansky, Dorothy. *Composing Ourselves: The Little Theatre Movement and the American Audience*. Carbondale: Southern Illinois University Press, 2004.
Chant, Sylvia. "Men in Crisis? Reflections on Masculinity, Work and Family in North-West Costa Rica." *European Journal of Development Research* 12, no. 2 (December 2000), 199–218.
Charles, Jeffrey A. *Service Clubs in American Society: Rotary, Kiwanis, and Lions*. Urbana: University of Illinois Press, 1993.
Chaudhuri, Nupur, and Margaret Strobel. *Western Women and Imperialism: Complicity and Resistance*. Bloomington: Indiana University Press, 1992.
Chomsky, Aviva. *West Indian Workers and the United Fruit Company in Costa Rica, 1870–1940*. Baton Rouge: Louisiana State University Press, 1996.
Chornook, Kay, and Wolf Guindon. *Walking with Wolf*. Hamilton OT: Wandering Words Press, 2008.
Christian, Michelle. "'. . . Latin America without the Downside': Racial Exceptionalism and Global Tourism in Costa Rica." *Ethnic and Racial Studies* 36 no. 10 (2013): 1599–618.
Cinel, Dino. *From Italy to San Francisco: The Immigrant Experience*. Palo Alto CA: Stanford University Press, 1982.
Cleveland, Harlan. "The Pretty American," *Harper's*, March 1959, 39.

Cleveland, Harlan, Gerard J., Mangone, and John Clarke Adams. *The Overseas Americans.* New York: McGraw-Hill, 1960.

Cohen, Benjamin B. "Networks of Sociability: Women's Clubs in Colonial and Postcolonial India." *Frontiers: A Journal of Women Studies* 30, no. 3 (2009): 169–95.

Cohen, Deborah. *Household Gods: The British and Their Possessions.* New Haven CT: Yale University Press, 2006.

Cohen, Eric. "Expatriate Communities." *Current Sociology* 24, no. 3 (January 1977): 5–90.

Cohen, Lizabeth. *A Consumers' Republic: The Politics of Mass Consumption in Postwar America.* New York: A. A. Knopf, 2003.

———. "From Town Center to Shopping Center: The Reconfiguration of Community Marketplaces in Postwar America." *American Historical Review* 101, no. 4 (October 1996): 1050–81.

Colby, Jason M. *The Business of Empire: United Fruit, Race, and U.S. Expansion in Central America.* Ithaca NY: Cornell University Press, 2011.

Cole-Christensen, Darryl. *A Place in the Rain Forest: Settling the Costa Rican Frontier.* Austin: University of Texas Press, 1997.

Columbus, Christopher. *Four Voyages to the New World: Letters and Selected Documents.* Translated and edited by R. H. Major. New York: Corinth Books, 1961.

"Contacts," *Mother Earth,* September 1973, 104 (obtained at LOC).

Cortés, Carlos. *La invención de Costa Rica y otras invenciones.* San José: Editorial Costa Rica, 2003.

Croucher, Sheila. "Americans Abroad: A Global Diaspora?" *Journal of Transnational American Studies* 4, no. 2 (2012): 1–35.

———. "The Gendered Spatialities of Lifestyle Migration." In Janoschka and Haas, *Contested Spatialities,* 15–28.

———. *The Other Side of the Fence: American Migrants in Mexico.* Austin: University of Texas Press, 2010.

———. "'They Love Us Here!': American Migrants in Mexico." *Dissent Magazine* 54, no. 1 (Winter 2007): 23–28.

Daniel, Yvonne Paynne. *Rumba: Dance and Social Change in Contemporary Cuba.* Bloomington: Indiana University Press, 1995.

Dashefsky, Arnold, and Karen Woodrow-Lafield. *Americans Abroad: A Comparative Study of Emigrants from the United States.* New York: Plenum, 1992.

Davis, Nathaniel P. *Few Dull Moments: A Foreign Service Career.* Philadelphia: Dunlap, 1967.

Dekkers, Onka. "Periodicals." *off our backs* 3, no. 1 (September 1972): 19.

Denevan, William M. "The Pristine Myth: The Landscape of the Americas in 1492." *Annals of the Association of American Geographers* 82, no. 3 (September 1992): 369–85.

Díaz-Arias, David. "Battle of Memories in Costa Rica: Inventions, Testimonies, and Violence during the Civil War of 1948." *Sociologies in Dialogue* 5, no. 2 (2019): 4–23.
Dolan, Marc. *Modern Lives: A Cultural Re-Reading of "The Lost Generation."* West Lafayette IN: Purdue University Press, 1996.
Dore, Elizabeth. *Gender Politics in Latin America: Debates in Theory and Practice*. New York: Monthly Review Press, 1997.
Douglas, Mary, and Baron Isherwood. *The World of Goods: Towards an Anthropology of Consumption*. London: Routledge, 1996.
Duany, Andres, Elizabeth Plater-Zyberk, and Jeff Speck. *Suburban Nation*. New York: North Point Press, 2000.
Emery-Waterhouse, Frances. *Banana Paradise: The Exciting Story of Central America's Banana Kingdom*. New York: Stephen-Paul, 1947.
Ergas, Yasmine. "Feminisms of the 1970s." In *History of Women in the West*. Vol. 7, *Toward a Cultural Identity in the Twentieth Century*, edited by Françoise Thébaud, 527–47. Cambridge MA: Belknap, 1996.
Escamilla Gutiérrez, Zaira, and Lorena Vargas Mora. "Peasant Women's Autobiographies: Women's Double Contribution to the Rural Economy." In *The Costa Rican Women's Movement: A Reader*, edited by Ilse Abshagan Leitinger, 89–98. Pittsburgh: University of Pittsburgh Press, 1997.
Escher, Anton, and Sandra Petermann. "Marrakesh Medina: Neocolonial Paradise of Lifestyle Migrants?" In Janoschka and Haas, *Contested Spatialities*, 29–46.
Ewing, Jack. *Monkeys Are Made of Chocolate: Exotic and Unseen Costa Rica*. Masonville CO: Pixyjack Press, 2005.
Fabre, Michel. *From Harlem to Paris: Black American Writers in France, 1840–1980*. Urbana: University of Illinois Press, 1991.
Facio, Rodrigo Brenes. "Means and Ends for a Better Costa Rica." In Palmer and Molina, *Costa Rican Reader*, 187–92.
Fallas, Carlos Luis. *Mamita Yunai: El infierno de las bananeras*. San José: Editorial Costa Rica, 1941.
Farrell, Amy Erdman. *Yours in Sisterhood: Ms. Magazine and the Promise of Popular Feminism*. Chapel Hill: University of North Carolina Press, 1998.
Fechter, Meike. "Living in a Bubble: Expatriates' Transnational Spaces." In *Going First Class?: New Approaches to Privileged Travel and Movement*, edited by Vered Amit, 33–52. New York: Berghahn, 2011. Kindle edition.
Finifter, Ada W. "American Emigration." *Society* 13, no. 5 (July–August 1976): 30–36.

Fishman, Robert. *Bourgeois Utopias: The Rise and Fall of Suburbia*. New York: Basic Books, 1987.
Friedan, Betty. *The Feminine Mystique*. New York: W. W. Norton, 1963.
Fuente, Alejandro de la. *A Nation for All: Race, Inequality, and Politics in Twentieth-Century Cuba*. Chapel Hill: University of North Carolina Press, 2001.
Gans, Herbert J. *The Levittowners: Ways of Life and Politics in a New Suburban Community*. New York: Columbia University Press, 1982.
García, Néstor Canclini. *Hybrid Cultures: Strategies for Entering and Leaving Modernity*. Translated by Christopher L. Chiappari and Silvia L. Lopez. Minneapolis: University of Minnesota Press, 1995.
Geertz, Clifford. *The Interpretation of Cultures*. New York: Basic Books, 1973.
Giglioli, Giovanna. "¿Mito o idiosincrasia?: Un análisis crítico de la literatura sobre el carácter nacional." In *Identidades y producciones culturales en América Latina*, edited by Marta Salvadora, 167–206. San José: Editorial de la Universidad de Costa Rica, 1996.
Glick Schiller, Nina, Linda Basch, and Christina Szanton Blanc. "From Immigrant to Transmigrant: Theorizing Transnational Migration." *Anthropological Quarterly* 68, no. 1 (January 1995): 48–63.
Gobat, Michele. "The Invention of Latin America: A Transnational History of Anti-Imperialism, Democracy, and Race." *American Historical Review* 118, no. 5 (December 2013): 1345–75.
Goebel, Michael. "Reconceptualizing Diasporas and National Identities in Latin America and the Caribbean, 1850–1950." In *Immigration and National Identities in Latin America*, edited by Nicola Foote and Michael Goebel, 1–30. Gainesville: University Press of Florida, 2017.
Goldman, Arieh. "Stages in the Development of the Supermarket." *Journal of Retailing* 51 (1976): 49–64.
Gonzáles, Luisa. "Women of the Barrio." In Palmer and Molina, *Costa Rica Reader*, 102–8.
Goody, Jack. *Cooking, Cuisine, and Class: A Study in Comparative Sociology*. New York: Cambridge University Press, 1982.
Gordimer, Nadine. "Hemingway's Expatriates." *Transition* 80 (1999): 86–99.
Granada, Daniel. *Del vocabulario rioplatense razonado*, Montevideo: Imprenta Rural, 1890.
Grandin, Greg. *Empire's Workshop: Latin America, the United States, and the Rise of the New Imperialism*. New York: Metropolitan Books, 2010.
Grazia, Victoria de. *Irresistible Empire: America's Advance through 20th-Century Europe*. Cambridge MA: Harvard University Press, 2005.

Grazia, Victoria de, and Ellen Furlough, eds. *The Sex of Things: Gender and Consumption in Historical Perspective.* Berkeley: University of California Press, 1996.

Grewal, Inderpal. *Home and Harem: Nation, Gender, Empire and the Cultures of Travel.* Durham NC: Duke University Press, 1996.

Grossman, James R. "Introduction." In Grossman, *Frontier in American Culture,* 1–6.

Grossman, James R., ed. *The Frontier in American Culture.* Berkeley: University of California Press, 1994.

Gudmundson, Lowell. *Costa Rica before Coffee: Society and Economy on the Eve of the Export Boom.* Baton Rouge: Louisiana State University Press, 1986.

Gudmundson, Lowell, and Justin Wolfe, eds. *Blacks and Blackness in Central America: Between Race and Place.* Durham NC: Duke University Press, 2010.

Guindon, Lucille (Lucky). "Frugality." In Guindon et al., *Monteverde Jubilee Family Album,* 210.

———. "A Letter." In Guindon et al., *Monteverde Jubilee Family Album,* 209.

———. "We Were Not the First." In Guindon et al., *Monteverde Jubilee Family Album,* 51–52.

Guindon, Lucille, Martha Moss, Marvin Rockwell, John Trostle, and Sue Trostle, eds. *Monteverde Jubilee Family Album.* Monteverde, Costa Rica: Asociación de Amigos de Monteverde, 2001.

Guindon, Wolf. "Homesteading." In Guindon et al., *Monteverde Jubilee Family Album,* 105.

Gutiérrez, Manuel E. *La casa de adobes costarricense.* San José: Editorial de la Universidad de Costa Rica, 1972.

Hagan, John. *Northern Passage: American Vietnam War Resisters in Canada.* Cambridge MA: Harvard University Press, 2001.

Harpell, Ronald. "White Zones: American Enclaves Communities of Central America." In Gudmundson and Wolfe, *Blacks and Blackness in Central America,* 307–33.

Harter, Eugene C. *The Lost Colony of the Confederacy.* College Station: Texas A&M University Press, 2000.

Harvey, David. *Justice, Nature, and the Geography of Difference.* Malden MA: Blackwell, 1996.

Hawkins, Gladys, Jean Soper, and Jane Henry. *Your Maid from Mexico.* San Antonio TX: Naylor, 1959.

Hayes, Matthew. *Gringolandia: Lifestyle Migration under Late Capitalism.* Minneapolis: University of Minnesota Press, 2018.

———. "'It Is Hard Being the Different One All the Time': Gringos and Racialized Identity in Lifestyle Migration to Ecuador." *Ethnic and Racial Studies* 38, no. 6 (2015): 943–58.

Herzfeld, Anita, and Teresa Cajiao Salas. *El teatro de hoy en Costa Rica: Perspectiva, crítica y antología*. San José: Editorial Costa Rica, 1974.

Herzog, Arthur. *Vesco: From Wall Street to Castro's Cuba: The Rise, Fall, and Exile of the King of White-Collar Crime*. Lincoln NE: Universe, 2003.

Hiltunen Biesanz, Mavis, Richard Biesanz, and Karen Zubris Biesanz. *The Ticos: Culture and Social Change in Costa Rica*. Boulder CO: L. Rienner, 1999.

Hoey, Brian A. "From Pi to Pie: Moral Narratives of Noneconomic Migration and Starting Over in the Postindustrial Midwest." *Journal of Contemporary Ethnography* 34, no. 5 (October 2005): 586–624.

Holdridge, Desmond. "Toledo: A Tropical Refugee Settlement in British Honduras." *Geographical Review* 30, no. 3 (July 1940): 376–93.

Hollen Lees, Lynn. "Urban Civil Society: The Context of Empire." *Historical Research* 84, no. 223 (February 2011): 135–47.

Holt, Thomas C. "The First New Nations." In Appelbaum, Macpherson, and Rosenblatt, *Race and Nation in Modern Latin America*, vii–xiv.

Horowitz, Daniel. *Betty Friedan and the Making of "The Feminine Mystique": The American Left, the Cold War, and Modern Feminism*. Amherst: University of Massachusetts Press, 1996.

Hulme, Peter, and Tim Youngs, eds. *The Cambridge Companion to Travel Writing*. Cambridge, UK: Cambridge University Press, 2002.

Instituto Nacional de Estadística y Censos. *Censo de población y vivienda*. San José, 1950, 1963, 1973. Obtained from ANCR.

Isla, Ana. *The "Greening" of Costa Rica: Women, Peasants, Indigenous Peoples, and the Remaking of Nature*. Toronto: University of Toronto Press, 2015.

Jackson, Kenneth T. *Crabgrass Frontier: The Suburbanization of the United States*. New York: Oxford University Press, 1985.

James, Daniel. *Doña María's Story: Life, History, Memory and Political Identity*. Durham NC: Duke University Press, 2000.

Janoschka, Michael. "Imaginarios del turismo residencial en Costa Rica: Negociaciones de pertenencia y apropiación simbólica de espacios y lugares: una relación conflictive." In *Construir una nueva vida: Los espacios del turismo y la migración residencial*, edited by Mazón, Tomás, Raquel Huete, and Alejandro Mentecón, 81–102. Santander: Milrazones, 2011.

Janoschka, Michael, and Heiko Haas. "Introduction: Contested Spatialities of Lifestyle Migration: Approaches and Research Questions." In Janoschka and Haas, *Contested Spatialities*, 1–12.

Janoschka, Michael, and Heiko Haas, eds. *Contested Spatialities, Lifestyle Migration and Residential Tourism*. London: Routledge, 2013.

Joseph, Gilbert M., Catherine LeGrand, and Ricardo D. Salvatore, eds. *Close Encounters of Empire: Writing the Cultural History of U.S.-Latin American Relations*. Durham NC: Duke University Press, 1998.

Joseph, Gilbert M., and Daniela Spenser, eds. *In from the Cold: Latin America's New Encounter with the Cold War*. Durham NC: Duke University Press, 2008.

Kantor, Harry. "A 'New Deal' Government." *World Affairs* 117, no. 1 (Spring 1954): 11–13.

Katzman, David M. *Seven Days a Week: Women and Domestic Service in Industrializing America*. New York: Oxford University Press, 1978.

Kennedy, John F. "Address at a White House Reception for Members of Congress and for the Diplomatic Corps of the Latin American Republics, March 13, 1961." John F. Kennedy Presidential Library. https://www.jfklibrary.org/archives/other-resources/john-f-kennedy-speeches/latin-american-diplomats-washington-dc-19610313.

Kessler-Harris, Alice. *In Pursuit of Equity: Women, Men, and the Quest for Economic Citizenship in 20th Century America*. New York: Oxford University Press, 2001.

———. *Out to Work: A History of Wage-Earning Women in the United States*. New York: Oxford University Press, 1983.

Kikumura, Akemi. "Family Life History: A Collaborative Venture." In Perks and Thompson, *Oral History Reader*, 140–44.

King, Antony D. *The Bungalow: The Production of a Global Culture*. New York: Oxford University Press, 1995.

Kirk, Andrew G. *Counterculture Green: The Whole Earth Catalog and American Environmentalism*. Lawrence: University Press of Kansas, 2007.

Kockelman, Paul. *The Chicken and the Quetzal: Incommensurate Ontologies and Portable Values in Guatemala's Cloud Forest*. Durham NC: Duke University Press, 2016.

Kolodny, Annette. *The Land before Her: Fantasy and Experience of the American Frontiers, 1630–1860*. Chapel Hill: University of North Carolina Press, 1984.

Kopytoff, Igor. "The Cultural Biography of Things: Commoditization as Process." In *The Social Life of Things: Commodities in Cultural Perspective*, edited by Arjun Appadurai, 64–94. New York: Cambridge University Press, 1988.

Kordick, Carmen. "Constructing Costa Rica's Inter-American Highway and Building U.S. Empire: Social, Economic, and Political Change at the Local Level, 1941–44." *Journal of Iberian and Latin American Research* 23, no. 2 (May 2017): 122–42.

———. *The Saints of Progress: A History of Coffee, Migration, and Costa Rican National Identity.* Tuscaloosa: University of Alabama Press, 2019.
Kusch, Frank. *All American Boys: Draft Dodgers in Canada from the Vietnam War.* Westport CT: Praeger, 2001.
LaFeber, Walter. *Inevitable Revolutions: The United States in Central America.* 2nd ed. New York: Norton, 1983.
Láscaris, Constantino. "In Defense of the Corner Store." In Palmer and Molina, *Costa Rica Reader*, 192–97.
Leech, Kenneth. *Youthquake: The Growth of the Counter-Culture through the Decades.* London: Sheldon Press, 1973.
Leeds, Asia. "Representations of Race, Entanglements of Power: Whiteness, Garveyism, and Redemptive Geographies in Costa Rica, 1921–1950." PhD diss., University of California Berkeley, 2010.
Lesser, Jeffrey. *Immigration, Ethnicity, and National Identity in Brazil, 1808 to the Present.* Cambridge, UK: Cambridge University Press, 2013.
Lesser, Jeffrey, and Raanan Rein. "Challenging Particularities: Jews as a Lens on Latin American Ethnicity." *Journal of Latin American and Caribbean Ethnic Studies* 1, no. 2 (September 2006): 249–63.
Levenstein, Harvey. *Paradox of Plenty: A Social History of Eating in Modern America.* Berkeley: University of California Press, 1993.
Levitt, Peggy, Josh DeWind, and Steven Vertovec. "International Perspectives on Transnational Migration: An Introduction." *International Migration Review* 37, no. 3 (Fall 2003): 565–75.
Light, Paul C. *Baby Boomers.* New York: W. W Norton, 1990.
Limerick, Patricia Nelson. *The Legacy of Conquest: The Unbroken Past of the American West.* New York: W. W. Norton, 1988.
Linde, Charlotte. *Life Stories: The Creation of Coherence.* New York: Oxford University Press, 1993.
Lohse, Russel. "Cacao and Slavery in Matina, Costa Rica, 1650–1750." In Gudmundson and Wolfe, *Blacks and Blackness in Central America*, 57–91.
Longley, Kyle. "Resistance and Accommodation: The United States and the Nationalism of José Figueres, 1953–1957." *Diplomatic History* 18, no. 1 (Winter 1994): 1–28.
———. *The Sparrow and the Hawk: Costa Rica and the United States during the Rise of José Figueres.* Montgomery: University of Alabama Press, 1997.
Longstreth, Richard W. *The Drive-In, the Supermarket, and the Transformation of Commercial Space in Los Angeles, 1914–1941.* Boston: MIT Press, 2000.
Lundestad, Geir. "'Empire by Invitation' in the American Century." *Diplomatic History* 23, no. 2 (Spring 1999): 189–217.
Macunovich, Diane J. *Birthquake: The Baby Boom and Its Aftershocks.* Chicago: University of Chicago Press, 2002.

Madison, Greg. "Existential Migration: Conceptualising out of the Experiential Depths of Choosing to Leave 'Home.'" *Existential Analysis* 17, no. 2 (2006): 238–60.

Mahler, Sarah J., and Patricia R. Pessar. "Gendered Geographies of Power: Analyzing Gender Across Transnational." *Global Studies in Culture and Power* 7, no. 4 (2001): 441–59.

Mallon, Florencia. "Introduction." In *When a Flower Is Reborn: The Life and Times of a Mapuche Feminist*, written by Rosa Isolde Reuque Pillalef, edited by Florencia Mallon, 1–33. Durham NC: Duke University Press, 2007.

Mann, Susan A. "Pioneers of U.S. Ecofeminism and Environmental Justice." *Feminist Formations* 23, no. 2 (Summer 2011): 1–25.

Marañón, Jon. *The Gringo's Hawk*. Eugene OR: Kenneth Group, 2001.

Marois, Thomas. "From Economic Crisis to a 'State' of Crisis?: The Emergence of Neoliberalism in Costa Rica." *Historical Materialism: Research in Critical Marxist Theory* 13 (2005): 101–34.

Masing, Ulv. "Foreign Agricultural Colonies in Costa Rica: An Analysis of Foreign Colonization in a Tropical Environment." PhD diss., University of Florida, 1964.

Massey, Douglas, et al. "Theories of International Migration: A Review and Appraisal." *Population and Development Review* 19, no. 3 (September 1999): 431–66.

Mathews-Gardner, Lanethea. "From Woman's Club to NGO: The Changing Terrain of Women's Civic Engagement in the Mid-Twentieth Century United States." PhD diss., Syracuse University, 2003.

May, Elaine Tyler. *Homeward Bound: American Families in the Cold War Era*. 2nd ed. New York: Basic Books, 2008.

McAdams, Dan P. *The Redemptive Self: Stories American Live By*. New York: Oxford University Press 2006.

McClintock, Anne. *Imperial Leather: Race, Gender and Sexuality in the Colonial Contest*. New York: Routledge, 1995.

McCoy, Alfred W., and Francisco A. Scarano, eds. *Colonial Crucible: Empire in the Making of the Modern American State*. Madison: University of Wisconsin Press, 2009.

McCoy, Alfred W., Francisco A. Scarano, and Courtney Johnson. "On the Tropic of Cancer: Transitions and Transformations in the U.S. Imperial State." In McCoy and Scarano, *Colonial Crucible*, 3–33.

McGranahan, Carole, and John F. Collins, eds. *Ethnographies of U.S. Empire*. Durham NC: Duke University Press, 2018.

McKeon, Michael. *The Secret History of Domesticity: Public, Private, and the Division of Knowledge*. Baltimore: Johns Hopkins University Press, 2007.

McMahon, Joseph H. "City for Expatriates." *Yale French Studies* 32 (1964): 144–58.
Meagher, Thomas Francis. "Holidays in Costa Rica." In Vargas, *Tropical Travel*, 255–320.
Meléndez, Carlos Chaverri, and Quince Duncan. *El negro en Costa Rica*. San José: Editorial Costa Rica, 1981.
Meléndez-Obando, Mauricio. "Los últimos esclavos de Costa Rica." *Revista de Historia* 39 (1999): 51–138.
Meléndez-Obando, Mauricio, and Tatiana Lobo Wiehoff. *Negros y blancos, todo mezclado*. San José: Editorial Universidad de Costa Rica, 1997.
Melman, Billie. "Under the Western Historian's Eyes: Eileen Power and the Early Feminist Encounter with Colonialism." *History Workshop Journal* 42 (Autumn 1996): 147–68.
———. *Women's Orients: English Women and the Middle East, 1718–1918*. Ann Arbor: University of Michigan Press, 1992.
Meltzer, Paige. "'The Pulse and Conscience of America': The General Federation and Women's Citizenship, 1945–1960." *Frontiers: A Journal of Women Studies* 30 (2009): 52–76.
"Men's Views of Women's Clubs. A Symposium, by Men Who Are Recognized Leaders in the Philanthropic and Reform Movements in America." *Annals of the American Academy of Political and Social Science* 28 (1906): 85–94.
Merleaux, April. *Sugar and Civilization: American Empire and the Cultural Politics of Sweetness*. Chapel Hill: University of North Carolina Press, 2015.
Meyerowitz, Joanne. "Beyond the Feminine Mystique: A Reassessment of Postwar Mass Culture, 1946–1958." In Meyerowitz, *Not June Cleaver*, 229–62.
———, ed. *Not June Cleaver: Women and Gender in Postwar America, 1945–1960*. Philadelphia: Temple University Press, 1994.
Miller, Daniel. "Why Some Things Matter." In *Material Cultures: Why Some Things Matter*, edited by Daniel Miller, 3–24. Chicago: University of Chicago Press, 1998.
Miller, Rory. *Britain and Latin America in the Nineteenth and Twentieth Centuries*. London: Longman, 1993.
Mintz, Sidney W., and Christine M. Du Bois. "The Anthropology of Food and Eating." *Annual Review of Anthropology* 31 (2002): 99–119.
Mohun, Arwen Palmer. *Steam Laundries: Gender, Technology, and Work in the United States and Great Britain, 1880–1940*. Baltimore: Johns Hopkins University Press, 1999.
"Monteverde Statement of Aims and Ideals, 1959." In Guindon et al., *Monteverde Jubilee Family Album*, 101.

Moore, Robin. "The Commercial Rumba: Afro Cuban Arts as International Popular Culture." *Latin American Music Review / Revista de Música Latinoamericana* 16, no. 2 (1995): 165–98.

Moraña, Mabel, Enrique Dussel, and Carlos Jáuregui, eds. *Coloniality at Large: Latin America and the Postcolonial Debate*. Durham NC: Duke University Press, 2008.

Morris-Crowther, Jayne. "Municipal Housekeeping: The Political Activities of the Detroit Federation of Women's Clubs in the 1920s." *Michigan Historical Review* 30, no. 1 (Spring 2004): 31–57.

Moya, José C. *Cousins and Strangers: Spanish Immigrants in Buenos Aires, 1850–1930*. Berkeley: University of California Press, 1998.

Muñoz-Pogossian, Betilde. "Gendered Language and (Unequal) Power: Deconstructing U.S.-Latin American Relations in the Early Cold War." *International Politics* 45, no. 6 (2008): 703–19.

Murchie, Anita Gregorio. *Imported Spices: A Study of Anglo-American Settlers in Costa Rica, 1821–1900*. San José: Ministry of Culture, Youth and Sports, 1981.

Nagar-Ron, Sigal, and Pnina Mutzafi-Haller. "'My Life? There Is Not Much to Tell': On Voice, Silence and Agency in Interviews with First-Generation Mizrahi Jewish Women Immigrants to Israel." *Qualitative Inquiry* 20, no. 10 (September 2011): 1–11.

Nash, Dennison. *A Community in Limbo: An Anthropological Study of an American Community Abroad*. Bloomington: Indiana University Press, 1970.

Nelson, Wilton. *Historia del protestantismo en Costa Rica*. San Francisco de Dos Ríos: Publicaciones Ilndef, 1983.

Nemcik, Christine Carol. "Germans, Costa Ricans, or a Question of Dual Nationalist Sentiments? The German Community in Costa Rica, 1850–1950." PhD diss., Indiana University, 2001.

Norgaard, Kari. "Moon Phases, Menstrual Cycles, and Mother Earth: The Construction of a Special Relationship between Women and Nature." *Ethics and Environments* 4, no. 2 (Autumn 1999): 197–209.

Nygren, Anja. "Deforestation in Costa Rica: An Examination of Social and Historical Factors." *Forest and Conservation History* 39, no. 1 (January 1995): 27–35.

Oldenziel, Ruth, and Karin Zachmann, eds. *Cold War Kitchen: Americanization, Technology, and European Users*. Cambridge MA: MIT Press, 2011.

Onis, Juan de. *The Green Cathedral: Sustainable Development of Amazonia*. Oxford: Oxford University Press, 1992.

O'Reilly, Karen. *The British on the Costa del Sol: Transnational Identities and Local Communities*. London: Routledge, 2000.

O'Reilly, Karen, and Michaela Benson. "Lifestyle Migration: Escaping to the Good Life?" In Benson and O'Reilly, *Lifestyle Migration*, 1–14.

Ortner, Sherry B. "Is Female to Male as Nature Is to Culture?" In *Woman, Culture, and Society*, edited by Michelle Rosaldo and Louise Lamphere, 68–87. Stanford CA: Stanford University Press, 1974.
Palma Mora, Mónica. *Norteamericanos en la Ciudad de México*. Mexico City: Gobierno del Distrito Federal, Instituto de Cultura de la Ciudad de México, 1999.
Palmer, Alexandra. *Dior*. London: Victoria and Albert Museum, 2009.
Palmer, Phyllis. *Domesticity and Dirt: Housewives and Domestic Servants in the US, 1920–1945*. Philadelphia: Temple University Press, 1989.
Palmer, Steven, and Iván Molina, eds. *The Costa Rica Reader: History, Culture, Politics*. Durham NC: Duke University Press, 2004.
Passerini, Luisa. "Mythbiography in Oral History." In *The Myths We Live By*, edited by Raphael Samuel and Paul Thompson, 51–71. London: Routledge, 1990.
———. "Work, Ideology and Consensus under Italian Fascism." *History Workshop Journal*, 8 (Autumn 1979): 82–108.
Pérez Navaro, Ricardo A. "Construcción de una communidad: Judios askenazi en Costa Rica (1939–1948)." *Revista de Historia de América* 153 (2017): 127–51.
Perkiss, Abigail. "Reclaiming the Past: Oral History and the Legacy of Integration in West Mount Airy, Philadelphia." *Oral History Review* 41, no. 1 (April 2014): 77–107.
Perks, Robert, and Elistair Thomson, eds. *The Oral History Reader*. London: Routledge, 2002.
Pickering, Lucy. "Past Imperfect: Displacing Hawaiians as Hosts in a 'Drop Out' Community in Hawaii." In Bönisch-Brednich and Trundle, *Local Lives*, 49–65.
———. "'Waiting for Chronic': Time, Cannabis and Counterculture in Hawaii." *Time and Society* 25, no. 3 (2016): 450–70.
Pike, Fredrick B. *United States and Latin America: Myths and Stereotypes of Civilization and Nature*. Austin: University of Texas Press, 1992.
Pizer, Donald. *American Expatriate Writing and the Paris Moment: Modernism and Place*. Baton Rouge: Louisiana State University Press, 1996.
Plan nacional de desarollo de los pueblos indígenas de Costa Rica. San José: Ministerio de Planificación Nacional y Política Económica, 2002.
Portelli, Alessandro. *The Death of Luigi Trastulli and Other Stories: Form and Meaning in Oral History*. Albany: State University of New York Press, 1991.
———. "What Makes Oral History Different." In Perks and Thomson, *Oral History Reader*, 32–42.
Potter, David M. *People of Plenty: Economic Abundance and the American Charter*. Chicago: University of Chicago Press, 1958.

Powell, George. "The Monteverde Preserve's Beginning." In Guindon et al., *Monteverde Jubilee Family Album*, 170–72.

Pratt, Marry Louise. "Fieldwork in Common Places." In *Writing Culture: The Poetics and Politics of Ethnography*, edited by James Clifford and George E. Marcus, 27–51. Berkeley: University of California Press, 1986.

———. *Imperial Eyes: Travel Writing and Transculturation*. London: Routledge, 1992.

———. "In the Neocolony: Destiny, Destination and the Traffic in Meaning." In Moraña, Dussel, and Jáuregui, *Coloniality at Large*, 459–78.

Preston-Werner, Theresa. "In the Kitchen: Negotiating Changing Family Roles in Costa Rica." *Journal of Folklore Research* 45, no. 3 (September–December 2008): 329–59.

Proshansky, Harold M., Abbe K. Fabian, and Robert Kaminoff. "Place-Identity: Physical World Socialization of the Self." *Journal of Environmental Psychology* 3, no. 1 (March–December 1983): 57–83.

Puga, Dolores. "Un lugar en el sol: Inmigración de jubilados hacia Costa Rica." In *Población del Istmo 2000: Familia, migración, violencia y medio ambiente*, edited by Luis Rosero Bixby, 253–66. San José: Centro Centroamericano de Población de la Universidad de Costa Rica.

Putnam, Lara. *The Company They Kept: Migrants and the Politics of Gender in Caribbean Costa Rica, 1870–1960*. Chapel Hill: University of North Carolina Press, 2002.

———. *Radical Moves: Caribbean Migrants and the Politics of Race in the Jazz Age*. Chapel Hill: University of North Carolina Press, 2013.

Putnam, Robert D. *Bowling Alone: The Collapse and Revival of American Community*. New York: Simon and Schuster, 2000.

Putz, Francis E., and Michele N. Holbrook. "Tropical Rain-Forest Images." In *People of the Tropical Rain Forest*, edited by Julie Sloan Denslow and Christine Padoch. Berkley: University of California Press, 1988.

Quijano, Anibal. "Coloniality of Power, Eurocentrism and Latin America." In Moraña, Dussel, and Jáuregui, *Coloniality at Large*, 181–224.

Rangel, Alberto. *Inferno verde: Cenas e Cenários do Amazonas*. Manaus: Editora Valer, 2008.

Rapport, Nigel. "Epilogue: The Cosmopolitan Justice of a Direction Home." In Bönisch-Brednich and Trundle, *Local Lives*, 183–92.

Reisman, David. *Abundance for What? And other Essays*. Garden City NY: Doubleday, 1964.

Renda, Mary A. *Taking Haiti: Military Occupation and the Culture of U.S. Imperialism*. Chapel Hill: University of North Carolina Press, 2001.

Reynolds, Winston A. "'Hispanism' in *Ms. Magazine*." *Hispania* 54, no. 4 (December 1974): 965–69.

Rivers-Moore, Megan. *Gringo Gulch: Sex, Tourism, and Social Mobility in Costa Rica*. Chicago: Chicago University Press, 2016.

———. "No Artificial Ingredients? Gender, Race and Nation in Costa Rica's International Tourism Campaign." *Journal of Latin American Cultural Studies* 16, no. 3 (2007): 341–57.

Rockwell, Dorothy. "What Did We Find to Feed the Family?" in Guindon et al., *Monteverde Jubilee Family Album*, 207.

Rodgers, Kathleen. *Welcome to Resisterville: American Dissidents in British Columbia*. Vancouver: University of British Columbia Press, 2014.

Rodriguez, Leila, and Jeffrey H. Cohen. "Generations and Motivations: Russian and Other Former Soviet Immigrants in Costa Rica." *International Migration* 43, no. 4 (November 2005): 147–65.

Romero, Mary. *Maid in the U.S.A.* London: Routledge, 1992.

Rosen, Ruth. *The World Split Open: How the Modern Women's Movement Changed America*. New York: Viking, 2000.

Rosenberg, Emily. "Consuming Women: Images of Americanization in the American Century." *Diplomatic History* 23, no. 3 (Summer 1999): 479–97.

Rossi, Anachristina. *La loca de Gandoca*. San José: Editorial Universitaria Centroamericana, 1991.

Roszak, Theodore. *The Making of a Counter Culture: Reflections on the Technocratic Society and Its Youthful Opposition*. Garden City NY: Doubleday, 1969.

Row, Philoméene, and Bruno Stagno. *Arquitectura de las ciudades bananeras*. San José: Instituto de architectura tropical, 2003.

Rutkow, Eric. *Longest Line on the Map: The United States, the Pan-American Highway, and the Quest to Link the Americas*. New York: Scribner, 2019.

Salas Víquez, José Antonio. "La búsqueda de soluciones al problema de la escasez de tierra en la frontera agrícola: aproximación al estudio del reformismo agrario en Costa Rica, 1880–1940." *Revista de Historia* número Especial Historia Agraria (1985): 97–149.

Sampar, Mario K. *Generations of Settlers: Rural Households and Markets on the Costa Rican Frontier, 1850–1935*. Boulder CO: Westview Press, 1990.

Samuel, Raphael, and Paul Thompson. *The Myth We Live By*. London: Routledge, 1990.

Sancho Jiménez, Mario. *Costa Rica, Suiza centroamericana*. San José: Editorial Costa Rica, 1982.

Sandoval-García, Carlos G., ed. *El mito roto: Inmigración y emigración en Costa Rica*. San José: Editorial Universidad de Costa Rica, 2008.

———. *Threatening Others: Nicaraguans and the Formation of National Identities in Costa Rica*. Athens: Ohio University Press, 2004.

Sarachild, Kathie. "Consciousness-Raising: A Radical Weapon." In *Redstockings: Feminist Revolution*, 144–50. New York: Random House, 1978.

Scarpellini, Emanuela. "Shopping American-Style: The Arrival of the Supermarket in Postwar Italy." *Enterprise and Society* 5, no. 4 (December 2004): 625–68.

Schama, Simon. *Landscape and Memory*. New York: Vintage, 1996.

Schell, William. *Integral Outsiders: The American Colony in Mexico City, 1876–1911*. Wilmington DE: SR Books, 2001.

Schifter, Jacobo. "Origins of the Cold War in Central America: A Study of Diplomatic Relations between Costa Rica and the United States 1940–1949." PhD diss., Columbia University, 1983.

Schreiber, Rebecca M. *Cold War Exiles in Mexico: U.S. Dissidents and the Culture of Critical Resistance*. Minneapolis: University of Minnesota Press, 2008.

Schrepfer, Susan R. *Nature's Altars: Mountains, Gender, and American Environmentalism*. Lawrence: University of Kansas Press, 2005.

Shaw, Gareth, Louise Curth, and Andrew Alexander. "Selling Self Service and the Supermarket: The Americanization of Food Retailing in Britain, 1945–1960." *Business History* 16 (2004): 568–82.

Shragai, Atalia. "Do Bananas Have a Culture? United Fruit Company Employees in Central America 1900–1960." *Iberoamericana* 11, no. 42 (2011): 65–84.

———. "In the Service of Their Homeland and Themselves: The U.S. Women's Club in Costa Rica 1945–1980." *Journal of Social History* 52, no. 2 (Winter 2018): 412–38.

Skidmore, Thomas E., Peter H. Smith, and James N. Green, eds. *Modern Latin America*. 8th ed. Oxford: Oxford University Press, 2013.

Skutch, Alexander F. *A Naturalist in Costa Rica*. Gainseville: University Press of Florida, 1971.

Slater, Candace. *Entangled Edens: Visions of the Amazon*. Berkley: University of California Press, 2003.

———. "Visions of the Amazon: What Has Shifted, What Persists, and Why This Matters." *Latin American Research Review* 50, no. 3 (2015): 3–23.

Smith, Peter H. *Talons of the Eagle: Latin America, the United States, and the World*. 4th ed. Oxford: Oxford University Press, 2012.

Snow, David A., and Leon Anderson. "Identity Work among the Homeless: The Verbal Construction and Avowal of Personal Identities." *American Journal of Sociology* 92, no. 6 (May 1987): 1336–71.

Solís, Manuel. *La institucionalidad ajena: Los años cuarenta y el fin de siglo*. San José: Editorial de la Universidad de Costa Rica, 2006.

Solís, Zecena, and Enrique Salvador. "El movimiento teatral costarricense, 1951–1971." *Escena Revista Teatral* 13–14, nos. 28–29 (1992): 70–79.

Sommer, Doris. *Foundational Fictions: The National Romances of Latin America*. Berkley: University of California Press, 1991.

Spencer, Anthony. "Americans Create Hybrid Spaces in Costa Rica: A Framework for Exploring Cultural and Linguistic Integration." *Language and Intercultural Communication* 11, no. 1 (February 2011): 59–74.

Spitzer, Loe. *Hotel Bolivia: The Culture of Memory in a Refuge from Nazism*. New York: Hill and Wang, 1999. Kindle edition.

Squire, Corinne. "Experience-Centered and Culturally-Oriented Approaches to Narratives." In *Doing Narrative Research*, 2nd ed., edited by Molly Andrews, Corinne Squire, and Maria Tamboukou. Thousand Oaks CA: SAGE, 2013.

Steinberg, Paul F. *Environmental Leadership in Developing Countries: Transnational Relations and Biodiversity Policy in Costa Rica and Bolivia*. Cambridge MA: MIT Press, 2001.

Stepan, Nancy Leys. *Picturing Tropical Nature*. Ithaca NY: Cornell University Press, 2001.

Stephens, Clyde S. "The Golfito Boat People." In Stephens, *Banana People*, 240–49.

Stephens, Clylde, ed. *Banana People: True Stories of the Tropics*. Ann Arbor MI: Dollar Bill Books, 2002.

Stoler, Ann Laura. *Carnal Knowledge and Imperial Power: Race and the Intimate in Colonial Rule*. Oakland: University of California Press, 2010.

———. "Intimidation of Empire: Predicaments of the Tactile and Unseen." In Stoler, *Haunted by Empire*, 1-22.

———. "Tense and Tender Ties: The Politics of Comparison in North America History and (Post) Colonial Studies." In Stoler, *Haunted by Empire* 23–70.

Stoler, Ann Laura, ed. *Haunted by Empire: Geographies of Intimacy in North American History*. Durham NC: Duke University Press, 2006.

Stovall, Tyler. "The Fire This Time: Black Americans Expatriates and the Algerian War." *Yale French Studies* 98 (2000): 182–200.

———. *Paris Noir: African Americans in the City of Lights*. Boston: Houghton Mifflin, 1996.

Strathern, Andrew, and Pamela J. Stewart. "Introduction," in *Landscape, Memory and History: Anthropological Perspectives*, edited by Strathern and Stewart. London: Pluto Press, 2003.

Strathern, Marilyn. "Artifacts of History: Events and the Interpretation of Images." In *Culture and History in the Pacific*, edited by Jukka Sikala, 25–44. Helsinki: Transactions of the Finnish Anthropological Society, 1990.

Suñol, Julio C. *Robert Vesco compra una república*. San José: Trejos, 1974.

Sutton, David E. *Remembrance of Repasts: An Anthropology of Food and Memory*. Oxford: Berg, 2001.

Swancutt, Katherine, and Mirelle Mazard. "Anthropological Knowledge Making, the Reflexive Feedback Loop, and Conceptualizations of the Soul." In *Animism beyond the Soul: Ontology, Reflexivity, and the Making of Anthropological Knowledge*, edited by Katherine Swancutt and Mirielle Mazard, 1–17. New York: Berghahn, 2018.

Theophano, Janet. *Eat My Word: Reading Women's Lives through the Cookbooks They Wrote*. New York: Palgrave Macmillan, 2003.

Theroux, Paul. "Tarzan Is an Expatriate." *Transition* 7, nos. 3–4 (75–76) (1997): 46–58.

Thomas, Charles. "Chilean Theatre in Exile: The Teatro del Angel in Costa Rica, 1974–1984." *Latin American Theatre Review* 19, no. 2 (Spring 1986): 97–101.

Thomson, Alistair. "Anzac Memories: Putting Popular Memory into Practice in Australia." *Oral History* 18, no.1 (1990): 25–31.

Tobia, Simona. *Advertising America: The United States Information Service in Italy, 1945–1956*. Milan: LED, 2008.

Tolia-Kelly, Divya P. "Mobility/Stability: British Asian Cultures of 'Landscape and Englishness.'" *Environment and Planning A: Economy and Space* 38, no. 2 (February 2006): 341–58.

Trejos, Alonso. *Costa Rica: Illustrated Geography*. 2nd ed. Curridabat, Costa Rica: Trejos Hermanos Sucesores, 1996.

Trundle, Catherine. "Against the Gated Community: Contesting the 'Ugly American Dream' Through Rural New Zealand Dreams." In Bönisch-Brednich and Trundle, *Local Lives*, 31–48.

———. *Americans in Tuscany: Charity, Compassion, and Belonging*. New York: Berghahn, 2014.

———. "Romance Tourists, Foreign Wives or Retirement Migrants? Cross Cultural Marriage in Florence, Italy." In Benson and O'Reilly, *Lifestyle Migration*, 51–67.

Tylor, Erin B. "A Reluctant Locality: The Politics of Place and Progress in Santo Domingo." In Bönisch-Brednich and Trundle, *Local Lives*, 101–18.

Unger, Nancy C. *Beyond Nature's Housekeepers: American Women in Environmental History*. New York: Oxford University Press, 2012.

U.S.A. Women's Club of Costa Rica. *Embassy Row Specialties*. San José: Self-published, 1963.

———. *Postres / Desserts*. San José: Self-published, n.d.

Van Noorloos, Femke. "Residential Tourism and Multiple Mobilities: Local Citizenship and Community Fragmentation in Costa Rica." *Sustainability* 5, no. 2 (2013): 570–89.

Vargas, Juan Carlos, ed. *Tropical Travel: A Representation of Central America in the 19th Century*. San José: Editorial UCR, 2008.

Venútolo, Patricia Alvarenga. "La inmigración extranjera en la historia costarricense." In Sandoval-Garcia, *El mito roto*, 3–24.

Vickery, Amanda. *Behind Closed Doors: At Home in Georgian England*. New Haven CT: Yale University Press, 2009.

Waldren, Jacqueline. *Insiders and Outsiders: Paradise and Reality in Mallorca*. New York: Berghahn, 1996.

Walke, Anika. "Memories of an Unfulfilled Promise: Internationalism and Patriotism in Post-Soviet Oral Histories of Jewish Survivors of the Nazi Genocide." *Oral History Review* 40, no. 2 (2013): 271–98.

Wallace, David Rains. *The Quetzal and the Macaw: The Story of Costa Rica's National Parks*. San Francisco: Sierra Club, 1992.

Warren, James Belasco. *Appetite for Change: How the Counterculture Took on the Food Industry*. Ithaca NY: Cornell University Press, 2007.

Warren, Robert, and Ellen Percy Kraly. *The Elusive Exodus: Emigration from United States (Population Trends and Public Policy, No. 8)*. Washington DC: Population Reference Bureau, 1985.

White, Richard. "Fredrick Jackson Turner and Buffalo Bill." In *The Frontier in American Culture*, edited by James R. Grossman, 7–66. Berkeley: University of California Press, 1994.

Whitehead, Neil L. "Amazonia: The Forest of Marvels." In Hulme and Youngs, *Cambridge Companion to Travel Writing*, 122–38.

Women's Club of Costa Rica. *Casseroles*. San José: Self-published, 1975.

Worin, Cindy, ed. *Kitchen Pleasures: A Book of Recipes from the Members of the Women's Club of Costa Rica 1940–2007*. Sun José: Litografia e Imprenta LIL, 2007.

Worster, Donald. *Under Western Skies: Nature and History in the American West*. New York: Oxford University Press, 1992.

Wright, Gwendolyn. *Building the Dream: A Social History of Housing in America*. Cambridge MA: MIT Press, 1981.

Yashar, Deborah. *Demanding Democracy: Reform and Reaction in Costa Rica and Guatemala*. Palo Alto CA: Stanford University Press, 1997.

Index

Page numbers in italics refer to illustrations.

Abrahams, Diane, 84
Africa, 143
agriculture, 45, 73; experiments of commune members in, 216; instructor in, 84, 168; land for, 75; settlements of, 68, 97–98, 104; sustainable, 71. *See also* deforestation; farming
Ahmed, Sara, 164
Albee, Edward, 89, 91
alcohol, 139; duties on, 270n97; as identity marker, 188–90; monopoly of Costa Rican government over, 188
Alice in Wonderland (Carroll), 89; poster for San José LTG production of, *90*
Allende, Salvador, 250n91
Alliance for Progress (1961), 13–14
All in the Family (U.S. American television sitcom), 52
Álvarez, Captain Guillermo, 52
Amazonia, 31
amenity migration, 4. *See also* migration
American Dream, 17
American Legion (AL), 82–83, 140
Ameringer, Charles, 13

Anderson, Leon, 3, 73, 81, 241n4
Anhalt, Diana, 246n16
anti-gringo movement, 14
Appadurai, Arjun, 61–62
Argentina, 7
Arlington, John, 206–7, 211, 229, 231
artifacts, 165; pre-Columbian, 104, 181, 268n74. *See also* material culture
Atlantic coast, 71–72, 76, 98, 125; southern, 177. *See also* Costa Rica
Auslander, Leora, 162, 174, 265n10
Austen, Jane: *Persuasion*, 152

baby boom / baby boomers, 2, 31, 38
Bach, Mark, 1, 19, 22, 34, 86
Backer, Dorothy, 21
Back to the Land movement, 71
Baird, Rosemary, 272n12
Baker, Josephine, 21
Baltimore, 118
banana republic, 8, 13, 76. *See also* Costa Rica
Barbas-Rhoden, Laura, 248n52
Barcelona, 63, 79; U.S. American women's club in, 249n78, 258n16

Bart, Theodor, 179, 181, 199, 204–7, 212, 225
Barthes, Roland, 81, 94, 181
beachfronts, 31, 60, 71, 118–23; development of, 120–23; real estate investment in, 54, 74–75; settlements in, 66–73, 93–94, 166, 169, 185. *See also* Costa Rica
beans, 101, 190, 197
beauty pageant, 140
Behadad, Ali, 94–95, 213
Benson, Michaela, 4, 35, 162, 269n90, 272n15
Biesanz, John, 53, 86
biodiversity, 96. *See also* nature
Blacks, 7, 66, 71, 135; Afro-descendants as cooks in U.S. American homes, 135; of Costa Rican colonial period, 235n22; of Costa Rican frontier, 98. *See also* cooking; race
Blunt, Alison, 162
Boggs, Henrietta, 15, 73–74, 125–26
Bolívar, Simon, 14
Bönisch-Brednich, Brigitte, 61
books, 179–80. *See also* material culture
Bozzoli de Wille, María, 98
Brazil, 7, 37, 275n2
Brenes, Rodrigo Facio, 9, 76
British empire, 87, 251n8
Brown, Jim, 73, 117
Brown, Joyce, 117–18, 177–78, 229, 231
Brown, Woodson, 65
brown rice, 190, 221
Burdick, Eugene, 259n24
Burnett, Ben, 165; "Peace and Plenty Found in Pensión," 165–66. *See also* "On Jungle Trails and Tropical Tales" (popular column)

Caamaño, Carmen, 241n9
cacao, 45
Cahuita, 72, 75
Calderón Guardia, President Rafael Ángel, 8–11, 236n29
California, 45, 47, 76, 100, 156, 176, 199
Cambodia, 206–7
Campbell, John, 174–75
campesinos (farmers), 67–68, 95; as national figures, 99; way of life of, 71, 170–71, 214; wisdom of, 107–8. *See also* Costa Rica; farming
Canada, 37, 44, 155; U.S. Americans as emigrants to, 242n19
capitalism, 2, 174, 247n36; ethos of land ownership of, 216. *See also* consumerism
Capote, Truman: *In Cold Blood*, 256n87
Caracas, 147
Caribbean islands, 98; U.S. American imperialism in, 271n113
Casa Tica (Tico House), 168–72, 266n22. *See also* housing
Casey, Edward, 61
Castro, President León Cortés, 8
Catholic Church, 11
cattle, 74–75, 101–2, 117–18
Central America: in Cold War, 31, 131; map of, 204–5; U.S. dominance in, 2, 4, 6, 13; U.S. empire in, 5
"Central America on a Shoe String" (travelogue column), 155–56

Central Valley, 6, 30, 45, 51, 60–62, 98–99, 156; cafeterias in English-speaking schools in, 191; Costa Rican women of rural community in, 256n75; counterculture lifestyle in, 178, 226; population of, 234n18; real estate in, 75–76, 248n54; settlements of U.S. Americans in, 66, 72–75, 118, 129, 138, 145, 163, 167; U.S. clubland in, 77–79, 87, 92. *See also* Costa Rica

Centro Israelita (Ashkenazi Jewish community), 77

Cerro de la Muerte, 9, 99, 171, 253n20

Chicago, 71, 216

Chicago Riots (1968), 44

china (maid), 144–45, 148–49, 261n65; hypersexuality of, 148. *See also* women

choza (dirt floor hut), 172. *See also* housing

Christian Dior, 173, 189, 197, 221, 267n38. *See also* material culture

Cinel, Dino, 241n10

citizenship: Costa Rican, 18–19, 21, 60, 244n67; U.S., 5, 18, 41, 203, 221, 238n62. *See also* nationality

Ciudad Colón, 66, 202–3

civil rights movement, 38, 200

civil war (Costa Rica), 11–12, 17, 88, 138, 236n29, 236n36. *See also* Costa Rica

Civil War (U.S.), 37. *See also* United States

Clairmont, Tom, 69, 70, 166, *167*, 218–19, 228

class: domestic work by women of lower, 155; and ethnicity, 146, 155, 158, 164; and gender, 187; and racial segregation, 258n15. *See also* ethnicity

Cleveland, Harlen, 38–39, 132–33, 260n37

climate, 1, 51, 54, 70; tropical, 109. *See also* Costa Rica; rainy season

Cocos Island, 119–20, 256n87. *See also* Costa Rica

coffee, 8–9, 64; duties on, 270n97; farm, 167; German oligarchy of, 236n29; instability of market for, 74

Cohen, Eric, 21, 81, 249n64

Cold War, 2–4, 10–14, 27, 38–40, 57, 80–83, 106, 222–23, 234n13; anxieties of, 144; interests of U.S. in Americas during, 129–33, 159, 236n30; rhetoric of, 158; U.S. propaganda of, 86, 135, 174

Cole-Christensen, Daryl: frontier experience of, 67, 100–103, 113, 116; home of, 169; land ownership according to, 105, 122; *A Place in the Rain Forest*, 67, 100–106, 109–16, 121–22; on rain forest, 106, 109–11, 255n60; on women, 255n71

Coleman, Jim, 55, 214–15, 274n48

colonialism, 19, 80, 126; British, 251n8, 262n73; discourses of, 110, 255n63; European, 95; histories of, 35; and nature conservation and preservation, 257n99. *See also* imperialism

colonization, 75–76; of indigenous lands in North America, 104; and land ownership, 216. *See also* imperialism; real estate

Colorado, 107, 117, 161, 228, 231

Columbus, Christopher, 93, 166, 273n27

Index 301

communes, 25–26, 48–51, 69–73, 108–9, 150; agriculture in, 216; of artists, 48, 204; beach, 181, 218–19, 225, 228; housing in, 170–71, 225; purchase of land for, 216–17; rain forest, 179; in U.S., 185, 199, 204–5. *See also* counterculture

communism, 2, 11–12, 37–38, 236n36; encroachment of, 144, 164

comparative religion, 71, 143, 216

conches, 120

Connecticut, 100

consciousness-raising groups, 150, 156–57; feminist, 264n95. *See also* feminism

consumerism, 2, 32, 163, 174–79, 186, 198. *See also* capitalism; materialism; United States

cooking: Afro-descendants as cooks in U.S. American homes, 135; and cookbooks and recipe books, 30, 132, 191–93, *194, 195, 196*, 197, 269n89, 270n111; Costa Rican style of, 182–83, 193, 197; counterculture style of, 185, 190, 197, 269n89; French style of, 197; as identity marker, 157, 164, 174, 182, 185–87, 190; ingredients for, 182–87, 190–92, 197; U.S. American style of, 30, 40, 174, 182–83, 188–93, 197; in U.S. Women's Club, 135, 143, 191–93. *See also* Blacks; culinary; culture; identity work; kitchen; material culture

Copey de Dota, 70, 73, 108, 171, 216

corn, 101

corruption, 229; U.S.-based, 237n49. *See also* Costa Rica; United States; Vesco, Robert

Costa Rica: abolishment of army of, 48; advertisement for Americans to joint homestead in, *50, 51*; advertisement of property in, *49, 51*; beautiful landscape of, 36, 48, 51, 70–71, 96, 163, 211–12; bureaucracy of, 54; close family ties of, 6; conservation policies of, 96, 121, 257n93, 257n99; constitutive myth of, 12, 234n18, 252n19; as ecological superpower, 257n99; economy of, 1, 6, 17, 74–76, 121; electricity sector of, 9; emigration to U.S. from, 241n9; European hegemony in, 15; fragmentation of expatriate community in, 25; frontier of, 97–106; handicrafts of, 215; as "imperial workshop" of U.S., 8; map of, *xx*; massive land-purchasing by Americans in, 14, 51, 104–6; national discourses of, 111; national ethos of, 241n9; police of, 105; as settler society, 7, 252n19; Spanish conquest of, 6, 120; style of cooking of, 182–83, 193, 197; U.S. American emigration to, 3, 14–19, *16*, 24, 31–39, 44–64, 74–75, 95, 100–101, 149, 173–75, 180, 199–220, 228–30, 239n67; U.S. Americans according to place of residence in, *62, 63*; welfare policies of, 74. *See also* Atlantic coast; banana republic; beachfronts; *campesinos* (farmers); Central Valley; civil war (Costa Rica); climate; Cocos Island; corruption; economy; immigration; nature; Pacific coast; rain forests; real estate;

San José; Switzerland of Central America
Costa Rica Academy, 65
Costa Rican Anti-Alcohol League, 139
Costa Rican Independence Day (Quince), 64
Costa Rican-North American Cultural Center / Centro Cultural Costarricense Norteamericano, 63, 86. *See also* U.S.-Costa Rican Cultural Center
Costa Rican Tourist Institute / Instituto Costarricense de Turismo (ICT), 53–54, 184
counterculture, 2–5, 17, 38, 46–48, 229, 271n7, 272nn14–15; artists of, 84, 89, 226; business venture of, 120; cooking style of, 185, 197; evolution of U.S. American, 243n55; gardening practices of, 71, 185; immigrants of, 21, 47, 51–55, 57–58, 68–73, 92, 95, 178–79, 199–220, 226–28; mysticism as part of, 200; parents of, 65; physical appearance of, 52, 53; scandal of, 72; settlements of, 68–74, 170–71, 178, 267n33; symbol of, 69. *See also* communes; culture; drug culture; hippies; identity; immigration
Country Day School, 65
cowboy, 102–3, 117
Creation myth, 97
Croucher, Sheila, 23, 43, 126, 146
Cuba, 7, 13
culinary, 181–97; Costa Rican, 182–83, 185, 192–93, 197, 270n106; counterculture, 185–86, 190; hybrid repertoires of, 181–86, 191–93, 197–98; of Quaker women, 184.

See also cooking; culture; identity work; kitchen; material culture
cultural capital, 201, 203
culture: Costa Rican, 187, 214; domestic, 32, 114, 129–43; and nature, 183, 198, 227; Pre-Columbian, 104, 167, 181; U.S. American, 95, 100, 214, 228. *See also* cooking; counterculture; culinary; culture shock; domesticity; ideology; material culture; popular culture; theater
culture shock, 84, 131, 178, 211–12. *See also* culture
Curridabat, 66

Davis, Ambassador Nathaniel, 11–12
de Beauvoir, Simone, 127
deforestation, 96, 99, 111; and agricultural development, 106; "primitive," 218; uncontrolled, 120–21, 257n92. *See also* agriculture; *denuncio* legislation
de Grazia, Victoria, 265n10, 268n53
Dekkers, Onka, 152
democracy, 11, 17
Denevan, William, 96–97
Dent, Thomas, 45
denuncio legislation, 99. *See also* deforestation; squatting
de Onis, Juan: *The Green Cathedral*, 251n8
development, 120–23, 253n32; and progress, 122. *See also* economy; investors; natural resources
dissident media, 14. *See also* dissidents; media
dissidents, 17, 35, 48; civilizing mission of, 228; in social and political protest movements of 1960s, 243n42. *See also* dissident media

Index   303

divorce, 157, 225, 231
domesticity, 114, 143–48, 164–65, 168–69; changes in U.S. American, 191–93; of Costa Rican women, 130, 146, 184; and domestic help, 175, 262n66, 262n69, 262n76, 264n92; revival of, 144; and supermarket shopping, 186; and traditional division of labor in family, 155; and wild nature, 116. *See also* culture; women
Dominical, 58, 71, 73, 107, 109, 118, 199, 208–9, 214, 217
Dowling, Robyn, 162
Dresner, Fay, 125, 141–42, 159
drug culture, 45–46, 73, 89, 108; in U.S., 143. *See also* counterculture
Durant, Marge, 146–47; "You Do It Yourself in Caracas," 147
Dyer, Dery, 29, 151, 159, 180
Dyer, Elizabeth, 29, *150*, 151–53, 157
Dyer, Richard, 29, 151

eco-feminist criticism, 255n67. *See also* feminism
ecological activism, 122
economy: access of U.S. American immigrants to U.S., 201; agricultural export-based, 8; crisis in Costa Rican, 1, 17, 77, 96, 201, 219, 248n53, 257n93; policies of, 121; stagnation of, 1. *See also* Costa Rica; development; plantation economy
ecotourism, 121–22. *See also* tourism
Ecuador, 34, 38, 63, 200, 245n82, 266n15, 271n5
Eden, 97, 221; patronizing of, 120–23. *See also* Garden of Eden; paradise

education, 180; of U.S. American palate, 271n113
Eigen, Barbara, 157
Eigen, Eric, 157
Eisenhower, President Dwight, 135
electrical home appliances, 174–78. *See also* material culture
Eliot, June, 167–68
emplacement, 94–95, 117, 162; and belonging, 246n26; practices of, 123, 185, 221. *See also* identity
enclave, 61; of counterculture, 72; in Ecuador, 63; upper-class U.S., 75, 84. *See also* social networks; U.S. clubland
Erikson, Richard, 41, 73, 212–13, 217–18
Escazú, 64–66, 157, 161; nutrition center in, 139–40; in pre-Columbian period, 263n80
ethnicity: class and, 146, 155, 158, 164; gender and, 3, 31, 113, 164; of U.S. Americans in Costa Rica, 188. *See also* class; identity
Europe, 37
Ewing, Jack, 121
exceptionalism, 5–8, 12, 17, 222–23, 234n18
existential mobility, 47. *See also* migration
expatriatism, 21–22, 25, 47–48, 77–91; administrative, 126; corporate, 126; of diverse nationalities, 226; enclaves of, 63, 86–91; as freedom, 239n75; post–World War I, 165; survey of U.S. emigration and, 242n11; theater of, 88–91; and U.S. consumer society, 179. *See also* colonialism; migration

farming, 73–74, 108–9; harmful methods of, 98; impoverish-

ment of Costa Rican, 74; practices of land management in, 121; in rain forest, 110; in U.S., 100. *See also* agriculture; *campesinos* (farmers)
Fechter, Meike, 79, 127, 133, 250n84
Federation of U.S. Women's Clubs, 137
Feminine Mystique, 137–43, 159; in domestic sphere, 164. *See also* women
feminism, 150–59; anonymous, 263n84; Costa Rican, 157–58; discourse of, 157, 248n52; second wave of, 258n15, 264n92; white liberal U.S. American, 152, 154–58, 264n92. *See also* eco-feminist criticism; U.S. women's liberation movement; women
feria (outdoor market), 187. *See also* shopping
Fernández, President Juan Mora, 6
Ferriss, Timothy, 245n82
Fiala, Elsie Mae, 67–68, 98, 103–4, 115–17, 161, 170, 175–76, 181, 184–85, 256n78
Fiala, Walter, 67, 104–5, *112*, 116–17, 181, 256n78
Figueres, President José (Pepe), 11–13, 15, 125, 237n37
Finifter, Ada, 38, 238n62
Fitzgerald, F. Scott, 21
Florida, 75
Foulks, John, 44–46, 59, 71–72, 222
Fourth of July, 78, 103, 134, 191
France, 37, 246n26
Fredrikson, Anna, 135, 149, 173, 188, 221–22, 225, 231
freedom: expatriatism as, 239n75; leisure and, 149; material, 58; migration and, 126, 145–47, 150, 158; purchase of, 48; from restraints, 22
French Existentialism, 46
Friedlander, Harvey, 238n60
frontera sur (southern frontier), 67, 96–106, 116; emergencies and accidents on, 113. *See also* frontier
frontier: Costa Rica as new, 96–106, 257n97; ethos of, 111; and indigenous peoples, 98–99, 102–6; perceptions of, 121–22; theory of, 106; in U.S. culture, 252n14; women on, 113–14, 255n71. See also *frontera sur* (southern frontier); indigenous peoples; rain forests
furniture: Costa Rican, 215; and home appliances, 178; imported, 161, 173; pedigree of, 173; physical translocation of, 165. *See also* home; material culture

gallo pinto (rice and beans), 190, 197, 270n106
García Canclini, Néstor, 101
Garden of Eden, 27, 209, 219. *See also* Eden; utopia
Geertz, Clifford, 30
gender: and class, 187; and ethnicity, 3, 31, 113, 164; geographies of power of, 127; and identity, 3, 10, 74, 96, 113; and immigration, 23, 126, 153, 157, 233n8, 240n81; and narratives, 240n85; and nationality, 83, 85; ratio of women to men in terms of, 16, *16*; roles, 42, 96, 112–13, 126–59, 184, 191–93; self-perceptions of, 177; sex and, 24; traditional relations of, 145–46, 151–54. *See also* gender work; machismo; women

Index 305

gender work, 112–18, 127; of consciousness-raising groups, 156–57; and identity work, 127–59; and women's liberation, 155. *See also* gender; identity work
geography of meaning, 4, 57–58, 127
German Club of Costa Rica, 77, 248n63
Germany, 8–9, 236n29, 248n63; U.S. Women's Club in, 261n53
GI Bill, 10, 17, 40–42, 145
Giglioli, Giovanna, 98, 234n18
Global North, 74
global power relations, 5, 97, 102, 222; and counterculture immigration of U.S. Americans, 200, 204, 216; and planetary gentrification, 74
Global South, 74
Gonzáles, Luiza, 258n20
Grandin, Greg, 8
granola, 190, 197
Great Depression, 38, 163, 191, 241n10
Green, Doris, 84
gringos, 3, 52, 59; alcoholism of, 189–90; good, 244n60; greed of, 216; guilt of, 172; in marriage, 230; "pacific invasion" of, 74–77; rich, 217
Gringo Trail, 73–74
Guanacaste, 68, *68*, 99, 103
Guatemala, 13, 33; indigenous population in, 156
Guindon, Lucille (Lucky), 67, 114–15, 184, 254n49; "Roots" drawing by, *115*
Guindon, Wilford (Wolf), 111, 114–15, 228
Guzmán, President Jacobo Árbenez, 13

Haas, Heiko, 4, 163, 247n36, 267n48
Hagan, John, 44
Hage, Sharon, 33, 47–49, 58, 71–73, 109, 171, 179, 186, 199–200, 213–14, 272n14
Haiti, 8
Harper's, 260n37
Harris, Elizabeth, 177
Hash House Harriers / House Harriers Club (HHH), 87–88, 250n88
Hawaii, 47, 51; change in perception of time among U.S. Americans in, 244n57, 254n55
Hayes, Matthew, 21, 52, 101, 200, 245n82, 266n15
Hemingway, Ernest, 21, 165
Hill-Webber, Karen, 59–60, 74, 205–8, 211
hippies, 25, 45, 51–52, *53*, 171, 223; commune of, 214; cultists and, 120. *See also* counterculture
history: ecological, 252n11; hearing of, 224; of imperialism, 35; migratory family, 41. *See also* oral history
home: in Cold War, 2; creation of new, 165; dislocation of, 164–65; freedom from restraints of, 22; as homesteading in Costa Rica, *50*; hybrid patterns of, 166–68; inability of women to work outside of, 43; memory of, 181–82; metaphor of, 172; trailer, 166–67; weekends of U.S. American husbands at, 73. *See also* furniture; housing; rancho
homosexuality, 89
Honduras, British, 37
House Beautiful magazine, 163
housing, 161–62; campesino, 170–71; corrugated iron roof, 170, 172, 266n22; and identity work of U.S. Americans in Costa Rica,

165–72, 197; narrowness of Costa Rican, 173, 197; permanent, 168–72; thatched-roof, 101, 166, 170–71, 266n22; transient, 165–68, 172. *See also Casa Tica* (Tico House); *choza* (dirt floor hut); home; material culture; rancho

identity: ecological, 229; formation of, 27; gender, 3, 28, 32, 146, 229; individual construction of, 247n36; migrant, 2, 61; national, 7–8, 19–20, 39–41, 123; pioneer, 96; place-based, 61–62, 66, 92, 95, 108, 118, 162; politics of, 122; professional, 229; of self-representation as child, 272n22; spiritual, 229; talk of, 22–30; transnational, 31, 60–61; of U.S. Americans in Costa Rica, 2–3, 19–29, 40–41, 60–62, 77–81, 95, 140, 173–74, 228–29. *See also* counterculture; emplacement; ethnicity; identity work; material culture; memory; nationality

identity work, 22–30, 39–41, 54, 60–61, 65–73, 77–95, 223–56; as agents of progress, 170; collective, 81, 95, 97, 138, 170–74, 182, 198, 202, 220; definition of, 241n4; gender work and, 127–59; health food and, 190; and identity talk, 199–220, 223–24, 243n27, 271n3; individual, 81, 95, 97, 115, 138, 174, 182, 198, 202, 220; of lifestyle or affluent immigrants, 163–64, 262n69; nature preservation as, 122–23; paradox of, 212–15; preservation of cultural identification as, 191–93, 197; service as key component of, 137–40, 144, 192; of U.S. Americans, 2–3, 19–29, 40–41, 60–62, 77–81, 95, 103–23, 129–45, 158, 170–93, 199–229. *See also* cooking; culinary; gender work; identity; life story; material culture

ideology, 31, 48; in Americas, 95; feminist, 153; of progress, 111; U.S. American culture and, 140. *See also* culture

immigration: accidental, 200–201, 206, 218; arrival scenes of, 205–12; Asian, 14; Black, 14, 235n23; British, 246n26; Caribbean, 246n9; Chinese, 7; collective experience of, 26, 200; Costa Rican, 235n24, 238n61, 241n9; counterculture, 199–220; countercurrent of, 1, 4–5, 31, 222; destination for, 94; dislocation of home in, 164–65; and dwellings, 161–68; and French Existentialism, 46–47; gender and, 23, 126, 153, 157, 233n8; Italian, 241n10; and marginality, 5, 80; memory-based inventories of U.S. American, 172–78, 181–82; and national identity, 7, 14; noneconomic, 126; Quaker, 51; return, 36; scholarly discourse on, 31, 36, 224, 240n81; small-scaled foreign, 243n40; Soviet and post-Soviet, 240n81; traditional definition of, 20; undocumented, 18; U.S. female, 23, 108, 126, 149–50, 155. *See also* Costa Rica; counterculture; lifestyle immigration; migration; privilege immigration; United States

Index 307

Immigration Act (1907), 36
imperialism: discourses of, 110; histories of, 35; narratives of, 200, 216, 220. *See also* colonization; U.S. imperialism
indigenous peoples, 6, 66, 253n38; of Costa Rican frontier, 98–99, 102–6; as helpers to white men, 113; as helpers to white women, 144–49; historical rights of, 105; masculinity of, 255n68; of rain forest, 67–68, 99, 104–6. *See also* frontier
individualism, 80, 101
informal U.S. empire, 5, 8, 235n26. *See also* United States
infrastructure, 64–65; poor, 71; settlement of Costa Rican frontier and, 99. *See also* Inter-American Highway
Inter-American Highway, 9–10, 67, 99; construction of, 218, 236n33, 247n27, 253n20; investments in land along future route of, 102. *See also* infrastructure
interesting groups, 17, 108. See also *juntitas*
International Club, 83
investors, 1, 67. *See also* development
Italian Club, 77

Jakarta, 79, 133; expatriate women in, 250n84, 259n22; U.S. American women's club in, 249n78, 258n16
James, Daniel, 27
Janoschka, Michael, 4, 163, 247n36, 267n48
Jefferson, President Thomas, 12, 242n11

Jesuits, 65
Jinesta, Carlos, 76–77
The Joy of Cooking (recipe book), 191, 270n108
jungle, 78, 109, 208–9, 251n8; civilization in, 170, 228; rain forest as, 96, 106, 114; representation of whites in, 101, 110–11, 218; tourist excursions into, 104; women in, 116. *See also* rain forests
junta, 11–12
juntitas, 142. *See also* interesting groups

Kaminar, Wendy, 256n76
Kennedy, President John F., 13–14, *15*, 134–35
King Kong (movie), 109
Kipling, Rudyard: *The Jungle Book*, 102, 251n8
kitchen, 147. *See also* cooking; culinary
Klee, Adam, 74, 231
Kordick, Carmen, 12, 235n24, 241n9
Korean War, 5, 17, 33, 35, 44, 66, 111, 223, 228. *See also* Quakers
Kraly, Ellen Percy, 37

La Hora, 52
La Liga Feminista Costarricense, 157. *See also* feminism; women
La Nación, 14, 54, 75, 120, *141*, 216, 237n49; "Costa Rica vende sus tierras a extranjeros" (series of reports), 56. *See also* Salguero, Miguel
Latin America Mission, 41, 68, 226
Latin American literature, 214
Latin dance, 142, 261n60

Lederer, William, 259n24
Lesser, Jeffrey, 228, 275n2
Levittown (New York), 174
Ley de Pensionados. *See* Pensionado Law (1964)
Life Magazine, 144, 174
life story, 40–41, 275n58; construction of, 219–20. *See also* identity work
lifestyle immigration, 4, 20, 24, 38, 96, 126, 163, 230, 251n9; beautiful landscapes and economic factor in, 241n8; domestic help in construction of identities in, 262n69; narratives of, 274n37; as neoliberal phenomenon, 241n8. *See also* immigration; privilege immigration
lifestyle migration. *See* lifestyle immigration
Limerick, Patricia Nelson, 255n71
Lincoln School, 63, 65
Linde, Charlotte, 26, 275n58
Little Theatre Group (LTG), 10, 30, 88–89, 90. *See also* theater
Los Angeles, 48, 72, 74, 108, 118, 171, 199, 204, 207–8
"Lost Generation," 37

machismo, 153–55, 263n89. *See also* gender
"Machismo and Marriage" (feminist column), 153–54
Madison, Greg, 126
Magellan, Ferdinand, 119
Mahler, Sara, 24, 127
Malinowski, Bronislaw: *Argonauts of the Western Pacific*, 273n33
Mallon, Florencia, 240n80
Manson, Charles, 72

Marañón, Jon, 93–97, 102–7, 111, 119, 122–23, 172, 180, 253n32
marine ecology, 213
market: indoor Costa Rican, 187; local Costa Rican, 183, 186–88, 227; local Spanish, 187; open-air Costa Rican, 187. *See also feria* (outdoor market); San José; shopping; supermarket
marriage: in Costa Rica, 40, 84; to Costa Rican men, 17, 34–35, 41–42, 59, 63–64, 83–84, 238n56; to Costa Rican women, 45; in U.S., 261n63
Marxism, 2; revolutionary ideas of, 13; subversive, 17
Massachusetts, 173
Massey, Douglas, 31, 34–35, 39, 272n12
material culture, 23, 32, 161–98; books of U.S. Americans as, 179–80; Costa Rican, 163, 168–75, 181; creation of production of locality through, 265n7; culinary practices of U.S. Americans as, 181–93, 197–98; differences in, 173–74, 179; dwellings of U.S. Americans as, 161–62, 165–72, 179; of hippies, 214; televisions of U.S. Americans as, 177. *See also* artifacts; books; Christian Dior; culinary; electrical home appliances; furniture; housing; identity; identity work; market; materialism; refrigerator; supermarket; washing machine
materialism, 35, 58, 179; opponents of, 216; way of life of, 200–201, 204. *See also* consumerism; material culture; United States

Index 309

May, Eileen Tyler, 144, 265n13
McAdams, Dan, 26–27, 201–2
McCarthy era, 37, 40
Meagher, Thomas Francis, 7–8, 168
media: Costa Rican, 52; U.S., 13. *See also* dissident media
Melman, Billie, 240n85, 264n101, 267n29
memory, 172–79; food and, 181–82; social construction of, 201. *See also* identity
mestizos, 7, 66, 105; girl, 144; lower-class, 102; as "natives," 276n12
Mexico, 33–34, 37–38, 45, 101, 206; desert of, 156; "privilege migrants" in, 239n69
Mexico City, 63, 212
Meyerowitz, Joanne, 264n92, 265n13
migration: affluent, 126, 162–63, 271n6; of Afro-Caribbean workers to Costa Rican Atlantic coast, 7; decision of, 35; and freedom, 126, 145–47, 150, 158; internal, 247n33; international flows of, 3–4, 20–21, 31, 34–35; retiree, 53; transnational, 241n98, 242n19. *See also* amenity migration; existential mobility; expatriatism; immigration; migration studies
migration studies, 5; locality in, 241n98. *See also* migration
Miller, Daniel, 174, 182, 267n40
missionaries, 16, 68, *68*, 161, 226; civilizing work of, 170, 214
modernity, 174, 182; progress and, 132; technology and, 10, 177
Molina, Ivan, 257n99
Monteverde, 17, 33–34, 44, 66, 111, 114, 169–70, 183–84, 254n49. *See also* Quakers; Santa Elena

Mora, Jane, 74, 176–78, 222, 227, 235n19
Morales, Kathrin, 40–42, 135–36, 231, 260n37
Moravia, 66
Morocco, 244n57, 254n55
Mother Earth magazine, 51
Movimiento para Liberación de la Mujer, 157–58. *See also* feminism; women
Moya, José, 39
Ms. magazine, 152, 154, 263n84, 263n89
mulatos, 7
myth: of agrarian equality, 235n23; constitutive myth of Costa Rica, 12, 234n18, 252n19; of Eldorado, 96, 104

narrative of transition, 158, 170, 264n93, 264n101, 267n29
Nash, Dennison, 79, 187, 270n103
National Geographic, 180
nationality, 3, 6, 228–29, 249n78; gender and, 83, 85, 146. *See also* citizenship; identity; patriotism
natural resources, 8; development of, 122. *See also* development; nature
nature: beauty of, 36, 48, 51, 70–71, 96, 163, 211–12, 241n8; and culture, 183, 198, 227; as feminine, 255n63; as Greater Household of Earth, 256n76; identity work of U.S. Americans in communes in, 170–72; physical distancing of U.S. Americans from, 175; preservation of, 257n97; pristine, 209; reserves of, 104, 114, 120–21. *See also* biodiversity; Costa Rica; natural resources

310 *Index*

New Deal, 12
New Jersey, 55
Newsweek magazine, 48
New York City, 75, 157
New York Times, 12
New Zealand, 38
Nicaragua, 1, 8, 16, 37, 236n30
Nicoya Peninsula, 75, 120, 231
Nixon, President Richard, 44, 177, 202, 214, 223, 237n49, 267n44
Nosara, 75, 181, 202
Novelas de la Selva, 251n8
nuclear weapons, 38, 164

off our backs (feminist periodical), 152
"On Jungle Trails and Tropical Tales" (popular column), 165. *See also* Burnett, Ben
oral history, 23, 27–28, 164, 274n48; snowball technique in, 240n86. *See also* history
O'Reilly, Jean: "The Housewife's Moment of Truth," 154
O'Reilly, Karen, 4, 22, 35, 162, 272n15
Orisí Valley, 104
Orlich, President Francisco, *15*, 134
Orosí, 170
Ortiz, Miguel, 147–49, 151, 155–56, 263n81. *See also* "Your Child's Health" (instructional column)
Osa Peninsula, 68–69, 111, 117, 123, 166, 185, 228

Pacific coast, 82; southern, 93, 117–21, 171–72, 183, 199, 208, 212–13, 225, 251n1. *See also* Costa Rica
pacifism, 48
Palma de Mallorca, 46, 265n7
Palmer, Steven, 257n99

Panama, 34, 38, 143; Canal Zone of, 52. *See also* Panama Canal
Panama Canal, 9, 11, 88, 167. *See also* Panama
Panama City, 210
Pan American Airways, 191
Pan American Congress (1940), 8
Pan American Highway. *See* Inter-American Highway
paradise: Costa Rica as, 69, 72, 93, 96–97, 205–8, 211, 229, 252n11, 273n27; destination of immigration as, 251n9; naturalist, 96; problems in, 72; tropical rain forest of Costa Rica as, 96. *See also* Eden; utopia
Pardo, Sue, 188
Partido Liberación Nacional (PLN), 11
Partido Republicano Nacional (PRN), 11
Partido Vanguardia Popular / Partido Comunista de Costa Rica (PCCR), 11
Passerini, Luisa, 274n48, 275n60
patriotism, 138, 174, 229; individualism and, 230. *See also* nationality
Peace Corps, 45
Pensionado Law (1964), 17, 52–57, 86, 238n59, 244n68; revision (1977) of, 245n79
pensionados (retirees), 52–58, 244n68; club de, 86; ley de, 17, 52–57, 238n59; U.S. American, 86–87. See also *rentistas*
Pensionados Club, 53–54, 86–87, 91
Pensión Morazán, 165. *See also* San José
Peru, 212
Pessar, Patricia, 24, 127
Philadelphia, 47

Index   311

philanthropy, 137–40, 144
Picado, President Teodoro, 11
Pickering, Lucy, 47
plantation economy, 7. *See also* economy
popular culture, 86–89, 100, 103, 177, 206; images of, 219. *See also* culture; television
Portelli, Alessandro, 25, 201, 224, 226
Potrero Grande, 67
Potter, David, 265n9
Powell, George, 114
Powell, Harriett, 114
Pratt, Mary Louise, 72, 252n12, 254n59, 273n34, 275n60
Preston-Werner, Theresa, 270n106
private property, 105, 244n68
privilege immigration, 19–20, 31–32, 60, 199–222, 230, 239n69. *See also* immigration; lifestyle immigration
prostitution, 130, 148, 153
Puerto Limón, 16, 45, 125, 173
Puerto Rico, 202
Puerto Viejo, 72
pulpería (stall / grocery store), 187, 190. *See also* shopping
Puntarenas, 16–17, 33, 66
Punta Uva, 45, 71
Putnam, Lara, 5, 225, 246n9

Quakers, 17, 33–35, 44, 51, 66–71, 111–14, 169–74, 183, 223, 228, 254n49, 274n42. *See also* Monteverde; Santa Elena
querencia (safe zone), 79, 83–84
Quijano, Aníbal, 35, 101

race, 6–7, 235n20; and racial segregation, 258n15. *See also* Blacks; "whiteness"

rain forests, 60, 106, 251n8, 256n75; conservation of, 121; as Costa Rican frontier, 98–106; Costa Ricans as guides in, 228; destructive power of, 110, 255n60; edge of, 114–15; gender work in, 112–18; heavy ground of, 183–84; natural ingredients in, 186; perceptions of, 95–96, 106–9, 120–21; real estate investment in, 74; relocation to, 117; research on, 114, 254n48; settlements in, 66–68, 71–73, 93–94, 101–6, 169, 179, 181, 185. *See also* Costa Rica; frontier; jungle
rainy season, 1, 199. *See also* climate
rancho, 69, 118, 169–70, 181, 185; A-frame, 171; sophisticated, 198; thatched-roof, 166–67. *See also* home; housing
Rangel, Alberto: *Inferno Verde*, 251n8
Rapport, Nigel, 108
rat race, 36, 49, 55, 58, 244n57
Reader's Digest, 98
real estate, 54, 74–77; Costa Rican, 248n54; and land speculation, 75–77; and settlement, 215–19. *See also* colonization; Costa Rica
reforestation, 121
refrigerator, 174–76, 197–98, 268n49. *See also* material culture
Registro Civil, 137
Rein, Raanan, 228
Renda, Mary A., 8
rentistas, 244n68. *See also pensionados* (retirees)
retirees, 1, 18, 21, 26, 35, 51–56, 87; housing of, 165; migration of, 53
Rivers-Moore, Megan, 98, 268n74

Robinson Settle de Oreamuno Flores, Elizabeth, 129
Rockwell, Dorothy: "What Did We Find to Feed the Family," 183
Roosevelt, President Franklin Delano, 12
Rosenberg, Emily, 132
Roszak, Theodor, 171
rural gentrification, 74–75
Russell, William, 75, 212

Salguero, Miguel, 54, 56, 75–76, 216–17, 248nn59–60. See also *La Nación*
San Antonio de Belén, 65
Sánchez, President Oscar Arias, 257n99
San Isidro de El General, 99
San José, 13–16, 25, 33, 41, 51–73, 53, 78–91, 117, 125–43, 168, 212; apartments in, 173, 176; arrival in, 207, 210–11; barrios of, 85; consciousness-raising groups around, 157; feminist parade in, 157–58; granola factory in, 190; lives of U.S. Americans in, 189, 191; local shops and markets around, 186; lower-class neighborhoods of, 258n20, 268n55; National Theater in, 88; sale of pre-Columbian artifacts in shops of, 104, 181; sights and places of interest around, 143; trailer parks in, 166; walking with mother-in-law in, 235n19. See also Costa Rica; market; Pensión Morazán; shopping
San José Pensionado Club. See Pensionados Club
San Pedro, 66
Santa Ana, 64, 66, 74, 84

Santa Elena, 33, 66. See also Monteverde; Quakers
Schama, Simon, 94
sexual harassment, 155
Sheinin, Linda, 109, 118, 199, 207–11, 274n48
shopping: in Costa Rica, 187–88; daily, 186; imported products in, 188; in U.S., 180, 187. See also *feria* (outdoor market); market; material culture; *pulpería* (stall / grocery store); San José; supermarket
Skutch, Alexander, 96, 104–7, 111, 113, 123, 251n6, 254n48
Slater, Candace, 95, 246n14
slavery, 6–7
Smithsonian Institution, 254n48
Snow, David, 3, 73, 81, 241n4
socialism, 2
social networks, 60–61, 92. See also enclave; U.S. clubland
social reforms, 11, 17
social work, 139
Soviet Union, 132, 186
soybeans, 190
Spain, 56; Costa del Sol region of, 239n75
Spanish empire, 6; conquest in Americas of, 120, 219
Spence, Antony, 239n67
Spitzer, Leo, 28, 81, 273n26
Spock, Dr. Benjamin, 263n81
squatting, 99, 105. See also *denuncio* legislation
Stam, Doris, 41, 68
Stam, John, 41, 68, *68*
Starthern, Andrew, 61
Stein, Gertrude, 21
Steinberg, Eileen, 93, 170–71, 216–17

Stephens, Clyde, 68–69
Stevens, Joan, 20, 51, 71, 84, 168, 173
Stewart, Pamela, 61
suburbs, 64–65
supermarket, 186–87, 269n91. *See also* market; shopping
Switzerland of Central America, 6, 18, 54. *See also* Costa Rica

Tamarindo, 120
technology: advantages of, 71; domestic, 267n44; and modernity, 10, 177; progress and, 110–11, 122
television, 38, 52, 177–78. *See also* popular culture
Texas, 74, 205, 228
theater: Costa Rican, 89, 250n91; U.S. American, 88–89. *See also* culture; Little Theatre Group (LTG)
Theroux, Paul, 78
Thompson, Mary, 42, 145, 147, 173, 191, 231
Thomson, Alistair, 23
Thoreau, H. D.: *Walden*, 254n46
ticos/ticas, 1, 135, 142, 230
Tico Times (*TT*), 1, 19, 29, 51–63, 72, 76, 101–2, 120–22, 128, 134, 145–58, *150*, 257n97; advertisements in, 177, 248n54; articles of, 233n2; bilingual recipes in, 191; ownership of, 151
Torres, Eric, 54
tourism, 24, 34, 53, 55, 130; communes and, 73; international campaign for, 97, 252n12; in Mexico, 101. *See also* ecotourism
trade unions, 12; repression of, 17
transnational cognitive spaces, 128–29

transnational gendered spaces, 158–59
travel writing, 94–95, 101, 156; arrival scenes in, 205–12, 256n84, 273n33; colonial, 255n63
Truman, Harry, 37
Trundle, Catherine, 47, 61, 126, 138, 182, 250n84, 259n28, 270n103
Turkey, 34
Turner, Fredrick Jackson, 103
Tuscany, 47, 138; Anglo-American charity associations in, 249n78, 250n84, 259n28, 260n41
Tussey, Mary Lou, 261n59
Tyler, Erin, 162

Ugly American, 83, 132, 135
The Ugly American (Burdick and Lederer), 259n24
Union Club, 85
United Fruit Company (UFC), 8–9, 14, 43, 68–69, 76, 167, 235n27; adventures in working for, 165; compounds of, 175; heritage of, 266n21; local branch of, 260n49; vessel of, 125, 173
United States, 1–2, 233n1; consumer society of, 198, 200; criticism of foreign policy of, 259n24; educational system of, 100, 103; emigration from, 36–38, 44, 47–49, 53, 241n9, 242n11, 242n19; emigration to Costa Rica from, 3, 14–19, *16*, 24, 31–39, 44–64, 74–75, 95, 100–101, 149, 173–75, 180, 199–220, 228–30, 239n67; as "empire by invitation," 204; frontier experience of, 95–106, 122; as global superpower, 2,

314 *Index*

13; immigration to, 241nn9–10; influence of Latin American practices and domestic culture on, 262n66; island colonies of, 8, 235n26; materialism of, 200–201, 204; militarism of, 33, 200, 204; overindustrialization of, 70; postwar, 174; U.S. intervention in Costa Rica to protect interests of, 8–9, 236n29; women's clubs in, 258n15. *See also* Civil War (U.S.); consumerism; corruption; immigration; informal U.S. empire; materialism; U.S. embassy; U.S. imperialism; Wild West

United States Information Service (USIS), 86

University of Costa Rica, 63, 157

urbanization, 248n53

Uruguay, 7

U.S.A. International Women's Club (1959–65), 65, 125, 136; application form for, *143*

U.S. antiwar movement, 2

U.S.A. Women's Club (1940–59), 83–84, 129

U.S. clubland, 30–31, 60–61, 77–91, 245n6. *See also* enclave; social networks

U.S.-Costa Rican Cultural Center, 85. *See also* Costa Rican-North American Cultural Center / Centro Cultural Costarricense Norteamericano

U.S. embassy, 63–64, 78, 85, 88. *See also* United States

U.S. imperialism, 2, 32, 35, 81, 234n13; in Central America, 8, 110–11; narratives of, 200. *See also* imperialism; United States

U.S.-Latin American relations, 255n63

U.S. State Department, 261n53

U.S. Women's Club, 10, 24–25, 32, 41, 128–43, 159, 169, 180, 191–92, 223; constitutions of, 132, 135, 137; criteria for membership in U.S. Women's Club in Barcelona, Jakarta, and Tuscany, 249n78; in Germany, 261n53

U.S. women's liberation movement, 32, 38, 129, 150–58; and Costa Rican feminism, 158. *See also* feminism; women

utopia: counterculture communes as, 171; in new world, 219; spiritual, 48. *See also* Garden of Eden; paradise

Uvita, 71, 73, 109, 119, 171, 179, 181

Vaccariello, Linda, 156

Valle del General, 104

Vesco, Robert, 14, 18, 54, 56, 120, 216, 237n49

Vickery, Amanda, 172

Vietnam, 206–7. *See also* Vietnam War

Vietnam War, 2, 5, 17, 22, 35–37, 44–46, 57; conscientious objectors to, 212, 223; sacrifices of, 122–23; veterans of, 34, 45, 171, 206–7, 229. *See also* Vietnam

violence: of civil wars, 12; politically motivated, 12; of second phase of counterculture, 48

Waldren, Jacqueline, 46, 265n7

Warren, Jane, 52, 166–67, 202–7, 214, 218

Warren, Michael, 52, 166–67, 202–7, 214, 224–25, 230

Warren, Robert, 37
washing machine, 174, 176–77, 198, 268n53. *See also* material culture
Washington, Larry, 161
White, Eric, 51, 70, 119, 178, 226
White, Michelle, 119
Whitehead, Neil, 106
"whiteness," 6–7, 66, 234n18; of Costa Ricans, 235n24; racialized, 203; symbolic attributes of, 126–27. *See also* race
Whole Earth Catalog, 185
Wild West, 96–106, 212, 221. *See also* United States
Willauer, Ambassador Whiting, 135
Williams, Albert, 88
Williams, Barbara, 123, 185
Wilson, Lisa, 56, 178, 210–11, 273n33
Wilson, President Woodrow, 8
The Wizard of Oz (U.S. American film), 206, 211
Wolf, Jerry, 55, 177
women, 125–59; activism of, 258n15, 258n20; agency of, 126; botanical drawings of, 115, *115*; British, 250n84; changing status of, 24, 42–43, 126–27; clubs for, 128–43, 147, 159, 191–93, 249n78, 258nn15–16; domestic emancipation of U.S. American, 144–49, 155, 159; feminine mystique of expatriate, 137–43, 153, 159, 192–93; on frontier, 113–16, 255n71; gender roles of, 243n36, 256n76, 258n18, 258n20, 265n10; home gardens of, 115; labor of Costa Rican, 130, 144, 155, 262n66; Latin American writings about bourgeois, 255n71; as mistresses, 153–54; rights of, 150; self-fulfillment of, 141–43; as settlers in Costa Rica, 104; social drinking of, 189–90; social spaces of, 79, 83–85, 129–43; and transnational gendered regimes, 24, 32; upper-class, 248n52; upward mobility of, 73, 127, 145–48, 175. *See also china* (maid); domesticity; Feminine Mystique; feminism; gender; La Liga Feminista Costarricense; Movimiento para Liberación de la Mujer; U.S.A. Women's Club (1940–59); U.S. women's liberation movement
"Women Here and Now" (feminist column), 151, 157
Women's Club of Costa Rica (WCCR), 83–85, 91, 117, 137–43, *141*; recipe book cover of, *195*, *196*
"Women's Lib and You" (feminist column), 151–56
Woodman, Julie, 190
World Affairs, 13
World Book Encyclopedia, 208
World War I, 21, 37, 241n10
World War II, 1, 4–5, 9–17, 35–43, 57, 69, 76–86, 120, 130–33, 138, 163–64, 221, 231; gendered aspects of sugar and sweets in, 271n113; impact of, on U.S. American immigration to Costa Rica, 10; U.S. American female work force in, 258n17
Wright, Richard, 37

yoga, 225
"Your Child's Health" (instructional column), 147–49, 151, 262n76. *See also* Ortiz, Miguel

www.ingramcontent.com/pod-product-compliance
Lightning Source LLC
Chambersburg PA
CBHW031900220426
43663CB00006B/701